hamlyn

D0491472

Guide to

Trees

of Britain
and Europe

C. J. Humphries
J. R. Press
D. A. Sutton

Illustrated by
I. Garrard
T. Hayward
D. More

Preface

This book is intended to provide the layman and the student with a simple means of identifying most of the common trees in Europe. Many genera have only one or two species and can be readily identified by the combined use of colour artworks and photographs in popular works. There are, however, many other genera which are well represented in the European flora, and the accurate determination of species often depends on the correct use of keys and specialist monographs. Unfortunately, specialist literature is generally beyond the scope of the beginner and layman since it presupposes some detailed knowledge of the organisms in question. As an alternative this book provides simple keys, illustrations and balanced simplified accounts of the form, variation and distribution of most of the common European tree species, and aims to provide the currently accepted treatment of some 400 species.

The policy in selection has been to include all but the rarest of the native trees together with the most important exotics of silviculture and horticulture. Since more than a thousand introductions to Europe have been recorded at one time or another, many of them occurring only in gardens and private collections, it would be impossible to include them all in this book. The result is that exact identification in the culturally exploited groups cannot always be guaranteed. In an effort to keep things simple in these cases, and in those groups which involve complex forms of variation, the reader is directed to alternative sources.

C.J.H., J.R.P., D.A.S.

Acknowledgements

The authors and publishers would like to thank Mr Keith Rushforth for reading the manuscript and Dr John Dransfield for supplying valuable reference material for the section on palm trees. We should also like to thank Mrs M. Humphries for typing the manuscript, and Mrs H. Press for the illustrations of the eucalyptus fruits. Finally, special thanks are due to Ian Garrard, whose cooperation and unflagging ability to produce plates of a uniformly excellent standard have contributed so much to this book.

First published by Hamlyn in 1981
Reprinted 1993

This edition published in 2000
by Hamlyn, an imprint of Octopus Publishing Group
2–4 Heron Quays
London E14 4JP

ISBN 0 600 60021 1

Previously published as the
Country Life Guide to Trees of Britain and Europe

A catalogue record for this book is available from the British Library

Design @ 2wo
Produced by Grafos S.A.
Printed in Spain

Contents

Contents (cont.)

How to use this book

The trees described in this book include nearly all native British species, most native European species, and many cultivated species if they are to be found in more than one European country. The geographical coverage follows the pattern adopted by *Flora Europaea*, which defines Europe according to its traditional boundaries. The area covered is shown in the map below. Trees not included in this book are rarities from remote or restricted areas of Europe, and those only grown in private collections or Botanic Gardens. Since the equability of the European climate makes it possible to cultivate a wide range of introductions from China, Japan, America and Australia for timber, shade and decoration on a reasonably wide scale, the criteria used for inclusion are independent of native, cultivated or naturalized status.

This book consists of four main parts: keys to genera and species; the colour plates; the detailed species descriptions, and the index. These can be used independently or together in order to determine the name of a tree. If you wish to identify a tree for the first time, use the keys (which are all given together before the main part of the book, starting on page 13). If you believe you know the name of a tree already it can be checked in the index and then found directly in the text. Almost all of the species described in the text are illustrated in the colour plates, which invariably occur above the relevant text. The main plant groups, e.g. the oaks, the conifers, etc., are all kept together so it is also possible just to thumb through the book to find the correct part.

Each description begins with the Latin name followed by the common English name, or the local European equivalent when an English name is not available.

In general, taxa below species level are only described when a variable species is represented in Europe by one particular subspecies or variety, or in the case of introduced trees represented only by artificially raised cultivars.

Al *Albania*
Au *Austria*
Be *Belgium*
Bl *Balearic Islands*
Br *Britain*
Bu *Bulgaria*
Co *Corsica*
Cr *Crete*
Cz *Former Czechoslovakia*
De *Denmark*
Fl *Finland*
Fr *France*
Ge *Germany*
Gr *Greece*
Ho *Holland*
Hu *Hungary*
Ic *Iceland*
Ir *Ireland*
It *Italy*
No *Norway*
Pl *Portugal*
Po *Poland*
Fu *Former USSR*
Ru *Rumania*
Sa *Sardinia*
Sd *Switzerland*
Si *Sicily*
Sp *Spain*
Sw *Sweden*
Tu *Turkey*
Yu *Former Yugoslavia*

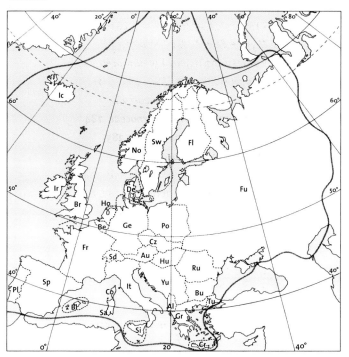

Introduction

What is a tree?

The feature common to both shrubs and trees is that their main stems and branches increase in length each year by the outgrowth of buds (shoots) at the tips, and in diameter by the concentric growth of new internal layers, called secondary thickening. The difference is that a tree has a single main stem (a trunk or bole) between the roots and a diffusely branching crown, while a shrub has several stems arising from ground level. This book is about trees, but it must be remembered that the distinction between shrubs and trees is not always clear-cut. For example, the Common Hawthorn, *Crataegus monogyna* is often seen as a hedge plant with many branches arising from ground level. However, because it can also occur as a tree with a distinct trunk up to 10m high it is included in this book. By the same token there are many shrub species, e.g. the Tree Heath, *Erica arborea*, which can grow to 7m or more but which rarely if ever produce a regular single trunk, and are thus excluded. For the purposes of this book, a tree can be defined as a woody plant that commonly achieves a height of 3m or more on a single stem.

The morphology and growth of trees

Shoots

The shoot (see fig. 1) consists of stems which bear the leaves and flowers or cones. In most trees the shoot consists of a central axis or main stem with side branches. The point where the leaf is attached to the stem is called the node. The angle which the leaf makes with the stem is called the axil, and borne in the axil there is frequently an axillary or lateral bud. The terminal bud is at the apex of the stem or shoot. The bud can be considered as a specialized overwintering organ for the protection of the growing point, and can be best observed during the winter. Fig. 1 illustrates a three-year-old Horse Chestnut twig (*Aesculus hippocastanum*), presented to indicate the distribution of terminal and lateral buds. In addition to the buds, the scars from previous years' bud scales are also visible, as are the horseshoe leaf-scars with their distinctive vascular pattern. The other marks on the young twigs are lenticels; these are microscopic holes packed loosely with tiny particles of cork to give a porous breathing surface to the twig.

The terminal buds provide the points of growth extension to the main stems, whereas side branches are formed by the growth of some of the lateral buds on the second-year twigs. None of the lateral buds grow out into branches during the first year, except when the terminal bud becomes damaged. In the second spring the lateral buds of the second-year twigs can produce side branches. After three years there is a main stem and two orders of side-branching.

Fig. 1

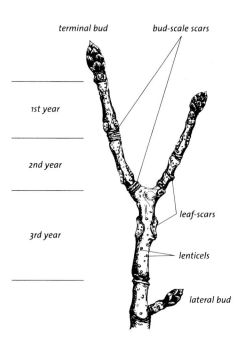

terminal bud   bud-scale scars

1st year

2nd year

3rd year

leaf-scars

lenticels

lateral bud

Habit and tree shape

Trees are extremely variable in their overall shape due to a combination of growth characteristics and environmental influences. Most people know the difference in growth characteristics between a Christmas tree and an oak tree: one is pointed and conical while the other is rounded and bushy. To look at the difference in more detail, the Christmas tree has a very distinct central axis with rather short, more or less horizontal side branches emerging alternately from the main stem; the oak tree has several main branches, none of which dominates the others, and no main stem is distinguishable within the crown. That the main stem in Christmas trees grows upwards and the side branches horizontally is a manifestation of a control system called apical dominance. The apex is the fastest-growing point of the tree and the growth of the whole tree is controlled by hormones passing down from the main shoot into the side branches. Should the apex become damaged one of the side branches bends upwards and assumes the role of the apical shoot.

By contrast, in mature flat-topped conifers, such as *Cedrus* and the Scots Pine, *Pinus sylvestris*, there has been a gradual loss of apical dominance. With time, the side branches have grown up towards the same level as the apex, giving the tree a flat-topped appearance. All trees with regular growth at the main apex controlling the growth of lateral branches will be conical in shape with a tall crown at maturity. Poplar trees, wild cherries and several other broad-leaved trees grow in this way for many years, but the majority soon lose the central control of the main apex and quickly develop diffused branch systems. In regular, rounded, bushy-topped trees such as the oak, the lack of apical dominance is apparent from very early on in life.

The other factor affecting tree shape is the physical environment. The two principal physical influences on tree shape are light and wind. Trees grown in the open tend to retain massive old branches only a short distance from the ground. They appear to have short but stout trunks and very full crowns. Plantation trees, by contrast, which are grown close together, develop tall slender branch-free trunks and small overlapping crowns; the lower branches are crowded out by shading. Foresters grow the trees in this way for timber.

Wind is probably a more important environmental factor determining tree shape. Trees growing in sites with a continuous prevailing wind from one direction have longer, healthier branches on the leeward side, so that the crown appears to be blowing with the wind. This is due mainly to the fact that young buds exposed to prevailing winds are liable to be killed off. In addition, such trees regularly have their branches broken off as a result of strong winds, and those growing close to the seashore also become affected by salt spray on one side.

Stem and wood structure

The thickened main stem of a tree is the trunk; that part below the lowest branches is called the bole.

A transverse section or slice across a mature trunk will reveal three obvious layers: the inner heartwood, or xylem, the outer layer of corky bark, and a middle layer, the bast, or phloem. The xylem forms the main part of the thickened stem and can be seen to be composed of two parts: a central, dark coloured heartwood that contains no sap, and an outer, lighter coloured sapwood that is filled with water and dissolved substances passing from the soil. The heartwood in other words is dead and has ceased to function. With time it gradually fills with the hard, durable thickening material called lignin, the substance we call wood. Surrounding the wood cylinder is the phloem, through which pass the food products manufactured in the leaves. Outside the phloem is another layer, the cork layer, which varies in thickness according to the species of the tree. Bark and cork are both protective dead tissues.

Gymnosperm heartwood is called softwood and is made up of only two types of cells. The main conductive elements, called tracheids, are long, thickened fibres running end to end in the wood. The other cells, called parenchyma, consist of thin-walled brick-shaped cells arranged in radiating rows known as medullary rays, and it is these which give the characteristic grain to finished timbers.

Angiosperm heartwood is called hardwood and differs from gymnosperm wood in that it consists of three, rather than two, types of cells. Instead of having the fibrous support and the conducting tissues functionally combined into a tracheid, hardwoods have separate large, hollow, rather thin-walled conductive cells called vessels, and rather more solid, thick-walled, sharp-pointed supportive cells called fibres. The parenchyma are arranged in medullary rays in much the same way as gymnosperm wood.

Leaves

The leaves are the food factories of plants. They are specialized organs which utilize water and dissolved minerals passed up by the roots and the stems from the soil, and carbon dioxide absorbed from the atmosphere through the stomata on the leaf surface, to manufacture complex food substances. They do this in the green part of the leaves, the chlorophyll, using sunlight as the energy source. The complex food substances, particularly carbohydrates, are redistributed around other organs of the plant by the phloem.

A typical leaf is composed of a leaf-stalk or petiole which attaches to the stem, and a blade (lamina) which is the functional part. In some cases the blade can be borne directly on the stem (in which case it is said to be sessile).

The leaf-blade is provided with a network of veins and the whole arrangement is called the venation pattern. The veins consist of xylem and phloem tissue, catering respectively for the transport of water and minerals into the leaf and the manufactured food substances out of the leaf. In some leaves there is one main vein which branches irregularly and further subdivides in a reticulate pattern – this is called net venation. Such a pattern is characteristic of elm, oak and maple leaves. In other species, particularly the monocotyledonous trees (the palms etc.) and conifers, instead of one main vein with branches there are several veins of equal size running parallel to each other, a pattern called parallel venation.

Reproductive structures
The sexual organs of gymnosperms and angiosperms are fundamentally quite different. The gymnosperm 'flowers' are almost always arranged in complex inflorescences called strobili or cones, and the two sexes are always borne in separate cones, although they may or may not be on the same tree. Angiosperm flowers by contrast are extremely variable. They may or may not be arranged into inflorescences, the inflorescences themselves are very variable, and a single flower can be entirely male, entirely female, or hermaphrodite.

Gymnosperms (see fig. 2)
The young female cone consists of a central axis upon which the reproductive organs are arranged in a close spiral. One or more ovules are situated at the base of a leaf-like stalked structure, the ovuliferous scale, and enclosed by a lower and smaller scale known as the bract scale. The ovuliferous scale and bract scales vary in their relative proportions and their degree of fusion, so that in some genera, such as *Abies*, the bract and scale are always distinguishable; in others, such as *Cupressus*, the two are fused at maturity so as to be indistinguishable to the naked eye. The young cones are green and soft, and at the time of pollination the two scales are slightly separated to give the pollen access to the ovule. After pollen grains have been drawn into the ovules, the female cone closes up again and sometimes even becomes sealed by a resinous exudation. After several months, or even years in some taxa, the ovules become fertilized and seed development takes place. While all this is going on the female cone has become brown. Eventually the scales move apart to release the ripe seeds.

There is considerable variation in female morphology. The following are some of the more extreme examples. *Juniperus* has the scales fused into a berry. *Taxus* has a single ovule borne

Fig. 2

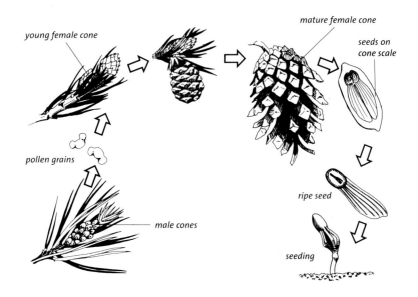

young female cone

mature female cone

seeds on
cone scale

pollen grains

male cones

ripe seed

seeding

apically on a relatively short shoot and is surrounded by a fleshy aril. *Cephalotaxus* has female strobili composed of opposite pairs of cup-shaped bracts with two ovules at the base of each, usually only one develops into an olive-like 'fruit'.

The male strobilus consists of a number of microsporophylls or stamens, arranged in catkin-like clusters. Each sporophyll bears pollen sacs (microsporongia) which are usually coloured yellow, violet or crimson, and which contain the pollen grains.

Angiosperms (see fig. 3)

The flower of the angiosperms, like that of gymnosperms, is a modified leaf-bearing shoot, and propagates sexually by means of seeds. The ovules of angiosperms, however, unlike those of gymnosperms, are enclosed in an ovary. (The terms are derived from the Greek *angeion* meaning a case or vessel, *gymnos*

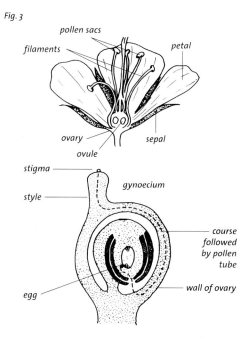

Fig. 3

meaning naked, and *sperma* meaning seed.) Another distinction is the presence of a stigma at the tip of the ovary, specialized to catch pollen which can no longer reach the ovule directly, as it can in the gymnosperms. The pollen of gymnosperms is usually wind dispersed and therefore the cones are relatively inconspicuous. Although a number of the angiosperms are wind pollinated, e.g. the catkin-bearing genera (which also have inconspicuous flowers), the great majority are pollinated by animals. Flowers and animal pollination always occur together. A flower is a conspicuous organ consisting of four distinct groups of parts: sepals to protect the developing flower bud; fragrant or colourful petals to attract the pollinators; the androecium, consisting of the stamens (pollen sacs borne on filaments), and the gynoecium, consisting of an ovary containing the ovules, the stigma and the style. Most angiosperm flowers are hermaphrodite, but well-known dioecious exceptions include willow, birch, hazel, beech, oak and ash, which are generally catkin-bearing wind-pollinated plants.

There is considerable variation in the arrangement and structure of the flower parts. Each set of four parts is arranged in a whorl. The individual whorls differ in certain characters, namely the position of attachment to one another, the number of parts within each whorl and the degree of fusion between each of the parts. The picture is further confused by the fact that in some species various parts can be lost, for example the petals in *Eucalyptus* and in various catkin-bearing plants.

Distribution of trees

There are two main reasons for the considerable diversity in the European tree flora: the first is a combination of the wide range of ecological and climatic conditions, which have given rise to a rich native flora; the second is the centuries of man's activity which has brought exotic trees and extended the distribution of native trees into silviculture and horticulture.

The 190 native species included in this book are representative of several distinct distribution patterns. At the global level there are families such as the Fagaceae, the Ulmaceae and the Aquifoliaceae which span the continents on both sides of the equator. The Fagaceae family, for example, which is well represented in Europe by *Quercus*, *Castanea* and *Fagus*, is an extremely ancient one probably dating back to the early Cretaceous period. The closest relative of the northern beech genus *Fagus*, so widespread in the northern hemisphere, is the southern beech genus *Nothofagus*, equally widespread in the temperate areas of Australia, New Zealand, South America and the mountains of New Guinea and New Caledonia. The divergence of these two genera probably dates back to the break-up of the ancient supercontinent (Pangaea).

Within the northern hemisphere there is only one species of tree, the Common Juniper, *Juniperus communis*, known to be widespread throughout Europe, Asia and North America. Nevertheless, there are quite a number of widely different genera which are represented by closely related species in the two separate continents. For example, the Eastern and Western

Plane Trees, respectively *Plantanus orientalis* and *P. occidentalis*, are now widely separated on the two northern land masses, but probably formed continuous populations at a time before the continents drifted apart. Despite a long separation, a hybrid between the two species, the commonly cultivated London Plane, *P. x hispanica*, is a living testament to the genetic similarity of the parental species.

In direct contrast to the intercontinental patterns are those genera strictly confined to either the New or the Old World. A classic Old World pattern for a relict distribution is seen in the Wing-nut genus *Pterocarya*, which has one species in the Caucasus, one in Japan and six in China. Another interesting example is the diverse genus *Cotoneaster*, which has some seventy species entirely restricted to the Old World mountain ranges. Much less diverse but showing another Old World distribution pattern is the genus *Laburnum*, which has three reasonably widespread species in southern Europe and western Asia.

Systematics, taxonomy and nomenclature

Systematics is the study of the relationships between organisms, and taxonomy is the process of making classification from that study. Most systems of classification are hierarchical, each level in the hierarchy being given a different name. Thus, a species is given a particular name, related species are put into the same genus, and in turn related genera are put into the same family. A Taxon (plural taxa) is a general term applied to any individual component or category within a classification; thus families, genera and species are all taxa, each at a different level.

Man has always given names to different organisms in order to distinguish one from another. In the case of plants and animals the most familiar in everyday language are the common names. But although common names are convenient in everyday speech they have many disadvantages. They come into existence haphazardly with little direction from any one authority; they do not come within the control of any international body; the same name often refers to different organisms even in different parts of the same country, and, above all, common names are incommunicable to people of different tongues. It is true that many common names can be given qualifying names so that they apply to one particular species; 'Holm Oak', for example, refers to the evergreen species *Quercus ilex* L., but even this common English name is meaningless to, say, the Maltese and the French, who respectively call the same species 'Ballut' and 'Chîne-vert'.

Scientific naming is given precision by the adoption of Latin as a common language, since it is common to scientists, and can be understood by people of all nationalities. In botanical nomenclature a species is always given a binomial, so that a particular species can be identified together with the genus to which it belongs. All of the oaks are placed in the one genus *Quercus* and our chosen example, the 'Holm Oak', is called *Quercus ilex*. The full name of the Holm Oak is, however, *Quercus ilex* L. The 'L.' is an abbreviation of Linnaeus, the Latinized version of the name Carl von Linné, who first described the species in 1753. To give consistency to nomenclature, the name of the author of the first validly published name combination is always added (usually in an abbreviated form) to distinguish his use of the name. Occasionally a later author might use the same name for a different species. For example, Loureio gave a Burmese species the name *Quercus ilex* Lour. This later use is rejected.

With time, taxonomic concepts change due to increases in the amounts of material available for study and to changes in systematic philosophy. Furthermore, early botanists generally had wider species and generic concepts than we do today, so that it has become necessary to create new genera for species removed from existing genera, to expand or contract species boundaries, or to reshuffle existing genera to accommodate new relationships. For example, Linnaeus first included the Common Alder in a broad genus of catkin-bearing trees, *Betula*, describing it as *Betula glutinosa* L. Another biologist, Phillip Miller, later considered that the name *Betula* should have a narrower range and be restricted to the Silver Birches. He described a new genus, *Alnus*, to accommodate the alders. It was left to a third author, Gaertner, to transfer the Common Alder to the genus *Alnus* Mill. The priority article in the Botanical Code of Nomenclature, the botanists' book of rules, insists that wherever possible the original specific epithet should be transferred to the new genus. The Common Alder thus became known as *Alnus glutinosa*. Since Linnaeus did not write the new combination but did coin the original specific epithet, his authority name is enclosed in parentheses at the end of the name and before the author who made the new valid combination. Hence the correct citation of the Common Alder is *Alnus glutinosa* (L.) Gaertner.

There are three infra-specific categories used in general tree taxonomy which cater for variation within species. The subspecies category caters for regionally distinct taxa which show some degree of intergradation with other regional variants of the same species. The variety category tends to cater for regional or sporadic variation on a smaller scale and at a level lower or less distinct than the subspecies. The application of names for both subspecies and varieties follow rules similar to those for species. The cultivar category caters for those variants which arise by deliberate selection, by cloning, or by mutation in trees raised in gardens and nurseries. Cultivars are given names according to the International code of nomenclature of cultivated plants, which differs from the botanical code in that authority names are not required. For example, the most commonly cultivated form of the Atlas Cedar, *Cedrus atlantica* (Endl.) Carrière is the Blue Atlas Cedar cv. '*glauca*', which has a glaucous blue waxy covering to the foliage.

Hybrids

A hybrid may be defined as the offspring of two dissimilar individuals. Since this book is concerned with different taxa (genera, species, subspecies, varieties and cultivars) the term can be restricted here to taxonomic hybrids, i.e. those involving crosses between individuals of different taxa. Thus hybrids can be intergeneric, interspecific, intervarietal, and so on.

Most of the hybrids described in this book are interspecific hybrids; in other words the parents belong to different species of the same genus. For example, the Hybrid Poplar is found in areas where its two parent species, the Grey Poplar, *Populus canescens* (Aiton) Sm., and the Aspen, *P. tremula* L., grow together. In Latin nomenclature, interspecific hybrids can be denoted in a variety of ways. When the male (pollen) and the female (ovule) parents are known it is conventional to put the female parent first. It is an unfortunate fact that the parental status of many hybrids is not really known, and that only the putative parents can be designated. Traditionally in such cases the names of the parents are given in alphabetical order with an 'x' between them, so that our example the Hybrid Poplar is given as *P. canescens* x *tremula*. Also, many of the hybrids which grow successfully in the wild are given single specific epithets in exactly the same way as conventional species, especially in the older taxonomic literature. In these cases an 'x' is given in front of the epithet to designate hybrid status. Thus the Hybrid Poplar can also be written as *P.* x *hybrida* Bieb.

The correct way to give the Latin name of an intergeneric hybrid (i.e. where the parents belong to species of different genera) is with a capital 'X' in front of the hybrid name. However, these are extremely rare amongst trees and the only one in this book is the Leyland Cypress, X *Cupressocyparis leylandii* (Jackson & Dallim.) Dallim., an intergeneric hybrid between the Nootka Cypress, *Chamaecyparis nootkatensis* (Lamb.) Spach, and the Monterey Cypress, *Cupressus macrocarpa* Hartw.

Identification

Using Keys

The keys on the following pages can be used for the identification of all genera in the book and of species in genera containing more than six species. The genera with separate species keys are marked with an asterisk in the main key and two cross-references are given, the first to the page number of the text account and the second to the page number of the species key. The shorter genera simply have a cross-reference to the page on which the text starts. The keys given here are of the bracketed type and are dichotomous throughout, i.e. at every stage a choice must be made between two contrasting alternatives which together make up a couplet. They are designed to be practical, using as many field characters as possible, particularly those of leaf, bark etc., in order to facilitate identification throughout the year.

To find a genus, or species, to which a specimen belongs, start at couplet no.1 and compare the specimen with the two alternative statements. For example, if it accords with the first line in couplet 1 of the generic key, proceed to couplet 2. However, if the specimen accords with the second line of couplet 1 then proceed to couplet 25. By continuing with the same process at each couplet, eventually the correct lead will be reached indicating the name of the genus, or species, to which the specimen belongs.

For most taxa the keys work reasonably well but sometimes they pose questions which appear to be entirely wrong for the specimen to hand. There can be a number of reasons for this, a common one being that the specimen to hand is an atypical plant – perhaps an obscure cultivar, or a rare species not actually included in the book. But perhaps the most likely reason is that there has been an error at one of the dichotomies in the key, probably due to misinterpretation of characters. The best remedy is to return to the first couplet and proceed through to the ambiguous dichotomy. If it is the case that a specimen does not exactly fit either lead one has to decide which of the two alternatives is the more relevant. In general the more reliable statement comes first. If, on the other hand, it is a case of total misjudgement at a particular couplet, the alternative lead must be taken and followed through to the appropriate part of the key.

Key to Genera

1	Leaves dark green, hard, narrow and usually spine-tipped, scale-like or needle like (except *Ginkgo*); veins parallel; usually annual growth in whorls; males and females always on separate trees; never with petals; fruit a cone or berry-like	***Ginkgo, conifers & taxads*** *Go to **2***
	Leaves lighter green, soft, leathery or hard, broad (rarely needle-like or linear); veins reticulate (except some monocotyledonous species); growth alternate or opposite, never in whorls; males and females hermaphrodite, monoecious or dioecious, with or without petals; fruit variable – a capsule, acorn, pod, nut, berry, winged or a pome etc.	***Broadleaved angiosperm trees*** *Go to **25***
2	Leaves fan-shaped, broadly 2-lobed, leathery, deciduous, fan-veined	***Ginkgo*** (p. 34)
	Leaves scale-like, linear or lanceolate, but never fan-shaped	*Go to **3***
3	Leaves appressed, opposite or whorled scales	*Go to **4***
	Leaves protruding scales, or not scale-like	*Go to **9***
4	Foliage in flattened, fern-like sprays	*Go to **5***
	Foliage in multidimensional plumes	*Go to **8***
5	Leaf scales 5mm or more wide, hard, glossy	***Thujopsis*** (p. 48)
	Leaf scales less than 5mm wide, if glossy then soft	*Go to **6***
6	Cones globose, woody when ripe	*Go to **7***
	Cones flask-shaped, leathery when ripe	***Thuja*** (p. 48)
7	Cones with 4 scales	***Tetraclinis*** (p. 48)
	Cones with 6–12 scales	***x Cupressocyparis*** (p. 38) ***Chamaecyparis*** (p. 36)
8	Free juvenile leaves at the base or the tip of the shoot	****Juniperus*** (p. 42; key p. 22)
	Leaves uniformly appressed scales	***Cupressus*** (p. 38) ***x Cupressocyparis*** (p. 38)
9	Leaves mostly in rosettes on spurs from 2nd year shoots	*Go to **10***
	Leaves opposite or spirally arranged, neither in rosettes nor spurs	*Go to **12***
10	Leaves soft, thin-textured, pale or bright green, deciduous	*Go to **11***
	Leaves hard, thick-textured, dark green, evergreen	***Cedrus*** (p. 60)
11	Spurs long and curved, leaves with pale margins	***Pseudolarix*** (p. 64)
	Spurs short and straight; leaves uniformly coloured	Larix (p. 62)
12	Fruits berry-like, without obvious scales	*Go to **13***
	Fruits cones, never berry-like, with obvious scales	*Go to **15***
13	Fruits single-seeded surrounded by a bright red aril	***Taxus*** (p. 34)
	Fruits several-seeded, blue, green or red	*Go to **14***
14	Fruits globose; leaves needle-like or scale-like, in pairs or whorls of three	****Juniperus*** (p. 42; key p. 22)
	Fruits ovoid; leaves linear-lanceolate spirally arranged	***Cephalotaxus*** (p. 34)
15	Leaves arranged in 2 flat rows on either side of the shoots	*Go to **16***
	Leaves spirally arranged on the shoots	*Go to **18***
16	Leaves and shoots alternate	*Go to **17***
	Leaves and shoots in opposite pairs	***Metasequoia*** (p. 52)
17	Female cone scales with short recurved spine	***Taxodium*** (p. 52)
	Female cone scales without spines	***Sequoia*** (p. 50)

18 Leaves broadly triangular, 3–4cm long x 1cm wide at the base	*Araucaria* (p. 36)
Leaves linear or linear-lanceolate, never more than 5mm wide	*Go to 19*
19 Leaves with 2 obvious white bands on the lower surface	*Go to 20*
Leaves without 2 obvious white bands on the lower surface	*Go to 22*
20 Cones erect, leaves with sucker-like base	***Abies*** (p. 54; key p. 22)
Cones pendent, leaves not expanded at the base	*Go to 21*
21 Leaves soft, but acute, cone bracts lobed	***Pseudotsuga*** (p. 72)
Leaves hard, but ovoid, cone bracts not lobed	***Tsuga*** (p. 72)
22 Leaves in bundles of 2,3 or 5	****Pinus*** (p. 74; key p. 23)
Leaves not in bundles	*Go to 23*
23 Bark scaly, never fissured or fibrous, leaves sharp but never incurving	****Picea*** (p. 66; key p. 23)
Bark fissured, very fibrous, leaves sharp with long incurving spines	*Go to 24*
24 Leaf-spine less than 1cm long, dull green or grey	***Sequoiadendron*** (p. 50)
Leaf-spine more than 1cm long, bright green	***Cryptomeria*** (p. 52)
25 Palm trees, with a single trunk and an unbranched crown of large compound leaves at the top	*Go to 26*
Flowering trees, usually with a single trunk and a branched crown of small leaves	*Go to 33*
26 Leaves pinnate 1–5m in length	*Go to 30*
Leaves palmate 60–120cm in diameter	*Go to 27*
27 Trunk covered by a 'petticoat' of dead leaves	***Washingtonia*** (p. 308)
Trunk covered by leaf-bases or fibres, or smooth	*Go to 28*
28 Leaves cut almost to the petiole with stiff straight segments	*Go to 29*
Leaves cut two-thirds of the way to the petiole with soft, drooping segments	***Livistona*** (p. 304)
29 Trunk densely covered with brown fibres, a moderate-sized tree 3–12m high	***Trachycarpus*** (p. 308)
Trunk smooth, a small tree 1–5m high	***Chamaerops*** (p. 304)
30 Trunks very broad, studded with old leaf-bases	***Phoenix*** (p. 306)
Trunks slender, smooth, ringed only by leaf-scars	*Go to 31*
31 Leaflets less than 2.5cm wide	***Arecastrum*** (p. 302)
Leaflets more than 2.5cm wide	*Go to 32*
32 Leaflets divided at the apex, petiole short with stiff hairy filaments	***Jubaea*** (p. 302)
Leaflets not divided at the apex, petiole up to almost 2m long	***Howeia*** (p. 302)
33 Leaves compound	*Go to 34*
Leaves simple	*Go to 53*
34 Leaves with 3 leaflets or digitately lobed	*Go to 35*
Leaves pinnate or twice-pinnate	*Go to 36*
35 Leaves with 3 leaflets	***Laburnum*** (p. 218) ***Acer griseum*** (p. 203)
Leaves 5–7 digitately lobed	***Aesculus*** (p. 242)
36 Leaves twice-pinnate	*Go to 37*
Leaves pinnate	*Go to 39*
37 Flowers lilac-coloured with 5 regular petals, leaflets toothed or lobed	***Melia*** (p. 224)
Flowers pink or yellow with 5 irregular petals in a pea-like corolla, leaflets entire	*Go to 38*

38 Flowers pink, leaves 30–45cm long with 6–12 pairs of main pinnae each with 20–30 pairs of pinnules	**Albizia** (p. 208)
Flowers yellow, leaves 6–15cm long with 15–20 pairs of pinnae each bearing up to 50 pairs of tiny pinnules	***Acacia** (p. 212; key p. 30)
39 Flowers without petals	*Go to 40*
Flowers with petals	*Go to 43*
40 Leaves opposite	***Fraxinus** (p. 286; key p. 33) **Acer negundo** (p. 234)
Leaves alternate	*Go to 41*
41 Leaflets 3–9	**Carya** (p. 110)
Leaflets 9–25	*Go to 42*
42 Bud without scales, fruit winged	**Pterocarya** (p. 112)
Bud with scales, fruit globose	**Juglans** (p. 112)
43 Leaflet margins entire	*Go to 47*
Leaflet margins toothed or sometimes lobed	*Go to 44*
44 Leaflet margins lobed	**Koelreuteria** (p. 242)
Leaflet margins toothed	*Go to 45*
45 Leaflets linear-lanceolate	**Schinus** (p. 226)
Leaflets rounded, ovate to ovate-lanceolate	*Go to 46*
46 Leaves pinnate, with a terminal leaflet, flowers in flat panicle-like cymes	**Sambucus** (p. 298)
Leaves regularly pinnate, flowers in clustered racemes	***Sorbus** (p. 170; key p. 28)
47 Flowers zygomorphic, fruit a pod	**(Leguminosae)** 48
Flowers radially symmetrical, fruit a samara or drupe	*Go to 51*
48 Leaflets lanceolate to ovate-lanceolate, acuminate at the apex	*Go to 49*
Leaflets ovate, truncate-mucronate or notched mucronate at the apex	*Go to 50*
49 Leaves with a terminal leaflet; lateral leaflets paired	**Sophora** (p. 220)
Leaves without a terminal leaflet; lateral leaflets alternate	**Gleditsia** (p. 210)
50 Trees with spines; leaves with 13–15 pairs of leaflets	**Robinia** (p. 220)
Trees without spines; leaves with 4–10 pairs of leaflets	**Ceratonia** (p. 210)
51 Fruit a drupe	*Go to 52*
Fruit a samara	**Ailanthus** (p. 224)
52 Leaflets petiolate	**Rhus** (p. 226)
Leaflets sessile	**Pistacia** (p. 228)
53 Leaves lobed	*Go to 54*
Leaves not lobed	*Go to 65*
54 Leaves opposite	*Go to 55*
Leaves alternate	*Go to 57*
55 Always a tree; flowers large, bell-shaped, blue, in profuse erect panicles	**Paulownia** (p. 296)
Usually a shrub or small tree; flowers small, white or yellow in flat panicles or loose clusters	*Go to 56*
56 Fruits composed of 2 dry, winged seeds, borne in loose hangings clusters	***Acer** (p. 230; key p. 31)
Fruits fleshy berries borne in flat panicles	**Viburnum** (p. 298)
57 Flowers with obvious petals	*Go to 58*
Flowers without petals	*Go to 60*

58 Leaves regularly lobed with a truncate apex and lateral lobes	*Liriodendron* (p. 148)
Leaves irregularly lobed with a pointed apex and a terminal lobe	*Go to* **59**

59 Shoots and leaves downy; stems not spiny, leaves slender, pointed with coarse teeth	*Corynabutilon* (p. 248)
Shoots and leaves not downy; stems spiny, leaves broadly pointed	***Crataegus*** (p. 184; key p. 29)

60 Leaves with rounded lateral lobes	*Go to* **61**
Leaves with pointed lateral lobes	*Go to* **62**

61 Evergreen tree with large, subshiny, dark green leaves *c.* 30 x 25cm	*Ficus* (p.144)
Deciduous tree with leaves smooth, glossy green or light green above and pubescent below, *c.* 10 x 8cm	*Morus* (p. 142)

62 Leaves somewhat palmate in outline with distinct wide-spreading lower lobes	*Go to* **63**
Leaves oblong-ovate with small irregular lobes all around	***Quercus*** (p. 124; key p.26)

63 Leaves white-felted below	***Populus*** (p. 104; key p. 25)
Leaves glabrous or pubescent below	*Go to* **64**

64 Bark pale to dark grey, fissured	*Liquidambar* (p. 152)
Bark dark grey or palish brown, flaking away to leave lighter patches beneath	*Platanus* (p. 156)

65 Leaves distinctly toothed or crenate	*Go to* **103**
Leaves entire	*Go to* **66**

66 Leaves more than 60cm long	*Go to* **67**
Leaves less than 30cm long	*Go to* **69**

67 Leaves linear-lanceolate with parallel longitudinal veins and without a petiole	*Go to* **68**
Leaves ovate-oblong with a central midrib and parallel right-angled veins	*Musa* (p. 300)

68 Inflorescence with 3 bracts; leaves 3–8cm wide	*Cordyline* (p. 300)
Inflorescence without bracts; leaves 3–4cm wide	*Dracaena* (p. 300)

69 Leaves scale-like or needle-shaped	***Tamarix*** (p. 264; key p. 32)
Leaves not as above	*Go to* **70**

70 Leaves with undulate or crinkled margins	*Go to* **71**
Leaves with flat margins	*Go to* **81**

71 Leaves evergreen	*Go to* **72**
Leaves deciduous	*Go to* **74**

72 Leaves pale bright green with strongly waved margins	*Pittosporum* (p. 154)
Leaves dark green or blackish with only slightly waved or crinkled margins	*Go to* **73**

73 Petiole red; leaf margins crinkled, glabrous below	*Laurus* (p. 150)
Petiole brown or green; leaf margin slightly undulate, hairy below	***Quercus*** (p. 124; key p.26)

74 Flowers with petals	*Go to* **75**
Flowers without petals	*Go to* **77**

75 Leaves dark glossy green above, underside lighter, glabrous to glabrescent	*Go to* **76**
Leaves pale yellow-green, pale and densely pubescent below	*Mespilus* (p. 182)

76 Bark black or dark pink-grey, regularly cracked into thick, small, square plates; flower urn-shaped, pendulous	*Diospyros* (p. 284)
Bark reddish-orange-brown, deeply fissured into ridges; flowers in globose heads spreading from the base of new shoots	*Maclura* (p. 144)

77	Flowers surrounded by 4 large white leafy bracts	*Cornus* (p. 280)
	Flowers not as above	*Go to* **78**
78	Petioles dark red	*Nyssa* (p. 260)
	Petioles green or brown	*Go to* **79**
79	Fruit an acorn	**Quercus* (p. 124; key p. 26)
	Fruit not as above	*Go to* **80**
80	Pubescence of stellate hairs	*Hamamelis* (p. 152)
	Pubescence of simple hairs	*Parrotia* (p. 152)
81	Leaves blue-grey, leathery, strongly aromatic	*Go to* **82**
	Leaves light to dark green, herbaceous to leathery, rarely aromatic	*Go to* **83**
82	Fruit a conical cylindrical capsule, opening by valves at the apex	**Eucalyptus* (p. 270; key p. 33)
	Fruit a flattened longitudinal pod, opening by longitudinal dehiscence	**Acacia* (p. 212; key p. 30)
83	Fruit an acorn	**Quercus* (p. 124; key p. 126)
	Fruit not as above	*Go to* **84**
84	Leaves deciduous	*Go to* **85**
	Leaves evergreen	*Go to* **93**
85	Leaves opposite (sometimes alternate at base)	*Go to* **86**
	Leaves invariably alternate	*Go to* **89**
86	Leaves 2–12cm long	*Go to* **87**
	Leaves 20–35cm long	*Go to* **88**
87	Flowers small, tubular, lilac or purple in terminal paired conical racemes; leaves long, acuminate, cordate	*Syringa* (p. 292)
	Flowers large, 3–4cm in diameter, solitary red with free petals; leaves acute, oblong-lanceolate to obovate	*Punica* (p. 280)
88	Bark dull pink and brown, scaling into flakes, or grey and fissured into flat ridges; lateral buds orange-brown	*Catalpa* (p. 294)
	Bark smooth, grey; lateral buds purplish	*Paulownia* (p. 296)
89	Trees (or shrubs) with peltate or stellate scale-like hairs	*Go to* **90**
	Trees with simple hairs, or hairless	*Go to* **91**
90	Dioecious; calyx 2-lobed	*Hippophäe* (p. 262)
	Polygamous; calyx 4-lobed	*Elaeagnus* (p. 262)
91	Stipules absent; leaves orbicular	*Cercis* (p. 210)
	Stipules present; leaves ovate to obovate-elliptic, or ovate-deltoid to deltoid	*Go to* **92**
92	Leaves ovate-deltoid to deltoid; flowers dioecious in long racemes	*Phytolacca* (p. 146)
	Leaves obovate to obovate-elliptic; flowers in umbel-like corymbs	**Pyrus* (p. 158; key p. 27)
93	Leaves opposite	*Go to* **94**
	Leaves alternate	*Go to* **97**
94	Leaves with scale-like hairs beneath	*Olea* (p. 290)
	Leaves glabrous or hairy below	*Go to* **95**
95	Flowers tubular	*Ligustrum* (p. 290)
	Flowers with separate petals and sepals	*Go to* **96**
96	Leaves aromatic when crushed; fruit a berry	*Myrtus* (p. 278)
	Leaves not aromatic when crushed; fruit a capsule	*Buxus* (p. 248)
97	Leaves more than 5cm long	*Go to* **98**
	Leaves less than 5cm long	*Cotoneaster* (p. 182)

| 98 | Leaves elliptic-obovate to ovate-acuminate, dark green; flowers white, yellow or greenish | *Go to* **99** |
| | Leaves oblong-lanceolate, obtuse, light green; flowers bright red | ***Embothrium*** (p. 146) |

| 99 | Flowers small, inconspicuous | *Go to* **100** |
| | Flowers large, petaloid | *Go to* **101** |

| 100 | Inflorescence subsessile; perianth 4-lobed | ***Laurus*** (p. 150) |
| | Inflorescence long-pedunculate; perianth 6-lobed | ***Persea*** (p. 150) |

| 101 | Fruit citrus-type; leaves sweetly and strongly aromatic when crushed | ***Citrus*** (p. 222) |
| | Fruit a cone, or a 2-bracted involucre; leaves not or only faintly aromatic when crushed | *Go to* **102** |

| 102 | Fruit a cone; flower large, solitary, with 6–15 tepals | ***Magnolia*** (p. 148) |
| | Ovaries in a 2-bracted involucre; flowers in a loosely globose inflorescence with 7 recurved slender white petals | ***Drimys*** (p. 148) |

| 103 | Leaves evergreen; usually dark green, leathery | *Go to* **104** |
| | Leaves deciduous; usually lighter green, herbaceous | *Go to* **112** |

| 104 | Leaves opposite | *Go to* **105** |
| | Leaves alternate | *Go to* **106** |

| 105 | Stipules present; petals absent | ***Rhamnus*** (p. 252) |
| | Stipules absent; petals present | ***Phillyrea*** (p. 292) |

| 106 | Leaves with irregular spines and somewhat undulate margins | ***Ilex*** (p. 244) |
| | Leaves with serrate or crenate and flat or revolute margins | *Go to* **107** |

| 107 | Leaf margins revolute | ***Myrica*** (p. 110) |
| | Leaf margins not revolute | *Go to* **108** |

| 108 | Leaves usually more than 12cm long | ***Eriobotrya*** (p. 180) |
| | Leaves usually less than 10cm long | *Go to* **109** |

| 109 | Petals united | *Go to* **110** |
| | Petals free | *Go to* **111** |

| 110 | Stamens as numerous as or less than the corolla lobes; fruit a drupe | ***Myoporum*** (p. 296) |
| | Stamens twice as numerous as the corolla lobes; fruit a globose berry | ***Arbutus*** (p. 282) |

| 111 | Some leaves apparently with 3 leaflets | ***Eucryphia*** (p. 260) |
| | Leaves not as above | ***Frangula*** (p. 252) |

| 112 | Leaves opposite | *Go to* **113** |
| | Leaves alternate | *Go to* **115** |

| 113 | Leaves finely serrate or crenate, cordate-obovate or lanceolate | *Go to* **114** |
| | Leaves with larger, irregular teeth, palmate | ****Acer*** (p. 230; key p. 31) |

| 114 | Petioles red; leaves cordate, crenate | ***Cercidiphyllum*** (p. 146) |
| | Petioles green; leaves lanceolate to ovate, serrate | ***Euonymus*** (p. 246) |

| 115 | Trees with spiny stipules | *Go to* **116** |
| | Trees with stipules not spiny, or stipules absent | *Go to* **117** |

| 116 | Young twigs minutely pubescent; fruit dry, winged | ***Paliurus*** (p. 250) |
| | Young twigs glabrous; fruit fleshy, unwinged | ***Zizyphus*** (p. 250) |

| 117 | Fruit a pome or drupe; flowers with distinct free petals | *Go to* **118** |
| | Fruit a nut, berry, acorn, samara or capsule; flowers without petals | *Go to* **125** |

| 118 | Carpels not joined to the flower tube; fruit a fleshy drupe | *Go to* **119** |
| | Carpels joined to the flower tube; fruit a pome | *Go to* **120** |

| 119 | Indumentum of simple hairs | ***Prunus*** (p. 192; key p. 29) |
| | Indumentum of stellate or scale-like hairs | ***Styrax*** (p. 284) |

| 120 | Flowers solitary | ***Cydonia*** (p. 158) |
| | Flowers in 2- to many-flowered inflorescences | *Go to* **121** |

| 121 | Carpel wall becoming stony in fruit; leaves irregularly lobed | ***Crataegus*** (p. 184; key p. 29) |
| | Carpel walls cartilaginous in fruit; leaves regular, serrate or crenate | **122** |

| 122 | Flowers in compound corymbs; leaves densely lanate below | ***Sorbus*** (p. 170; key p. 28) |
| | Flowers in umbels, racemes or few-flowered clusters | **123** |

| 123 | Petals linear to oblong-ovate, not clawed | ***Amelanchier*** (p. 180) |
| | Petals obovate or orbicular, distinctly clawed | **124** |

| 124 | Styles free; flesh of fruit with stone cells | ***Pyrus*** (p. 158; key p. 27) |
| | Styles connected at base; flesh of fruit with few or no stone cells | ***Malus*** (p. 166) |

| 125 | Flowers in catkins or dense heads | **130** |
| | Flowers not as above | **126** |

| 126 | Perianth of 2 markedly different whorls | **127** |
| | Perianth not as above | **128** |

| 127 | Inflorescence growing in the axil of a conspicuous bract partly joined to the peduncle | ***Tilia*** (p. 254; key p. 32) |
| | Inflorescence not as above | ***Davidia*** (p. 260) |

| 128 | Bark fissured; leaves double-toothed; flowers all hermaphrodite; fruit a samara | ***Ulmus*** (p. 134; key p. 27) |
| | Bark not fissured; leaves simply serrate; flowers male and hermaphrodite; fruit a drupe | **129** |

| 129 | Bark scaling; perianth segments joined; drupe dry | ***Zelkova*** (p. 138) |
| | Bark not scaling; perianth segments free; drupe fleshy | ***Celtis*** (p. 140) |

| 130 | Latex present; fruit or false fruit fleshy | **131** |
| | Latex absent; fruit dry | **132** |

| 131 | Buds with 3–6 scales; syncarp cylindrical or ovoid | ***Morus*** (p. 142) |
| | Buds with 2–3 scales; syncarp globose | ***Broussonetia*** (p. 144) |

| 132 | Dioecious; perianth absent | **133** |
| | Monoecious; perianth present | **134** |

| 133 | Buds with 1 outer scale; bracts entire; leaves linear-lanceolate | ***Salix*** (p. 90; key p. 25) |
| | Buds with several outer scales; bracts dentate or fringed; leaves ovate to deltoid | ***Populus*** (p. 104; key p. 25) |

| 134 | Styles 3 or more; flowers of both sexes with a perianth | **135** |
| | Styles 2; perianth present in flowers of 1 sex only | **138** |

| 135 | Male flowers in groups of 1–3 or pendent heads; buds spindle-shaped; nut sharply 3-sided | *Go to* **136** |
| | Male flowers in long erect or pendent catkins; buds ovoid, nut ovoid to subglobose | *Go to* **137** |

| 136 | Male flowers solitary, in pairs or groups of 3, sessile or shortly stalked; female flowers and nuts 3 in each involucre | ***Nothofagus*** (p. 122) |
| | Male flowers many-flowered; female flowers and nuts 2 in each involucre | ***Fagus*** (p. 122) |

137	Male catkins erect, with female flowers in lower part; cupule completely enclosing the nuts	*Castanea* (p. 124)
	Male catkins pendent; female flowers in separate inflorescences; cupule enclosing only lower half of nut	***Quercus** (p. 124; key p. 26)
138	Male flowers 3 to each bract; perianth present	*Go to 139*
	Male flowers 1 to each bract; perianth absent	*Go to 140*
139	Fruiting catkin cylindrical or narrowly ovoid; scales 3-lobed, falling with fruit; stamens 2, bifid below the anthers	*Betula* (p. 114)
	Fruiting catkin ovoid, cone-like, scales 5-lobed, woody and persistent; stamens 4, entire though with shortly forked connective	*Alnus* (p. 116)
140	Buds ovoid-obtuse; leaves usually with fewer than 8 pairs of veins; fruits in clusters of 1–4	*Corylus* (p. 120)
	Buds fusiform, acute; leaves with 9 or more pairs of veins; fruits numerous, in pendent spikes	*Go to 141*
141	Bark grey, smooth; male catkins appearing in spring; nut growing in the axil of a 3-lobed or serrate involucre	*Carpinus* (p. 118)
	Bark brown, rough, scaly; male catkins visible throughout winter; not enclosed in an entire, broadly pointed involucre	*Ostrya* (p. 118)

Juniperus Junipers (p. 42)

1	Leaves all juvenile, needle-like, jointed at the base, in whorls of 3; cones in axils of leaves	*Go to 2*
	Leaves of two sorts: juvenile leaves needle-like, not jointed at the base; adult scale-like, closely appressed; cones at tips of shoots	*Go to 3*
2	Leaves with a single white band above, cone 6–9mm long, blackish	*communis* (p. 42)
	Leaves with two white bands above, cone up to 1.5cm long, purplish	*oxycedrus* (p. 42)
3	Juvenile leaves usually in whorls of 3; scale-leaves with a narrow, pale margin	*Go to 4*
	Juvenile leaves in pairs; scale-leaves green at the margin	*Go to 5*
4	Juvenile leaves absent from adult shoots; scale-leaves blunt; cones dark red	*phoenicea* (p. 44)
	Juvenile leaves at the base of many adult shoots; scale-leaves pointed, cones bluish-white	*chinensis* (p. 46)
5	Cones 4–6mm long	*virginiana* (p. 46)
	Cones 0.7–1.2cm long	*Go to 6*
6	Twigs 0.6–0.8mm thick, rounded in cross-section; scale-leaves up to 1.5mm long	*excelsa* (p. 44)
	Twigs c. 1mm thick, squarish in cross-section; scale-leaves 1.5–2mm long	*Go to 7*
7	Twigs arranged irregularly; cones blackish	*foetidissima* (p. 44)
	Twigs arranged in two ranks, forming flattened sprays; cones dark purple	*thurifera* (p. 46)

Abies Silver Firs (p. 54)

1	Leaves flexible, blunt or slightly notched at the tip, those at the side of the shoot pointing forwards	*Go to* **2**
	Leaves stiff, pointed, radiating at right-angles all round the shoot	*Go to* **9**
2	Twigs with reddish hairs; leaves bluish-grey above	*Go to* **3**
	Twigs with greyish or brownish hairs, or hairless; leaves usually green or rarely dull grey above	*Go to* **4**
3	Twigs grey; cones 5–10cm, the bracts not protruding beyond the cone scales	***lasiocarpa*** (p. 56)
	Twigs brown; cones 12–20cm, the bracts protruding beyond the cone scales	***procera*** (p. 58)
4	Buds without resin; cones 10–20cm long	*Go to* **5**
	Buds exuding resin; cones 5–10cm long	*Go to* **6**
5	Twigs densely hairy; cones 3–4cm in diameter	***alba*** (p. 54)
	Twigs almost hairless; cones 4–5cm in diameter	***nordmanniana*** (p. 56)
6	Leaves not parted beneath the shoot, some pointing downwards; the bracts protruding beyond the cone scales	***delavayi*** (p. 54)
	Leaves distinctly parted beneath the shoot; the bracts not protruding beyond the cone scales	*Go to* **7**
7	Twigs with conspicuous grey down; leaves 1·5–2cm x 1–1·3mm	***sibirica*** (p. 58)
	Twigs almost smooth; yellowish or brownish-green leaves 2–6cm x 1·5–2·5mm	*Go to* **8**
8	Young twigs brownish-green; leaves 2–4cm long	***grandis*** (p. 56)
	Young twigs yellowish-green; leaves 4–6cm long	***concolor*** (p. 56)
9	Leaves 1–1·5cm long with grey or whitish bands above and below; bracts not protruding beyond the cone scales	***pinsapo*** (p. 58)
	Leaves 1·5–3·5cm long with grey bands below only; bracts protruding beyond the cone scales	***cephalonica*** (p. 54)

Picea Spruces (p. 66)

1	Leaves more or less 4-angled with whitish bands on all surfaces	*Go to* **2**
	Leaves flattened with 2 whitish bands on one surface only	*Go to* **7**
2	Leaves stiff with a spine-like tip, spreading all round the shoot	***pungens*** (p. 66)
	Leaves flexible, the tip not spine-like, parted beneath the shoot	*Go to* **3**
3	Twigs covered with dense down	*Go to* **4**
	Twigs smooth or with scattered hairs	*Go to* **6**
4	Leaves 0·6–1cm long, blunt	***orientalis*** (p. 68)
	Leaves 1–2·5cm long, pointed	*Go to* **5**
5	Twigs yellowish-brown; leaves 1·5–2·5cm long; cone scales narrowed into a squarish, irregularly toothed tip	***engelmannii*** (p. 68)
	Twigs brown; leaves 1–1·8cm long; cone scales rounded, sometimes slightly notched at the tip	***abies*** subsp. ***obovata*** (p. 66)
6	Leaves bluish-green, with fetid smell when crushed; cones 3·5–5cm long	***glauca*** (p. 68)
	Leaves dark, without fetid smell when crushed; cones 10–18cm long	***abies*** subsp. ***abies*** (p. 66)
7	Twigs long, slender and pendulous; cones 10–12cm long	***breweriana*** (p. 66)
	Twigs short and rather stiff; cones 5–10cm long	*Go to* **8**
8	Twigs downy; leaves 0·8–1·8cm long, blunt; cones 3–6cm long	***omorika*** (p. 70)
	Twigs smooth; leaves 1·5–2·5cm long. sharply pointed; cones 6–10cm long	***sitchensis*** (p. 70)

Pinus Pines (p. 74)

1	Leaves in groups of 3 or 5	*Go to* **2**
	Leaves in pairs	*Go to* **13**
2	Leaves in groups of 5	*Go to* **3**
	Leaves in groups of 3	*Go to* **8**
3	Seeds not winged	***cembra*** (p. 86)
	Seeds winged	*Go to* **4**
4	Leaves 12–25cm long	*Go to* **5**
	Leaves 2–12cm long	*Go to* **6**
5	Cones 15–25 x 3cm; seeds 8–9mm long with a wing 1–2cm long	***wallichiana*** (p. 86)
	Cones 8–20 x 3–4cm; seeds 5–8mm long with a wing 1·5–2·5cm long	***strobus*** (p. 88)
6	Leaves 2–5cm long	***aristata*** (p. 88)
	Leaves 8–12cm long	*Go to* **7**
7	Shoots bright green, glabrous	***peuce*** (p. 88)
	Shoots brownish to pale green, with short hairs at the base of the leaves	***strobus*** (p. 88)
8	Leaves up to 15cm long	*Go to* **9**
	Leaves 15–30cm long	*Go to* **10**
9	Leaves very slender, bright green, lax; cone 12cm long	***radiata*** (p. 76)
	Leaves stout, stiff; cones 4cm long	***rigida*** (p. 76)
10	Winter buds ovoid, not resiniferous	***canariensis*** (p. 84)
	Winter buds cylindrical, resiniferous	*Go to* **11**
11	Shoots red-brown or grey-brown, not glaucous	***ponderosa*** (p. 78)
	Shoots blue-white or pale blue-grey to more or less glaucous violet	*Go to* **12**
12	Leaves 12–20cm long; cone boss with recurved spine	***jeffreyi*** (p. 78)
	Leaves 20–30cm long; cone boss with straight spine	***sabiniana*** (p. 78)
13	Shoots grey-glaucous in 1st year	*Go to* **14**
	Shoots yellow to green or dark red in 1st year	*Go to* **17**
14	Seeds with well-developed wings	*Go to* **15**
	Seeds wingless, or wings less than 1mm long	***pinea*** (p. 84)
15	Leaves more than 1mm wide; resin canals central	*Go to* **16**
	Leaves less than 1mm wide; resin canals submarginal	***halepensis*** (p. 84)
16	Shoots glaucous for 3 years; exposed part of scale pyramidal with a recurved spine	***leucodermis*** (p. 82)
	Shoots turning green-brown in 2nd year; exposed part of scale flat with a short, erect, pointed spine	***heldreichii*** (p. 82)
17	Buds resiniferous; scales erect at apex	*Go to* **18**
	Buds not resiniferous; scale recurved at apex	*Go to* **19**
18	Resin canals median; cone 8–20 x 5–8cm	***pinaster*** (p. 74)
	Resin canals marginal or submarginal; cone 5–11 x *c.* 4cm	***brutia*** (p. 84)
19	Resin canals median	*Go to* **20**
	Resin canals marginal or submarginal	*Go to* **21**
20	Cone asymmetrical; leaves twisted	***contorta*** (p. 74)
	Cone more or less symmetrical; leaves not, or scarcely twisted	***nigra*** (p. 78)

21	Leaves dark green; cones strongly curved	**banksiana** (p. 76)
	Leaves light green or grey-glaucous; cones straight	*Go to* **22**
22	Shrub or small tree; leaves bright green, cone shining, patent	**mugo** (incl. **uncinata**) (p. 80)
	Always a tree; leaves glaucous; cone dull, pendulous	**sylvestris** (p. 80)

Salix Willows (p. 90)

1	Twigs long, slender, pendent (weeping)	*Go to* **2**
	Twigs not pendent	*Go to* **3**
2	Twigs yellow; indumentum silky	**x chrysocoma** (p. 92)
	Twigs brown; leaves glabrous at maturity	**babylonica** (p. 92)
3	Branches covered in a blue-white bloom, thinning to reveal purple bark with violet tinges	**daphnoides** (p. 102)
	Branches grey-brown or green	*Go to* **4**
4	Mature leaves glabrous	*Go to* **5**
	Mature leaves at least pubescent below	*Go to* **7**
5	Leaves glossy above, finely and evenly serrate with yellow glands; stamens 4–12, usually 5	**pentandra** (p. 90)
	Leaves not conspicuously glossy, rather coarsely serrate with white teeth; stamens 2–3	*Go to* **6**
6	Stipules persistent; bark of old stems flaking off; twigs tough	**triandra** (p. 94)
	Stipules falling early; bark of old stems not flaking off; twigs easily breaking off	**fragilis** (p. 90)
7	Leaves with rust-coloured hairs below	**atrocinerea** (p. 98)
	Leaves with white or grey hairs below	*Go to* **8**
8	Leaves with appressed silky white tomentum	*Go to* **9**
	Leaves woolly or pubescent but not appressed	*Go to* **10**
9	Leaves glabrous above, narrowly linear, more or less entire, with revolute margins	**viminalis** (p. 100)
	Leaves silky-tomentose above, lanceolate, finely serrated,	**flat alba** (p. 92)
10	Leaves 1·5–2 times as long as wide, ovate or obovate to ovate-oblong	**caprea** (p. 98)
	Leaves 2–14 times as long as wide, thin to lanceolate or oblanceolate	*Go to* **11**
11	Filaments joined for at least half their length	**elaeagnos** (p. 102)
	Filaments free	*Go to* **12**
12	Leaves turning black on drying, glabrous or more or less pubescent on both surfaces	**borealis** (p. 94)
	Leaves never turning black on drying, densely pubescent below	*Go to* **13**
13	Ovary and pedicel glabrous	**pedicellata** (p. 96)
	Ovary and pedicel pubescent	*Go to* **14**
14	2 to 4-year-old twigs without or with few inconspicuous ridges beneath the bark	*Go to* **15**
	2 to 4-year-old twigs with numerous very prominent ridges beneath the bark	**cinerea** (p. 96)
15	Stipules usually absent	**xerophila** (p. 100)
	Stipules well developed	**appendiculata** (p. 96)

Populus Poplars (p. 104)

1	Margins of leaves translucent, leaves usually densely hairy or whitish beneath	*Go to* **2**
	Margins of leaves not translucent, leaves usually glabrous and green beneath	*Go to* **5**
2	Petiole rounded in cross-section; crown columnar	***x berolinensis*** (p. 108)
	Petiole flattened; crown usually broad	*Go to* **3**
3	Teeth of leaf margins callus-tipped and with 2–5 glands beneath; stamens 30–60	***deltoides*** (p. 108)
	Teeth of leaf margins without calluses or glands; stamens 20–30	*Go to* **4**
4	Bole without bosses; leaves ciliate	***x canadensis*** (p. 108)
	Bole with bosses; leaves not ciliate	***nigra*** (p. 108)
5	Mature leaves woolly beneath	*Go to* **6**
	Mature leaves sometimes hairy but not woolly beneath	*Go to* **7**
6	Leaves with 3–5 lobes, hairy on the lower surface, white	***alba*** (p. 104)
	Leaves toothed, rarely lobed, hairs on lower surface grey	***canescens*** (p. 104)
7	Petiole strongly flattened; buds and young leaves not fragrant	***tremula*** (p. 106)
	Petiole rounded in cross-section; buds or young leaves fragrant	*Go to* **8**
8	Crown narrow, conical	***balsamifera*** (p. 106)
	Crown somewhat broad, domed	***trichocarpa*** (p. 106)

Quercus Oaks (p. 124)

1	Leaves deciduous or some remaining on the tree over winter, semi-evergreen soft or rarely leathery	*Go to* **2**
	Leaves evergreen, leathery	*Go to* **16**
2	Acorns ripening in the 2nd year on the leafless part of a twig	*Go to* **3**
	Acorns ripening in the 1st year among the leaves	*Go to* **8**
3	Tips of the involucre scales pressed closely together	*Go to* **4**
	Tips of the involucre scales spreading or reflexed	*Go to* **6**
4	Leaves divided to less than halfway to the midrib the lobes pointing forwards	*rubra* (p. 124)
	Leaves divided to more than halfway to the midrib, the lobes spreading widely	*Go to* **5**
5	Underside of the leaf with conspicuous tufts of brown hairs in the vein axils	*palustris* (p. 126)
	Underside of the leaf with the tufts of hairs very small or absent	*coccinea* (p. 126)
6	Leaves smooth and shiny; petioles up to 5mm long	*trojana* (p. 128)
	Leaves dull with soft or stiff hairs; petioles usually 1cm or more	*Go to* **7**
7	Leaves smooth above, the lobes with long bristle-like tips	*macrolepis* (p. 128)
	Leaves rough above, the triangular lobes blunt or rarely with short points	*cerris* (p. 128)
8	Leaves semi-evergreen, glaucous beneath	*canariensis* (p. 132)
	Leaves not semi-evergreen; tomentose, pubescent or rarely smooth below, but not glaucous	*Go to* **9**
9	Scales of the involucre more or less fused; fruits on a long stalk	*Go to* **10**
	Scales of the involucre distinct and separate; fruits on a very short stalk, or stalkless	*Go to* **11**
10	Underside of leaves with grey down	*pedunculiflora* (p. 130)
	Underside of leaves smooth	*robur* (p. 130)
11	Young twigs smooth; the petioles grooved	*Go to* **12**
	Young twigs downy; the petioles not grooved	*Go to* **13**
12	Involucre more or less hairless; adult leaves smooth beneath	*dalechampii* (p. 130)
	Involucre with short down; adult leaves downy beneath	*petraea* (p. 130)
13	Leaves with more than 8 pairs of distinct side veins	*frainetto* (p. 132)
	Leaves with less than 8 pairs of distinct side veins	*Go to* **14**
14	Scales of involucre blunt, not pressed closely together	*pyrenaica* (p. 132)
	Scales of involucre pointed, pressed closely together	*Go to* **15**
15	Petiole 0·5–1·2cm long	*pubescens* (p. 132)
	Petiole 1·5–2·5cm long	*virgiliana* (p. 132)
16	Bark thick and corky, with orange under bark; midrib of leaf sinuous	*suber* (p. 128)
	Bark not thick and corky; midrib of leaf more or less straight	*Go to* **17**
17	Mature leaves hairy beneath; petiole 0·5–1·5cm long	*ilex* (p. 126)
	Mature leaves smooth beneath; petiole 1–4mm long	*coccifera* (p. 126)

Ulmus Elms (p. 134)

1	Pedicels much longer than the flowers; the fruits with the wings fringed with white hairs, pendulous on long stalks	***laevis*** (p. 138)
	Pedicels shorter than the flowers; the fruits not fringed with hairs, or pendulous, almost stalkless	*Go to* **2**
2	Base of the leaf with the longer half overlapping the petiole; seed in the centre of the fruit	***glabra*** (p. 134)
	Base of the leaf with the longer half not overlapping the petiole; seed above the centre of the fruit	*Go to* **3**
3	Leaves up to 15cm long, smooth above; the petiole 1–2cm long	***x hollandica*** (p. 134)
	Leaves 6–10cm long, rough or smooth above; the petiole 1–5cm long	*Go to* **4**
4	Leaves rounded, rough above; fruit about as long as wide	***procera*** (p. 134)
	Leaves ovate, obovate or oblanceolate; fruit longer than wide	*Go to* **5**
5	Twigs with dense white down; leaves with 12–16 pairs of veins, the underside with dense grey down	***canescens*** (p. 136)
	Twigs almost smooth; leaves with 7–12 pairs of veins, the underside with tufts of hairs in the vein axils	*Go to* **6**
6	Leaves with a very unequal base, the midrib curving towards the short side	***coritana*** (p. 136)
	Leaves with the base almost equal or somewhat unequal, the midrib more or less straight	*Go to* **7**
7	Young twigs short and rather stiff; leaves often concave	***angustifolia*** (p. 136)
	Young twigs long and pendulous; the leaves flat	*Go to* **8**
8	Leaves usually widest above the middle, the base of the longer half turning at right-angles towards the petiole	***carpinifolia*** (p. 136)
	Leaves usually widest at the middle, the base of the longer half rounded	*Go to* **9**
9	Crown dense, small branches ascending to a symmetrical tip	***minor*** (p. 136)
	Crown slender, arching out a little and thinning out markedly below a slightly leaning, one-sided tip	***plotii*** (p. 136)

Pyrus Pears (p. 158)

1	Fruit with a deciduous calyx	***cordata*** (p. 160)
	Fruit with a persistent calyx	*Go to* **2**
2	Fruit 5–16cm, flesh sweet-tasting	***communis*** (p. 164)
	Fruit not more than 5.5cm long, flesh hard, usually bitter	*Go to* **3**
3	Leaves not more than 1.5 times as long as wide	***pyraster*** (p. 160)
	Leaves more than 1.5 times as long as wide	*Go to* **4**
4	Mature leaves glabrous or papillose beneath	*Go to* **5**
	Mature leaves hairy or woolly beneath	*Go to* **6**
5	Leaves toothed, rounded at the base	***bourgaeana*** (p. 160)
	Leaves entire to slightly toothed, wedge-shaped at the base	***amygdaliformis*** (p. 162)
6	Styles densely hairy at least at the base	*Go to* **7**
	Styles more or less glabrous	*Go to* **9**
7	Styles hairy to the middle	***elaeagrifolia*** (p. 162)
	Styles hairy only at the base	*Go to* **8**

8	Fruit 2.5–3cm long	*nivalis* (p. 164)
	Fruit 3–5cm long	*salicifolia* (p. 158)
9	Leaves usually less than 3.5cm wide, entire	*salvifolia* (p. 162)
	Leaves usually more than 3.5cm wide, toothed towards the apex	*austriaca* (p. 164)

Sorbus Whitebeams, Rowans and Service Trees (p. 170)

1	Leaves all pinnate	*Go to 2*
	At least most leaves simple	*Go to 9*
2	Leaves with terminal leaflet about the same size as the others, not deeply lobed	*Go to 4*
	Leaves with terminal leaflet much larger than the others, usually deeply lobed	*Go to 3*
3	Leaves with 2 pairs of free leaflets	*hybrida* (p. 178)
	Leaves with 4–5 pairs of free leaflets	*meinchii* (p. 178)
4	Ripe fruits orange or scarlet	*Go to 7*
	Ripe fruits greenish, brownish, pink or white	*Go to 5*
5	Ripe fruits greenish or brownish, ovoid or pear-shaped	*domestica* (p. 170)
	Ripe fruits pink or white, globose	*Go to 6*
6	Leaf-rachis grooved on the upper surface, reddish	*hupehensis* (p. 172)
	Leaf-rachis not grooved on upper surface, green	*vilmorinii* (p. 170)
7	Leaves with 5 or fewer pairs of leaflets, hairy on the lower surface; flowers opening in June	*sargentiana* (p. 172)
	Leaves with 5 or more pairs of leaflets, glabrous or glabrescent on the lower surface; flowers opening in May	*Go to 8*
8	Inflorescence 10–15cm in diameter; bud dark purple	*aucuparia* (p. 172)
	Inflorescence less than 10cm in diameter; bud shiny red	*commixta* (p. 170)
9	Leaves lobed	*Go to 12*
	Leaves entire	*Go to 10*
10	Leaves with teeth curved on the outer edge; fruit with numerous lenticels	*Go to 11*
	Leaves with symmetrical teeth; fruit with few large lenticels	*graeca* (p. 174)
11	Leaves with 10–14 pairs of veins; fruits more or less ovoid	*aria* (p. 174)
	Leaves with 7–9 pairs of veins; fruits globose	*rupicola* (p. 174)
12	Ripe fruits red	*Go to 13*
	Ripe fruits brown or yellow	*Go to 15*
13	Leaves yellowish-grey-tomentose beneath	*Intermedia* (p. 176)
	Leaves whitish-grey-tomentose beneath	*Go to 14*
14	Leaves 1.5–2 times as long as wide; fruit ovoid with few small lenticels	*mougeotii* (p. 176)
	Leaves 1.25 times as long as wide; fruit globose with numerous large lenticels	*austriaca* (p. 176)
15	Leaves lobed more than quarter way to the midrib, glabrous below	*torminalis* (p. 174)
	Leaves lobed usually to less than quarter way (sometimes to halfway) to the midrib, tomentose below	*Go to 16*
16	Leaves grey-hairy below; ripe fruit brown	*latifolia* (p. 178)
	Leaves white-hairy below; ripe fruit yellow	*umbellata* (p. 176)

Crataegus Hawthorns (p. 184)

1	Lateral veins of leaves ending only in the lobe apices or teeth	*Go to* **2**
	Lateral veins of leaves ending both in the apices and sinuses of the lobe or teeth	*Go to* **3**
2	Leaves unlobed, simply and acutely serrate above, entire at base	***crus-galli*** (p. 184)
	Leaves with 7–11 lobes, sharply and irregularly serrate to the base	***nigra*** (p. 188)
3	Styles 4–5	*Go to* **4**
	Styles 1–3	*Go to* **5**
4	Leaves sparsely villous with well-developed petioles; inflorescence lax; fruit black, more or less globose, rarely exceeding 1·1cm in diameter	***pentagyna*** (p. 188)
	Leaves lanate or with silky hairs and with poorly developed petioles; inflorescence compact; fruit orange or red often more than 1·1cm in diameter	***orientalis*** (p. 190)
5	Styles 2–3	*Go to* **6**
	Styles 1	*Go to* **7**
6	Leaves shallowly lobed with well-developed petioles; inflorescences lax; fruit rarely exceeding 1·1cm in diameter	***laevigata*** (p. 184)
	Leaves laciniate with short petioles; inflorescences compact; fruit exceeding 1·1cm in diameter	***azarolus*** (p. 190)
7	Leaf-lobes with more or less entire margins or a few apical teeth; sepals more or less triangular or broadly lanceolate; fruit globose to ovate	***monogyna*** (p. 186)
	Leaf-lobes with margins more or less serrate to base; sepals narrowly lanceolate; fruit narrowly ovate	***calycina*** (p. 186)

Prunus Cherries and Plums (p. 192)

1	Ovary and ripe fruit smooth	*Go to* **2**
	Ovary and ripe fruit hairy	*Go to* **20**
2	Flower solitary, or in clusters, or in heads with all the stalks arising from the same point (umbels)	*Go to* **3**
	Flowers in branched heads, with the stalks arising from many different points (racemes or corymbs)	*Go to* **15**
3	Fruit-stalk much longer than the ripe fruit; flower stalks rarely 1cm, usually 1·5–8cm long (if less than 1·5cm long, then petals exceeding 1·5cm)	*Go to* **4**
	Fruit-stalk shorter than, or about as long as ripe fruit; flower stalks 0·1–1·5cm rarely up to 2cm (if more than 1·5cm then petals less than 1·5cm)	*Go to* **9**
4	Flower-tube urn-shaped, more or less constricted at the mouth	*Go to* **5**
	Flower-tube narrowly or broadly bell-shaped, not constricted at the mouth	*Go to* **6**
5	Leaves 1–3cm wide; petioles 6–7cm long	***serrula*** (p. 202)
	Leaves 4–7cm wide; petioles 2–5cm long	***avium*** (p. 198)
6	Leaves 3–8cm long; flower-tube broadly bell-shaped	***cerasus*** (p. 198)
	Leaves 8–20cm long; flower-tube narrowly bell-shaped	*Go to* **7**
7	Young twigs downy; flowers in clusters of 5–6	***x yedoensis*** (p. 200)
	Young twigs smooth; flowers in clusters of 2–4	*Go to* **8**
8	Teeth of leaves drawn out into hairlike points; flowers white or pink, the petioles 1·5–8cm long	***serrulata*** (p. 200)
	Teeth of leaves sharp but not with hairlike points; flowers deep pink; petioles 1–2cm long	***sargentii*** (p. 200)
9	Flower-tube urn-shaped, constricted at the mouth	***subhirtella*** (p. 202)
	Flower-tube broadly bell-shaped, not constricted at the mouth	*Go to* **10**
10	Petals pink; the flowers without peduncles	***persica*** (p. 192)
	Petals white or rarely pinkish; the peduncles 0·5–2cm long	*Go to* **11**
11	Young twigs smooth and glossy	*Go to* **12**
	Young twigs dull and hairy	*Go to* **14**
12	Leaves with large, pointed teeth	***brigantina*** (p. 194)
	Leaves with rounded or very small forward-pointing teeth	*Go to* **13**
13	Flowers usually solitary, the peduncles *c.* 1·5cm long	***cerasifera*** (p. 194)
	Flowers in clusters of 2–4, the peduncles 2–4mm long	***cocomilia*** (p. 196)
14	Bark blackish; branches spine-tipped; fruit less than 2cm long, more or less erect	***spinosa*** (p. 196)
	Bark brown; branches without spines, or rarely spine-tipped; fruit 2cm long or more, pendulous	***domestic*** (p. 196)
15	Flowers in short rounded heads (corymbs) of up to 10 flowers	***mahaleb*** (p. 202)
	Flowers in elongated heads (racemes) of 12–100 flowers	*Go to* **16**
16	Leaves deciduous, thin and soft	*Go to* **17**
	Leaves evergreen, thick and rather leathery	*Go to* **19**
17	Petals 6–9mm; stone grooved	***padus*** (p. 204)
	Petals 3–5mm; stone smooth	*Go to* **18**

18 Bark bitter and aromatic; fruit purplish-black	*serotina* (p. 204)	
Bark not aromatic; fruit deep red	*virginiana* (p. 204)	
19 Flower-heads 8–13cm long, shorter than the leaves	*laurocerasus* (p. 206)	
Flower-heads 15–28cm long, longer than the leaves	*lusitanica* (p. 206)	
20 Leaves about as long as wide	*armeniaca* (p. 194)	
Leaves more than twice as long as wide	Go to **21**	
21 Petals deep pink; outer layer of ripe fruit succulent	*persica* (p. 192)	
Petals while or pinkish; outer layer of ripe fruit leathery	*dulcis* (p. 192)	

Acacia Wattles or Mimosas (p. 212)

1 Adult leaves twice-pinnate	Go to **2**	
Adult leaves flattened phyllodes	Go to **5**	
2 Stipules spiny; leaves deciduous with 2–8 pairs of pinnae	Go to **3**	
Stipules rudimentary; leaves evergreen with 7–20 pairs of pinnae	Go to **4**	
3 Leaflets 3–5mm long, stipules up to 2·5cm long on old branches	*farnesiana* (p. 216)	
Leaflets 0·6–1cm long; stipular spines up to 10cm long on old branches	*karoo* (p. 216)	
4 Twigs and young leaves whitish-tomentose; leaflets 3–4mm long; legume 1–1·2cm wide, not or scarcely constricted between the seeds	*dealbata* (p. 212)	
Twigs and young leaves yellowish-villous; leaflets 2mm long; legumes 5–7mm wide, distinctly constricted between the seeds	*mearnsii* (p. 214)	
5 Flowers in axillary spikes; legume terete	*longifolia* (p. 214)	
Flowers in heads in groups of 2–3 or racemes; legume flattened	Go to **6**	
6 Phyllodes with 2–6 veins	Go to **7**	
Phyllodes with a single vein	Go to **8**	
7 Flowers yellow	*cyclops* (p. 216)	
Flowers creamy-white	*melanoxylon* (p. 214)	
8 Phyllodes falcate, oblong-lanceolate to obovate; 10–20 heads in each raceme	*pycnantha* (p. 216)	
Phyllodes not or scarcely falcate, linear to lanceolate or oblanceolate; 2–9 heads in each raceme	Go to **9**	
9 Capitula 1–1·5cm in diameter; legume distinctly constricted between the seeds; stalk encircling seed short, whitish	*cyanophylla* (p. 212)	
Capitula 4–6mm in diameter; legume not or scarcely constricted between seeds; stalk encircling seed scarlet	*retinodes* (p. 216)	

Acer Maples (p. 230)

1	Leaves pinnate, with 3–7 leaflets	*Go to* **2**
	Leaves simple, undivided or palmately lobed	*Go to* **3**
2	Bark peeling in papery strips; leaves with 3 dark green leaflets	***griseum*** (p. 230)
	Bark smooth or shallowly fissured, never peeling; leaves with 3–7 light green leaflets	***negundo*** (p. 234)
3	Leaves undivided, or sometimes with 3–5 very shallow lobes	*Go to* **4**
	Leaves with 3–7 distinct lobes	*Go to* **5**
4	Wings of fruit subparallel, red; petiole grooved	***tataricum*** (p. 240)
	Wings of fruit almost horizontal, green; petiole not grooved	***davidii*** (p. 230)
5	Wings of fruit making an acute angle, or more or less parallel; leaves usually leathery, sometimes evergreen	*Go to* **11**
	Wings of fruit making an obtuse angle or more or less horizontal; leaves usually not leathery,	***deciduous*** 6
6	Middle lobe of leaf separated nearly to the base; wings of fruit usually strongly curved	***heldreichii*** (p. 230)
	Middle lobe of leaf not separated to more than one-third of the way to base; wings of fruit usually not strongly curved	*Go to* **7**
7	Fruits 5cm long or more, the wings horizontal	*Go to* **8**
	Fruits 5cm long or less, the wings usually making an obtuse angle, or sometimes horizontal	*Go to* **9**
8	Fruit 5–6cm long, green or reddish; leaves with 3–5 lobes, ciliate	***campestre*** (p. 230)
	Fruit 6–10cm long, yellow; leaves with 5–7 lobes, not ciliate	***platanoides*** (p. 238)
9	Flower clusters pendent; fruit 2cm long or more	*Go to* **10**
	Flower clusters erect; fruit 2cm long or less	***palmatum*** (p. 236)
10	Leaves with 7–11 lobes; wings of fruit making an obtuse angle	***japonicum*** (p. 236)
	Leaves with 5 lobes, wings of fruit making or nearly making a right-angle	***pseudoplatanus*** (p. 238)
11	Margins entire, leaves with 3 lobes	*Go to* **12**
	Margins toothed, leaves usually with more than 3 lobes	*Go to* **13**
12	Leaves evergreen, green and glabrous below	***sempervirens*** (p. 232)
	Leaves somewhat leathery but deciduous, slightly bluish and hairy below	***monspessulanum*** (p. 232)
13	Leaves silvery below	*Go to* **14**
	Leaves green or whitish below, but not silvery	*Go to* **15**
14	Leaf sinuses cut less than halfway to the base, margins coarsely toothed; fruit 1cm long, red	***rubrum*** (p. 240)
	Leaf sinuses cut more than halfway to the base, margins deeply toothed; fruit 5–6cm long, green	***saccarhinum*** (p. 240)
15	Leaf lobes triangular-ovate, cut less than halfway to the base	*Go to* **17**
	Leaf lobes parallel-sided, cut halfway to the base	*Go to* **16**
16	Leaf up to 7cm long, densely hairy on lower surfaces	***granatense*** (p. 232)
	Leaf up to 10cm long, more or less glabrous on the lower surface	***hyrcanum*** (p. 232)
17	Leaf lobes blunt, persistently hairy on the lower surface	***obtusatum*** (p. 234)
	Leaf lobes acute, lower surface glabrescent	***opalus*** (p. 234)

Tilia Lime Trees (p. 254)

1	Leaves white beneath with a layer of stellate hairs; staminodes present	*Go to* **2**
	Leaves smooth beneath or with simple hairs; staminodes absent	*Go to* **3**
2	Petioles up to 5cm long, usually less than half as long as the leaf blade	***tomentosa*** (p. 254)
	Petioles up to 12cm long, usually more than half as long as the leaf blade	***petiolaris*** (p. 254)
3	Flowers in erect cymes; fruit shell membranous	***cordata*** (p. 256)
	Flowers in pendent cymes; the fruit shell thick and woody	*Go to* **4**
4	Fruit strongly ribbed	*Go to* **5**
	Fruit weakly ribbed or smooth	*Go to* **6**
5	Leaves with teeth ending in a hairlike tip	***rubra*** (p. 256)
	Leaves with teeth pointed but not hairlike at the tip platy	***phyllos*** (p. 256)
6	Flowers yellowish-white; underside of leaves with whitish hair tufts in the vein axils	***x vulgaris*** (p. 258)
	Flowers rich yellow; underside of leaves with reddish-brown hair tufts in the vein axils	***x euchlora*** (p. 258)

Tamarix Tamarisks (p. 264)

1	Perianth segments 4 in each whorl	*Go to* **2**
	Perianth segments 5 in each whorl	*Go to* **4**
2	Inflorescence 0·7–1cm wide; bracts exceeding the calyx	***dalmatica*** (p. 268)
	Inflorescence 3–7mm wide; bracts not exceeding the calyx	*Go to* **3**
3	Bark black; bracts herbaceous in proximal half; petals more than 2mm long	***tetrandra*** (p. 266)
	Bark brown to purple; bracts entirely scarious; petals less than 2mm long	***parviflora*** (p. 266)
4	Inflorescence 0·8–1·2cm wide	***dalmatica*** (p. 268)
	Inflorescence 3–8mm wide	*Go to* **5**
5	Petals 2–3mm long	*Go to* **6**
	Petals 1·25–2mm long	*Go to* **7**
6	Sepals 1·5mm long	***africana*** (p. 264)
	Sepals 2–2·5mm long	***tetrandra*** (p. 266)
7	Bracts equalling or exceeding the calyx; petals not more than 1·5mm long	***canariensis*** (p. 264)
	Bracts not extending beyond the calyx; petals 1·5–2mm long	*Go to* **8**
8	Petals elliptical to elliptic-obovate, more or less flat	***gallica*** (p. 266)
	Petals ovate-orbicular, strongly keeled	***smyrnensis*** (p. 268)

Eucalyptus Eucalypts (p. 270)

1	Fruits more than 1cm long; flowers solitary	***globulus*** (p. 276)
	Fruits up to 1cm long; flowers in umbels	*Go to* **2**
2	Fruits distinctly pedicellate	*Go to* **3**
	Fruits sessile or subsessile	*Go to* **7**
3	Inflorescence with 3 (occasionally 5) flowers	*Go to* **4**
	Inflorescence with 5–10 flowers	*Go to* **5**
4	Mature leaves 10–25cm long	***citriodora*** (p. 270)
	Mature leaves 4–7cm long	***gunnii*** (p. 278)
5	Peduncles terete or nearly so	***camaldulensis*** (p. 274)
	Peduncles compressed, angular, or strap-shaped	*Go to* **6**
6	Fruit 1·2–1·5cm long, cylindrical to flask-shaped, valves enclosed or very slightly projecting	***robustus*** (p. 272)
	Fruit 5–8mm long, ovoid to hemispherical; valves strongly projecting	***resinifer*** (p. 272)
7	Inflorescence 3-flowered	***viminalis*** (p. 278)
	Inflorescence with 5–10 (rarely 3) flowers	*Go to* **8**
8	Bark smooth; leaves c. 20cm long; fruit glaucous	***maidenii*** (p. 276)
	Bark fibrous; leaves 10–17cm long; fruits not dull	*Go to* **9**
9	Peduncles 0·7–1cm long; fruit 7–9 x 7–9mm long, barrel-shaped or cylindrical	***botryoides*** (p. 270)
	Peduncles 2·5–3·5cm long; fruit 1·3–2 x 1·1–1·5cm long, bell-shaped	***gomphocephalus*** (p. 274)

Fraxinus Ashes (p. 286)

1	Corolla present; flowers appearing after the leaves	***omus*** (p. 286)
	Corolla absent; flowers appearing before the leaves	*Go to* **2**
2	Calyx present; body of samara terete	*Go to* **3**
	Calyx absent; body of samara flattened	*Go to* **4**
3	Wing of samara decurrent on the body; base of blade usually decurrent on the petiolule	***pennsylvanica*** (p. 286)
	Wing of samara not decurrent on the body; base of blade not decurrent on the petiolule	***americana*** (p. 286)
4	Buds black; leaflets with more teeth than lateral veins	***excelsior*** (p. 288)
	Buds brown; leaflets with as many teeth as lateral veins	*Go to* **5**
5	Twigs, petiole and leaf-rachis densely hairy; samaras finely hairy	***pallisiae*** (p. 288)
	Twigs, petiole and leaf-rachis glabrous; samaras glabrous	***angustifolia*** (p. 288)

Gymnosperms

Maidenhair Tree Family
Ginkgoaceae

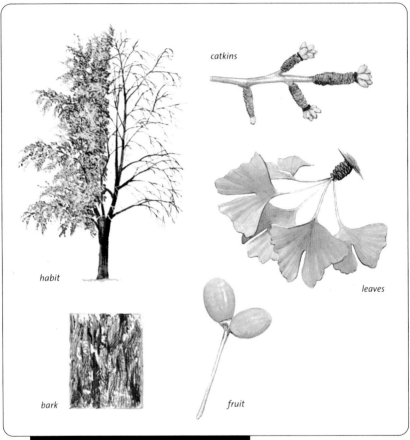

catkins

leaves

habit

bark

fruit

Ginkgo biloba L. Maidenhair Tree

An irregularly or narrowly conical, deciduous, dioecious tree up to 30m high, with one to several trunks. **Bark** Rather corky, grey-brown with interconnecting ridges separated by wide fissures. **Branches** Spreading; the shoots of 2 kinds: long shoots, greenish-brown with widely spaced leaves; and short shoots borne on the long shoots, brown, with closely spaced leaves or leaf-scars. **Leaves** Up to 12 x 10cm, fan-shaped with radiating veins, usually with one or several deep and several shallow divisions around the margin, yellowish to dark green, smooth; the petiole is 1–4·5cm long, somewhat grooved above. **Flowers** Male flowers occur in thick yellowish, upright, spreading catkins, in clusters of up to 6 on the short shoots; female flowers occur singly or in pairs on a pedicel c. 5cm long. **Fruit** 2·5–3cm long, globose or sometimes ovoid, fleshy, smooth, turning yellow with a greyish bloom, becoming foul-smelling when ripe and containing a single seed in a stony layer. Male cones shed pollen in March–April. **Distribution** A species almost unknown in the wild (reputed wild in Chekiang Province, China) but cultivated for centuries in China for its edible fruits. It is widely planted in gardens and parks in much of Europe.

Yew Family
Taxaceae

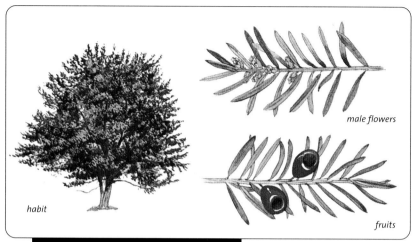

habit

male flowers

fruits

Taxus baccata L. Common Yew

A broadly conical dioecious evergreen tree or shrub up to 25m, the bole often long and sinuous. **Bark** Reddish-brown, flaking and peeling to reveal reddish patches. **Branches** Rather stout, level or ascending, the twigs arising irregularly, somewhat pendulous. **Leaves** 1–4cm x c. 3mm, linear, flattened, abruptly narrowing into a sharp point, entire, tapering at the base, glossy or dull, dark green above, with 2 pale yellowish-green bands below, sessile, arising spirally but flattened into a row on either side of the twig. **Flowers** Male flowers are solitary, consisting of a globose cluster of up to 14 anthers, yellowish; female flowers are minute, solitary or in pairs, green. **Fruits** 0·6–1cm long, ovoid to globose with a depression at the tip, the outer fleshy aril usually scarlet as it ripens in September. Male cones shed pollen in February–April. **Distribution** A native of much of Europe, some areas of N. Africa and parts of SW. Asia, usually on lime-rich soils. Many different cultivated varieties are planted widely for ornament, shelter and timber. All except Cr Ic.

Cow Tail Pine Family
Cephalotaxaceae

habit

fruits

Cephalotaxus harringtonia (Forbes) C. Koch Cow Tail Pine

A species similar to Taxus baccata, infrequently planted for ornament in parks and gardens.

Monkey Puzzle Family
Araucariaceae

habit

shoot with male cone

bark

female cone

Araucaria araucana (Molina) C. Koch Monkey Puzzle

An evergreen, dioecious, broadly conical or domed tree up to 30m tall with a long cylindrical bole, sometimes suckering from the roots. **Bark** Dark grey, becoming wrinkled and ridged and marked with rings of old branch scars around the trunk. **Branches** Mostly horizontal to somewhat pendent, regularly arranged around the trunk; the shoots are densely covered with spirally arranged leaves. **Leaves** 3–4cm long, ovate to triangular, gradually tapering into a sharp brown point, thick and leathery, dark glossy green. **Cones** Male cones are *c.* 10 x 6cm long, occurring in clusters on the shoot tips, brown; female cones are 10–17cm long, globose, erect, occurring on the upper side of a shoot, green until the second year and breaking up on the tree; each scale ends in a gradually tapering, outward-curving point. Male cones shed pollen in June–July. **Seeds** *c.* 4cm long, brown, edible. **Distribution** A native of Chile and Argentina, commonly planted for ornament in parks and gardens of W. Europe.

Cypress Family
Cupressaceae

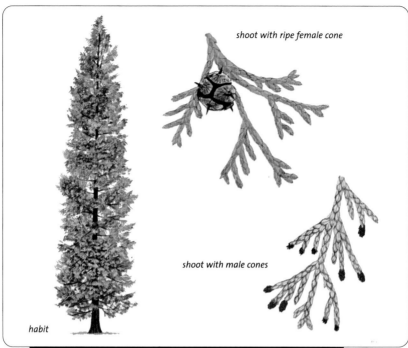

shoot with ripe female cone

shoot with male cones

habit

Chamaecyparis lawsoniana (A. Murray) Parl.
Lawson Cypress

A narrowly conical, dioecious tree up to 45m high, the trunk often forking. **Bark** Becoming cracked into long vertical grey-brown plates. **Branches** Numerous and small; the young shoots pendulous, forming flattened sprays. **Leaves** Opposite, the adjacent pairs at right-angles to each other, 0·5–2mm long, scale-like, closely pressed together, the smaller vertical pairs with translucent glands, whitish below, where they join. **Cones** Male cones are *c.* 4mm long, pink or red, occurring at the tips of the twigs; female cones are *c.* 8mm in diameter, globose, green with a bluish bloom, becoming yellowish-brown; the scales occur in 4 pairs, each depressed in the centre, with a transverse ridge. Male cones shed pollen in March. **Seeds** 2–5 on each scale with broad wings and large resiniferous tubercles. **Distribution** A native of the W. United States, widely planted for ornament (as cultivars), shelter and timber; sometimes naturalized. Au Br De Fr Ge Ir It No Po Ru Tu.

shoot with female cone

Chamaecyparis obtusa
(Siebold & Zucc.) Siebold & Zucc. in Endl. **Hinoki Cypress**

Like C. lawsoniana but the bark is reddish and shallowly fissured into long thin strips; the leaves are blunt with a minute gland and a conspicuous white marking underneath. **Distribution** A native of Japan, commonly planted for ornament.

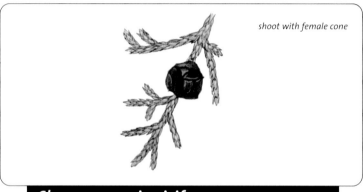

shoot with female cone

Chamaecyparis pisifera
(Siebold & Zucc.) Siebold & Zucc. in Endl. **Sawara Cypress**

A species also like C. lawsoniana but the bark is reddish-brown with ridges and deep cracks, and the leaves have sharp, incurved tips with indistinct glands. **Distribution** Another Japanese native, commonly planted for ornament.

female cone

Chamaecyparis nootkatensis
(Lamb.) Spach **Nootka Cypress**

Like C. lawsoniana but the female cones are c. 1cm in diameter, green with a bluish bloom, becoming dull brown; and each of the 4–6 scales has a long curved spine. **Distribution** A native of N. America, planted infrequently for ornament.

male cones

habit

female cone

X Cupressocyparis leylandii
(A.B. Jackson & Dallimore) Dallimore **Leyland Cypress**

A narrowly conical to columnar monoecious tree up to 35m tall. **Bark** Dark reddish-brown shallow fissures. **Branches** Numerous, regular, ascending almost vertically, the foliage remaining alive at the base; the lateral shoots often arise on one side of the leading shoots. **Leaves** Opposite, the adjacent pairs at right-angles to each other, 0·5–2mm long, scale-like, closely pressed together, pointed, dark green. **Cones** Male and female cones are rare; male cones are c. 3mm in diameter, yellow, occurring at the tips of twigs; female cones are 1–3cm in diameter, globose, each of the 4–8 scales with a large process in the centre, green becoming brown and shiny. Male cones shed pollen in March. **Taxonomic notes** The Leyland Cypress is a vigorous hybrid between the Nootka Cypress (Chamaecyparis nootkatensis) and the Monterey Cypress (Cypressus macrocarpa). There are two distinct sorts of cultivar: 'Haggerston Grey', with the Nootka Cypress as the female parent, has branches in several planes producing plumes of greyish foliage; and 'Leighton Green', with the Monterey Cypress as the female parent, has branchlets more or less restricted to one plane, producing flattened sprays of greenish foliage.

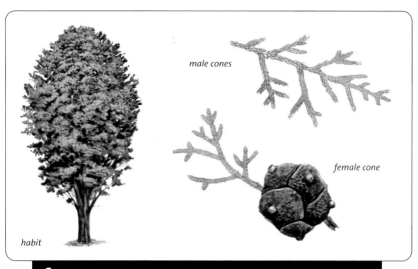

male cones

female cone

habit

Cupressus macrocarpa Hartweg Monterey Cypress

An evergreen monoecious tree up to 35m tall, pyramidal while young, but becoming broadly domed at maturity. **Bark** Ridged and scaly, reddish-brown. **Branches** Numerous, rather stout, steeply ascending on young trees, much more spreading on old trees; the young shoots are stiffly forward-projecting, arranged irregularly around the leading shoot; the leaves are opposite, the adjacent pairs at right-angles, 1–2mm long, scale-like with a sharp point and a pale margin. **Cones** Male cones are 3–5mm in diameter, yellow, carried on the lower pads of shoots, below the females; female cones are 2–4cm in diameter, globose to ellipsoid, bright green becoming purplish-brown and shiny; the scales occur in 4–7 pairs, each with a shortly pointed central protuberance. Male cones shed pollen in June. **Seeds** 8–20 on each scale, pale brown, with a papery wing. **Distribution** A native of S. California. Commonly planted in W. and S. Europe for ornament and shelter or occasionally for timber. Br Fr Ir It Pl Si Sp.

female cone

Cupressus lusitanica
Miller **Cedar of Goa, Mexican Cypress**

Similar to C. macrocarpa but the bark is brown with peeling strips; the branches are spreading, more or less pendent at the tips; the leaves have spreading, sharp points; the female cones are 1–1·5cm in diameter, globose to ellipsoid, bluish-grey when young but becoming brown and shiny; and the scales number 6–8. **Distribution** A native of Mexico and Guatemala, planted for ornament and timber particularly in S. Europe. Fr It Pl Sp.

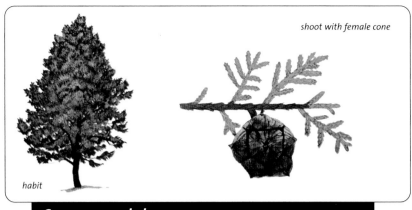

shoot with female cone

habit

Cupressus glabra Sudworth Smooth Arizona Cypress

Similar to C. macrocarpa but the bark flaking to reveal yellow or red-brown patches; the branches are widely spreading and ascending at the tips; the young shoots spread at right-angles to the leading shoot; the leaves are greyish-green, occasionally with a central white spot; the female cones are 1·5–2·5cm in diameter, greenish-brown with a slight bloom; the scales each with a small, rather blunt protuberance. **Distribution** A native of C. Arizona, occasionally planted for ornament or shelter in parks and gardens.

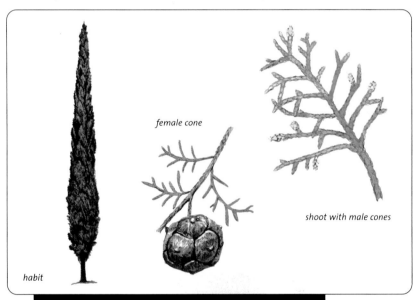

female cone

shoot with male cones

habit

Cupressus sempervirens L. Italian Cypress

A narrow columnar or occasionally pyramidal evergreen tree up to 30m tall. **Bark** Shallowly, often spirally ridged, grey-brown. **Branches** Upright or occasionally diverging; the young shoots are somewhat 4-angled, arising irregularly around the leading shoot, curved upwards at the tips. **Leaves** Opposite, the adjacent pairs at right-angles to each other, 0·5–1mm in diameter, scale-like, blunt, dark green, all similar, closely pressed together. **Cones** Male cones are 4–8mm in diameter, greenish-yellow; female cones are 2·5–4cm in diameter, ellipsoid-oblong, green becoming yellowish-grey in the second year; the scales occur in 4–7 pairs and are blunt except for a small point at the tip, the margins somewhat wavy. Male cones shed pollen in March. **Seeds** 8–20 on each scale, narrowly winged. **Distribution** The wild form has rather spreading branches, forming a pyramidal tree, but the fastigiate form is much more widely planted and a conspicuous feature of Mediterranean landscapes. A native of SE. Europe and planted in other parts of S. Europe for ornament and timber. Al Bl Bu Co Cr Fr Fu Gr It Pl Sa Sd Si Sp Tu Yu.

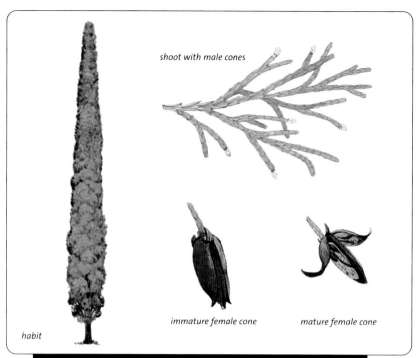

shoot with male cones

immature female cone

mature female cone

habit

Calocedrus decurrens   (Torrey) Florin Incense Cedar

A monoecious, narrowly columnar evergreen tree up to 35m high and rounded at the top. **Bark** Cracked into large flakes, dark reddish-brown. **Branches** Numerous, short, ascending towards the tips; the shoots are covered with contiguous leaf-bases, green, becoming reddish-brown. **Leaves** Occurring in whorls of 4, scale-like, narrow with short, incurving, acute tips, closely pressed together, all similar. **Cones** Male cones are 3–6mm in diameter, ovoid, deep yellow, occurring at the tips of lateral shoots; female cones 2–3cm in diameter, oblong-ovoid, pointed; the two large fertile scales each with a short, outward-pointing, acute tip. Male cones shed pollen in January. **Distribution** A native of N. America, occasionally planted for ornament in large parks and gardens in Europe.

Juniperus L. Junipers

A genus of some 60 species of evergreen trees and shrubs

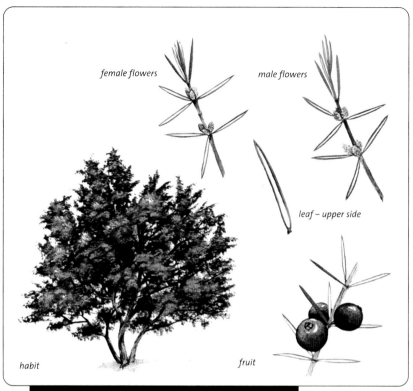

female flowers

male flowers

leaf – upper side

habit

fruit

Juniperus communis L. Common Juniper

A dioecious shrub or small tree up to 15m high, initially conical, becoming much broader. **Bark** Reddish-brown, peeling in papery sheets. The twigs are slender, with ridges on the 3 angles, pale brown. **Leaves** All juvenile, 0·8–2 x 0·1–0·2cm, linear, spreading at right-angles, in whorls of 3, jointed at the base, sharply pointed at the tip, rigid, the upper surface with a single, broad, whitish stomatiferous band, rarely divided by a faint midrib near the base, lower surface faintly keeled, sessile. **Cones** Male cones are solitary, yellow, produced in the leaf axils; female cones are 6–9mm long, ovoid to globose, ripening in the 2nd or 3rd year, changing from green to glaucous-blue to black when fully ripe. Male cones shed pollen in March. **Seeds** Usually 3. **Distribution and taxonomic notes** There are 2 further shrubby subspecies of the Common Juniper found mostly in mountainous regions of Europe. J. communis subsp. nana Syme in Sowerby has short, closely set leaves up to 1·5cm long, and often mat-like growth and grows on high mountains or occasionally near the coast in N. and NW. Europe. J. communis subsp. hemisphaerica (J. & C. Presl.) Nyman can be distinguished by its broad leaves, up to 2mm wide. It is a native of Europe, often found on lime-rich soils in the Mediterranean region, SW. Asia to the W. Himalayas and N. America. Found in all Europe.

fruit

leaf – upper side

habit

Juniperus oxycedrus L. Prickly Juniper

A dioecious shrub or small tree up to 14m high. **Bark** Reddish-grey. The twigs are stout. **Leaves** All juvenile, 0·4–2·5 x 0·1–0·2cm, linear, in whorls of 3, swollen and jointed at the base, sharply and stiffly pointed at the apex, the upper surface with 2 glaucous bands of stomata separated by a raised green midrib, the lower surface sharply keeled, sessile. **Cones** Female cones are c. 1·5cm in diameter, more or less globose to pear-shaped, initially reddish and becoming yellow at maturity. **Distribution and taxonomic notes** The Prickly Juniper is native to S. Europe and is an extremely variable species. It can be divided into 3 subspecies: subsp. oxycedrus, with leaves c. 2mm wide and ripe cones 0·8–1cm in diameter, occurs in dry hills and mountainous tracts (to 1900m) almost throughout the range of the species; subsp. macrocarpa (Sibth. & Sm.) Ball, with leaves up to 2·5mm in diameter and cones 1·2–1·5cm in diameter, occurs in rocky places and maritime sands throughout much of the range; and the shrubby subsp. transtagana Franco, with leaves only 1–1·5mm wide and cones up to 1cm in diameter, is confined to maritime sands of SW. Portugal. Al Bl Co Fr Fu Gr It Pl Sa Si Sp Tu Yu.

female cone

leaves

habit

Juniperus phoenicea L. Phoenician Juniper

A small dioecious tree up to 8m high or a procumbent shrub. **Branches** The twigs are c. 1mm in diameter, rounded in cross-section, scaly. **Leaves** Of 2 sorts: juvenile leaves are 0·5–1·4cm x 0·5–1mm, linear, sharply pointed at the tip, the upper and lower surfaces with 2 whitish stomatiferous bands, carried usually in whorls of 3, spreading at right-angles; adult leaves are 0·7–1mm long, scale-like, ovate to somewhat rhombic, obtuse to subacute, the margins whitish, the back of the leaf with a conspicuous furrowed gland, carried in opposite pairs or whorls of 3, closely appressed. **Cones** Male cones are produced at the tips of branchlets; female cones are 0·6–1·4cm long, globose to ovoid, ripening in the 2nd year, initially blackish, changing to green or yellowish and to dark red when fully ripe. Male cones shed pollen in March. **Seeds** 3–9. **Distribution** A native of the Mediterranean region and the Atlantic coast of Portugal. Al Bl Co Cr Fr Gr It Pl Sa Si Sp Yu.

female cone

habit

Juniperus excelsa Bieb. Grecian Juniper

A dioecious or monoecious tree, conical when young, later becoming a broad open pyramid up to 20m high at maturity. **Branches** The twigs are 0·6–0·8mm wide, rounded in cross-section, scaly. **Leaves** Of 2 sorts: juvenile leaves are very few, 5–6mm long, linear, sharply pointed at the tip, with 2 whitish stomatiferous bands on the lower surface, carried in decussate pairs, spreading at right-angles; adult leaves are 1–1·5mm long, scale-like, ovate to rhombid, pointed, with an ovate or linear gland in the centre of the lower surface, carried in decussate pairs and mostly closely appressed. **Cones** Male cones are produced at the tips of branchlets; female cones are c. 8mm long, globose, ripening in the 2nd year, becoming dark purplish-brown with a slight bloom when ripe. Male cones shed pollen in March. **Seeds** 4–6. **Distribution** A native of the Balkan Peninsula and the Crimea. Bu Cr Fu Gr Yu.

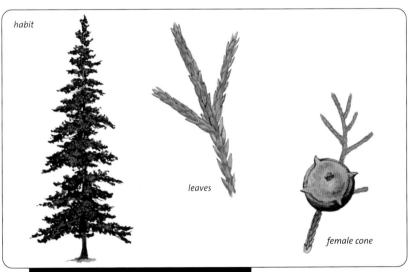

habit

leaves

female cone

Juniperus foetidissima Willd.

A dioecious or monoecious, columnar or narrowly conical tree up to 17m high. **Branches** The twigs are c. 1mm wide, distinctly 4-angled, scaly, irregularly arranged, fetid when crushed. **Leaves** Of 2 sorts: the few juvenile leaves are 5–6mm long, linear, sharply pointed at the tip, with 2 whitish stomatiferous bands on the lower surface, carried in decussate pairs, spreading at right-angles; adult leaves are c. 1·5mm long, ovate to rhombic, short or long-pointed, mostly without a whitish margin or gland, carried in decussate pairs, appressed but free at the apices. **Cones** Male cones are produced at the tips of branchlets; female cones are 0·7–1·2cm long, ripening in the 2nd year, becoming dark reddish-brown or blackish when ripe. Male cones shed pollen in April. **Seeds** 1–3. **Distribution and taxonomic notes** A species very similar to J. excelsa with which it is often confused. A native of mountainous parts of the Balkan Peninsula and the Crimea. Bu Cr Fu Gr Yu.

Juniperus thurifera L.

A rather similar species to *J. foetidissima* but with the twigs regularly arranged in 2 ranks. **Leaves** Adult leaves are 1·5–2mm long, the margins sometimes slightly toothed, the back of the leaves with an oblong, furrowed gland. **Cones** Female cones are 7–8mm long, becoming dark purple. **Seeds** 2–4. **Distribution** A native of the French Alps and mountains of S., C. and E. Spain. Fr Sp.

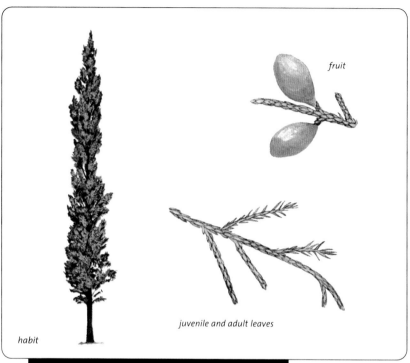

fruit

juvenile and adult leaves

habit

Juniperus virginiana L. Pencil Cedar

A pyramidal or columnar, usually dioecious tree up to 30m high. **Branches** The twigs are 0·6–0·8mm in diameter, very slender, rounded in cross-section, scaly. **Leaves** Of 2 sorts: juvenile leaves 5–6mm long, linear, sharply pointed at the tip, the upper surface with a broad bluish stomatiferous band, the lower surface green, carried in decussate pairs, spreading often at the end of an adult shoot; adult leaves 0·5–1·5mm long, scale-like, ovate, with a sharp, often tapering tip, the back of the leaf with a small gland, carried in decussate pairs, appressed but usually free at the apices. **Cones** Male cones are yellow, produced at the tips of branchlets; female cones are 3–6mm long, ovoid, ripening in the first year, changing from bluish-green to brownish-violet when ripe. Male cones shed pollen in March. **Seeds** 1–2. **Distribution** A native of N. America, planted for timber in C. and S. Europe, and several cultivated varieties, differing in habit and colour of the leaves, are frequently planted in gardens and parks for ornament. Fr Hu It Ru.

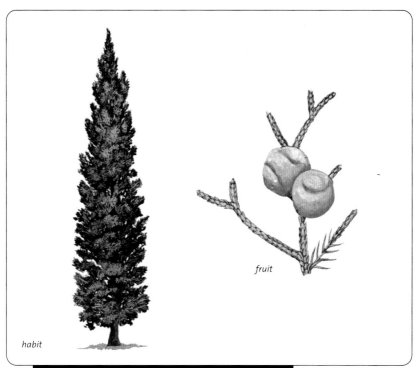

fruit

habit

Juniperus chinensis L. Chinese Cedar

A dioecious tree or shrub up to 18m high, often narrowly conical but of variable habit. **Branches** The twigs are 0.7–1mm in diameter, rounded in cross-section or slightly ridged on juvenile twigs. **Leaves** Of 2 sorts: juvenile leaves are *c*. 8mm long, linear, sharply pointed at the tip, the upper surface with 2 broad bluish stomatiferous bands separated by the midrib, the lower surface green, usually carried in whorls of 3 or occasionally paired, spreading or at right-angles, often at the base of adult shoots; adult leaves are *c*. 1.5mm long, scale-like, rhombic, blunt or slightly pointed, the back of the leaf with a small glandular depression, carried in, decussate pairs and closely appressed. **Cones** Male cones are yellow, produced at the tips of branchlets; female cones are 6–7mm long, almost globose to top-shaped, ripening in the 2nd year, changing from bluish-white to purplish-brown when ripe. Male cones shed pollen in March and April. **Distribution** A native of Japan and China, commonly planted for ornament in gardens, parks and churchyards. Many cultivated varieties differing in habit and leaf colour are known.

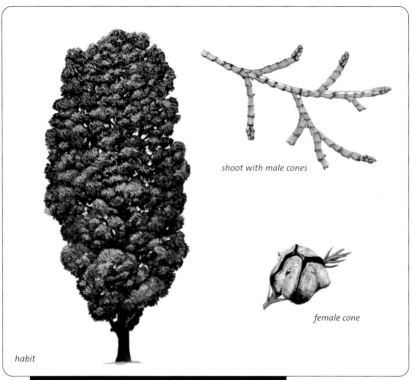

shoot with male cones

female cone

habit

Tetraclinis articulata (Vahl) Masters

A monoecious evergreen tree up to 15m high with a stout reddish-brown trunk. **Branches** The twigs are erect, arranged in flattened sprays and regularly jointed. **Leaves** In whorls of 4, the lateral pair larger than the central pair. **Cones** Solitary at the tips of branchlets; female cones are 0.8–1.3cm in diameter. Male cones shed pollen in February and March. **Distribution** A drought-resisting species restricted to SE. Spain, Malta and N. Africa. Si Sp.

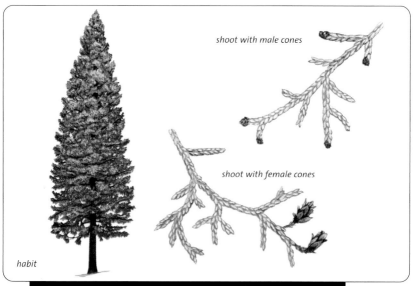

shoot with male cones

shoot with female cones

habit

Thuja plicata D. Don ex Lamb. **Western Red Cedar**

A narrowly conical to pyramidal, evergreen monoecious tree up to 65m high in its native state, eventually with a broadly buttressed trunk. **Bark** Dark reddish-brown with wide ridges, soft, shedding irregular plates. **Branches** The twigs are covered with leaf-bases, forming flattened sprays of foliage. **Leaves** Opposite and decussate, the lateral pair larger, 2–3mm long, scale-like, ovate with an acute or rather blunt apex, closely appressed, glossy and dark green above, paler and usually with whitish markings beneath, aromatic. **Cones** Male cones are minute, initially pale yellow; female cones are c. 1·2cm long, ovoid to conical, acute, brown when ripe; the scales number 10–12, each with a thickened protuberance on the inner side, projecting beyond the recurved spine-tipped apex. Male cones shed pollen in March. **Seeds** 2–3 on each scale, elliptical, winged. **Distribution** A native of W. N. America, commonly planted for ornament and shelter and sometimes for timber. It is occasionally naturalized. Several other related species are occasionally planted, mainly for ornament. Au Br De Ge It No Pl.

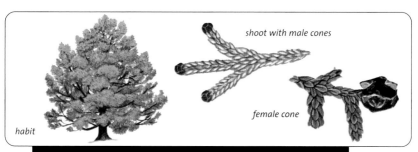

shoot with male cones

female cone

habit

Thujopsis dolabrata (L.fil.) Siebold & Zucc. **Hiba**

A monoecious, narrowly or broadly conical, evergreen tree up to 30m high, or sometimes a pyramidal shrub, the trunk often divided near ground level. **Bark** Dark reddish-brown, usually shredding into fine strings or papery strips. **Branches** The twigs are rather pendulous, covered with scale-leaves, flattened, regularly arranged in flattened sprays. **Leaves** Opposite and decussate, the lateral pairs rather larger, 4–7mm long, scale-like, broadly triangular, the apex pointed, incurved, appressed, glossy and dark green above, the underside with broad white markings, aromatic. **Cones** Solitary; male cones are blackish-green, female cones are 1·2–1·9cm long, irregularly globose, bluish-brown when ripe; the scales are 6–8, wedge-shaped, each with a triangular boss near the apex. Male cones shed pollen in April or May. **Seeds** rounded, winged, 3–5 on each scale. **Distribution** A native of Japan, commonly planted for ornament.

Deciduous Cypress Family
Taxodiaceae

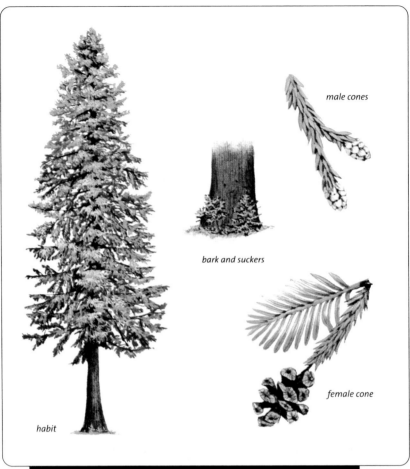

male cones

bark and suckers

female cone

habit

Sequoia sempervirens (Lamb.) Endl. Coast Redwood

A large monoecious evergreen tree up to 100m high in its native state, conical when young, becoming broadly columnar with a stout, sometimes buttressed trunk, often sprouting and suckering from the base, occasionally forming a clump of trees. **Bark** Dark reddish-brown, the outer layers scaling away to reveal the thick, soft and fibrous, bright orange-red layers beneath. **Branches** Horizontal or somewhat pendulous. The twigs are irregularly whorled, green. **Buds** Surrounded by brown scales. **Leaves** Spirally arranged and of 2 sorts: those on leading shoots are 6–8mm long, linear, sharply pointed, loosely appressed; those on side-shoots are flattened into 2 rows, 0·6–2 x 0·2cm, linear to linear-oblong, pointed, flat, dark green above, the underside with a white band on either side of the midrib. **Cones** Male cones are terminal, on young shoots, c. 2mm long, yellow; female cones are on stouter shoots, 1·8–2·5cm long, globose to ovoid, woody, ripening reddish-brown in the 2nd year; the 14–20 scales are spirally arranged, rhomboidal, wrinkled. Male cones shed pollen in February. **Seeds** c. 1·5mm long, winged, 3–7 on each scale, light brown. **Distribution** A native of the W. United States, planted for ornament in parks and large gardens, or occasionally for timber. Br Fr Ir It.

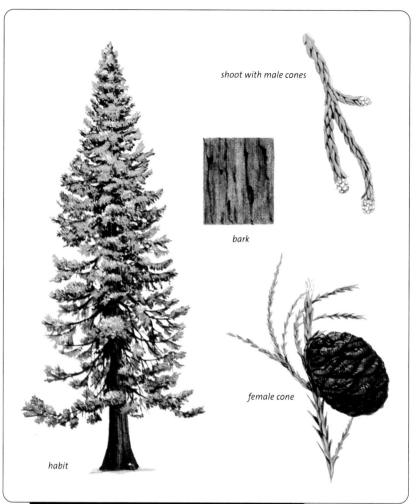

shoot with male cones

bark

female cone

habit

Sequoiadendron giganteum (Lindley)
Californian Big Tree, Giant Redwood or Wellingtonia

A large monoecious evergreen tree up to 90m high in its native state, the crown narrowly conical, becoming rounded. The trunk of old trees is up to 7m in diameter, buttressed at the base, tapering and bare of branches in the lower half. **Bark** Dark, reddish-brown or blackish, thick, fibrous, shredding from the ridges to reveal brighter reddish-brown layers beneath, deeply furrowed. **Branches** Ascending, becoming more pendulous below but upturned at the tips. The twigs are stout, turned upwards, covered with scale-leaves, green, becoming brown. **Buds** Without protective scales. **Leaves** Spirally arranged, crowded, 0·4–1cm long, all scale-like, ovate to lanceolate, acute, flat above, convex beneath, initially bluish at the base, becoming shiny dark green, appressed or spreading towards the tips. **Cones** Male cones are solitary on the tips of young shoots, 6–8mm long, pale yellow; female cones are solitary or in pairs on stouter shoots, 5–8 x 2·5–5cm, ovoid, woody, ripening dark reddish-brown in the 2nd year; the 25–40 scales are spirally arranged, rhomboidal, each with a slender spine in the central depression, wrinkled. Male cones shed pollen from March to April. **Seeds** 3–6mm long, oblong, winged, 3–7 on each scale, light brown. **Distribution** A native of the western slopes of the Sierra Nevada in the W. United States, often planted for ornament in parks and the largest gardens; or occasionally for timber. Au Br Fr.

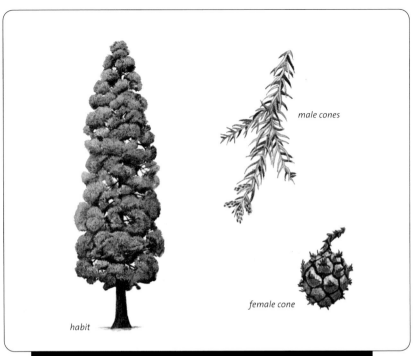

male cones

female cone

habit

Cryptomeria japonica (L. fil.) D. Don Japanese Red Cedar

A narrowly conical or pyramidal, monoecious evergreen tree up to 50m high in its native state, with a dense crown and eventually a rounded apex, the trunk becoming buttressed at the base. **Bark** Orange-brown, becoming dark brown, thick, fibrous, shredding away in strips. **Branches** Irregular whorled, level or the lowermost ones drooping. The twigs are sparsely branched, often pendulous, green. **Buds** Protected by small immature leaves. **Leaves** Spirally arranged, 0·6–1·5cm long, linear, acute, curved inwards at the tips, rhombic in cross-section, bright green. **Cones** Male cones are towards the tips of young twigs, in clusters of *c.* 20 in the leaf axils, 6–8mm long, bright yellow or orange; female cones are terminal on stouter branchlets, 1·2–3cm long, almost globose, woody, ripening in the first year; each of the 20–30 scales usually with 5 recurved spines at the tip. Male cones shed pollen in March. **Seeds** *c.* 6mm long, very narrowly winged, dark brown, 2–5 on each scale. **Distribution** A native of China and Japan with many different cultivars commonly planted for ornament in parts of W. and S. Europe. Br De It.

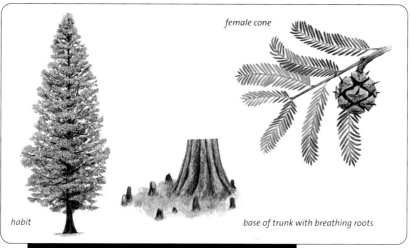

female cone

habit

base of trunk with breathing roots

Taxodium distichum (L.) L.C.M. Richard
Swamp Cypress

A monoecious deciduous tree up to 50m high in its native state, narrowly conical, becoming broad and domed at maturity; plants near water produce some 'breathing roots' near the base of a fluted trunk. **Bark** Pale, reddish-brown; fibrous, scaling or peeling in strips, fissured. **Branches** Upright or spreading. The shoots are of 2 sorts: long shoots with spirally arranged leaves; and alternate side-shoots, *c.* 10cm long with flattened leaves arranged into 2 ranks. **Buds** Scaly. **Leaves** Alternate, 0·8–2cm long, linear, flat, pale green, the underside with a greyish band on either side of the midrib. **Cones** Male cones are in slender branched heads, 5–15cm long, produced at the end of previous year's shoots, dull yellow or purplish; female cones are solitary or in small clusters near end of twigs, 1·2–3cm long, globose to obovoid, woody, ripening purplish-brown in the first year, the scales few, rhomboidal, each with a small recurved spine; the pedicels are *c.* 3mm long. Male cones shed pollen in April. **Seeds** *c.* 3mm long, 3-angled, narrowly winged, 2 to each scale. **Distribution** A native of swamps in SE. and S. United States, often planted in parks and gardens, and sometimes for timber in S. Europe. Bu Fr Ge It Ru.

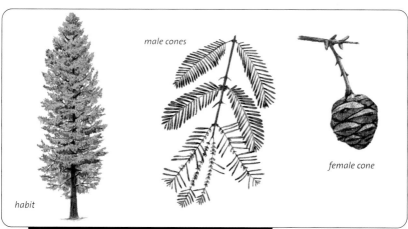

male cones

female cone

habit

Metasequoia glyptostroboides
Hu & Cheng Dawn Redwood

Similar to *Taxodium distichum* but side-shoots and leaves arranged in opposite pairs. **Leaves** 1·2–4cm (occasionally 6cm) long, linear, soft, flat, pale green, greyish-green beneath; male cones clustered at the base of leaves towards the ends of shoots; female cones with 20–30 scales in opposite and decussate pairs, each scale grooved, with 2–9 ovules; pedicel *c.* 5cm long. **Distribution** A native of E. Szechuan and NE. Hupeh in SW. China, frequently planted for ornament in parks and gardens in Europe.

Pine Family
Pinaceae

Abies Miller Silver Firs

About 50 species of evergreen resiniferous trees from the temperate northern hemisphere, many of which are cultivated for timber or ornament.

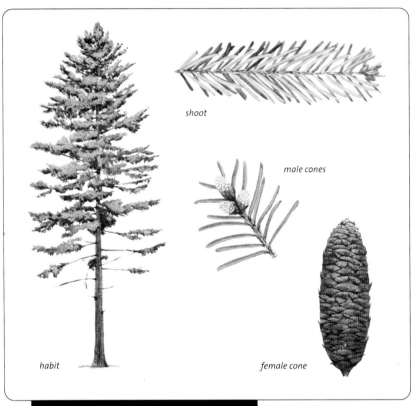

shoot

male cones

habit

female cone

Abies alba Miller Common Silver Fir

A pyramidal tree up to 50m high with a stout trunk. **Bark** Smooth, becoming fissured to form scales, greyish-brown. **Branches** The young twigs are densely pubescent, greyish. **Buds** Not resiniferous. **Leaves** 1·5–3cm x 1·5–2mm, shallowly notched at the tip, thick but flexible, the underside with 2 white bands, spreading horizontally from the sides of the twigs, more or less erect above but spreading to leave a distinct gap above the centre of the twig. **Cones** Female cones are 10–20 x 3–4cm, cylindrical, ripening pale brown, with a projecting spine beneath each scale, becoming bent backwards. Male cones shed pollen in April. **Distribution** A distinctive native forming natural forests in the mountainous parts of C. Europe, from N. Spain to Macedonia, and from S. Italy and Corsica to E. Poland. It is widely planted for timber elsewhere and also for ornament. Al Au Be Br Bu Co Cz De Fr Ge Gr Hu It No Pl Po Ru Sd Sp Sw Yu.

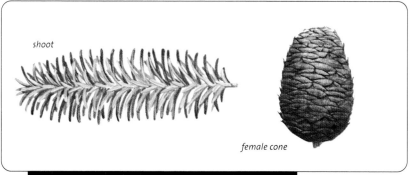

shoot

female cone

Abies delavayi Franchet Delavay's Silver Fir

Similar to A. alba but young twigs almost smooth or sometimes downy, reddish-brown; winter buds resiniferous. **Leaves** 2–4cm long, usually notched or sometimes pointed, glossy dark green, the margin revolute, partly hiding the broad white bands beneath. **Cones** Female cones are 6–10 x 2·5–4·5cm, cylindrical or oblong-elliptical, dark purplish or bluish-green, with a long projecting spine, usually becoming bent backwards, beneath each scale. **Distribution** A native of China, from W. and SW. Szechuan to the Yunnan. A. delavayi var. forrestii (C.C. Rogers) A.B. Jackson is the most commonly planted variety, recognizable by its deeply notched leaves and the rather shorter, narrower spines on the cones. It is grown for ornament in parks and large gardens.

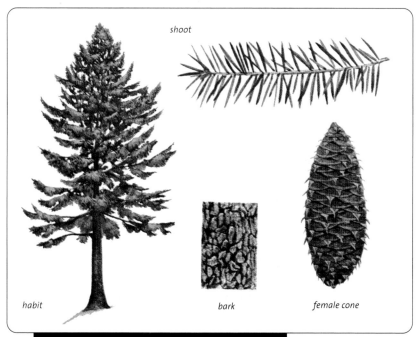

shoot

habit

bark

female cone

Abies cephalonica Loudon Grecian Fir

A pyramidal tree up to 30m high with a fairly stout trunk. **Bark** Greyish-brown, smooth, eventually becoming fissured into oblong plates. **Branches** The young twigs are hairless, light brown. **Buds** Very resiniferous. **Leaves** Densely arranged on the stems, projecting evenly at right-angles from the upper surface and sides of the twig but usually leaving a gap beneath, 1·5–3·5cm x 2–2·5mm, sharply pointed, thick, rigid, glossy green above, with two white bands beneath. **Cones** Female cones are 12–16 x 4–5cm, cylindrical, ripening yellowish-brown; each scale with a projecting triangular backward-pointing spine. **Distribution** A native to the mountains of Greece up to 1700m altitude, planted for timber in Italy and for ornament elsewhere. Gr It.

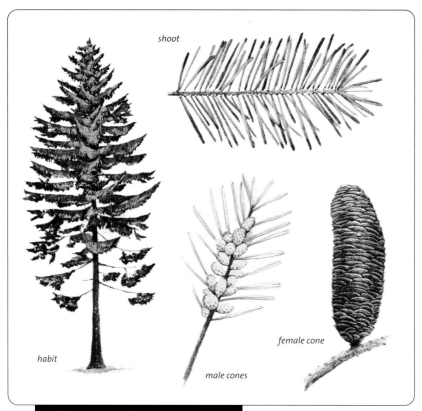

shoot

habit

male cones

female cone

Abies grandis Lindley **Giant Fir**

A narrowly conical tree, becoming broadly columnar, up to 100m tall in its native state with a fairly stout trunk. **Bark** Smooth except for resin blisters when young, becoming cracked and scaling, dark brown. **Branches** The young twigs are olive-green, covered with scattered, minute hairs. **Buds** Resiniferous. **Leaves** 2–6cm x 1·5–2·5mm, notched at the tip, dark glossy green above, the underside with 2 silvery-white bands, the margin sometimes revolute. **Cones** Female cones are 5–10 x 3–4cm, cylindrical, becoming tapered towards the tip, ripening dark brown; scales are rounded, concealing the pointed bracts. Male cones shed pollen in April. **Distribution** A native of W. N. America, planted for timber in N. and C. Europe and for ornament elsewhere. Br Cz De Ge Ir It No Sd.

Abies concolor (Gordon) Hildebrand **Colorado White Fir**

Similar to A. grandis but up to 55m high. **Bark** Blackish-grey, becoming deeply fissured. **Branches** The young twigs sometimes smooth, yellowish-green. **Buds** Very resiniferous. **Leaves** In 2 ranks, curving upwards to almost vertical, 4–5·5cm x c. 2mm, shortly pointed at the tip, bluish-grey, the underside with 2 faint bluish bands. **Cones** The female cones 12–15 x 3–7cm, cylindrical to barrel-shaped. **Distribution** A variable native of W. N. America, frequently planted for ornament in parks and gardens.

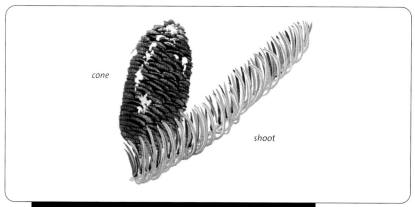

Abies lasiocarpa (Hooker) Nutt. Alpine Fir

Similar to A. grandis but up to 48m high in its native state, with a slender pyramidal crown and a slender trunk. **Bark** Silvery-grey, slightly fissured. **Branches** Drooping; the young twigs with scattered reddish hairs, sometimes almost smooth, grey. **Leaves** Arranged irregularly in 2 ranks or curving upwards, those on the upper surface pointing forwards to obscure the upper surface of the twig. **Cones** The female cones 5–10 x 3·5cm, dark purplish, becoming brown. **Distribution** A native of W. N. America, occasionally planted for timber in N. Europe and sometimes cultivated for ornament elsewhere. Ic Sw.

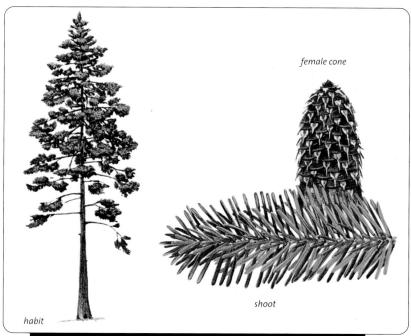

Abies nordmanniana (Steven) Spach Caucasian Fir

A conical to narrowly columnar tree up to 70m high with a stout trunk. **Bark** Smooth but gradually becoming fissured to form scales or plates, grey-brown. **Branches** The young twigs have scattered short hairs, brown or greyish-brown. **Buds** Not resiniferous. **Leaves** 1·5–3·5cm x 1·5–2mm, notched at the tip, thick but flexible, glossy green above, the underside with 2 conspicuous white bands. **Cones** The female cones are 12–18 x 4–5cm, cylindrical, ripening dark brown; with a projecting, strongly deflexed spine beneath each scale. Male cones shed pollen in April. **Distribution** A native to NE. Turkey and the W. Caucasus, widely planted for timber, especially in C. Europe, and frequently cultivated for ornament. Au Cz De It Pl Ru Sw Tu.

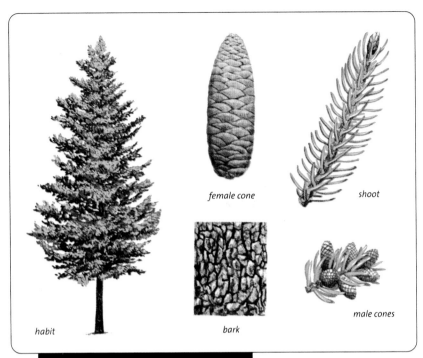

female cone

shoot

habit

bark

male cones

Abies pinsapo Boiss. Spanish Fir

A pyramidal tree up to 30m high with a fairly stout trunk. **Bark** Smooth, gradually becoming irregularly fissured into plates, dark grey or blackish. **Branches** The young twigs are greenish-brown, without hairs. **Buds** Resiniferous. **Leaves** Densely but evenly arranged at right-angles to the twig, on all sides, 1–1·8 x 0·2–0·3cm, thick, stiff, sometimes curved, the tip sharply pointed, bluish-grey above, with 2 grey bands beneath. **Cones** Female cones are 10–16 x 3–4cm, cylindrical, gradually tapering towards the tip, ripening brown, each scale rounded, concealing the short spine-tipped bract. Male cones shed pollen in May. **Distribution** A native of the mountains of SW. Spain, near Ronda, where it grows on limestone slopes up to 2000m. It is occasionally planted for ornament in large gardens, parks and churchyards or sometimes for timber. Au Pl Sp.

Abies x insignis Carrière ex Bailly

A hybrid between A. pinsapo and A. nordmanniana with leaves 1–3·3cm x 1·5–2·5mm, arranged all round the twig or with a gap on the underside; the female cones are 11–20 x 3·5–5cm with some of the pointed bracts slightly projecting from the scales. It is frequently planted for ornament in parks and large gardens.

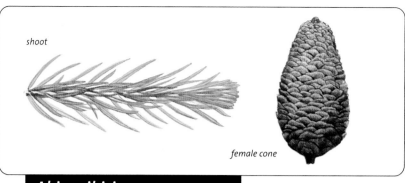

shoot

female cone

Abies sibirica Ledeb. Siberian Fir

Similar to A. pinsapo but with a slender trunk. **Bark** Has resin blisters. **Branches** Young twigs grey with scattered hairs. **Buds** Very resiniferous. **Leaves** Spreading horizontally from the sides of the twigs, leaving a gap below, those on the upper surface pointing forwards and upwards, obscuring the surface of the twig, 1·5–3cm x 1–1·3mm, thin, flexible, blunt or slightly notched, bright green above, the underside with 2 greyish bands. **Cones** Female cones 6–8 x 3cm, cylindrical, bluish while young, becoming brown. **Distribution** A species forming large natural forests in N. and E. Russia, planted for timber in some parts of Europe. De Fi Fu Ic.

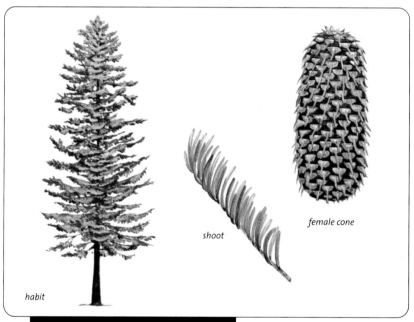

female cone

shoot

habit

Abies procera Rehder Noble Fir

A narrowly conical tree, eventually becoming broadly columnar with a rounded top, up to 80m high usually with a stout trunk. **Bark** Smooth except for resin blisters, gradually becoming deeply fissured, grey and eventually brown on old trees. **Branches** The young twigs are reddish-brown, densely covered with reddish hairs. **Buds** Resiniferous at the tip. **Leaves** 1–3·5cm x 1–1·5mm, blunt at the tip, slender, flexible, greyish-green above, the underside with 2 greyish bands, spreading horizontally from the sides of the twig, curving upwards, leaving a gap below, those from the upper surface spreading forwards and curving upwards. **Cones** Female cones are 12–20 x 5–8cm, cylindrical, tapered towards the tip, ripening purplish-brown; with a protruding, backward-pointing, green spine beneath each scale. Male cones shed pollen in May. **Distribution** A native of W. N. America, planted for timber in N. and W. Europe and widely planted for ornament in parks and gardens, especially those forms with bluish-white foliage. Br De Ge Ir No.

Cedrus Trew Cedars

A small genus of 4 evergreen tree species. They are very similar to one another and sometimes regarded as geographical races of the same species.

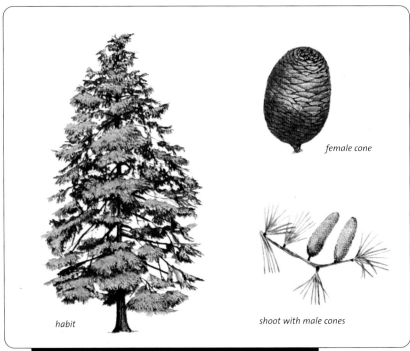

female cone

habit

shoot with male cones

Cedrus deodara (D. Don) G. Don in Loudon
Deodar, Himalayan Cedar or Indian Cedar

A conical tree initially with a slender pointed apex, eventually broader, up to 65m high in its native state. **Bark** Greyish-brown, irregularly fissured into oblong plates. **Branches** Pendulous or more or less level on old trees. The young shoots are pendulous, densely pubescent; the short shoots with 15–20 leaves in a cluster. **Leaves** 2–5cm long, dark green with faint grey lines. **Cones** Male cones are 5–12cm long, dark purple before shedding pollen; the female cones are 8–12 x 5–8cm, rounded at the apex. **Distribution** A species frequently planted for ornament in parks and large gardens and cultivated for timber in S. Europe. A native to Afghanistan and the NW. Himalayas. Fr Gr It Pl.

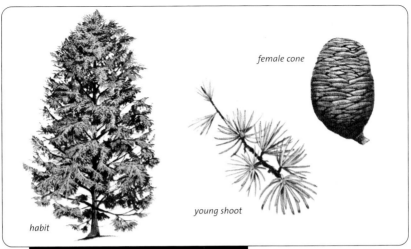

female cone

young shoot

habit

Cedrus atlantica (Endl.) Carrière
Atlas Cedar or Atlantic Cedar

A pyramidal tree becoming broadly domed, up to 40m high. **Bark** Dark grey, becoming cracked into large plates, then deeply fissured. **Branches** Ascending, or level on the oldest trees. The young shoots are ascending, rather stiff, downy; the short shoots with 10–45 leaves in a cluster. **Leaves** 1–3cm long, shiny deep green or bluish-green. **Cones** Male cones are 3–5cm long, pinkish-yellow; female cones are 5–8 x 3–5cm, squarish or often sunken with a central boss at the tip. **Distribution and taxonomic notes** A native of the mountains of Algeria and Morocco, planted for ornament or for timber in S. Europe. The most common cultivar is the Blue Atlas Cedar, cv. 'Glauca', with bright bluish-grey or whitish leaves. It is a pollution-tolerant species and is widely planted in town parks and gardens, occasionally as fastigiate or pendulous cultivars.

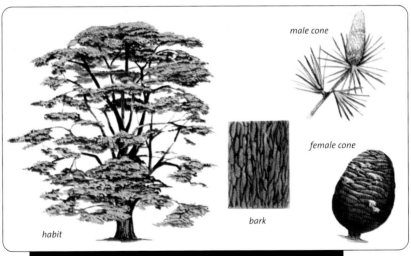

male cone

female cone

bark

habit

Cedrus libani A. Richard in Bory **Cedar of Lebanon**

A medium-sized tree, conical when young, becoming broadly domed or flat-topped, up to 40m high at maturity, often with a very stout trunk. **Bark** Dark grey with short ridges, scaling, becoming deeply fissured and dark brown. **Branches** Ascending in young trees, becoming level, forming a massive flat surface of foliage, the lowermost branches descending to the ground. The young shoots are spreading, hairless, the short shoots with 10–15 leaves in a cluster. **Leaves** 2–3cm long, dark green. **Cones** Male cones are 5–7.5cm long, greyish-green; female cones are 7–12 x 5–7cm, blunt at the tip. **Distribution** A native of SE. Turkey, Syria and the Lebanon. Very commonly planted for ornament in gardens, parks and churchyards. It is particularly tolerant of air pollution.

Larix Miller Larches

A small genus of some 10 species from the colder parts of the northern hemisphere.

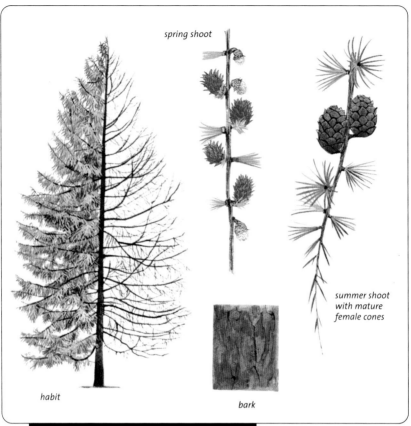

spring shoot

summer shoot
with mature
female cones

habit

bark

Larix decidua Miller Common Larch

A narrowly conical tree up to 35m (sometimes up to 50m) high. **Bark** Greyish, becoming brown, fissured and scaling away, very thick at the base of old trees. **Branches** Rather short, level except for lowest descending branches on old trees. The long shoots are rough with old leaf-bases, pendulous, hairless, yellowish or greyish. **Buds** Terminal, globose, shortly pointed, yellowish-brown. **Leaves** In clusters of 30–40, 1·2–3cm long, soft, blunt or slightly pointed, light green above, with 2 greenish stomatiferous bands below. **Cones** Female cones are with conspicuous red or white bracts while young, 2–3·8 x 1·5–2·5cm, conical-ovoid, ripening brown; the scales are 40–50, rounded, entire, loosely appressed, with fine linear markings, covered with soft brown hairs, the pointed tips of the bracts sometimes protruding. Male cones shed pollen in March and April. **Distribution and taxonomic notes** A native of the Alps and W. Carpathian mountains, widely planted for timber, shelter, along roadsides or for ornament in parks. Trees from the Carpathians with smaller cones and more concave scales than the typical form are sometimes treated as a separate subspecies, L. decidua subsp. polonica (Racib.) Domin, the Polish Larch. Au Be Br Cz Fi Fr Fu Ge It No Po Sd Sw Yu.

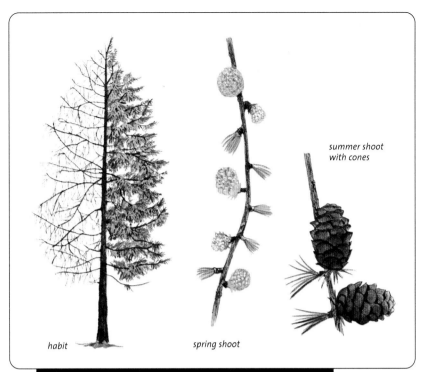

habit

spring shoot

*summer shoot
with cones*

Larix kaempferi (Lamb.) Carrière Japanese Larch

A broadly conical tree up to 40m high. **Bark** Reddish-brown, scaling. **Branches** Long, widely spreading. The long shoots are stiff, usually reddish-brown with a greyish waxy bloom, smooth or with soft brownish hairs. **Buds** Terminal, conical, pointed, reddish-brown, resiniferous. **Leaves** In clusters of c. 40, 1·5–3cm long, pointed or blunt, greyish-green above, the underside with 2 conspicuous white stomatiferous bands. **Cones** Female cones are with pointed, reflexed, greenish bracts when young, 1·5–3·5 x 1·2–3cm, ovoid, ripening brown; the scales are c. 40, the tips rounded and curved outwards, slightly downy, more or less concealing the bracts. Male cones shed pollen in March. **Distribution** A native of Japan, commonly planted for timber in NW. Europe and occasionally for ornament. Au Be Br De Fi Fr Fu Ge Ho Ir Sw.

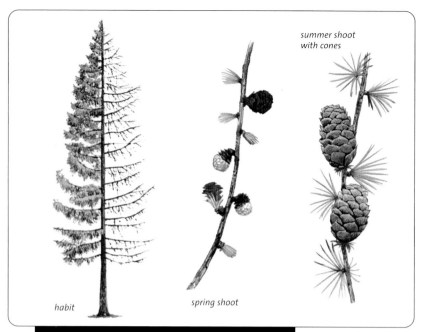

summer shoot
with cones

habit

spring shoot

Larix x eurolepis A. Henry Dunkeld Larch

A vigorous conical tree up to 35m high. **Bark** Greyish to reddish-brown, becoming fissured and scaling. The long shoots are yellowish-brown, with a slight grey waxy bloom, hairless or slightly downy. **Buds** Terminal, pale reddish-brown, not resiniferous. **Leaves** In clusters of c. 40, up to 5cm long, pointed or blunt, greyish-green above, the underside with 2 greyish stomatiferous bands. **Cones** Female cones are with pinkish reflexed bracts while young, 3–4 x 2–2.5cm, conical, ripening to pale brown; the scales are rounded, loosely appressed, the margins slightly exposed. Male cones shed pollen in March. **Distribution and taxonomic notes** A rather variable hybrid between the Common Larch Larix decidua and the Japanese Larch, L. kaempferi. Most of the characteristics are rather intermediate between the two parent species although the hybrid is usually more vigorous than either parent. It is much planted for timber or shelter belts in NW. Europe, although a precise distribution cannot be given, since it intergrades with L. decidua.

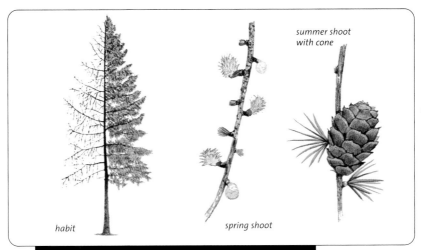

summer shoot
with cone

habit   spring shoot

Larix gmelinii (Rupr.) Kuzen. Dahurian Larch

A conical or rather slender tree up to 30m high. **Bark** Reddish-brown with irregular scales. **Branches** More or less level, sometimes forming a large flat surface. The long shoots are yellowish or reddish-brown, often with a covering of soft hairs. **Buds** Terminal, yellowish-brown, not resiniferous. **Leaves** Occur in clusters of c. 25, 1·2–4cm x 0·5mm, blunt, bright green above, the underside with 2 pale greenish stomatiferous bands. **Cones** Female cones are with pinkish or yellowish-green bracts while young, 2–2·5 x 1·8cm, ovoid, blunt, ripening pale brown; the scales are c. 20, rounded, hairless, squarish at the tip with the margins slightly curved outwards, the points of the bracts often projecting. Male cones shed pollen in March. **Distribution** A native of E. Asia, sometimes planted for timber or rarely for ornament in N. Europe. De Fi No.

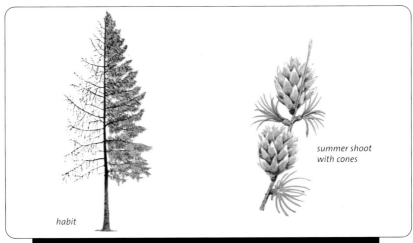

summer shoot
with cones

habit

Pseudolarix amabilis (A. Nelson) Rehder Golden Larch

A deciduous conical tree up to 40m high. **Bark** Light reddish-brown, becoming fissured. **Branches** Irregularly whorled, level, producing flattened plates of foliage. The long shoots are reddish-brown, hairless, with scattered, spirally arranged leaves; the short shoots are with clusters of 15–30 leaves. **Leaves** Up to 6·5 x 0·3cm, pointed, bright yellowish-green above, the underside with 2 greyish bands. **Cones** Male and female cones occur on the same tree from short shoots; the male cones densely clustered, c. 2·5cm long, cylindrical; female cones are 5–7 x 4–5cm, ovoid, woody, ripening light brown in the first year; the scales are triangular, blunt or notched, eventually falling away. Male cones shed pollen in May and June. **Seeds** Winged, 2 to each scale. **Distribution** A native of E. China, occasionally cultivated for ornament, especially in S. Europe.

Picea A. Dietr. Spruces

About 50 species from the temperate northern hemisphere, many of which are planted for timber or ornament.

shoot with male cones

bark

female cone

habit

Picea abies (L.) Karsten **Norway Spruce**

A conical tree up to 65m high. **Bark** Reddish-brown, scaling. **Branches** Short, the lowermost on old trees descending. The young twigs are reddish-brown, usually hairless or with scattered hairs. **Buds** c. 6mm long, pointed, reddish-brown. **Leaves** 1–2·5cm long, 4-angled in cross-section, stiff, pointed, dark green with greyish lines, spreading from the sides of the twig, exposing the under surface; those above point forwards and upwards, concealing the twig. **Cones** Female cones are usually 10–18cm long, cylindrical, ripening brown; the scales are irregularly rhombic and usually squarish or notched at the tip. Male cones shed pollen in May. **Distribution and taxonomic notes** Two subspecies are currently recognized: P. abies subsp. obovata (Ledeb.) Hultén, the Siberian Spruce, is a smaller tree than typical P. abies, only up to 30m high; the twigs are densely pubescent; the leaves are 1–1·8cm long; the female cones are 6–8cm long, with scales more rounded; restricted to NE. Europe and N. Asia. Typical P. abies subsp. abies is found from N. Europe to the S. Alps and the Balkan Peninsula. It is commonly planted for timber, ornament or in plantations for Christmas trees. Al Au Be Br Bu Cz De Fi Fr Fu Ge Ho Hu Ir It No Po Ru Sd Sp Sw Yu.

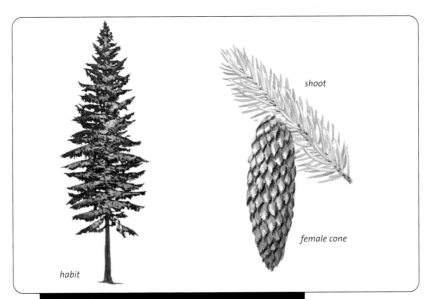

shoot

female cone

habit

Picea pungens Engelm. Colorado Spruce

Similar to P. abies but up to 50m high. **Bark** Brownish-grey. **Branches** The twigs are hairless, yellowish-brown. **Buds** 0·6–1·6cm long. **Leaves** 2–3cm long, bluish-green, sharply pointed, spreading almost around the shoot. **Cones** Female cones are 6–10cm long, cylindrical, initially purplish, ripening to greyish-brown; the scales tapering to a squarish, irregularly toothed apex. **Distribution** A native of N. America, commonly planted for ornament and for timber in C. and NW. Europe. Au Br Fr Ge Ho Ir It No.

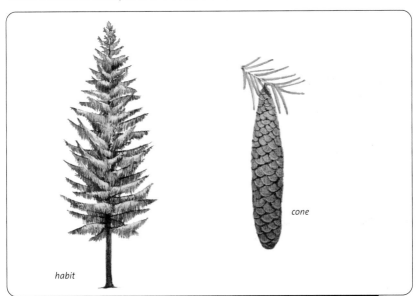

cone

habit

Picea breweriana S. Watson Brewer's Weeping Spruce

Similar to P. abies but up to 40m high. **Bark** Grey, flaking. **Branches** Short, curving upwards except for the lowermost ones; the side-shoots are long and slender, pendent with greyish hairs. **Buds** c. 3mm long, blunt. **Leaves** 2·5–3cm long, flattened, dark green with 2 whitish bands beneath. **Cones** Female cones are 6–13 x 2–2·5cm, cylindrical, purplish becoming reddish-brown; the scales have rounded margins. **Distribution** A native of the W. United States, frequently planted for ornament in parks and gardens.

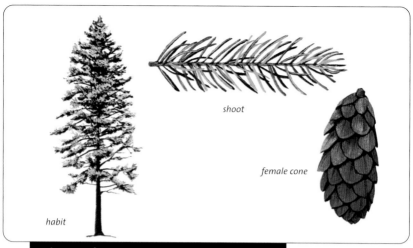

shoot

female cone

habit

Picea glauca (Moench) Voss White Spruce

A narrowly conical tree, gradually becoming more rounded at maturity, up to 30m high. **Bark** Greyish-brown, becoming cracked into rounded plates. **Branches** Somewhat deflexed, turning upwards at the tips. The twigs are hairless, greyish, becoming yellowish-brown. **Buds** c. 6mm long, ovoid, blunt. **Leaves** 1·2–1·3cm long, stiff, 4-angled in cross-section, pointed or somewhat blunt, pale green or bluish, emitting a fetid smell when crushed, mostly spreading from the sides and the upper surface of the twig. **Cones** Female cones are 2·5–6 x 1·2–2cm, more or less cylindrical, ripening orange-brown; the scales have rounded margins. Male cones shed pollen in April. **Distribution** A native of Canada and N. United States, frequently planted for timber and occasionally for ornament in N. Europe. Au Be De Fi Ic No.

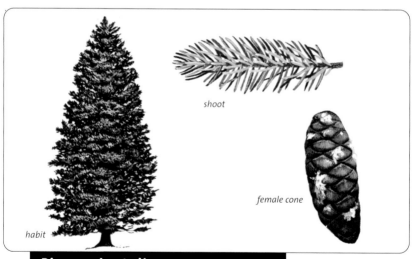

shoot

female cone

habit

Picea orientalis (L.) Link Oriental Spruce

A tree up to 40m (occasionally 60m) high with a dense conical crown. **Bark** Pale brown, cracking into small scales which gradually flake away. **Branches** Rather slender, ascending or level; the twigs are densely hairy, whitish, becoming pale brown. **Buds** c. 3mm long, conical, pointed, reddish-brown. **Leaves** Dense, spreading more or less horizontally from the sides of the stems, exposing the lower surface, those from the upper surface pointing forwards and upwards, concealing the twig, 0·6–1cm long, 4-angled in cross-section, usually blunt, glossy dark green. **Cones** Female cones are 6–9cm long, elongated-ellipsoid, slightly purplish, ripening to shiny brown; the scales are rounded. Male cones shed pollen in April. **Distribution** A native to E. Turkey, the Caucasus and parts of SW. Asia. Frequently planted for ornament in parks and gardens, and occasionally for timber. Au Be It Tu.

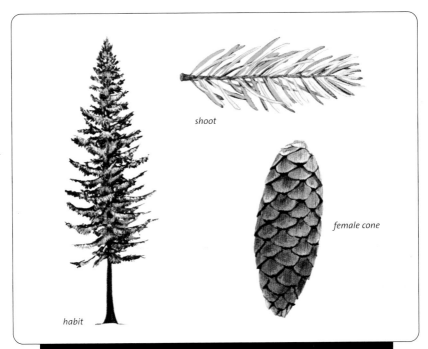

shoot

female cone

habit

Picea engelmannii Parry ex Engelm. **Engelmann Spruce**

A slender conical or pyramidal tree up to 50m high. **Bark** Reddish or greyish-brown, becoming scaly. **Branches** Ascending or curved upwards at the tips. The young shoots are slender, pendulous, covered with minute glandular hairs, pale yellowish-brown. **Buds** c. 1·5cm long, conical, blunt. **Leaves** 1·5–2·5cm long, flexible, 4-angled in cross-section, pointed, bluish-green, emitting a somewhat fetid smell when crushed, spreading more or less horizontally from the side of the twig, exposing the lower surface; those from the upper surface point forwards and upwards, concealing the twig. **Cones** Female cones are 3·5–7·5cm long, oblong-elliptic but tapered towards the tip, initially crimson-tinged, becoming shiny brown when ripe; the scales are elongated-rhombic, squarish at the tip with small irregular teeth. Male cones shed pollen in May. **Distribution** A native of W. N. America, planted for timber in N. Europe and occasionally for ornament in parks and gardens. Au Be De Fi Ic No.

shoot

young female cones

habit

bark

mature female cone

Picea sitchensis (Bong.) Carrière Sitka Spruce

A conical tree with a slender tapering apex, up to 60m high, the trunk stout and sometimes buttressed. **Bark** Greyish-brown, becoming darker, purplish-grey with thin lifting scales. **Branches** Ascending. The side-shoots are slightly pendent, stiff, hairless, greyish becoming light brown. **Buds** *c.* 6mm long, ovoid, rather blunt, pale brown. **Leaves** 15–30cm long, sharply pointed, thick and rigid, flattened, bright green above, the underside with 2 broad white bands, spreading all round the shoot but becoming parted below to spread more horizontally, those on the upper side of the twig pointed forwards, obscuring the twig. Female cones are 6–10 x 2·5–3cm, cylindrical, rather blunt at the top, initially pale, olive-green ripening to light brown; the scales are elongated, rhombic, tapering to a squarish, irregularly toothed apex. Male cones shed pollen in May. **Distribution** A native of W. N. America, commonly planted as a timber tree or for ornament in NW. Europe and parts of C. Europe. Au Br Fr Ge Ho Ic Ir No.

shoot

habit

bark

female cone

Picea omorika (Pančić) Purkyně Serbian Spruce

A narrowly columnar or somewhat conical tree up to 30m high with a very slender trunk.
Bark Reddish or orange-brown, with thin scales or roughly rectangular plates on older trees.
Branches Short, ascending or level, the lowest descending then curving upwards. The side-shoots are often somewhat pendent, covered with rather stiff persistent hairs, light brown.
Buds *c.* 6mm long, conical, reddish-brown. **Leaves** 0.8–2cm long, the apex sharp or blunt on old trees, rather flexible, flattened, dark bluish-green above, the underside with 2 broad white bands, spreading more or less horizontally from the sides of the twigs, curving downwards, those from the upper surface pointing forwards, overlapping and obscuring the surface of the twig. **Cones** Female cones are 3–6 x 1.5–3cm, oblong-ovoid to somewhat conical, bluish-black or bluish-green, ripening to dark brown; the scales are almost orbicular, the tips with very small irregular teeth. Male cones shed pollen in May. **Distribution** The Serbian Spruce has a natural distribution restricted to the Drina basin of C. Yugoslavia, growing on limestone rocks up to 1800m. It is planted for timber in other parts of Europe, especially in Scandinavian countries, and since it is tolerant of air pollution it is frequently planted in town gardens and parks. De Sw Yu.

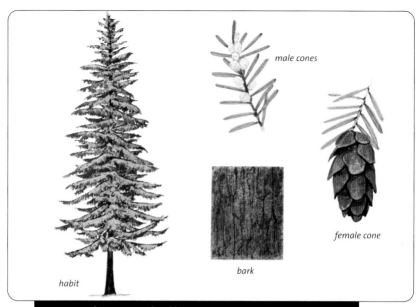

male cones

female cone

bark

habit

Tsuga heterophylla (Rafin.) Sarg. Western Hemlock

An evergreen tree with a dense, narrowly conical or somewhat columnar crown up to 70m high in its native state. **Bark** Reddish-brown, becoming fissured with scaling ridges. The young shoots are slender, pendulous at the tips, greyish-brown, covered with long pale brown hairs. **Buds** Globose, greyish-brown. **Leaves** 0·6–2cm long, oblong, flattened, blunt, the margins minutely toothed, dark green above, the underside with 2 whitish stomatiferous bands; one resin canal is present. **Cones** Male cones are in the leaf axils of the previous year's shoots, globose; female cones are solitary, terminal on the previous year's wide shoots, 2–2·5cm long, ovoid, blunt, pendent, ripening reddish-brown in the first year; the scales are roundish, entire, exceeding the bracts, persistent. Male cones shed pollen in April. **Seeds** Winged, 2 to each scale. **Distribution** A native of W. N. America, occasionally planted for ornament or as a timber tree in NW. Europe. De Fr Ge Ir No.

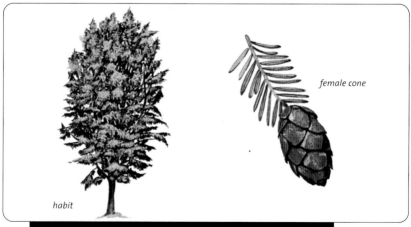

female cone

habit

Tsuga canadensis (L.) Carrière Eastern Hemlock

Like T. heterophylla but broader, up to 30m high, often with a forked trunk. **Buds** Ovoid. **Leaves** Spreading on the side of the twig but some obscuring the upper surface, 0·8–1·8cm long, rather narrowed towards the tip, the underside with 2 narrow white stomatiferous bands. **Cones** Female cones 1·5–2cm long, dark brown. **Distribution** A native of N. America with many cultivars differing mostly in habit; frequently planted for ornament and occasionally as a timber tree. Ge.

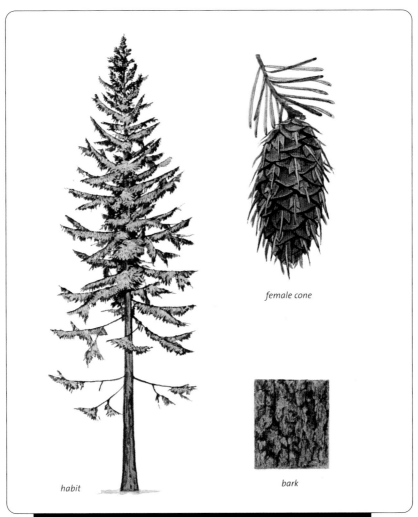

female cone

habit

bark

Pseudotsuga menziesii (Mirbel) Franco **Douglas Fir**

An evergreen resiniferous tree with a conical crown up to 100m high in its native state. **Bark** Greyish-green, smooth but with resin blisters, becoming dark, reddish-brown and ridged on old trees. The shoots are yellowish to greyish-green with slightly projecting elliptical leaf-scars, downy. **Buds** Ovoid, slender, sharply pointed, brown. **Leaves** 2–3·5cm, linear, blunt or pointed at the tip, dark green and grooved above, the underside with 2 distinct white stomatiferous bands; 2 resin canals are present. **Cones** Male cones are in the leaf axils of the previous year's shoots, conical, yellow; female cones are usually terminal on the previous year's shoots, 5–10 x 2–5cm long, oblong-ovoid, pendent, ripening light brown in the first year, the scales rounded, entire, minutely pubescent, persistent, the bracts 3-pointed, projecting beyond the scales. Male cones shed pollen in May. **Seeds** Winged, 2 to each scale. **Distribution** A native of the Pacific coast of N. America, widely planted for timber in much of Europe and for shelter or occasionally ornament in large gardens. Au Be Br Bu Cz De Fi Fr Ge Gr Ir It Pl Po Ru Sd Sw Yu.

Pinus L. Pines

Evergreen trees or shrubs with a conical habit and horizontal branches disposed in regular whorls; the mature crowns may become flat, round or spreading. Isolated trees are usually large at the base, tapering rapidly as they advance in height. Plantation trees have long clean columnar trunks, losing their lower branches early. **Bark** Usually thick, rough and deeply furrowed or thin and scaly. **Leaves** Of 3 kinds: (i) primordial leaves of seedlings are solitary, spirally arranged, linear-lanceolate and toothed; (ii) scale-leaves are triangular-lanceolate, falling early, bearing short shoots in the axils; (iii) adult leaves are needle-like, persistent for two or more years, borne in clusters of 2, 3 or 5, although some species are inconstant in number. **Cones** The flowers are borne separately on strobili; male strobili are catkin-like, clustered at the base of young twigs, shedding pollen in May–June; female strobili are borne at the tips of new shoots, or in whorls some way below the tip. Cones develop from the enlarging female strobili and are at least 2 years old when ripe; the scales are woody; the exposed part of the scale has a prominent protuberance usually ending in a spine or prickle.

habit

shoot with winter bud

leaf bundles

habit

mature cone

Pinus contorta Douglas ex Loudon

A small to large tree 3–30m tall with short contorted branches; young trees have a broad bushy base and a vigorous central shoot; old trees usually tall and narrow, densely bushy-domed or spired. **Branches** The shoots are glabrous, green in the 1st year, orange-brown and striped white in the 2nd year. **Leaves** 3–7cm x *c.* 1mm, sharply pointed, very densely set over young shoots, spreading on older shoots, appearing in pairs, and twisted. **Cones** Male strobili occur in dense whorls; female strobili occur in clusters of 2–4, at or just below the tip of the shoot. The cone is 2–6 x 2–3cm, ovoid-conical, symmetrical, pale brown-yellow, shining; each scale has a slender, fragile, sharp tip. **Seeds** 4–5mm long with a wing up to 8mm long. **Distribution and taxonomic notes** A very variable species of Pacific United States origin, widely planted for timber on peatlands and moors throughout much of C. or NW. Europe. Be Br Cz De Fi Ge Ic Ir It No Ru Sw. *Pinus contorta* var. *latifolia* S. Watson, Lodgepole Pine, is similar to the type but has a less dense crown; the bark has shallow fissures, forming scales; the leaves are broader and those of each pair spread apart more widely. Planted for timber in similar regions to the type.

*shoot
with female
summer buds*

habit

leaf bundle

cone

Pinus pinaster Aiton Maritime Pine

A large tree 30–40m tall; young trees with broad whorls of widely spaced branches; the trunks of old trees bare for a greater part of their length, with wide flat crowns. **Bark** Thick, deeply fissured, dark red-brown. **Branches** The shoots are glabrous, dark red or pale green when young, becoming pink-brown above, pale olive below. **Leaves** 10–25cm x c. 0·2mm, spiny, stout, rigid, occurring in pairs, pale grey-green. **Cones** Male strobili are scattered along the basal third of new shoots; pink, female strobili are in groups of 3–5 around the terminal bud. The cones are 8–22 x 5–8cm, conical, ovoid, symmetrical or almost so, light brown and shining; the exposed part of the scale is rhomboidal, keeled with a prominent prickly protuberance. **Seeds** 7–8mm long with a wing up to 3cm long. **Distribution** A native of the Mediterranean region growing on light soils and sea sand, now cultivated as far eastward as Greece and reaching the Atlantic shores of France and Portugal. Al Br Co Cr Fr Gr It Pl Sa Si Sp.

leaf clusters

cone

habit

Pinus radiata D. Don Monterey Pine

A long pointed conical tree when young but dense and high domed when mature, 30–40m high. **Bark** Rugged, deeply fissured into thick, more or less vertical parallel ridges, dull grey on older trees. **Branches** The main branches are heavy, wide and spreading and sometimes touching the ground. The young shoots are glabrous, pale grey or white-green. **Buds** Winter buds are ovoid, short-pointed, with close-fitting, resiniferous, brown scales. **Leaves** 10–15cm long, in clusters of 3, persisting for 3–4 years, with finely toothed margins, a sharp apex and central resin canal. **Cones** Male strobili are crowded at the base of new shoots, bright yellow at flowering time; female strobili occur in clusters of 3–5 around the shoot tip. The mature cones are 7–15 x 6–9cm; the scales are broad, thick and woody, rounded on the outer, exposed sides. **Seeds** Up to 6mm long, black with a well-developed wing. **Distribution** A species of rather restricted distribution in Monterey County, Guadalupe Island and Baja California, now widely planted as a shelter tree in W. Europe, particularly near sea coasts and on light soils. Br Fr Ir It Pl Sp.

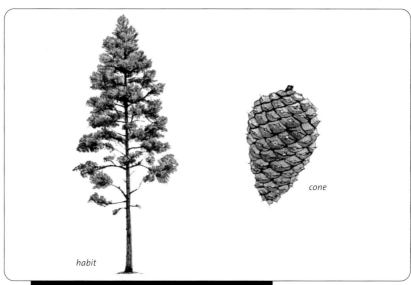

cone

habit

Pinus rigida Miller Northern Pitch Pine

A conical tree up to 25m, with rigid horny leaves occurring in clusters of 3, and small cylindrical or barrel-shaped cones with thin scales. **Distribution** A N. American, Atlantic species planted for timber on a small scale in Europe.

cone

branch
with winter bud
and leaf clusters

habit

Pinus banksiana Lamb. Jack Pine

A variable tree in habit, 8–25m (rarely 30m) high, the branches forming a thin and irregular, somewhat oval crown on young trees but tough and wide-spreading on mature trees. **Bark** Reddish-brown, vertically striped, with a grey finish. **Branches** The young shoots are smooth, glabrous, initially pale yellow-green, becoming reddish-brown in the 2nd year. **Buds** Winter buds are cylindrical, 3–6mm long, resiniferous, with closely appressed scales. **Leaves** 1·5–3·5cm long, in pairs, lasting 2 or 3 years, olive-green, stiff, with minutely toothed margins, a sharp pointed apex, and marginal resin canals. **Cones** Male strobili are numerous on the smaller shoots, yellow; female strobili are globose, pale red. The cones are 3–6 x 1–2cm, curving forwards, lumpy, pointed, persisting unopened for years on mature trees; the scales are 1·5 x 0·5cm, spineless. **Seeds** Up to 4mm long, triangular, blackish-brown, mottled. **Distribution** An E. Canadian species originating from the McKenzie river in the Arctic Circle, and common in the Canadian forest belt. Because of its hardiness it is widely planted for timber on well-drained soils of cold, exposed places. Au Br Cz De Ge Ru.

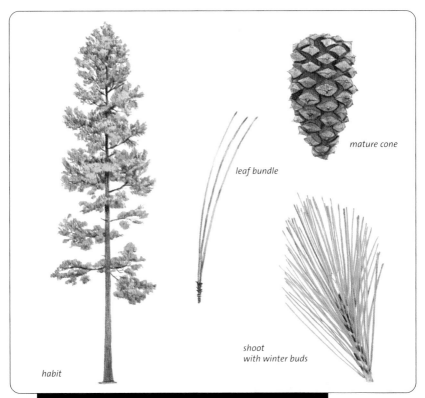

leaf bundle

mature cone

shoot
with winter buds

habit

Pinus ponderosa Douglas Western Yellow Pine

A tall tree up to 50m high (70m in the wild) with a straight clean trunk and a long spire-like crown. **Bark** Yellowish or dark reddish-brown, breaking up into irregularly shaped scaly plates which become very large and thick in old trees. **Branches** The shoots are glabrous, orange-brown or green at first, becoming black at maturity. **Leaves** Occurring in threes, persisting for 3 years; 15–30 x *c.* 0·3cm, spreading, densely crowded on the shoots, curved, rigid, with minutely toothed margins and a sharp horny apex. **Cones** Subterminal, either solitary or occurring in clusters, ovoid, 7–15 x 3·5–5cm, sessile or on short peduncles, light reddish-brown, often leaving a few of the basal scales attached to the branchlets when falling off; the scales are oblong, *c.* 3 x 1·5cm, the exposed part of the scale swollen, rhomboidal, transversely ridged; the central boss is armed with a minute prickle. **Seeds** *c.* 5cm long, oval, mottled, with a wing up to 2cm long. **Distribution and taxonomic notes** A wide-ranging tree of W. N. America planted in Europe on a small scale for timber, but mostly for ornament. Au Ge Gr It Ru. Related species planted on a lesser scale include: *P. jeffreyi* Balf., Jeffrey Pine, with a darker bark, larger cones with recurved prickles and heavier seeds; and *P. sabiniana* Douglas, the Digger Pine, a very slender tree with blue-white foliage.

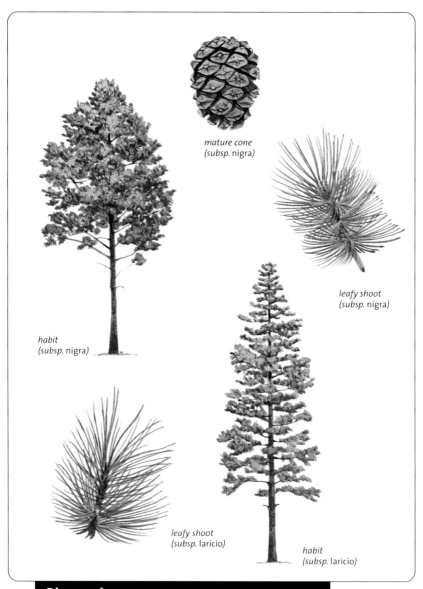

mature cone
(subsp. nigra)

leafy shoot
(subsp. nigra)

habit
(subsp. nigra)

leafy shoot
(subsp. laricio)

habit
(subsp. laricio)

Pinus nigra Arnold Austrian Pine or Corsican Pine

A large tree 40–50m high, pyramidal when young, becoming flat-topped when mature. **Bark** Greyish-brown or dark brown and very rough when mature. **Branches** Densely crowded. The shoots are glabrous, yellowish-brown and ridged; the branchlets become roughened by persistent leaf-bases as they lose their leaves. **Leaves** Occurring in pairs, persisting very densely on the branchlets for about 4 years; they are 10–15cm long, stiff, stout, straight or curved, with minutely toothed margins and a thickened apex; the resin canals are central and the basal sheaths initially *c.* 1·5cm long but gradually getting shorter with age. **Cones** Solitary or in clusters, 5–8cm long, up to 3cm wide, subsessile; the scales are 2–2·5cm long, transversely keeled near the apex and terminating with a persistent prickle. **Seeds** *c.* 3mm long, greyish-brownish with a long wing. **Distribution and taxonomic notes** A very variable and wide-ranging species with several distinct varieties described. It can be broadly divided into 2 main types: the Austrian Pine, subsp. *nigra*, with broad, rigid, persistent leaves; and the Corsican Pine, subsp. *laricio* (Poiret) Maire, with soft narrow leaves. It succeeds on poor chalky or neutral soils in C. European and S. coastal areas and is widely planted for timber, as a windbreak and as a sand dune stabilizer. Al Au Be Br Bu Co Cr Cz De Fu Ge Gr Ho Ir It Ru Sd Si Sp Sw Tu Yu.

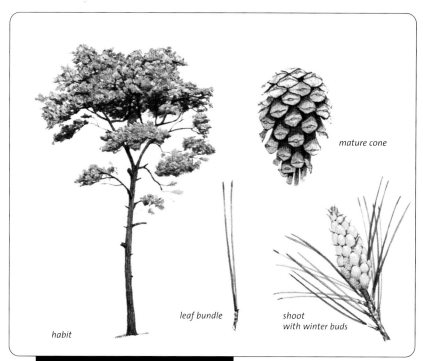

mature cone

leaf bundle

*shoot
with winter buds*

habit

Pinus sylvestris L. Scots Pine

A moderate-sized tree 25–35m (occasionally up to 50m) tall with a straight cylindrical bole up to 3·5m in diameter. **Bark** On the main portion of the bole fissured into irregular longitudinal plates, reddish-brown or greyish-brown, but light red to orange and in papery scales towards the top. **Branches** Usually regularly whorled in young trees, but in old trees branching only at the top, giving rise to a flat crown. The shoots are initially green, smooth and shining, becoming greyish-brown in the 2nd year, somewhat marked by the bases of the scale-leaves. **Buds** Winter buds are *c.* 1cm long, oblong-ovate with lanceolate fringed scales, the upper ones free at the apex. **Leaves** 2·5–8cm long, in pairs, grey-green, glaucous, short-pointed with finely toothed margins and well-defined lines of stomata on the flat inner surface, but with interrupted lines on the outer surface; the resin canals are marginal; the basal sheaths are initially white, later becoming grey, about 1cm long. **Cones** Solitary or in groups of 2–3 on short peduncles, usually ovoid-conical, 2–8cm long, grey or dull brown; the scales are narrowly oblong, the exposed part flat or protruding, the central boss terminating in a small prickle. **Seeds** 2–4mm long, black or dark grey, with a wing up to 1·5cm long. **Distribution and taxonomic notes** The Scots Pine has the widest distribution of all the pines, occurring as a native on light montane soils throughout Europe and W. and N. Asia. In the British Isles it survives as a native only in Scotland. More than 150 variants have been described, some regarded as subspecies, but the variation is somewhat continuous and often difficult to determine. However, it may be distinguished from other 2-leaved pines by its glaucous twisted foliage, the reddish upper trunk and its characteristic spire-like mature crown. All except Co Cr Ic. *P. resinosa* Aiton, the Red Pine from E. N. America, resembling *P. ponderosa* with the bark of *P. sylvestris*, is grown on a small scale for timber in Europe.

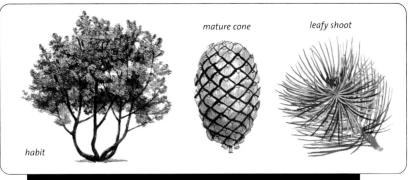

mature cone *leafy shoot*

habit

Pinus mugo Turra Mountain Pine (incl. *P. uncinata* Miller)

A shrub or small tree with many crooked, irregularly spreading branches. **Bark** Grey-black and scaly. **Buds** Ovoid-cylindrical and very resiniferous. **Leaves** 3–8cm x 1·5–2mm, in pairs, bright green, curved, rigid, persisting 5 years or more. **Cones** Subterminal, solitary or in groups of 2–3, ovate to ovate-conical, up to 5cm long x 1·5–2·5cm wide; the exposed part of the scale is flat, or convex above and concave below; the boss is central or below the middle with a small prickle. **Seeds** small. **Distribution** A common species to the mountains of C. Europe and the Balkan Peninsula. It is frequently planted for sand binding and shelter in N. Europe. Al Au Bu Cz Fr Fu Ge Gr It Po Ru Sw Yu.

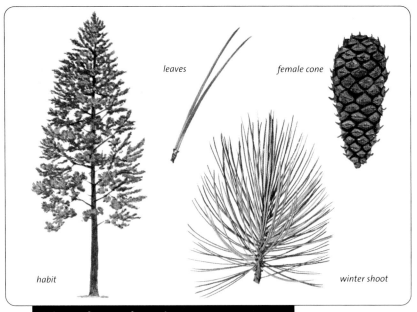

leaves *female cone*

habit *winter shoot*

Pinus leucodermis Antoine Bosnian Pine

A stout pyramidal tree up to *c.* 30m, the trunk with a girth of up to 2m. **Bark** Ash-grey, dividing into irregular plates. **Branches** The young twigs are glabrous but glaucous for about the first 3 years. The winter buds are dark brown but not resiniferous. **Leaves** 7–9cm x *c.* 1·2mm, occurring in pairs, densely covering the shoots, dark green, rigid, erect, pungent, with minutely toothed margins, sharply pointed apices, stomatic lines on both surfaces, and 4–6 central resin canals. **Cones** Ovoid-conical, 7–8 x *c.* 2·5cm, shortly stalked, dull brown and somewhat shining; the exposed part of the scale is pyramidal with a recurved prickle. **Seeds** *c.* 7mm long with a wing up to 2·5cm long. **Distribution and taxonomic notes** The Bosnian Pine is closely allied to *P. nigra* and considered by some authors to be a montane form of it, although it is readily recognized by the compact branching system and denser foliage. A SW. Italian and Balkan species, occurring on dry limestone; it is frequently cultivated in other parts of Europe. Bu Gr It Yu.

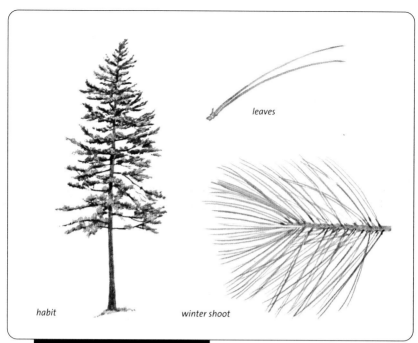

leaves

habit   winter shoot

Pinus heldreichii Christ

A tree or shrub up to 20m tall with a rounded pyramidal crown. **Bark** Ashy-grey, flaking to leave yellowish patches. **Branches** The twigs are glabrous but glaucous in their first year. **Buds** Green, not resiniferous. **Leaves** 6–9cm x *c.* 1·5mm, occurring in pairs, rigid, more or less spine tipped; there are 2–11 central resin canals. **Cones** 7–8 x 2–5cm, brown and slightly shining; the exposed part of the scale is flat with a very short straight prickle. **Seeds** *c.* 7mm long with a wing *c.* 2–5cm long. **Distribution and taxonomic notes** Many authorities consider *P. leucodermis* and *P. heldreichii* as the same species but the latter can be distinguished by the brown 2nd year twigs, the exposed part of the scale being flat and the short, acute prickles. A resistant montane species occurring on limestone in the Balkan Peninsula. Al Gr Yu.

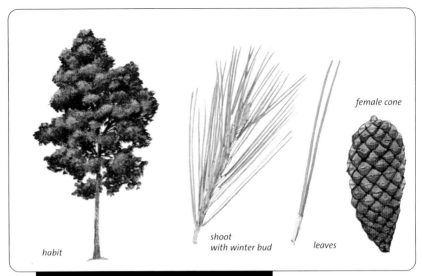

female cone

shoot with winter bud

leaves

habit

Pinus halepensis Miller Aleppo Pine

A stout tree (at maturity) rarely exceeding 20m high, with twisting branches and fine twigs and a bole with a girth up to 5m. **Bark** Smooth, silvery-grey and shining at first, becoming reddish-brown, fissured and scaly on old boles. **Branches** The shoots are grey-glaucous and glabrous, remaining grey for many years but eventually becoming green. **Buds** Winter buds are conical, *c.* 8mm long, with fringed scales and often reflexed at the tips. **Leaves** 6–15cm x 0·7mm, occurring in pairs, persisting for *c.* 2 years, slender, clear green, curved, twisted above, with minutely toothed margins and a short horny apex; there are 3–8 submarginal or central resin canals. **Cones** 5–12 x 4cm, ovate-conical, solitary or in groups of 2–3, spreading or deflexed, reddish, occurring on thick scaly peduncles up to 2cm long; the scales are shiny, *c.* 2·5cm long; the exposed part is convex. **Seeds** *c.* 7mm long with a wing up to 2cm long. **Distribution** A species common to the countries surrounding the Mediterranean; being particularly drought-resistant it is commonly planted in hot dry places to check soil erosion and as a windbreak. Bl Co Cr Fr Gr It Pl Sa Si Sp Yu.

Pinus brutia Ten Calabrian Pine
Closely related to *P. halepensis* but the leaves are longer (8–12cm x *c.* 1–1·5mm), darker green and more rigid; the cones are more spreading, never deflexed. **Distribution** It occurs in similar localities in Calabria, Crete and Turkey. Cr It Tu.

Pinus canariensis Sweet & Sprengel Canary Island Pine
Superficially similar to *P. halepensis* but the leaves are 20–30cm long, occurring in threes; the shoots are yellow in colour; the bud scales are fringed, and the cones are very large. **Distribution** It is planted in Italy and on a smaller scale in other Mediterranean countries as a timber tree.

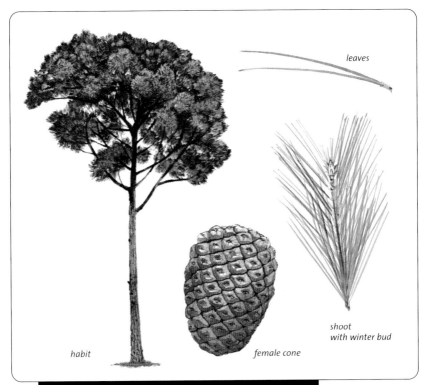

leaves

*shoot
with winter bud*

habit

female cone

Pinus pinea L. Stone Pine or Umbrella Pine

A stout, parasol-shaped tree up to 30m tall. **Bark** On old trees reddish-grey with deep longitudinal fissures, flaking to leave reddish-orange patches. **Branches** The twigs are glabrous, greyish-green, becoming brown at maturity. **Buds** Winter buds are 0·5–1·2cm long, with reflexed scales. **Leaves** 10–20cm x 1·5–2mm, occurring in pairs, persisting for 2–3 years, slightly twisted, acute, with 12 stomatic lines on the outer surface and 6 on the inner surface; the resin canals are marginal. **Cones** 8–14 x 10cm, ripening shining brown after 3 years, the exposed part of the scale weakly pyramidal. **Seeds** 1·5–2 x 0·7–1·1cm with a wing less than 1mm long. **Distribution** A native of light sandy soils in Mediterranean Europe. Al Bl Co Cr Fr Gr It Pl Sa Si Sp Tu Yu.

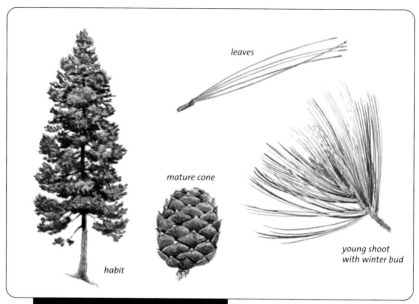

leaves

mature cone

young shoot
with winter bud

habit

Pinus cembra L. Arolla Pine

A pyramidal tree 20–40m high with stout spreading branches. **Bark** Reddish-grey, separating into thin scaly patches on older trees and sometimes covered with blisters of resin. **Branches** The twigs are strongly pubescent with an orange-brown tomentum. **Buds** Winter buds are about 5mm long, dotted with long, pointed, dull resiniferous scales. **Leaves** In groups of 5, persisting for 3–5 years, 5–8cm x 1mm, rather rigid, erect and crowded on the shoot, with toothed margins, the stomata confined to the inner surfaces in 2 faint lines; there are 2 central resin canals. **Cones** 5–8 x 3·5–5cm, less than one and a half times as long as wide, on short peduncles, violet-tinged at first, later purplish-brown when ripe; the scales are rounded in outline, c. 2·5 x 2cm, with a thickened apex, minutely downy on the outer surface. **Seeds** Virtually or completely wingless. **Distribution** A tree readily distinguished from other 5-leaved species by its distinct habit and the shaggy orange-brown pubescence of the young shoots. It is native to the Alps and Carpathians, seldom found below 1700m and often occurring up to the tree line. It is often planted in other parts of N. Europe for its light wood. Au Cz Fi Fr Fu Ge Ic It No Po Ru Sd Sw Yu.

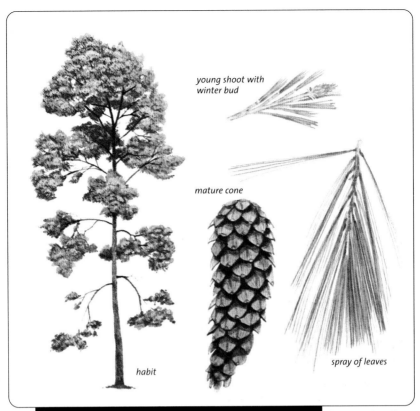

young shoot with winter bud

mature cone

spray of leaves

habit

Pinus wallichiana A.B. Jackson Bhutan Pine

A slender, elegant tree up to 50m high, with horizontal spreading branches below and ascending branches above. **Bark** Thin, smooth, resiniferous and grey-brown on young trees, becoming shallowly fissured when older. **Branches** The young shoots are glabrous, yellowish-green at first, becoming brownish-yellow. **Buds** Winter buds are cylindrical or conical, up to 6mm long, with dull lance-like scales often matted with resin. **Leaves** In fives, persisting for 3–4 years, those on the young shoots more or less erect, the older ones spreading or drooping, 8–20cm x 0·7mm, flexible, greyish-green, minutely toothed on the margins, the apex pointed; the resin canals are marginal. **Cones** 15–25 x 3cm, cylindrical, straight, becoming pendent, light brown when mature, very resiniferous; the scales are *c.* 3·5 x 2·5cm, wedge-shaped, longitudinally grooved with a thickened apex, the basal ones sometimes reflexed. **Seeds** Oval-shaped, with a wing up to 2cm long, shed readily, leaving empty cones on the tree. **Distribution** A native of the temperate Himalayas at 2000–4200m, the Bhutan pine is planted on a small scale in Italy for timber and in other parts of N. Europe as an ornamental.

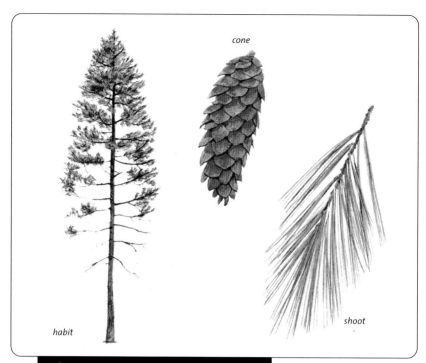

cone

shoot

habit

Pinus peuce Griseb. Macedonian Pine

A narrowly conical tree up to 30m tall with a thin trunk, and with a narrow dense pyramidal crown. **Bark** Greyish-green and smooth on young trees, becoming brown and fissured on old trees. **Branches** The young shoots are smooth, glabrescent or remaining hairy at the leaf-traces, becoming greyish-brown in the 2nd year. **Buds** The winter buds are ovoid, sharply and abruptly pointed, about 1cm long and somewhat resiniferous. **Leaves** 7–12cm x *c.* 0·7mm, in clusters of 5, persisting for about 3 years, slender, flexible, suberect on the branches, with finely toothed margins, a sharp apex and with marginal resin canals. **Cones** Male strobili are in clusters at the base of the shoot, conical, pointed, purplish-yellow; female strobili are terminal, slender ovoid, initially pale green but rapidly becoming purple. The cones are 8–20 x 3–4cm, subterminal, pendent, subcylindrical and often curved near the apex; the scales are broadly wedge-shaped, grey-tipped and convex with incurving tips. **Seeds** 5–8mm long with a wing up to 2·5cm long. **Distribution** A restricted native of Europe found in small montane localities of the Balkan Peninsula between 600–2000m. Its robust habit and resistance to extreme environments has led to high altitude planting in Germany. Al Bu Ge Gr Yu.

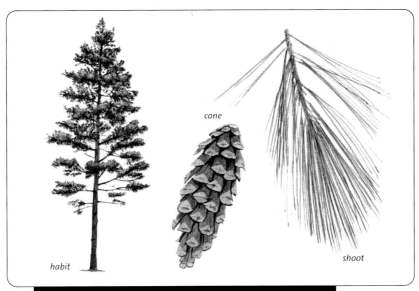

cone

habit

shoot

Pinus strobus L. White Pine or Weymouth Pine

A moderately large tree up to 50m with a tapering trunk. The branches of old trees form a round-topped or conical crown with the leaves in horizontal masses. **Bark** Thin, smooth and greyish-green on young trees, becoming rugged, fissured and brown on old trees. **Branches** Young twigs are slender with tufts of short hairs below the insertion of the leaf-bundles but glabrescent elsewhere. **Buds** Winter buds are conical with a sharp point, *c.* 3mm long, resiniferous, with some of the scales free at the tips. **Leaves** 5–14cm long, slender, sharply pointed, bluish-green, flexible, with finely toothed margins, and marginal resin canals. **Cones** 8–20 x 3–4cm, subterminal, pendulous, cylindrical, often curved near the apex; the scales are thin, smooth, light brown. **Seeds** 5–8mm long with a rounded wing 1·8–2·5cm long. **Distribution** A species easily recognized by its horizontal masses of bluish-green foliage and tufts of hairs below the point of insertion of leaves, the Weymouth Pine is one of the most distinctive N. American species, now planted on a wide scale particularly in C. Europe as a timber tree. Au Be Bu Cz De Fr Fu Ge It Po Ru Sd Sw Tu.

habit

Pinus aristata Engelm. Bristle-cone Pine

A small slow-growing tree only attaining 10m in European conditions. **Leaves** 2–4cm long, in groups of 5, deep green, often flecked with white resin, and persisting for 14 years or more. **Cones** 5–8cm long when mature, with a spreading spine up to 6mm long on each scale. **Distribution** A relatively rare species originating from the Rocky Mountains of the SW. United States. It is usually found in private collections and cultivated on a small scale for its timber.

Angiosperms

Willow and Poplar Family
Salicaceae

Salix L. Willows

Dioecious trees or shrubs. **Leaves** Alternate and stipules are present. **Flowers** Arranged in catkins, each growing in the axil of an entire bract with 1–2 small nectaries but no perianth; male flowers usually have 2, 3 or 5 stamens; the female flowers have numerous ovules. **Taxonomic notes** Many species hybridize with one or more different species, creating confusion as to their correct identity.

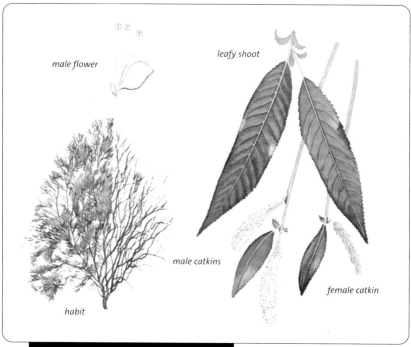

male flower

leafy shoot

male catkins

female catkin

habit

Salix fragilis L. Crack Willow

A tree up to 25m high with a broad tapering crown. **Bark** Blackish-grey, scaly, becoming thickly ridged. **Branches** Curving upwards. The 1-year-old twigs are very easily snapped off at the base. **Buds** Pointed, conical, yellow, pale green or brown. **Leaves** 6–15 x 1·5–4cm, lanceolate, usually 4–9 times as long as wide, with a slender, tapering, somewhat twisted apex, rather coarsely serrate, glabrous, shiny green above, bluish-green or greyish-green beneath; the petiole is 1–2cm long with 2 glands at the top; the stipules usually fall early. **Flowers** The catkins appear with the leaves, drooping, densely cylindrical; males are 2–5cm long, yellow; females are *c.* 10cm long, green, with 2 nectaries. **Flowering period** May. **Distribution and taxonomic notes** An abundant species around lowland rivers and streams in much of Europe except the Arctic. The hybrid *S.* x *rubens* Schrank (*S. fragilis* x *alba*) is perhaps the most common *Salix* hybrid. Its resemblance and similar habitat to *S. fragilis* means that the two are often confused. It differs in having silky leaves.

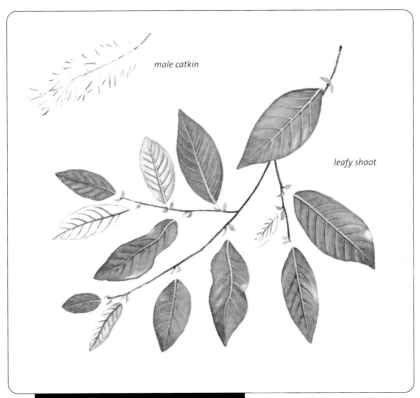

male catkin

leafy shoot

Salix pentandra L. Bay Willow

A shrub or small tree up to 7m high, forming a densely branched, broad, rounded crown. **Bark** Greyish-brown with fine pale fissures. **Branches** Twigs are glabrous, shining. **Buds** 5mm long, more or less conical, pale brown. **Leaves** 5–12cm long, elliptic to somewhat oblong, 2–4 times as long as wide, acuminate, rounded or broadly wedge-shaped at the base, finely and evenly serrulate, dark shiny green above, whitish beneath, with yellow glands, somewhat leathery when mature, sticky and fragrant when young; the petiole is up to 8mm long with 1–3 pairs of glands near the top; the stipules are small, falling early. **Flowers** The catkins are 2–5 x 1cm, cylindrical, bright yellow, appearing after the leaves on leafy pubescent peduncles; males have 4–12 but usually 5 stamens; females are smaller with 2 nectaries. **Flowering period** May–June. **Distribution** A species widespread along river banks and wet meadows in much of Europe except the extreme N. and S. and most of the islands. Al Au Be Br Bu Cz De Fi Fr Fu Ge Ho Hu Ir It No Po Ru Sp Sw Yu.

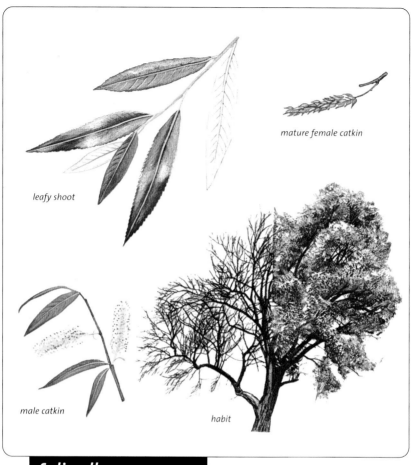

leafy shoot

mature female catkin

male catkin

habit

Salix alba L. White Willow

A stout tree up to 25m high (although often pollarded); the crown is a rather irregularly shaped dome. **Bark** Does not flake, but has thick interconnecting ridges. **Branches** Ascending, silvery-grey. The shoots are slender, silky pubescent when young, soon becoming glabrous, grey to greenish-brown. **Buds** 2mm long, with a curved tapering tip, reddish-tinged and covered with a grey down. **Leaves** 5–10cm long, usually *c.* 5–8 times as long as wide, acuminate, sometimes slightly asymmetrical at the apex, wedge-shaped at the base, finely serrate, covered with long white hairs which are pressed closely to the surface of the leaf; the petiole is *c.* 5mm long, and without glands. The stipules usually fall early. **Flowers** The catkins appear with the leaves; male catkins are most abundant, 7–8cm long, slender, curved upwards, yellow with 2 stamens; occasionally female flowers with 1 nectary occur with the males; female catkins are 4–6cm long, green, soon becoming white with seed. **Flowering period** May–June. **Distribution and taxonomic notes** A very common species of waterways and wet woods in Europe, N. Africa and Asia. Al Au Be Br Bu Co Cr Cz De Fi Fr Fu Ge Gr Ho Hu Ir It No Pl Po Ru Sa Si Sp Sw Tu Yu. There are many described variants and it frequently hybridizes with other species. Subsp. *coerulea* (Sm.) Rech. f. is frequently cultivated, particularly in the British Isles, for the manufacture of cricket bats. The hybrid *Salix* x *chrysocoma* Dode (= *S. alba* subsp. *vitellina* (L.) Arcangeli x *babylonica*), the Weeping Willow, is a favourite cultivar in many parts of Europe since it combines the silky indumentum of *S. alba* with the weeping habit of *S. babylonica*.

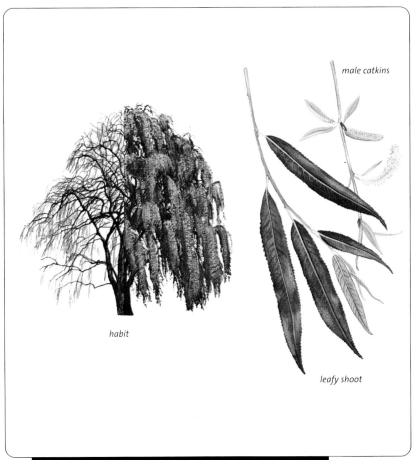

male catkins

habit

leafy shoot

Salix babylonica L. Chinese Weeping Willow

A graceful tree up to 20m high. **Branches** The branches and twigs are long, pendent, drooping almost entirely to the ground. **Leaves** 8–16 x 0·8–1·5cm long, narrowly lanceolate or linear-lanceolate, acuminate at the apex, finely toothed, usually glabrous at maturity; the petiole is 3–5mm long. **Flowers** The catkins are up to 2cm long x 0·3–0·4cm wide; the bracts are all the same colour, becoming smooth; female flowers have 1 nectary; the ovary is glabrous, sessile. **Flowering period** May. **Distribution** A species of Chinese origin widely cultivated in many parts of Europe and frequently naturalized. It has browner twigs and poorer growth characteristics than the Weeping Willow, which is usually cultivated in preference.

male flower

male catkin

habit

female catkin

leafy shoot

Salix triandra L. Almond Willow

A shrub or more rarely a small tree 4–10m high. **Bark** Smooth, flaking off in patches. **Branches** The shoots are glabrous, except initially, rather fragile, olive or reddish-brown. **Buds** Ovoid, brown, glabrous. **Leaves** 5–10cm long, usually *c.* 3–8 times as long as wide, oblong-ovate or oblong-lanceolate, acuminate or acute, symmetrical, rounded at the base, serrate, glabrous, dark, somewhat glossy green above, glaucous or less often pale beneath; the petiole is 0·6–1·5cm long, glabrous, with 2–3 glands near the top; the stipules are ovate, dentate, 0·5–1cm long, usually persistent. **Flowers** The catkins are cylindrical and erect, appearing with the leaves on short leafy shoots; males are 3–5cm long, slender, greenish-yellow, persistent, with obovate scales of a single colour and 3 stamens having yellow anthers and filaments hairy at the base; females are denser and shorter, each with 1 nectary and sometimes a short style diverging at a wide angle and shallowly notched at the tip, and a pedicel ultimately 3–4 times as long as the nectary. **Flowering period** March–May (and sometimes July–August). **Distribution and taxonomic notes** A widespread and rather common species of pond and river banks in much of Europe, except the Arctic, and rather local in the Mediterranean region. The shrubbery forms are frequently confused with such hybrids as *S.* x *mollissima* Hoffm. ex Elwert (*S. triandra* x *viminalis*), *S.* x *speciosa* Host (*S. fragilis* x *triandra*) and *S.* x *leiophylla* E. G. & A. Camus (*S. purpurea* L. x *triandra*), which occur in similar habitats and are frequently planted as Osiers. Al Au Be Br Bu Cz Fi Fr Fu Gr Ho Hu Ir No Pl Po Ru Sa Sd Sp Sw.

leafy shoot

habit

female catkin

male catkin

Salix borealis Fries

A shrub or small tree. **Branches** Irregularly thick, erect. The young shoots have a dense white indumentum. **Leaves** 2–7cm (occasionally to 10cm) long, *c.* 1–4 times as long as broad, orbicular-ovate to more or less elliptical, acute or shortly acuminate, often deeply serrate with large glands, leathery, somewhat glaucous beneath with long whitish hairs and a prominent network of veins. **Flowers** The catkins appear with the leaves on thick woolly peduncles; the males are 1·5–2·5cm long, subsessile, ovoid or oblong with free stamens and yellow anthers. The females are 1·5–3cm long in flower, lengthening to 5–8cm long in fruit, rather lax, with long slender styles and stigmas; the pedicel is 3–4 times as long as the nectary. **Distribution and taxonomic notes** A species of wetlands in N. Scandinavia and Russia. Fi Fu. It is frequently confused with the more widespread shrubby *S. nigricans* Sm., the Dark-leaved Willow, which has more slender, glabrescent twigs and branches, more glaucous leaves (which turn black on drying), longer, more slender styles and stigmas; and which occurs on lakesides and streamsides in much of N. and C. Europe.

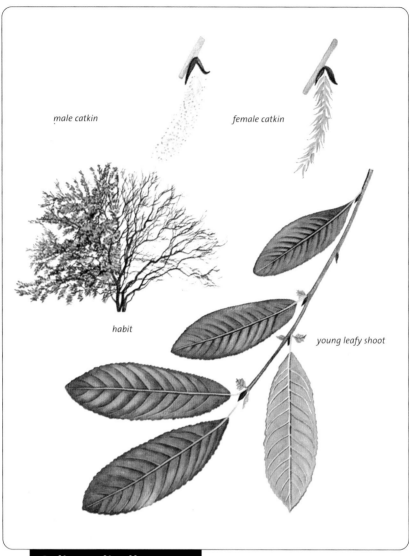

male catkin

female catkin

habit

young leafy shoot

Salix pedicellata Desf.

A tall shrub or tree up to 10m high. **Bark** Grey. **Branches** Numerous prominent ridges on the peeled wood. The young shoots are grey-tomentose, gradually becoming glabrescent as the trees get older. **Leaves** Oblong or obovate-lanceolate, crenate to almost entire, glabrescent above and thinly pubescent beneath; the lateral veins occur in 10–12 pairs, connected by a fine network of veins, impressed above but prominent beneath; the stipules are large, deciduous, dentate, semicordate. The bracts have short hairs. **Flowers** The catkins are 3–6 x 1–1.5cm; the females have short or moderately long styles; the pedicels are 3–4mm long and the ovary is glabrous. **Distribution** An indistinct species found in wet places in the Mediterranean region. Co Gr It Sa Si Sp Tu.

male catkin

female catkin

leafy shoot

Salix appendiculata Vill.

A tall shrub or small tree up to 3m high. **Branches** Short, spreading at a wide angle, the peeled wood displaying somewhat indistinct ridges. The young shoots are pubescent with short hairs, eventually becoming glabrescent. **Leaves** Extremely variable in size and shape, up to 14cm long x 1·5–3cm (occasionally to 5cm) wide, usually widest above the middle, more or less dark green and glabrous above but paler, light green and pubescent beneath, the margins roughly and irregularly toothed to entire, somewhat asymmetrical at the apex and the veins distinct beneath; the petiole is *c.* 1cm long; the stipules are prominent, semicordate and coarsely serrate. **Flowers** The catkins are *c.* 3 x 1cm, very lax; the filaments in the male flowers have a few long hairs near the base; the pedicel is as long as or longer than the grey pubescent ovary. **Distribution and taxonomic notes** An alpine or montane species invariably above 500m in the Alps of C. Europe, the Apennines and the NW. Balkan Peninsula. It readily hybridizes with other montane species, particularly *S. caprea* L. (*S.* x *macrophylla* Kerner). The hybrids invariably inherit its distinctive rough leaf character and the prominent veins. Au Fr Ge It Sw Yu.

Salix cinerea L. Grey Willow or Common Sallow

A shrub or very rarely a tree up to 6m high. **Branches** Readily recognized by its rather stout, persistently grey-tomentose twigs, and the fine raised linear markings on the 2-year-old wood when the bark is stripped off. **Leaves** 2–4 times as long as broad, the short styles and the pedicel 2–5 times as long as the nectary. **Flowering period** March–April. **Distribution** It is extremely common in much of Europe, although rare in the west and the Mediterranean region. Al Au Be Br Bu Co Cz De Fi Fr Fu Ge Gr Ho Hu It No Po Ru Sw Tu Yu.

male catkins

female catkin

habit

leafy shoot

Salix atrocinerea Brot. Common Sallow

A tall shrub or small tree up to 10m high. **Branches** The young shoots are initially brown-pubescent, becoming reddish in winter and remaining thinly pubescent or becoming glabrous. The buds are thinly pubescent or glabrous. **Leaves** Usually reddish-green or fawn, pubescent above when young, thinly and shortly pubescent on the veins beneath, glaucous at maturity and with some or all of the bristly hairs rust-coloured, more or less prominently veined; the stipules are usually small. **Flowers** The catkins are the same as those of *S. cinerea*. **Distribution and taxonomic notes** A prominent species of woods, heaths, ponds and stream sides, and in marshes and fens throughout W. Europe from Britain to Portugal. The pure form is often difficult to find since it freely hybridizes with *S. aurita* L., the Eared Sallow, *S. caprea* L., and *S. cinerea* whenever they meet. Be Br Fr Ir Pl Sp.

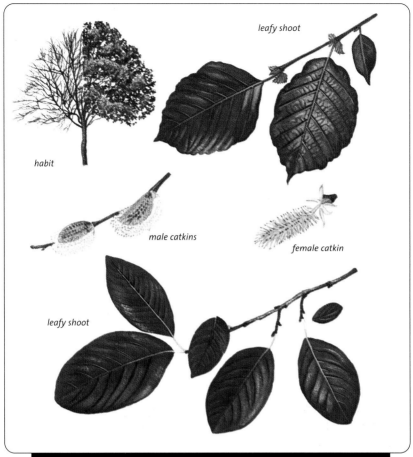

leafy shoot

habit

male catkins

female catkin

leafy shoot

Salix caprea L. Pussy Willow, Great Sallow or Goat Willow

A dioecious shrub or small tree 3–10m high, often with a short, twisting bole. **Bark** Light greyish-brown and shallowly fissured. **Branches** The shoots are rather stout, covered with long grey hairs, becoming smooth, shiny and reddish-brown. **Leaves** Rather variable, 6–11 x 3–6cm, usually broadly ovate to ovate-oblong, the base rounded, sinuate-dentate or almost serrate, dark green and eventually almost glabrous above, persistently softly and densely grey-tomentose beneath; the margins are somewhat undulate, shallowly toothed or entire; there are 6–9 pairs of lateral veins, forming almost a right-angle with the midrib and very distinctive on the lower surface; the petiole is *c.* 1cm long, dark red; the stipules are semicordate and very large. **Flowers** The catkins are dense, subsessile and appear before the leaves; male catkins are 2–3·5 x 1·5–2cm, oblong-ovoid, initially with projecting silvery hairs, later with yellow stamens; female catkins are eventually 3–7cm long, looser than the males, initially pale green with projecting styles, later covered with long wavy hairs which turn from brown to white at maturity; the bracts are blackish at the apex; both male and female flowers have 1 nectary. **Distribution and taxonomic notes** A species of woods, scrub and hedgerows from lowland to montane stations in much of Europe. Au Be Br Bu Co Cz De Fi Fr Fu Ge Gr Ho Hu Ir It No Po Ru Sd Si Sp Sw Tu Yu. The European Sallows or Pussy Willows are a difficult group to identify as there are many different subspecies and hybrids. The Sallows range from shrubs to trees. Scandinavian and Scottish plants with the 2nd year twigs hairy, and cuneate leaves hairy above, are generally given a different name – *S. coaetanea* (Hartman) B. Flod.

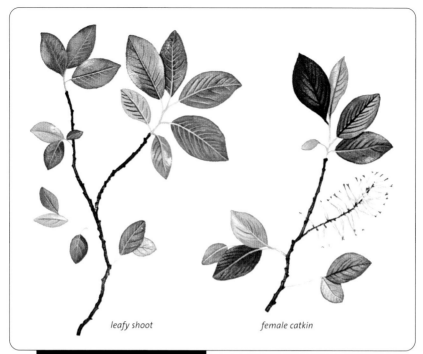

leafy shoot　　　　　*female catkin*

Salix xerophila B. Flod.

A shrub and more rarely a tree up to 5m high. **Branches** Erect. The shoots are dull and more or less woolly. **Buds** Conical, somewhat right-angled and reddish-brown. **Leaves** Oblanceolate, woolly-grey, with appressed, somewhat curved hairs, entire margins and 7–8 pairs of lateral veins; stipules are usually absent. **Flowers** The catkins are 1·5–3 x 0·5–1cm long, lax on peduncles up to 2·5cm long; the bracts are obovate, brown; the nectaries are slender, ovate, one-quarter to one-third as long as the bracts; the filaments are hairy; the stigmas are divergent, cylindrical, usually deeply cleft. **Distribution** A waterside species of N. Finland, Norway and Russia. Fi Fu No.

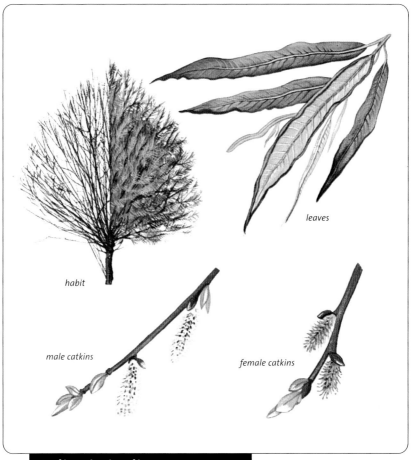

leaves

habit

male catkins

female catkins

Salix viminalis L. Common Osier

A shrub or small tree 3–5m (rarely up to 10m) high. **Branches** Long, straight, leafy, flexible. The young shoots are densely pubescent, becoming glabrous later, without linear markings beneath the bark. **Buds** Ovoid-oblong, acute to acuminate, pubescent. **Leaves** 10–25cm long, *c.* 1·5cm wide when mature, 4–18 times as long as broad, narrowly linear, with a very narrow cuneate base, dark green and glabrous above, silvery silky-tomentose beneath; the margins are wavy, revolute when young, entire or nearly so, with 20–35 pairs of lateral veins; the petiole is up to 1·2cm long; the stipules are small, linear-lanceolate, usually falling early. **Flowers** The catkins are subsessile; the bracts are black at the tip, the nectaries are long, linear; the males appear before the leaves, 2·5–4cm long, ovoid-oblong, with free stamens and bright yellow anthers; the females appear with the leaves, cylindrical and up to 6cm long in fruit; the capsule is ovoid-conical, silky-tomentose, sessile or subsessile; the style is very long – more than half as long as the ovary in fruit and as long as the flowers; the stigmas are entire, slender and bifid. **Flowering period** April–May. **Distribution and taxonomic notes** A native species of streams and pond sides and in marshes and fens, mostly in C. Europe, extending westwards to Ireland and eastwards to the Ukrainian Carpathians and Bulgaria. Au Be Br Cz Fr Fu Ge Gr Ho Hu Ir Po Ru Sd Yu. It is frequently planted as an osier in De Fi It No Pl Sp Sw. In Russia *S. viminalis* is largely replaced by *S. rossica* Nasarov, which differs in its more obtuse buds, the leaves rounded at the base and its shorter styles. *S. viminalis* is difficult to determine anywhere in its pure form because it is so similar to *S. caprea*, *S. cinerea* and *S. aurita* L. and readily produces shrubby hybrids with them, many of which are cultivated and frequently escape into the wild.

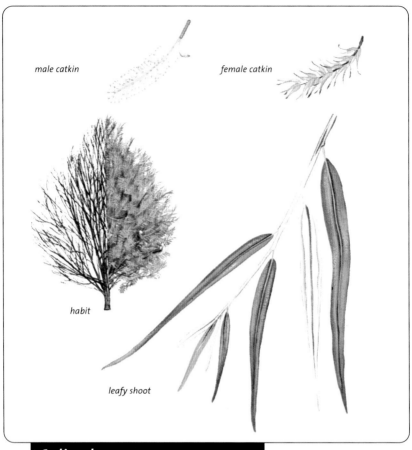

male catkin

female catkin

habit

leafy shoot

Salix elaeagnos Scop. Hoary Willow

A shrub up to 6m high or more rarely a tree up to 16m high. **Branches** The shoots are slender, thinly covered with whitish hairs when young, yellowish to reddish-brown. **Leaves** 5–12cm long, up to 1cm wide, 6–14 times as long as wide, erect, linear-lanceolate to narrowly linear, tapering at both ends, densely lanate on both surfaces when young but becoming more or less glabrescent above, remaining lanate beneath, dull, margin deflexed or revolute and finely glandular-serrate, particularly in the apical part; the veins are more or less impressed above and slightly prominent beneath although often not visible because of the dense indumentum; the petiole is up to 5mm long; stipules are usually absent. **Flowers** The catkins are up to 6 x 0·8cm on peduncles up to 1cm long, bearing small lanceolate leaves; the bracts are about half as long as the ovary; the filaments are united at the base or up to the middle and hairy at or near the base; the ovary is glabrous and the pedicel is about one-quarter as long as the ovary. **Distribution and taxonomic notes** A species of lowland or montane valley waterways, usually occurring in large stands with other trees. It is common in C. Europe extending to France, Spain, Italy and the Ukrainian Carpathians. Al Au Bu Co Cz Fr Fu Ge Gr Ho Hu It Po Ru Sp Sw Yu. It is an extremely variable species and hybrids are common along riversides in the Alps. It readily hybridizes with *S. cinerea*, *S. viminalis* and *S. nigricans* Sm. as well as several other shrubby species. The most prominent inherited characters from *S. elaeagnos* are the long, narrow, curved catkins, and leaves with more or less parallel margins and lanate undersides.

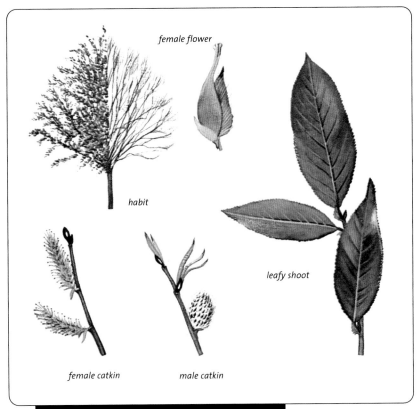

female flower

habit

leafy shoot

female catkin *male catkin*

Salix daphnoides Vill. Violet Willow

A tall shrub or a tree 7–10m tall with slender branches. **Branches** The shoots are dark shining purple and covered with a waxy bloom. **Buds** Narrowly conical, blackish-purple. **Leaves** 5–10cm long, *c.* 2–4 times as long as wide, oblong-lanceolate or oblong-ovate, acute or acuminate, glandular-serrulate, soon glabrous dark green and shining above, glaucous, pale yellow beneath, with 8–12 pairs of lateral veins and a broad white midrib; the petiole is 2–4mm long, crimson above; the stipules are large, cordate. **Flowers** The catkins are 3–5cm long, appearing before the leaves, subsessile, cylindrical, dense; the tracts are ovate, hairy and black at the apex; male catkins are bright yellow; females are more slender and green. **Flowering period** March. **Distribution** A native of Europe to N. Scandinavia, also the Himalayas and C. Asia, widely planted in C. and S. Europe for its colourful violet-tinged year-old shoots, which are especially attractive in winter. Au Fr Ge No Sw.

Populus L. Poplars

Deciduous dioecious fast-growing, often large trees. The flowers are borne in pendulous catkins and appear before the leaves.

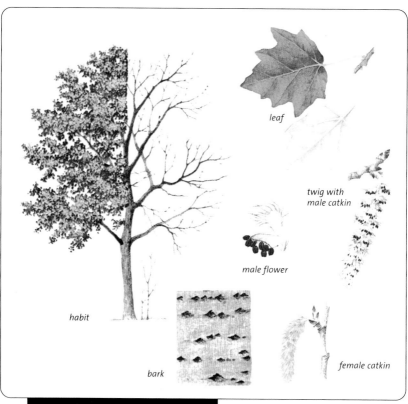

leaf

twig with male catkin

male flower

habit

bark

female catkin

Populus alba L. White Poplar

A medium-sized tree up to 30m high with a broad and often one-sided crown and a sturdy bole with numerous suckers around the base. **Bark** On immature trees and young branches smooth and white or greyish-green, becoming rougher and much darker with age. **Branches** Horizontal or slightly pendent, and twisted. **Buds** Small, ovoid, orange-brown and covered with white down. **Leaves** Those of the long shoots are 6–12cm long, ovate with 3–5 lobes, the lobes coarsely toothed or with 1–2 lobules on each side, dark greyish-green above, downy-white beneath; those of the short shoots are smaller and narrower, with wavy dentate margins and a greyish down beneath; the petiole is 3-4cm long, flattened and covered with a white down. **Flowers** The catkins are 4–8cm long in flower, 8–10cm long in fruit; males are grey, each flower with 6–10 crimson stamens; females are green. **Flowering period** March–April. **Distribution** A species of wet and well-watered places, and also of sandy coasts where it is resistant to salt and winds. It is frequently planted in gardens, streets and parks for ornament and for shelter along coasts. Al Au Be Br Bu Cz De Fr Fu Ge Gr Ho Hu It Pl Po Ru Sa Sd Sp Tu Yu.

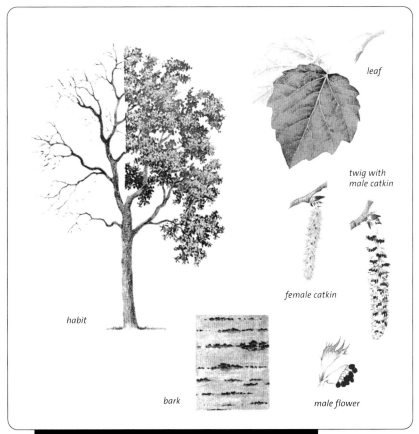

leaf

twig with
male catkin

female catkin

habit

bark

male flower

Populus canescens (Aiton) Sm. Grey Poplar

Similar to but larger than *P. alba*, up to 30m high; the crown conical when young but broad and many-domed in older specimens. **Bark** Has diamond-shaped pits on young trees, becoming coarse and rugged and changing from dark grey to brown or black in mature trees. **Branches** Relatively few, massive and ascending, the twigs dense and rather pendulous, covered with white or greyish hair. **Buds** Red-brown, hairy towards the base, glabrous towards the tip. **Leaves** Those of the long shoots are triangular-ovate, slightly heart-shaped at the base, toothed or lobed, dark glossy green above, downy grey beneath; those of the short shoots are ovate to more or less orbicular, becoming glabrous. **Flowers** The catkins are 3–4cm long in flower, the male flowers with 8–15 reddish-purple stamens. **Flowering period** Early February. **Distribution and taxonomic notes** It is usually found in river valleys. It is intermediate and thought to be a hybrid between *P. alba* and *P. tremula*. Au Be Br Bu De Fr Fu Ge Gr Ho Hu Ir It Po Pl Ru Sd Sp Sw. *Populus* x *hybrida* Bieb. (*P. canescens* x *P. tremula*), the Hybrid Poplar, may be found in areas where the parents grow together and is sometimes planted.

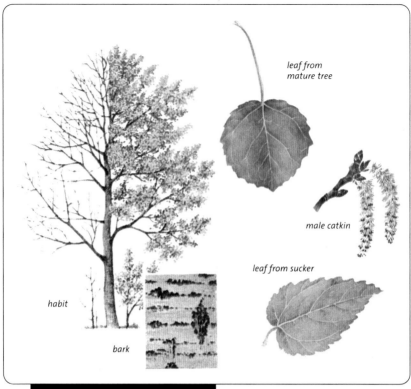

leaf from mature tree

male catkin

leaf from sucker

habit

bark

Populus tremula L. Aspen

A short-lived tree up to 20m high, the crown open, narrow or conical when young, becoming broader and irregular, the bole often leaning and suckering freely at the base at maturity. **Bark** Smooth with diamond-shaped depressions, greyish-green. **Buds** Ovoid, pointed, glabrous and slightly viscid; the leaf buds yellow and brown and appressed against the twig; the flower buds are broader, *c.* 1cm long, brown, shiny, and borne towards the tip of the twig. **Leaves** 3–8cm long (up to 15cm on young plants and suckers), suborbicular with a sinuate margin and short blunt teeth, thin, green or greyish-green above, paler below; the petiole is 4–6cm long, laterally flattened and rather pale. **Flowers** The catkins are about 4cm long, the flowers having numerous white hairs. The male flowers are thicker than the female, with 5–12 stamens; the female catkins are up to 12cm long in fruit. **Flowering period** March. **Distribution and taxonomic notes** A typical species of damp and muddy areas of hillsides, valleys, hedgerows and copses. In S. Europe it is restricted to montane areas. The flattened petiole allows easy movement of the leaf, giving rise to the name Trembling Aspen. Al Au Be Br Bu Co Cz De Fi Fr Fu Ge Gr Ho Hu Ic Ir It No Po Ru Sa Sd Sp Sw Tu Yu. Several exotic species are planted in Europe, eg. the hybrid *P. tremula* x *tremuloides* Mich., common in Scandinavia and Austria, *P. gileadensis* Rouleau, planted for timber and occasionally naturalized in N. Europe, and *P. simonii* Carrière, grown for timber and for ornament in C. Europe.

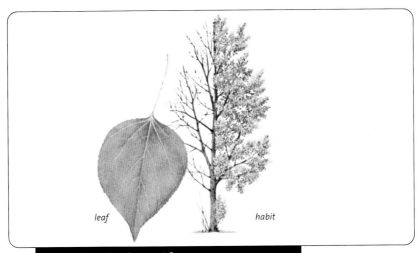

leaf   *habit*

Populus balsamifera L. Balsam Poplar

A tree up to 30m high though often much smaller, with a domed crown, the bole producing numerous suckers at the base. **Bark** Rather thin and shallowly fissured. **Branches** Erect or ascending, the young shoots terete, smooth and thickly covered with resin, giving a varnished appearance. **Buds** May be up to 2·5cm long, pointed, and also thickly covered in resin. **Leaves** 5–10cm long, those on vigorous suckers often much larger, more or less ovate, long-pointed, the margins with small blunt teeth, dark shiny green above, paler or whitish and somewhat downy beneath. The petiole is 1·5–5cm. **Flowers** Male catkins are 7·5cm long; female catkins are 10–12·5cm long. **Flowering period** May. **Distribution** A common species of wet woods, along rivers and shorelines in northern N. America. Cultivated in Europe for timber and sometimes for the fragrant balsam resin. Only male plants appear to be in cultivation.

leaf

habit

Populus trichocarpa Torrey & A. Gray ex Hooker
Western Balsam Poplar

A medium-sized fragrant resiniferous tree up to 35m high with a narrow conical crown. **Distribution** A fast-growing native of western N. America, sometimes planted in Europe. It is very similar to *P. balsamifera* and hybrids between the two are often planted in damp soils.

Populus candicans Aiton Balm of Gilead

An open-crowned, freely suckering tree with downy shoots and resin-covered buds.
Leaves Heart-shaped, fragrant when young, ciliate and downy below; the petiole downy.
Distribution It is commonly cultivated in Europe and frequently confused with the closely
related Balsam Poplar, *P. balsamifera*.

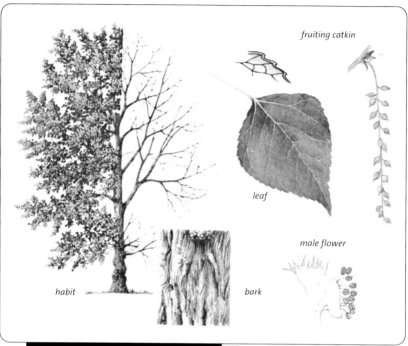

fruiting catkin

leaf

male flower

habit

bark

Populus nigra L. Black Poplar

A medium-sized tree up to 30m high with an uneven, broadly domed crown and a short
bole which usually bears large bosses and burrs but rarely suckers. **Buds** Ovoid and slightly
pointed; the lateral leaf buds appressed, pale brown; the flower buds larger, less appressed,
green. **Leaves** Those of the long shoots are 5–10cm long, ovate-rhombic, pointed, with
minute forward-pointing teeth, pale green below; those of the short shoots are smaller and
broader; the petiole is flattened. **Flowers** Male catkins are 5cm long, grey at first, becoming
crimson, each flower with 20–30 stamens; female catkins are greenish, 6–7cm long in
flower, 10–15cm long in fruit. **Flowering period** March. **Distribution and taxonomic notes** A
species of roadsides and fields. A native of S., C. and E. Europe, frequently planted elsewhere
and naturalized in places. Al Au Be Br Bu Co Cr Cz De Fu Ge Gr Ho Hu Ir It Po Pl Ru Sa Sd Si Sp
Tu Yu. *Populus nigra* cv. 'Italica', the Lombardy Poplar, has a narrow columnar habit and is
more common in cultivation than *P. nigra*.

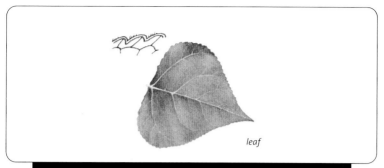

leaf

Populus x canadensis Moench Hybrid Black Poplar

This name covers a number of hybrids between *P. deltoides* and *P. nigra*. All are similar to *P. nigra* in general features but lack bosses on the bole, and have ciliate leaves.

Populus x berolinensis C. Koch Berlin Poplar

A columnar, densely branched tree with angular yellowish twigs and ovate or somewhat rhombic leaves. **Distribution** It is frequently planted for shelter in C. and S. Europe and believed to be a hybrid between *P. laurifolia* Ledeb. and *P. nigra* cv. 'Italica'.

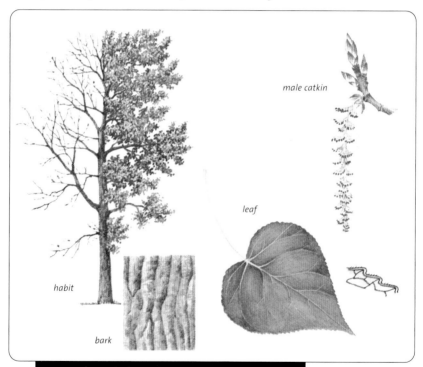

male catkin

leaf

habit

bark

Populus deltoides Marshall Cottonwood

A fast-growing tree up to 30m high with a broad crown. **Branches** Slightly ascending, the twigs markedly angled, greenish when young, becoming greyish or brownish. **Buds** Terminal bud viscid and glabrous. **Leaves** 10–18cm long, somewhat variable in shape but longer than wide, typically broadly triangular, truncate or heart-shaped at the base, densely covered with ciliate hairs, shortly pointed at the tip, with sharp-toothed margins, the teeth callus-tipped and with 2–5 glands at each base. **Flowers** Male flowers have 30–60 stamens. Female catkins are 15–20cm long in fruit. **Distribution** A species of low woods and moist prairies throughout E. N. America. In Europe it is planted as a timber tree and along roadsides, and has become naturalized in a number of areas. Au Be Br Bu Ge Gr Ho Hu It Pl Sp Yu.

Bog Myrtle Family
Myricaceae

flowering twig

fruit

Myrica faya Aiton

A small evergreen dioecious tree or shrub up to 8m high. **Branches** The twigs are covered with small reddish-brown, peltate hairs. **Leaves** Alternate, 4–11cm long, widest above the middle, entire, the margins rolled downwards, glabrous. **Flowers** Solitary in the axils of bracts, grouped in branched catkins on new wood; male flowers lack bracteoles; female flowers have 2 or more bracteoles. **Fruit** A somewhat fleshy drupe. **Flowering period** April–May. **Distribution** A species of the drier parts of broad-leaved evergreen forest in the Atlantic islands. A doubtful native but certainly naturalized in C. and S. Portugal. Pl.

Walnut Family
Juglandaceae

Carya Nutt. Hickory .

Deciduous monoecious trees. **Branches** The twigs have a continuous pith. The buds are sessile, enclosed in scales. **Leaves** Alternate, pinnate with a terminal leaflet. **Flowers** The male catkins are in groups of 3 or more, on 1-year-old wood; the female flowers are clustered at the tips of the new twigs. Flowers appear in May or June. **Fruit** A large drupe, dehiscing by 4 valves.

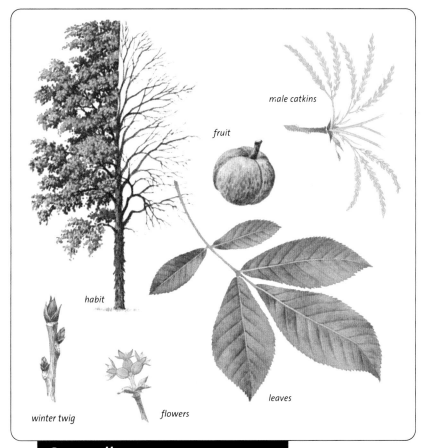

male catkins

fruit

habit

leaves

winter twig

flowers

Carya alba (L.) Nutt. Shagbark Hickory

Up to 40m high with a broad crown. **Bark** Grey, split into long scales. **Branches** Few and widely arched; the twigs are reddish-brown. **Buds** 10–12 overlapping scales, the outer dark, the inner yellowish or purplish. **Leaves** The leaflets are 10–20cm long in groups of 5 (rarely 3 or 7), the upper 3 largest, the terminal one with a stout petiole, all elliptic, oblong-lanceolate, acuminate, the margins sharply toothed except at the base, with tufts of white hairs between the teeth, hairy beneath, becoming glabrous later. **Flowers** The male catkins are 10–15cm long. **Fruit** 3·5–6cm long, more or less globose or broadly ovoid, not winged, the pericarp splitting to the base. **Seed** White and somewhat angled. **Distribution** A native of E. N. America, planted for timber in central Europe. Cz Ge Ru.

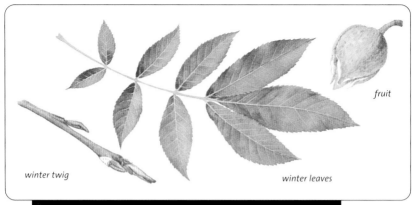

fruit

winter twig

winter leaves

Carya cordiformis (Wangenh.) C. Koch **Bitternut**

Up to 30m high with a conical crown. **Bark** Greyish and smooth, becoming wrinkled and scaly, showing orange where the scales have lifted. **Branches** Numerous, straight, ascending. **Buds** 4–6 scales, the scales touching one another but not overlapping, all bright yellow. **Leaves** The leaflets are 8–15cm long, 9 (rarely 5–8), the terminal one sessile, ovate-lanceolate to lanceolate, acuminate, the margins sharply toothed, hairy beneath when young. **Flowers** The male catkins are 5–7cm long. **Fruit** 2–3·5cm long, more or less globose or pear-shaped, 4-winged above the middle, the pericarp splitting to below the middle. **Seed** Grey, more or less smooth. **Distribution** A native of E. N. America, used as a timber tree in Germany. Ge.

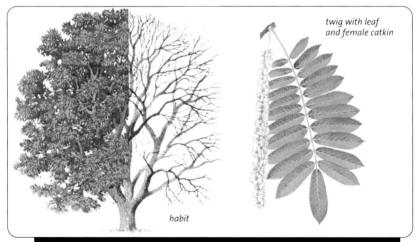

twig with leaf and female catkin

habit

Pterocarya fraxinifolia (Poiret) Spach. **Caucasian Wing-nut**

A tree up to 30m high, with a rounded crown and a short solitary bole or with many long, twisted boles, suckering freely around the base. **Bark** Deeply fissured, grey. **Branches** The pith of the twigs has transverse walls. **Buds** Without scales, stalked, dark brown. **Leaves** The leaflets are up to 18cm long, in 11–20 pairs, ovate-lanceolate, acuminate, the margins sharply toothed, the midrib with long brown or white stellate hairs below. **Flowers** Male catkins are solitary; female catkins are pendent with numerous flowers. **Fruit** A broad-winged nut. **Flowering period** April. **Distribution** A SW. Asian native, frequently planted on a small scale in Europe.

Juglans L. Walnuts

Deciduous monoecious trees, the pith having transverse walls. **Buds** Sessile, enclosed in scales. **Leaves** Alternate, pinnate with a terminal leaflet, aromatic. **Flowers** Male catkins are solitary, occurring on the previous year's wood; female flowers are few, in terminal racemes on the current year's wood. **Fruit** A large indehiscent drupe.

habit

*leafy twig
with fruits*

Juglans regia L. Common Walnut

A moderate tree up to 30m high with a wide spreading crown. **Bark** Smooth, becoming deeply fissured and grey at maturity. **Branches** The lower ones are large and sinuous, the smaller shoots crowded and twisted. **Buds** Dark purplish-brown. **Leaves** The leaflets are 6–15cm long, 7–9, elliptical or widest above the middle, thick, leathery, acute or acuminate, becoming glabrous, the margins almost entire. **Flowers** Male catkins are 5–15cm long, yellow; female flowers are in clusters of 2–5, with greenish hairs. **Fruit** 4–5cm long, more or less globose, smooth, dotted with glands, green, glabrous. **Seed** Ovoid, wrinkled and splitting easily. **Flowering period** May–June. **Distribution** A native of the Balkans, it has been planted and become naturalized in much of Europe. Al Au Br Bu Co Cr Fr Fu Gr Hu It Pl Sa Sd Si Sp Yu.

*leafy twig
with fruits*

Juglans nigra L. Black Walnut

Up to 50m high, the crown tall and domed. **Bark** Has a diamond pattern of deep fissures, black or dark brown. **Branches** The main ones are slightly sinuous. **Buds** Pale brown. **Leaves** The leaflets are 6–12cm long, 15–23, ovate, acuminate, the margins irregularly toothed, becoming glabrous above, hairy and glandular below. **Flowers** Male catkins are 5–15cm long, green at first, becoming yellow; female flowers 5, with greyish-green hairs. **Fruit** 3·5–5cm long, globose or slightly pear-shaped, smooth, green, hairy, not splitting. **Seed** Ovoid, ridged. **Flowering period** May–June. **Distribution** A N. American species widely planted as a timber tree in parts of C. E. Europe. Au Cz De Ge It Ru.

Juglans cinerea L. Butter-nut

Up to 30m high with a conical crown. **Bark** Grey, fissured. **Buds** Pink or white. **Leaves** The leaf-scars have a hairy band on the upper edge; the 11–19 leaflets are finely hairy above, hairy and glandular below. **Flowers** Male catkins are 5–8cm long. **Fruit** 4–6·5cm long, ovoid-oblong, hairy. **Seed** Ridged, not splitting. **Distribution** A N. American species sometimes planted for timber. De Ru.

Birch and Alder Family
Betulaceae

Betula L. Birches

Monoecious trees or shrubs. The flowers are in catkins; the pendent male flowers have a minute perianth and 2 stamens; the female flowers are in groups of 3 and lack a perianth. The fruiting catkins are cylindrical or narrowly ovoid.

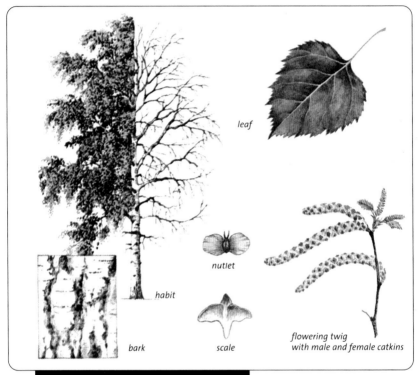

leaf

nutlet

habit

bark

scale

flowering twig with male and female catkins

Betula pendula Roth Silver Birch

A medium-sized tree up to 30m high with a narrow, pointed crown when young, becoming broader with age. **Bark** Fissured at the base, forming rectangular plates, smooth above and silvery-white, sometimes with scaly patches showing darker grey. **Branches** Erect on young trees, becoming pendulous with age; the young twigs are slender, pendulous, glabrous and brown, with numerous white resin glands. **Leaves** 2–7cm long, ovate-triangular, pointed at the apex, the margins with protruding primary teeth separated by several smaller secondary teeth, thin and more or less glabrous when mature; the petiole is glabrous. **Flowers** Male catkins are 3–6cm long, in groups of 2–4 at the tips of small twigs, brownish in winter, becoming yellowish and maturing with the young leaves; female catkins are borne in the axils of leaves, greenish at first, becoming brown. The fruiting catkins are 1·5–3·5cm long; the scales have 2 broad, curved lateral lobes and a somewhat triangular central lobe. **Fruit** The wing of the fruit is 2–3 times as wide as the nutlet. **Flowering period** April–May. **Distribution** A pioneer species, forming woods on light soils. It is short-lived, does not grow in shade and is eventually replaced by other, larger species. In S. Europe it is local and confined to mountains. It is sometimes grown in gardens as an ornamental and is often used as a street tree. All except Bl Cr Fi Gr Ic Sa Tu.

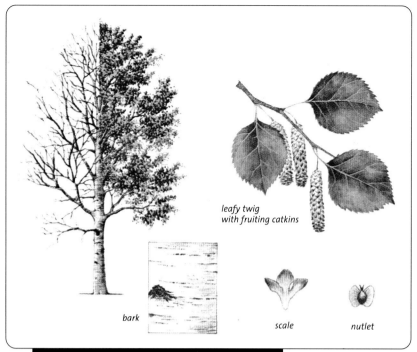

*leafy twig
with fruiting catkins*

bark   *scale*   *nutlet*

Betula pubescens Ehrh. Downy Birch

A small tree up to 25m high, or sometimes a shrub, with an irregular crown. **Bark** Brown or greyish, never fissured into rectangular plates at the base, being entirely smooth or with faint patterning. **Branches** Dense and twisted, spreading but not pendulous; the twigs lack resin glands but have a covering of soft white hairs. **Leaves** Similar to those of Silver Birch but usually more rounded, the teeth coarse and equal, with white hairs in the axils of the veins beneath; the petiole is hairy. **Flowers** The catkins are similar to Silver Birch but the scales have slightly broader lateral lobes and an oblong central lobe. **Fruit** The wing of the fruit is 1–1·5 times as wide as the nutlet. **Flowering period** April–May. **Distribution** A very variable species forming extensive woods and scrub on poor, especially peaty, soils in N. Europe and the mountains of S. Europe. Au Be Br Cz De Fi Fr Fu Ge Hu Ir It No Po Pl Ru Sd Sp Sw Yu.

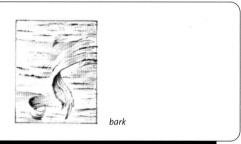

bark

Betula papyrifera Marshall Paper-bark Birch

A N. American species. **Bark** Peeling. **Leaves** Ovate, more or less glabrous leaves up to 10cm long, male catkins up to 10cm long and scales with suberect lateral lobes. **Distribution** It is sometimes planted in gardens and parks.

Alnus Miller Alders

Monoecious trees or shrubs. **Flowers** Similar to the birches but the males have 4
stamens, with anthers separated by a forked connective, and 2 female flowers in the axil of
each bract. The fruiting catkin is ovoid and cone-like with persistent, woody, 5-lobed scales.

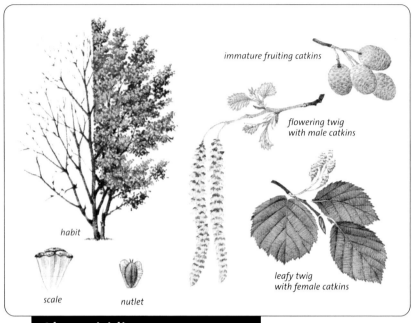

immature fruiting catkins

*flowering twig
with male catkins*

*leafy twig
with female catkins*

habit

scale

nutlet

Alnus viridis (Chaix) DC. **Green Alder**

A small tree up to 5m high, or sometimes a shrub. **Buds** 1·2–1·5cm long, pointed, sessile,
shiny and reddish. **Branches** The twigs are glabrous or minutely hairy, greenish or reddish.
Leaves 6cm long, elliptic to suborbicular, sharply double-toothed, hairy on the midrib and in
the axils of the veins beneath, sticky when young. **Flowers** The catkins appear with the
leaves; the male catkins are 5–12cm long, yellow; females are 1cm long, green when young,
becoming reddish, in slender, stalked clusters of 3–5. The fruiting catkins are up to 1·5cm
long, green at first, blackish when mature, persisting until the spring. **Fruit** The nutlet has a
broad, membranous wing. **Flowering period** April. **Distribution** A montane species with
variable leaves and indumentum. Au Bu Co Cz Fr Fu Ge Hu It Po Ru Sd Yu.

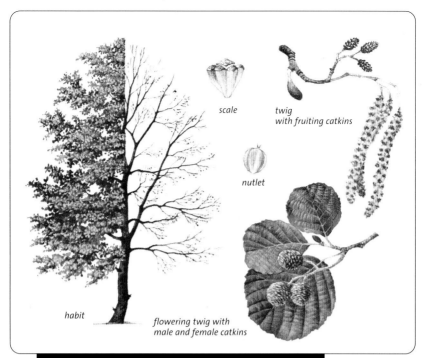

scale

twig
with fruiting catkins

nutlet

habit

flowering twig with
male and female catkins

Alnus glutinosa (L.) Gaertner **Common Alder**

A small tree up to 20m high or sometimes a shrub, with a broad conical crown. **Bark** Fissured into square or oblong, grey or brown plates. **Branches** Ascending, spreading later; the twigs are glabrous, sticky when young, with raised orange lenticels. **Buds** 7mm long, narrow, with a stalk about 3mm long. **Leaves** 4–10cm long, widest above the middle, or more or less orbicular, sometimes notched at the apex, doubly toothed or wavy at the margins, with 5–8 pairs of veins and long yellowish hairs in the axils of the veins beneath. **Flowers** The catkins appear before the leaves; male catkins are 2–3cm long, in clusters of 2–3, purplish in winter; female catkins are 0·8–1·5cm long, pedunculate, purplish-red when young, becoming green, in inflorescences of 3–8. The fruiting catkins are 1–3cm long, dark brown, persisting until the following spring. **Fruit** The nutlet has a narrow wing. **Flowering period** February–March. **Distribution and taxonomic notes** Common Alder is frequently found growing by water throughout Europe. All except Bl Cr Fi Ic. Three other related species occur in Europe: *A. incana* (L.) Moench, the Grey Alder is similar to *A. glutinosa* but has sessile female catkins and is native to mountain regions of Europe; *A. cordata* (Loisel.) Loisel., Italian Alder, is distinguished by having female catkins in clusters of 1–3, grey pubescent twigs and pale grey bark, is native to Corsica and S. Italy and sometimes planted in parks and by roadsides. *A. rugosa* (Duroi) Sprengel, Smooth Alder, has leaves with red hairs in the axils of the veins, and is a N. American species frequently planted in C. Europe.

Hornbeam and Hazel Family
Corylaceae

Carpinus Hornbeams

Deciduous monoecious trees or shrubs. **Buds** Tapered at each end, acute at the tip. **Leaves** Alternate, simple, with 9 or more pairs of veins. **Flowers** The male catkins have solitary flowers in the axil of each bract, but lack bracteoles and a perianth. The female flowers are in pairs in the axil of each bract with obvious bracteoles and perianth. **Fruit** A nut, borne in the axil of a lobed or toothed involucre, occurring in groups of drooping spikes.

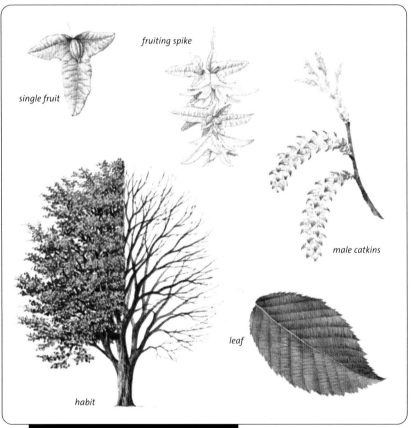

fruiting spike

single fruit

male catkins

leaf

habit

Carpinus betulus L. Hornbeam

A distinctive tree up to 30m high, the bole often twisted and gnarled. **Bark** Silvery-grey, often with darker bands and deep fissures. **Branches** Ascending, sinuous; the twigs sparsely hairy, greyish-brown. **Leaves** 4–10cm long, ovate to oblong-ovate, shortly pointed, rounded at the base, sharply double-toothed, with about 15 pairs of veins, and hairy on the veins below; the petiole is about 1cm long. **Flowers** The male catkins are up to 5cm long, greenish-yellow with reddish outer scales. **Fruit** The fruiting spike is 5–14cm long with about 8 pairs of nuts; the involucre is 3-lobed. **Flowering period** April–May. **Distribution and taxonomic notes** It is common as a hedgerow tree and in deciduous woods, sometimes forming pure stands. It is sometimes pollarded and the cv. 'Fastigiata' is frequently planted as a boulevard and park tree. Native to much of Europe. Al Au Be Br Bu Cz De Fr Fu Ge Gr Ho Hu It Po Ru Sd Sw Tu Yu.

single fruit

Carpinus orientalis Miller Eastern Hornbeam

A small tree or shrub up to 11m high. **Bark** Purplish with pale brown marks. **Leaves** 2–6cm long, ovate or elliptical, shortly pointed, tapering or rounded at the base, the margins doubly toothed, with 11–15 pairs of veins, and sparsely hairy on the veins below. **Fruit** The fruiting spike is 3–5cm long; the involucre is toothed but not lobed. **Distribution** A native of SE. Europe, reaching Italy and Sicily. Al Bu Fu Gr Hu It Ru Si Tu Yu.

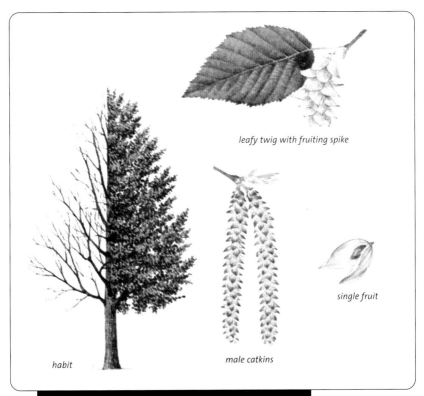

leafy twig with fruiting spike

single fruit

habit

male catkins

Ostrya carpinifolia Scop. Hop Hornbeam

A deciduous monoecious tree with a conical crown, and sometimes several spreading boles. **Bark** Brown, smooth at first, later fissured and sometimes peeling. **Branches** The twigs are hairy, brown with raised orange lenticels. **Buds** Tapered at each end, acute at the tip. **Leaves** 5–8cm long, alternate, simple, ovate with a pointed tip, sharply double-toothed, with 12–15 pairs of veins, hairy when young, becoming glabrous. **Flowers** The male catkins are up to 10cm long, pendulous, with solitary flowers in the axil of each bract; bracteoles and perianth absent; the female flowers are in pairs in the axils of each bract. **Fruit** The fruiting head is 3–5cm long, compact and semicylindrical; the involucre is 1·5–2cm long, elliptical, with a short, hairy point, bladder-like, white or greenish with long hairs, enclosing a single nut. **Flowering period** April. **Distribution** A native of S. and SE. Europe. Al Au Bu Co Fr Gr Hu It Sa Sd Si Yu.

Corylus L. Hazels

Deciduous monoecious trees or shrubs. **Buds** Ovoid, obtuse. **Leaves** Alternate, simple, with less than 8 pairs of veins. **Flowers** The male catkins have solitary flowers in the axils of the bracts; bracteoles 2, perianth absent. The female flowers are in short bud-like inflorescences; the prominent stigmas are red. **Fruit** A large nut, solitary or in clusters of 2–4, surrounded by a tubular involucre which is toothed or irregularly divided above.

habit

twig with male and female flowers

cluster of nuts

leaf

Corylus avellana L. Common Hazel

A small tree or shrub up to 12m high with a broad and bushy crown and a rather short bole. **Bark** Brown, smooth, shiny, peeling in strips. **Branches** The twigs are covered with stiff glandular hairs. **Buds** Ovoid and smooth. **Leaves** Up to 10cm long, more or less orbicular, heart-shaped at the base, sharply double-toothed, sometimes lobed, stiffly hairy, the hairs white on the veins beneath; the petiole is densely glandular-hairy. **Flowers** The male catkins are up to 8cm long, pendulous, pale yellow when open. **Fruit** The fruiting head has 1–4 nuts; the involucre is about as long as the nut, divided to about half its length into irregular teeth or lobes. The nut is 1·5–2cm long, brown when ripe with a woody shell. **Flowering period** January–April. **Distribution** Common as coppice in hedgerows and as undershrub in woods throughout Europe, and frequently planted in gardens. All except Bl Cr Ic.

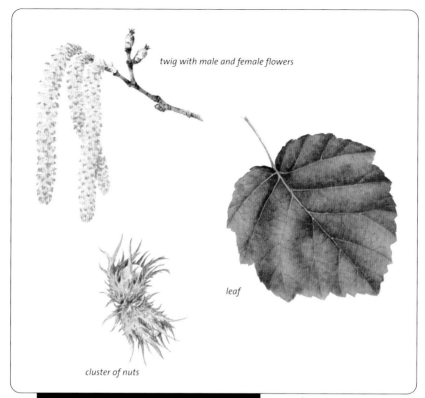

twig with male and female flowers

leaf

cluster of nuts

Corylus colurna L. Turkish Hazel

A small tree up to 22m high with a conical crown and a stout bole. **Bark** Rough. **Branches** Horizontal and often twisted; the twigs are covered in glandular hairs. **Leaves** Up to 12·5cm long, ovate or widest above the middle, heart-shaped at the base, abruptly pointed at the tip, double-toothed and sometimes almost lobed. **Flowers** The male catkins are up to 12cm long, pendulous. The involucre is much longer than the nut and deeply divided into toothed lobes which are often recurved. **Fruit** The nut is slightly larger than that of Corylus avellana. **Flowering period** February. **Distribution** A native of SE. Europe and Asia Minor but introduced in other parts of Europe. Al Bu Gr Ru Tu Yu.

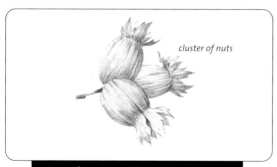

cluster of nuts

Corylus maxima Miller. Filbert

A small tree or shrub up to 6m high. It is very similar to C. avellana except for the nuts. They are solitary or in clusters of 2–3, and completely enclosed by a tubular involucre, constricted above the nut and toothed or lobed at the apex. **Distribution** A native of the Balkan Peninsula, it is often planted for its nuts in other countries and has become naturalized in parts. A purple-leaved form, var. atropurpureus, is frequently grown as a garden ornamental. Gr It Tu Yu.

Beech Family
Fagaceae

A large family of deciduous and evergreen trees, or sometimes shrubs

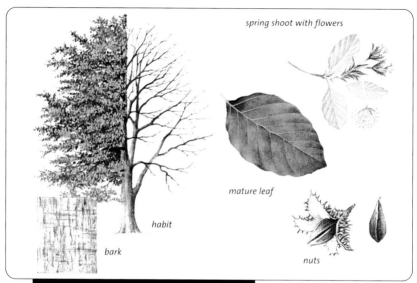

spring shoot with flowers

mature leaf

habit

bark

nuts

Fagus sylvatica L. Common Beech

A large broadly domed deciduous tree up to 40m. **Bark** Smooth and grey, or sometimes slightly rough. **Branches** Main ones numerous, usually ascending but sometimes arching; twigs dull purplish-brown, smooth. **Buds** c. 2cm long, slender, with a long tapering point, reddish-brown, smooth. **Leaves** 4–10cm long, ovate to elliptical, pointed, the margin wavy and fringed with hairs when young, sometimes with short teeth, dark green, covered with silky hairs when young, becoming more or less smooth, with 5–8 pairs of almost parallel veins; petiole 1–1·5cm. **Flowers** Unisexual; the male flowers are numerous, carried in terminal clusters, long-stalked, with a perianth divided almost to the base. The female flowers are surrounded by a 4-lobed involucre, and usually occur in pairs on a short stalk. **Fruit** The nuts are 1·2–1·8cm long, 3-angled, brown, usually occurring in pairs in the cupule. **Flowering period** May. **Fruiting** September–October. **Distribution** In woods on well-drained soils, especially on chalk. Widespread in W. and C. Europe, cultivated for timber, shelter and ornament. Al Au Be Br Bu Co Cz De Fr Fu Ge Gr Ho Hu It No Po Ru Sd Si Sp Sw Yu.

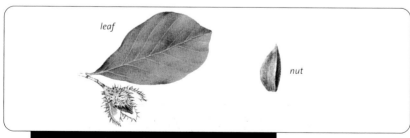

leaf

nut

Fagus orientalis Lipsky Oriental Beech

Similar to F. sylvatica but the bark may be furrowed. **Leaves** 9–14cm long, with 7–12 pairs of veins. **Flowers** Male flowers have perianth divided up to one-third of its length, and a cupule with narrowly oblong scales above and paddle-shaped scales below. **Distribution** Usually in more sheltered localities than F. sylvatica. SE. Europe and Asia Minor. Bu Fu Gr Ru Tu.

spring shoot with flowers

nuts

habit

Nothofagus procera (Poeppig & Endl.) Örsted **Rauli**

A large, broadly conical tree up to 30m. **Bark** Greenish-grey with wide, vertical, dark cracks. **Branches** Main ones level below, ascending above, twigs stout, green, becoming dark brown. **Buds** c. 1cm, narrowly conical, reddish-brown. **Leaves** 4–8cm, ovate to oblong-ovate, acute or somewhat blunt, the margin wavy, finely toothed, the underside with silky hairs on the veins; there are 14–20 pairs of lateral veins; petiole is 0·5–1cm. **Flowers** Male flowers are solitary in leaf axils towards the tip of the shoot. **Fruit** The nuts are c. 1cm long, usually occurring in threes, in a 4-lobed, deeply fringed cupule. **Flowering period** May. **Fruiting** September. **Distribution** A native of Chile and Argentina, now planted in small forestry plantations in Britain and for ornament.

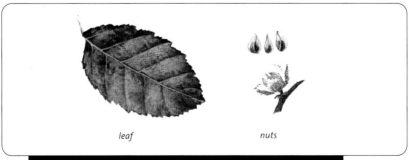

leaf

nuts

Nothofagus obliqua (Mirbel) Blume **Roble Beech**

Like N. procera but the bark becoming cracked into small square flakes. **Branches** Twigs slender, branching in a regular alternating pattern. **Buds** c. 5mm, light brown. **Leaves** Irregularly toothed margin, with 7–11 pairs of veins. **Fruit** Nuts c. 5mm long, enclosed in a cupule with short projecting scales. **Distribution** A native of Chile and W. Argentina. Planted in Britain for timber and ornament.

Castanea Miller Chestnuts

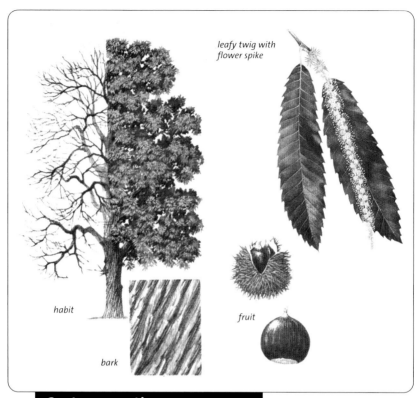

leafy twig with flower spike

habit

bark

fruit

Castanea sativa Miller
Sweet Chestnut or Spanish Chestnut

A domed deciduous tree up to 30m high. **Bark** Smooth and silvery-grey, becoming dark brownish-grey with longitudinal, often spirally twisted fissures. **Branches** Lower ones massive and spreading, upper ones twisting. **Buds** Ovoid, obtuse, red-brown. **Leaves** 10–25cm, oblong-lanceolate, acute, the base slightly heart-shaped, dark green above and paler beneath, more or less smooth and glossy, the margins with large spine-tipped teeth; the lateral veins are parallel, irregularly alternate, about 20 on either side of the main vein; the petiole is c. 2·5cm long, yellowish or red. **Flowers** In erect bunches of insect-pollinated catkins; male flowers are a mass of whitish-yellow stamens; female flowers have 7–9 slender white styles, usually in threes in a rosette of bright green spines carried at the base of the bisexual catkins. **Fruit** Produced in bunches of 2–3, the green outer cupule with branched radiating spines, splitting into 4 irregular lobes to release usually 3 large shiny red-brown nuts. **Flowering period** June–July. **Fruiting** October–November. **Distribution** Well-drained, usually acidic soils in woods, often on mountain slopes. It is cultivated in S. Europe from Italy eastwards, N. Africa and W. Asia. Naturalized in W., C. and N. Europe. Al Au Be Br Bu Co Cr Cz De Fr Fu Ge Gr Ho Hu Ir It Pl Ru Sa Sd Si Sp Sw Tu Yu.

Quercus L. Oaks

Large deciduous trees or sometimes shrubs. **Leaves** Usually toothed or lobed, though sometimes entire. **Flowers** Of 2 sexes, in wind-pollinated catkins; male flowers with 6–12 stamens in slender, pendent, many-flowered catkins; female flowers with 3–6 styles, in separate few-flowered catkins, each flower in a small cup-like involucre. **Fruit** A single-seeded, oblong or ellipsoidal nut (acorn) carried in the enlarged, cup-like involucre or cupule. **Taxonomic notes** Hybrids are common in areas where related species grow together (eg. Q. x hispanica Lam. = Q. cerris x Q. suber), tending to make identification difficult.

leaf

habit

bark

acorn

Quercus rubra L. Red Oak

A large, broadly-domed deciduous tree up to 35m high. **Bark** Smooth and silvery-grey, the old trees sometimes having shallow fissures. **Branches** Main ones straight and radiating; the twigs are stout, reddish-brown. **Leaves** 12–22 x 10–15cm, ovate to obovate with several lobes on either side, dividing the leaf about halfway to the midrib, each with 1-3 large whisker-tipped teeth, matt green above, matt greyish and smooth below except for slight downiness in the axils of veins; the petiole is 2–5cm long, yellowish with a swollen reddish base. **Fruit** The acorn ripens in the 2nd year, the shallow cup 1·8–2·5cm wide with thin oval scales closely pressed together, finely downy, carried on a 1cm stout stalk. **Flowering period** May. **Fruiting** October of the following year. **Distribution** An E. N. American species, commonly planted for ornament, timber and shelter, especially in C. Europe. Au Be Br Cz De Fr Fu Ge Gr Hu It Pl Po Ru Sd Sp Sw.

acorn

leaf

Quercus palustris Muenchh. **Common Sallow**

Similar to Q. rubra but with more slender, often pendulous twigs. **Buds** c. 3mm, pale brown.
Leaves Deeper cuts, more ragged lobes, the underside with conspicuous tufts of brown
hairs in the axils of the veins. **Fruit** The acorn cup is 1–1·5cm wide. **Distribution** Another
species from E. N. America, but planted less commonly than Q. rubra for ornament and
timber, especially in E. C. Europe. Au Br De Ge Hu Ru.

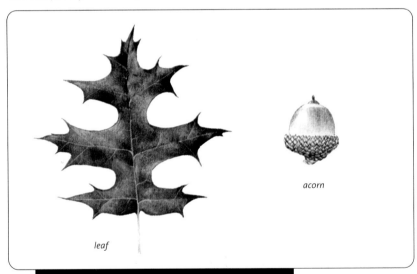

acorn

leaf

Quercus coccinea Muenchh. **Scarlet Oak**

Similar to Q. rubra but with leaves 7·5–15 x 5–12cm, more deeply cut, the middle lobe longest,
shiny on both sides; fewer hair tufts. **Fruit** The acorn cup is 1–2cm wide. **Distribution** A
species of E. and C. North America. Planted less commonly than Q. rubra for ornament. Br.

habit *leaf* *acorn*

Quercus coccifera L.

An evergreen shrub or rarely a small tree up to 5m tall. **Bark** Dull grey, finely scaled in old trees. **Branches** Main branches are numerous, ascending and repeatedly divided; twigs are yellowish-brown, covered with stellate hairs, soon becoming smooth and grey. **Leaves** 1·5–4cm, ovate to oblong with a heart-shaped or rounded base, the margin wavy with spiny teeth, the blade with a rigid texture, the veins slightly raised on the dark green upper surface. **Fruit** The acorns ripen in the 2nd year, the cup c. 1·8cm wide, the scales rigid, almost spiny. **Flowering period** April–May. **Fruiting** October–November of the following year. **Distribution** A native of the Mediterranean region, except for much of Italy. The host plant for coccid insects from which important red dyes were extracted in antiquity. Al Bl Bu Co Cr Fr Gr It Po Sa Si Sp Tu Yu.

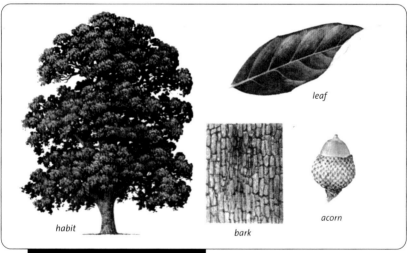

leaf *habit* *bark* *acorn*

Quercus ilex L. Holm Oak

A broadly domed evergreen tree up to 25m high. **Bark** Brownish-black, cracked into shallow square plates. **Branches** Main ones ascending, almost straight, often emerging from near the bottom of the trunk; twigs are slender, grey-brown and tomentose. **Buds** 1–2mm long, light brown, grey-tomentose. **Leaves** 4–10 x 3–8cm, oblong-ovate to lanceolate with a pointed tip, rounder or shortly tapering at the base, the margin wavy, entire or with spiny teeth on young trees, the blade with a thick but not rigid texture, dark green, becoming smooth above, grey-tomentose with raised veins below, 7–11 pairs of veins from a straight midrib; the petiole is 0·6–2cm long and densely hairy; the stipules are very narrow, hairy. **Fruit** The acorns ripen in the first year, the cup c. 1·2cm wide, enclosing the bottom third to half of the nut, the scales flat and pressed together, felted. **Flowering period** Late June. **Fruiting** October. **Distribution** A native of the Mediterranean region, widely planted for ornament; rarely naturalized in W. and S. Europe. Al Bl Br Co Cr Fr Fu Gr It Po Sa Sd Si Sp Tu Yu.

leaf

habit

bark

acorn

Quercus suber L. Cork Oak

An evergreen tree up to 20m. **Bark** Thick and corky, forming sinuous interconnecting ridges; pale greyish-brown when present but revealing a smooth and red-brown bole when stripped. **Branches** Main ones low, massive and twisting; the twigs are grey-green, tomentose. **Buds** c. 2mm long, ovoid, dark purple. **Leaves** 3–7 x 2–3cm, ovate-oblong, pointed, the margin wavy, with spine-tipped teeth, dark green and smooth above, grey-pubescent beneath; 5–8 pairs of lateral veins emerge from a somewhat sinuous midrib; the petiole is 0.8–1.5cm long, densely pubescent. **Fruit** The acorns ripen in the 2nd year on spring-flowering trees and on some autumn-flowering trees in the following season; the cup is 1.2–1.8cm wide, enclosing about half of the nut, the scales long and projecting at right-angles, the lower ones shorter and pressed together. **Flowering period** May–June. **Fruiting** October. **Distribution** A common species of the W. Mediterranean region, widely planted elsewhere for its bark (the cork of commerce) or for ornament. Co Fr It Pl Sa Si Sp Yu.

habit

leaf

acorn

Quercus cerris L. Turkey Oak

A broadly domed deciduous tree up to 35m. **Bark** Greyish and deeply fissured, eventually cracking to form square convex plates. **Branches** Main ones long and ascending, swollen at the base; twigs rough, brownish or green-grey, shortly pubescent. **Buds** Ovoid, pale brown, hairy, surrounded by long thin twisted stipules. **Leaves** 9–12 x 3–5cm, oblong or wider above the middle, rounded or slightly tapering at the base, the margin with 4–10 pairs of lobes or teeth, blunt or rarely with a small point, slightly rough with stiff hairs above, pubescent or almost smooth below; petiole 0.8–1.5cm long. **Fruit** Acorns ripen in the 2nd year, half to two-thirds enclosed in a cup 1.5–2.2cm wide, the scales long, pointed, curving outwards, downy. **Flowering period** May–June. **Fruiting** October. **Distribution** C. S. and SE. Europe, planted elsewhere for ornament. Al Au Be Br Bu Cr Cz Fr Ge Gr Hu It Ru Sd Si Tu Yu.

acorn

leaf

Quercus macrolepis Kotschy

Like Q. cerris, but semi-evergreen and rarely more than 15m tall. The leaves are 6–10cm long, the margin with 3–7 pairs of triangular, bristle-tipped lobes; the petiole 1·5–4cm long. The acorn cup is up to 5cm wide, the scales wide, thick, flat, usually projecting at right-angles. At one time an important cultivated crop for the high tannin content of the acorn cups. **Distribution** SE. Italy, the Aegean and the Balkan Peninsula. Al Cr Gr It Tu Yu.

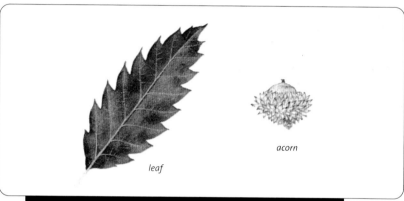

acorn

leaf

Quercus trojana Webb in Loudon **Macedonian Oak**

Like Q. cerris but semi-evergreen, up to 15m tall. The leaves are 3–7cm long, the margin with 8–14 pairs of slightly spiny teeth, smooth and shiny on both sides; the petiole 2–5mm long. The acorn cup is 1·5–2·2cm wide, enclosing about two-thirds of the acorn, the lowest scales pressed together, the upper spreading or incurved. **Distribution** SE. Italy and the Balkan Peninsula. Al Bu Gr It Tu Yu.

acorn

habit

leaf

Quercus petraea (Mattuschka) Liebl.
Sessile Oak or Durmast Oak

A domed deciduous tree up to 40m high. **Bark** Finely fissured, mostly forming vertical ridges, grey. **Branches** Main ones radiate from a straight bole; the young twigs dark, purplish-grey, glabrous, becoming greyish-bloomed. **Buds** 4–8mm long, ovoid, the apex slightly pointed, orange-brown, with long white hairs. **Leaves** 7–12 x 4–5cm, obovate, acute, the base cuneate or slightly heart-shaped, the margin with 5–9 pairs of rounded regular lobes, dark green above, paler beneath with very fine appressed hairs and tufts of brownish hairs in the axils of the veins; the lateral veins often with several smaller veins leading to the sinuses; petiole 1·8–2·5cm. **Fruit** The acorns ripen in the first year, the cup 1·2–1·8cm wide; the scales are ovate-lanceolate, thin, not tuberculate, downy, up to 6 nuts grouped together, sessile or on a peduncle up to 1cm long. **Flowering period** May. **Fruiting** October. **Distribution** A widespread and often dominant tree in woods, especially on lighter, more sandy soils. It is found throughout Europe except for the extreme N. and NE. and parts of the Mediterranean region. Al Au Be Br Bu Co Cz De Fr Fu Ge Ho Hu Ir It No Po Ru Sd Si Sp Sw Tu Yu.

leaf

acorn

Quercus dalechampii Ten.

Like Q. petraea but the leaves have 4–7 pairs of narrow, subacute, irregular lobes with a petiole 1·5–2cm long. The acorn cup has diamond-shaped blunt scales, is strongly tuberculate and very shortly downy or almost smooth, greyish. **Distribution** SE. Europe. Au Bu Gr Hu It Ru Si Yu

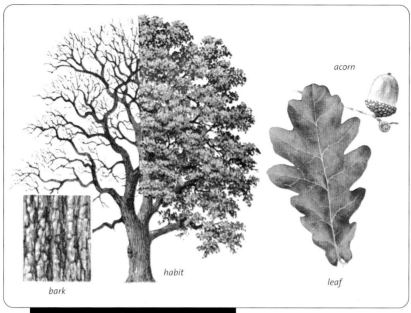

acorn

habit

bark

leaf

Quercus robur L. English Oak

A large irregularly domed deciduous tree up to 45m. **Bark** Fissured, forming narrow, vertical, pale grey plates. **Branches** The few main ones are massive, twisting, usually carried low on the trunk; young twigs brownish-green, pubescent, becoming greyish-bloomed and glabrous. **Buds** 3–6mm long, ovoid-conical, blunt or slightly pointed, light brown, smooth. **Leaves** 10–12 x 7–8cm, obovate, blunt, the base usually with a pair of auricles, the margin with 5–7 pairs of wavy-edged lobes, dark green above, paler beneath and sometimes pubescent when young; the lateral veins make various angles with the midrib, some leading to the sinuses; petiole 0·4–1cm long. **Fruit** The acorns ripen in the first year, the cup 1·1–1·8cm (or up to 2·3cm) wide; the scales flat, slightly downy, joined together except at the tips; up to 3 nuts are carried on a peduncle 4–8cm long. **Flowering period** May–June. **Fruiting** October. **Distribution** A widespread and often dominant species especially on heavy basic soils. Distributed throughout Europe except for the extreme N. and parts of the Mediterranean region. Al Au Be Br Bu Cz De Fi Fr Fu Ge Ho Hu Ir It No Pl Po Ru Sa Sd Si Sp Sw Yu.

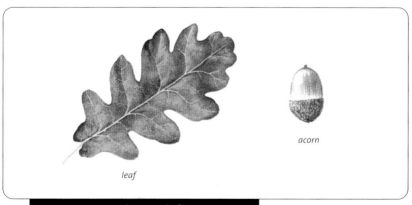

leaf

acorn

Quercus pedunculiflora C. Koch

Like Q. robur but with leaves somewhat glaucous above, the lateral veins making an acute angle with the midrib then curving out to the margin, the underside with a persistent yellow-grey tomentum. Acorn cup up to 2cm wide, the scales warty, more closely joined together, with yellowish down. **Distribution** SE. Europe. Bu Fu Gr Ru Tu.

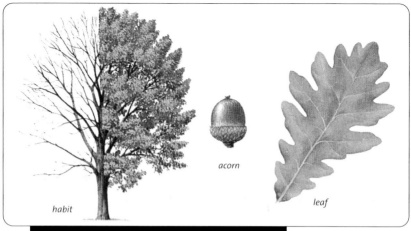

habit　　*acorn*　　*leaf*

Quercus frainetto Ten. Hungarian Oak

A domed deciduous tree up to 30m. **Bark** Closely and deeply fissured, forming short small ridges, pale grey or brownish. **Branches** Main ones long and straight, radiating from a stout bole; twigs grey-green or brownish, softly downy. **Buds** *c.* 1cm long, ovoid, grey-brown, surrounded by persistent stipules. **Leaves** Clustered towards the end of the branches, 10–25 x 8–14cm, obovate, the base tapered often with a pair of auricles, the margin deeply pinnatifid with 7–10 pairs of broad, oblong, often wavy-edged lobes, dark green above, the underside paler with grey or brownish down; the main lateral veins are parallel with a few smaller veins leading to the sinuses; petiole 2–6mm. **Fruit** The acorns ripen in the first year, the cups 0·6–1·2 x 1·2–1·5cm, the scales oblong, blunt, downy, loosely overlapping. **Flowering period** May. **Fruiting** October. **Distribution** The Balkan Peninsula, Hungary, Rumania and S. Italy. Al Bu Gr Hu It Ru Tu Yu.

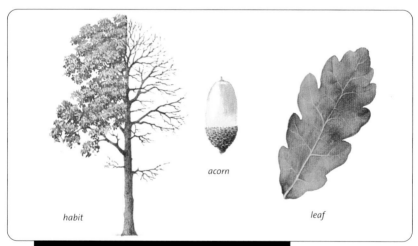

habit　　*acorn*　　*leaf*

Quercus pubescens Willd. Downy Oak

A deciduous tree up to 25m, or sometimes a shrub. **Bark** Finely and deeply fissured, forming small rough plates, dark grey. **Branches** Main ones swollen where they join the bole; twigs brown, densely grey-pubescent. **Buds** 4–7mm long, orange-brown, grey-pubescent. **Leaves** 4–13 x *c.* 6cm, obovate, broadly cuneate at the base, the margin sinuate to pinnatifid with 4–8 pairs of broad, rounded, forward-directed lobes, becoming grey-green and glabrous above, densely tomentose beneath when young, becoming almost smooth; petiole 0·5–1·2cm, densely pubescent. **Fruit** The acorns ripen in the 1st year, the cup up to 1·5 x 1·4cm, the scales lanceolate, acute or obtuse, pubescent, pressed closely together. **Flowering period** End of May. **Fruiting** October. **Distribution** S., C. and W. Europe and W. Asia. Al Au Be Bu Co Cz Fr Fu Ge Gr Hu It Po Ru Sa Sd Si Sp Tu Yu.

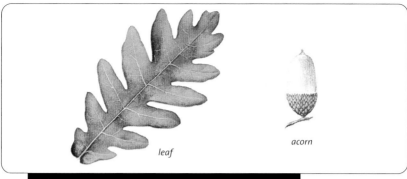

leaf

acorn

Quercus pyrenaica Willd. Pyrenean Oak

Like *Q. pubescens* but often suckering and with pendent twigs; leaves up to 20cm long with narrow, rather pointed lobes, completely downy at first, becoming more or less smooth above with dense white down below; petiole up to 2·2cm. Acorn cup with blunt, loosely overlapping scales. **Distribution** SW. Europe and N. Italy. Fr It Po Sp.

leaf

acorn

Quercus virgiliana (Ten.) Ten.

Like *Q. pubescens* but leaves up to 16cm, the lobes often wavy-edged; petiole 1·5–2·5cm; acorn cup with the scales loosely pressed together, the tips erect. **Distribution** S. Europe. Bu Co Cr Hu It Ru Sa Si Tu Yu.

leaf

acorn

Quercus canariensis Willd. Mirbeck's Oak or Algerian Oak

Like *Q. pubescens* but semi-evergreen, young shoots densely woolly, becoming almost smooth. **Leaves** Up to 18cm, the margin with 9–14 pairs of almost acute teeth, woolly when young, becoming almost smooth, glaucous beneath; petiole 0·8–3cm. **Fruit** Acorn cup with the lower scales tuberculate, the upper ones pressed closely together. **Distribution** Hybridizes extensively with *Q. pubescens* in Spain. SW. Europe, N. Africa. Pl Sp.

Elm Family
Ulmaceae

Ulmus L. Elms

Large deciduous trees, often forming suckers. The bark is fissured and cracked. The leaves are simple, alternate, with an asymmetrical base, a double-toothed margin and paired lateral veins. The flowers are hermaphrodite, appearing in clusters before the leaves on the previous year's twigs. The fruit is dry and flattened, forming a broad papery wing encircling the seed.

leafy twig

habit

fruit

flowering twig

Ulmus glabra Hudson Wych Elm

A broad, multiple-domed tree up to 40m, very rarely producing suckers. **Bark** Smooth and grey when young, becoming cracked and ridged, turning grey-brown. **Branches** The few main ones spread outwards and often become almost level; young twigs are stout, dark red-brown, with short stiff hairs, becoming smooth and grey. **Buds** Winter buds are ovoid, blunt, reddish-brown with reddish hairs. **Leaves** 10–18cm, almost round or obovate to elliptical; the tip tapers into a long point; the base is very unequal with the long side overlapping the petiole; the veins are in 10–18 pairs; the upper side of the leaf has short stiff hairs while the underside has fewer, soft hairs; the petiole is 2–5mm, thick and hairy. **Flowers** The dense flower clusters have purplish-red anthers. **Fruit** 1·5–2cm, obovate, borne on a very short pedicel. **Flowering period** Late February–March. **Fruiting** May–July. **Distribution** Woods and hedges, especially by water. Al Au Be Br Bu Cz De Fi Fr Fu Ge Gr Ho Hu Ir It No Po Ru Sd Sp Sw Yu.

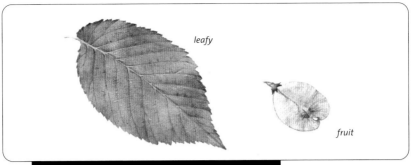

leafy

fruit

Ulmus x *hollandica* Miller Dutch Elm

A hybrid between *U. glabra* and species of the *U. minor* group. Cv. 'Hollandica' and cv. 'Vegeta' are the common clones in Britain, but many others are planted elsewhere in Europe. Dutch Elms usually have large broad leaves; up to 15 x 8cm, like *U. glabra*, but with more or less shiny upper surfaces, a very unequal base and a petiole 1–2cm long. 'Hollandica' has numerous suckers with corky flanges up to 2cm wide on the stems. The hybrids are commonly planted. Au Be Br Fr Ge Ho Ir Sd.

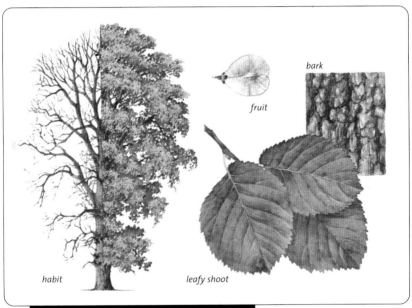

bark

fruit

habit

leafy shoot

Ulmus procera Salisb. English Elm

A domed tree up to *c.* 35m commonly producing numerous suckers. **Bark** Dark brown and deeply fissured, forming square plates. **Branches** The few main ones are large and ascending; the twigs are rather stout, reddish-brown, and remain densely hairy. **Buds** Winter buds are 2–3mm, ovoid, pointed dark brown and slightly hairy. **Leaves** Up to 10cm, oval to rounded with a short tapering tip, the base unequal but not overlapping the petiole, the veins in 10–12 pairs; the upper side of the leaf is rough while the lower side has white down on both sides of the main vein; the petiole is 1–5mm long, finely downy. **Flowers** The flowers have dark red anthers. **Fruit** 1–1·7cm, rounded, borne on a very short pedicel, often sterile. **Flowering period** Late February–March. **Fruit** When present fruits are shed from May–July. **Distribution** Hedgerows. Br Bu Fr Gr Hu Ru Sp Yu (planted in Ir).

Ulmus minor Miller

An open, narrowly crowned tree up to 30m, commonly producing suckers. **Bark** Greyish-brown with long deep furrows and ridges. **Branches** The main ones are narrowly ascending to almost upright; young twigs are slender, commonly pendulous, pale brown and becoming smooth. **Buds** Winter buds are ovoid, shiny dark red and somewhat downy. **Leaves** 6–8cm (up to 12cm), obovate or ovate to oblanceolate, tapering to a slender point; the veins are in 7–12 pairs; the upper side of the leaf is shiny and dark green, the underside has downy tufts in the axils of the veins; petiole c. 5mm, downy. **Flowers** Red with white stigmas. **Fruit** 0·7–1·8cm, elliptical, with the seed above the centre, close to the notch in the wing. **Flowering period** March. **Fruiting** July. **Distribution and taxonomic notes** The name *U. minor* has been applied to include the 4 species described below. The species are not easily distinguished and hybrids have been reported between each of them, and with *U. glabra*. By roads and in hedges, commonly in deep, moist soils. Widely planted as an amenity tree around towns and along roads. Native to much of Europe, N. Africa and SW. Asia. Al Au Be Br Bu Co Cr Cz De Fr Fu Ge Gr Ho Hu It Pl Po Sd Si Sp Ru Tu Yu.

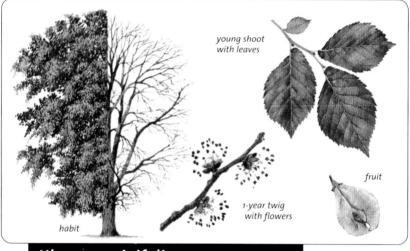

young shoot with leaves

fruit

1-year twig with flowers

habit

Ulmus carpinifolia G. Suckow Smooth Elm

The crown is domed, young twigs are long and pendulous. Leaves are usually widest above the middle with the midrib almost straight, the base is rather unequal, the margin of the longer side is straight in the lower one-third to one half, turning at right-angles into the petiole. **Distribution** Throughout the range of *U. minor*.

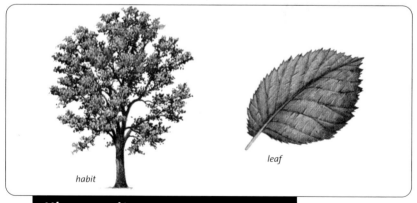

leaf

habit

Ulmus coritana Melville Coritanian Elm

The crown is rather spreading, young twigs are stout. Leaves are usually widest at or below the middle with the midrib curving towards the short side; the base is very unequal with the longer side often forming a rounded lobe. **Distribution** SE. Britain. Br.

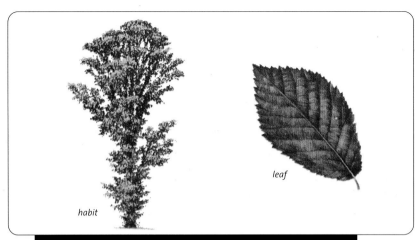

habit

leaf

Ulmus angustifolia (Weston) Weston **Cornish Elm**

The crown is narrow and somewhat conical, especially when young; twigs are short and rather stiff. Leaves are usually broadest above the middle, often concave, with the midrib more or less straight; the base is more or less equal. **Distribution** SW. Britain; may also be native in France. Br Fr.

leaf

habit

Ulmus plotii Druce **Plot's Elm**

The crown is narrow and upright with an arching, one-sided leading shoot; young twigs are long and pendulous. Leaves are rather narrow, widest near the middle with the midrib almost straight and the base more or less equal; some short shoots proliferate and produce smaller, rounder leaves. **Distribution** Br.

leaf

Ulmus canescens Melville

This species closely resembles *U. minor* but the young twigs have a dense soft white down. Leaves are ovate-elliptic with rounded teeth and have a dense grey down; lateral veins are in 12–16 (sometimes 18) pairs. **Distribution** C. and E. Mediterranean region. Al Cr Gr It Ru Si Yu.

leaf   1-year twig with flower   fruit

Ulmus laevis Pallas European White Elm

A wide-spreading tree up to 35m with a rather open crown. **Bark** Brownish-grey, smooth when young, becoming deeply furrowed with broad ridges. **Branches** Young twigs dark red-brown with a soft grey down, becoming smooth. **Buds** Winter buds small, pointed and dark orange-brown. **Leaves** 6–13cm, almost round to oval with a short tapering point, the base very unequal; the veins are in 12–19 pairs, the longer side with 2–3 extra veins; the upper surface is smooth or occasionally with stiff hairs, the lower surface is usually clothed with a soft grey down; the petiole is 3–5mm long. **Flowers** Borne in clusters on long pedicels 3–6 times as long as the flowers. **Fruit** Pendulous, 1–1·2cm, obovate, the two halves of the wing fringed with white hairs and curving together above the notch. **Flowering period** March. **Distribution** Sometimes planted as a shelter tree. Al Au Be Bu Cz Fr Fu Ge Gr Hu Po Ru Sd Sw Yu (planted in It).

Zelkova Spach

Large deciduous trees or shrubs. The simple leaves are alternately arranged with a slightly asymmetrical or level base and a toothed margin. Flowers appear in the axils of leaves on young stems; male flowers are at the base of new growth, sometimes at the tip; the lobes of the perianth are leaf-like and joined together, enclosing an erect cluster of stamens. Fruits are dry and form single-seeded nutlets. **Distribution** This small genus from Caucasus, Crete and E. Asia is closely related to the elms, but differs mainly in having separate male and female flowers, and fruits without an encircling wing.

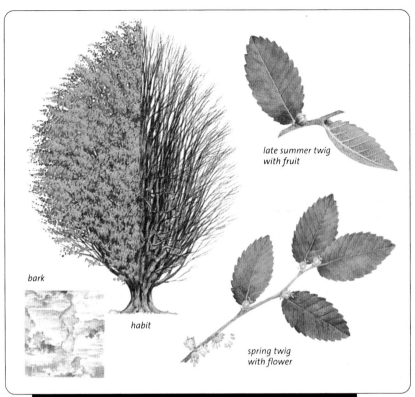

bark

habit

late summer twig
with fruit

spring twig
with flower

Zelkova carpinifolia (Pallas) C. Koch **Caucasian Elm**

An unusual, often many-stemmed tree up to 30m withs a domed crown, sometimes producing suckers. The short fluted bole is usually 1–3m. **Bark** Smooth, greyish- or greenish-brown, flaking away as rounded scales, revealing orange underneath. **Branches** Main ones very numerous and almost upright; the twigs are slender, greyish- or greenish-brown, covered with a white down. **Buds** Winter buds are ovoid, blunt, dark reddish-brown with a white down. **Leaves** 5–10cm, oval or elliptic, pointed, with large rounded teeth; the side veins are in 6–12 pairs; the upper surface of the leaf is dark green, often with scattered stiff hairs, the underside has stiff white hairs either side of the veins; the petiole is 1–2mm. **Flowers** Male flowers have clusters of yellow stamens and are borne on the lower, leafless portion of young twigs, female flowers being carried in the axils of terminal leaves. **Fruit** 5mm, globose with 4 distinct ridges or small wings. **Flowering period** April. **Distribution** A native of the Caucasus mountains infrequently planted for ornament in C. and W. Europe.

late summer twig
with fruit

Zelkova serrata (Thunb.) Makino **Keaki**

Young twigs have fine stiff white hairs, but soon become smooth. The leaves differ from *Z. carpinifolia* in having more pointed teeth and a smooth underside. The fruit is smooth and rounded. **Distribution** Infrequently planted for ornament in parks or gardens. Japan.

Elm Family *Ulmaceae*

Celtis L. Nettle-trees

Deciduous trees or shrubs. The bark is smooth or sometimes wrinkled, but does not form scales. The alternately arranged simple leaves are level at the base; the middle section of the margin has usually uneven teeth but these are often absent from the base and the tapering tip; three prominent veins diverge from the base; the stipules soon fall off. Flowers appear in the axils of leaves on young stems; male flowers are at the base of new growth with hermaphrodite flowers towards the tip; the lobes of the perianth are brownish and separate, enclosing a cluster of upright stamens with yellow anthers. The fruit is small and fleshy, enclosing a single seed with a stony layer. A genus of about 70 species from the northern hemisphere and the tropics.

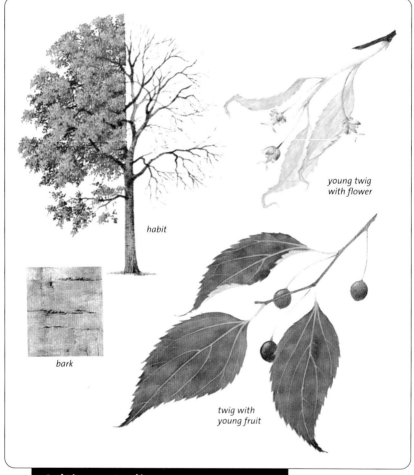

*young twig
with flower*

habit

bark

*twig with
young fruit*

Celtis australis L. Southern Nettle-tree

A round-domed tree up to 25m. **Bark** Grey and pale brown. **Branches** Young twigs are reddish-brown. **Leaves** 4–15cm, lance-shaped to narrowly oval, with a long tapering tip which is often twisted; the base is rounded or heart-shaped; the margin is often wavy and has sharp pointed teeth; the upper side of the leaf has short, stiff hairs while the underside has white down, especially on the veins and petiole. **Fruit** Fleshy, 0·9–1·2cm in diameter, globose, smooth and brownish-red, becoming blackish when ripe; the outer layer of the stone has irregular projections. **Flowering period** May. **Fruiting** September. **Distribution** Native to S. Europe and SW. Asia. Planted in France and Italy as a street tree, occasionally for ornament elsewhere. The fruits are edible though rather small. Al Bu Co Cr Fr It Po Ru Sd Sp Yu.

fruiting twig

habit

Celtis tournefortii Lam.

A shrub or small tree up to 6m. **Branches** Young twigs are reddish-brown with whitish down. **Leaves** 5–8cm, broadly oval with a short tapering apex; the base is rounded; the margin has rounded teeth, each with a small point; the dark green upper surface of the leaf has short stiff hairs or is almost smooth, while the underside is paler and slightly downy. **Fruit** Fleshy, 0·7–1·1cm, ovoid, brownish-yellow when ripe; the outer layer of the stone has 4 ridges. **Distribution** Bu Fu Gr Si Yu.

Mulberry and Fig Family
Moraceae

Morus L. Mulberries

Large monoecious or dioecious trees with flowers on catkins. The compound 'fruit' is composed of closely packed drupes, each enclosed by persistent fleshy sepals.

leafy twig
with male
and female flower

fruit

habit

Morus alba L. White Mulberry

A deciduous tree up to *c*. 15m with a narrow to rounded crown of brittle branches and a broad bole up to 2m in girth. **Bark** Sinuously ridged, generally grey but may have a pinkish appearance. **Branches** The shoots are slender, initially bearing fine hairs. **Buds** Minute, narrowly conical, dark brown. **Leaves** 6–18cm long, broadly ovate with a heart-shaped base, thin, flat, coarsely toothed, usually smooth, glossy green above, glabrous or pubescent on the veins and midrib beneath; the petiole is up to 2·5cm long, finely hairy and with a groove on the upper side. **Flowers** Female flowers occur on stalked cylindrical spikes up to 1·5cm long; male spikes are longer. **Fruit** 1–2·5cm long, white, pinkish or purplish, edible although insipid long before being ripe. **Flowering period** May. **Distribution** A native of China and other parts of Asia, and cultivated for centuries in many S. European and oriental countries as food for silkworms and as a roadside tree. It has frequently become naturalized in SE. Europe and occasionally elsewhere. Al Au Bu Cr Fu Gr Ru Tu.

leafy twig with male flower

fruit

habit

Morus nigra L. Common Mulberry or Black Mulberry

A deciduous tree up to *c.* 12m high with a rugged aspect, forming a dense spreading crown of twisted branches usually wider than the tree is high, the short rough bole with many bosses and burrs. **Bark** Dark orange-brown, fraying or shredding along the sides of wide cracks. **Branches** The young shoots are pubescent, exuding a milky juice when cut, initially pale green and later becoming purple-grey. **Buds** Squat and pointed, the scales dark, glossy and purple-brown. **Leaves** 6–20cm long, broadly ovate, with a deep heart-shaped base, curled, acute, irregularly dentate or lobed, shiny green above, paler and pubescent below; the petiole is stout, 1·5–2·5cm long, hairy. **Flowers** The flower spikes are cylindrical, occurring on downy peduncles. The male flower spikes are *c.* 2·5cm long, pallid; the females are about half as long. **Fruit** 2–2·5cm long, dark red to deep purple, very acid until ripe, when they have an agreeable flavour. **Flowering period** May. **Fruiting** July–September. **Distribution** Although undoubtedly an oriental native, the Common Mulberry has been in cultivation for so long that its native boundaries have been obliterated. It is mostly cultivated for its fruit and has become naturalized in S. Europe. Al Bu Cr Gr It Ru Sp.

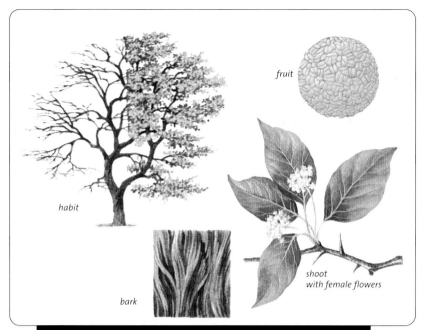

fruit

habit

shoot with female flowers

bark

Maclura pomifera (Rafin) C. K. Schneider **Osage Orange**

A deciduous dioecious tree up to 14m tall or higher, with spiny branches forming an irregular domed crown. **Bark** Cracked and ridged, with an orange coloration. **Branches** The young shoots are initially downy, soon becoming glabrous. **Leaves** 5–12cm long, oval or ovate to oblong-lanceolate, acuminate, mostly rounded at the base, dark glossy green above, downy beneath and paler, especially on the veins and midrib. **Flowers** The male flowers are in dense clusters or more rarely racemes, green, inconspicuous on short peduncles; female flowers are in dense globose or subglobose inconspicuous clusters, and develop into compound fruits which are orange-shaped, pitted, covered with a white inedible pulp and a tough bright yellowish-green rind. **Flowering period** June. **Fruiting** October–November. **Distribution** A native of the S. and C. United States, cultivated in Europe as a hedge plant and for ornament. It has become locally naturalized in some parts of S. Europe. Fu It Ru.

fruiting shoot

Ficus carica L. Fig

A deciduous dioecious tree or shrub with a low spreading crown and robust branches. **Bark** Smooth, pale grey, with a tracery of darker markings. **Leaves** Alternate, 10–20cm long and wide, usually 3–5 palmately lobed, the lobes rounded, heart-shaped at the base, and usually with a scalloped toothed margin, sparsely hispid and rough to the touch, especially below, dark green, thick, leathery, with prominent veins below; the petiole is 5–10cm long. **Flowers** Produced on the inner surface of a pear-shaped receptacle almost enclosed at the top, which develops later into the sweet, succulent fig. **Distribution and taxonomic notes** A species perhaps native to SW. Asia, the Iberian Peninsula and the Balkan Peninsula, now extensively cultivated for its fruit and widely naturalized in S. Europe but also found in gardens throughout N. and W. Europe. Many different cultivars exist and the fruits are eaten both fresh and dried. Al Au Bl Co Cr Cz Fr Fu Gr Hu It Pl Sa Sd Si Sp Tu. Its evergreen relative *F. elastica* Roxb. with entire, glossy dark green leaves is the commonly cultivated 'Rubber' plant, forming large trees in the Mediterranean countries.

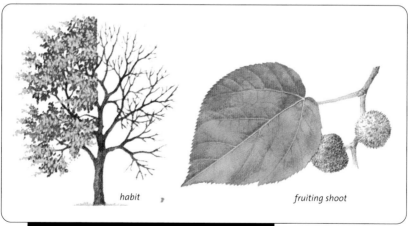

habit *fruiting shoot*

Broussonetia papyrifera (L.) Vent.

A small dioecious tree with villous twigs. **Leaves** 7–20cm long, ovate, serrate or sometimes lobed, rough to the touch above, grey-tomentose below. **Flowers** Male flower a catkin-like inflorescence with a 4-partite perianth; there are 4 stamens, somewhat inflexed in bud; female flowers occur in dense globose tomentose heads; the perianth has 4 very small teeth and forms a layer of pulp in the ripe fruit. **Distribution** An uncommon E. Asian tree planted in S. Europe for ornament, sometimes becoming naturalized. Fr It Ru Si.

Protea Family
Proteaceae

habit

flowering shoot

Embothrium coccineum J.R. & G. Forst. **Chilean Firebush**

A small evergreen tree up to 12m tall. **Bark** Slightly flaking, dark purplish to grey, with a slender crown. **Branches** Sinuous, leaning outwards; the shoots are somewhat pendulous, pale green, smooth. **Leaves** Variable, 5–15cm (rarely up to 22cm) long, elliptic to lanceolate, cuneate or rounded, entire, pale to deep bluish-green; the petiole is *c.* 1cm long, bright green. **Flowers** Axillary or terminal clusters of bright red flowers; the flowers are 5–10cm long, swollen at the apex and divided into 4 segments. **Fruit** A capsule, 3 x 1cm, oblong, grooved, on a dark red peduncle and bearing a dark red style up to 3cm long at the tip. **Flowering period** Late May and June. **Distribution** A S. American species from Chile and Argentina planted for ornament in W. Europe. Br.

Phytolacca Family *Phytolaccaceae*

leafy twig with fruit

Phytolacca dioica L. **Phytolacca**

A small evergreen dioecious tree. **Branches** Robust, brown, glabrous. **Leaves** 6–12 x 2·5–6cm, entire, elliptical to ovate, acute, glabrous, petiolate, rich green with a prominent vein. **Flowers** An axillary, drooping cylindrical raceme up to *c.* 12cm with a peduncle up to 1·5cm long; the flowers are green, spotted with white, pubescent; males slender, *c.* 1·5cm long with pointed membranous petals; female flowers are more robust with elliptical, obtuse petals and 7–10 styles. **Fruit** A subglobose berry with 7–10 carpels joined only at the base, compressed, about 3mm long and 7·5mm wide, purplish-black. **Flowering period** June–August. **Distribution** A native of temperate and subtropical S. America planted for ornament and shade in the Mediterranean region and locally naturalized. Fr Gr It Si Sp.

Katsura Family
Cercidiphyllaceae

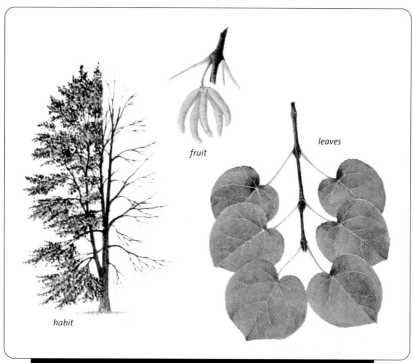

fruit

leaves

habit

Cercidiphyllum japonicum Sieb. & Zucc. **Katsura Tree**

A moderate-sized dioecious tree up to 25m with an ovoid-conical crown and a solitary trunk or divided into many stems. **Bark** Dull greyish-brown, becoming vertically fissured and eventually peeling in strips. **Branches** Slender, curving upwards, covered with opposite pairs of buds; the buds are dark brown, glossy. **Leaves** Opposite, *c.* 8 x 7cm, ovate or round, obtuse, cordate with small, rounded teeth, emerging as a pink colour, becoming green, turning red in the autumn. **Flowers** Occurring at the nodes; male flowers are clusters of red stamens, appearing before the leaves; female flowers are 5–6mm, with clusters of dark red twisted styles. **Fruit** In clusters of 4–6, 1·5–5cm, bluish-grey, later becoming green then brown. **Flowering period** April. **Distribution** A Japanese species frequently planted in gardens for ornament.

Magnolia and Tulip Tree Family
Magnoliaceae

flowering shoot

habit

Liriodendron tulipifera L. Tulip Tree

A large deciduous glabrous tree up to 45m tall. The crown is slender, more or less parallel-sided when young, becoming domed, often with massive lowest branches when old. **Bark** Grey, becoming brown or somewhat orange at maturity, with a network of low ridges. **Buds** c. 1cm, broadest above the middle, glossy, reddish-brown with stipules enclosing the bud and each of the young leaves. **Leaves** 7–18 x 15–20cm, with 4 large lobes and a broad squarish or notched apex, shiny green above, somewhat waxy and dull below; the lower lobes project at right-angles, triangular or somewhat oval with pointed tips; the upper lobes are narrowly triangular, spreading either side of the apex; the petiole is slender, 5–10cm long. **Flowers** Borne at the tips of shoots, at first cup-shaped, later opening wider, the petaloid perianth segments yellowish-green with a pale orange band near the base enclosing a greenish-blue area; the stamens are up to 5cm long, fleshy, yellowish-white, erect becoming spreading; the central conical mass of ovaries is yellowish with a green tip. **Fruit** Conical, 5–8·5cm long, consisting of numerous dark brown carpels, overlapping, erect and pointed, each with a terminal wing and indehiscent when separating from the axis. **Distribution** A N. American species introduced into Europe in the 17th century, widely planted as a timber tree and for ornament. Au Br De Ge. A close relative, the Chinese Tulip Tree, *L. chinense*, is less widely planted.

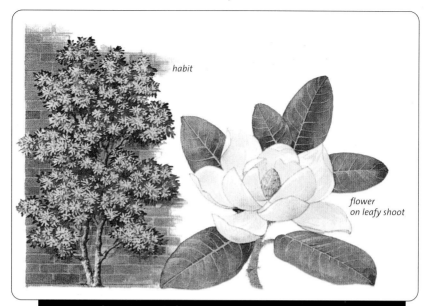

habit

flower on leafy shoot

Magnolia grandiflora L. Evergreen Magnolia or Bull Bay

A medium to large evergreen tree up to 30m high with large spreading branches. The crown is broadly conical. **Bark** Dull grey and smooth. **Branches** Shoots are thickly covered with a reddish-brown down. **Buds** Up to 1·5cm long, conical with a reddish tip. **Leaves** 8–16 x 5–9cm, elliptical or broader above the middle, the margin without teeth but sometimes wavy, thick and leathery, shiny above but rusty-pubescent below; the petiole is 2–2·5cm long, covered with a dense down. **Flowers** Borne at the tips of shoots, initially conical, later cup-shaped, up to 25cm in diameter with 6 thick creamy-white petal-like segments. **Fruit** Conical, 5–6 x 2–3cm, comprised of separate carpels on an orange-brown stalk, marked where the stamens and petal-like segments have fallen away. **Flowering period** July–November. **Distribution** A native of the SE. United States, introduced to W. Europe in the early 18th century and now one of the most popular cultivated trees, commonly grown against walls or free-standing in milder areas. There are some 35 other species of *Magnolia*, many of which are cultivated.

flowering shoot

Drimys winteri Forst. Winter's Bark

A small evergreen of the *Winteraceae* with glossy green leaves and panicles of white flowers. **Distribution** A S. American species cultivated in gardens of SW. Europe.

Bay Family
Lauraceae

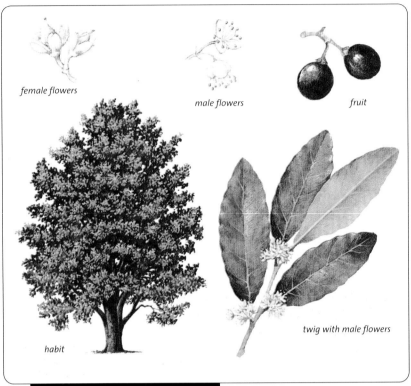

female flowers

male flowers

fruit

twig with male flowers

habit

Laurus nobilis L. Sweet Bay

A medium-sized evergreen tree or shrub up to 20m high with a broadly conical crown and covered in all parts with aromatic oil glands. **Bark** Usually smooth, dark grey to black. **Branches** Ascending, usually dark grey, the twigs slender, glabrous, reddish near the tip, green on the lower parts of the shoot. **Buds** 3mm long, narrowly conical, dark red. **Leaves** 5–10 x 2–4cm (rarely up to 7·5cm), alternate, narrowly lanceolate, leathery, dark green above, paler beneath, the margins crinkled, glabrous, dotted with glands and aromatic when crushed; the petiole is dark red. **Flowers** The inflorescence has a short peduncle; the perianth is deeply 4-lobed and not differentiated into sepals and petals. The flowers are dioecious, borne in pairs beneath each leaf, *c.* 1cm in diameter, red and green in bud and yellow when open; the male flowers have 8–12 stamens usually arranged in 4 whorls, each with 2 glands at the base, the anthers opening by 2 valves; the female flowers each have 2–4 staminodes and a simple style. **Fruit** An ovoid berry, 1–1·5cm long when mature, shiny green at first, later turning black. **Flowering period** June. **Distribution** A native of the Mediterranean region, the Sweet Bay is cultivated in many parts of Europe as far north as Britain, often as a shrub or half-standard, and has become naturalized in some places. The 'Laurel' from which poets' wreaths were made in classical times, it is now widely used as a pot herb. Al Co Cr Fr Gr It Pl Sa Sp Tu Yu.

flowering twig

flower

habit

fruit

Persea americana Miller Avocado

A much-branched evergreen tree 7–9m high, although in natural habitats reaching 18m or more, the crown rounded, covered in all parts with aromatic oil glands. **Leaves** 10–20cm long, elliptic or ovate, acute or shortly pointed, leathery, glabrous, dark green above, bluish-green beneath, entire; pinnately veined or 3-veined. **Flowers** The inflorescence is elongated with many flowers, each *c.* 2cm across, greenish, grey-pubescent; the perianth is 6-lobed, the lobes either equal in length or with 3 smaller outer lobes; the anthers open by 4 valves. **Fruit** A berry *c.* 10cm long, pear-shaped, oblong or globose, seated on a persistent perianth tube, the skin thick and sometimes woody, varying in colour from green through yellow to brown or purple; the soft flesh is greenish, becoming bright yellow when ripe; the seed is single, large and shiny. **Distribution** The origin of the Avocado is unknown but it is generally thought to be a native of C. America. It is grown as an orchard tree in many parts of the world including the Mediterranean countries. Cultivated plants are generally much smaller and of a bushier habit than wild plants. There are a number of cultivars with fruits of varying sizes and textures occurring at different times of the year. The Avocado is grown for the soft, edible flesh which surrounds the seed.

Witch Hazel Family
Hamamelidaceae

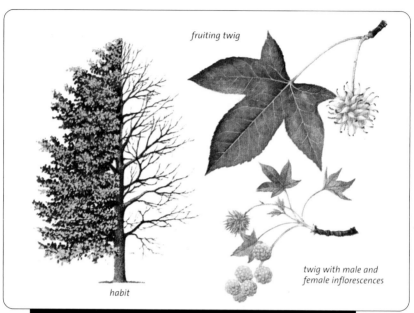

fruiting twig

twig with male and female inflorescences

habit

Liquidambar orientalis Miller Oriental Sweet Gum

A small deciduous tree up to 7·5m high with a dense spreading crown. **Bark** Dark orange-brown, fissured and flaking. **Branches** The young shoots are slender, red-brown above, green beneath, glabrous. **Buds** Ovoid with about 6 outer scales, red-brown, glossy. **Leaves** 4–6cm wide, alternate, usually 5-lobed, the lobes ovate, the margins coarsely toothed and finely glandular, glabrous; petiole is *c.* 3·5cm. **Flowers** Monoecious; male flowers are intermixed with small scales in catkins 5–7·5cm long, and consist of stamens only; female flowers are in greenish or yellowish globose heads and consist only of 2-beaked ovaries in the axils of minute scales. The fruiting inflorescence is about 2·5cm in diameter. **Fruit** A dehiscent capsule containing 1 or 2 seeds, with a slender beak. **Flowering period** May. **Distribution** Originally from Asia Minor, this species is cultivated in Europe for the fragrant resin called liquid storax which is obtained from the inner bark. In N. Europe the plants are usually small.

Liquidambar styraciflua L. Sweet Gum
A large tree up to 28m, twigs initially downy; leaves up to 15cm, downy beneath on the veins; the petiole is 10–15cm. **Distribution** A native of E. and S. United States, frequently planted in NW. Europe for ornament.

leaf *flowering twig* *fruit*

Hamamelis L. Witch Hazels

Small deciduous trees or shrubs. **Branches** Usually spreading, stellate-hairy at least when young. **Leaves** Alternate, ovate, the margins toothed; the petiole is short; the stipules are large, falling early. **Flowers** In few-flowered short-stalked clusters emerging from the leaf axils, in most species appearing before the leaves. The calyx consists of 4 rounded sepals; the 4 petals are long, narrow, strap-like, yellow. **Fruit** A capsule containing 2 seeds, exploding when ripe. **Seeds** Black and shiny. **Distribution and taxonomic notes** Four species are commonly planted: the spring-flowering species, *Hamamelis mollis* Oliver, Chinese Witch Hazel, and *H. japonica* Siebold & Zucc., Japanese Witch Hazel, with their hybrid, *Hamamelis* x *intermedia* Rehder and the autumn-flowering *Hamamelis virginiana* L., Virginian Witch Hazel.

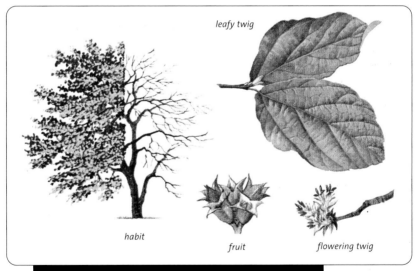

leafy twig

habit *fruit* *flowering twig*

Parrotia persica C.A. Meyer Persian Ironwood

A small deciduous tree 9–12m high with a spreading crown and a short bole. **Bark** Smooth, flaking, grey to greyish-brown, revealing pinkish-brown or yellow patches beneath. **Branches** The twigs are stellate-hairy when young. **Buds** Purplish-black, hairy. **Leaves** 5–25 x 2·5–7·5cm, stipulate, ovate or obovate, rounded to tapering at the base, the margins shallowly or unevenly toothed, sometimes only wavy towards the apex, glabrous above, sparsely stellate, hairy below, becoming glossy green; the petiole is 4–5mm long, hairy. **Flowers** Borne in crowded short-stalked clusters, opening before the leaves. **Fruit** A capsule with 2 recurved beaks each splitting into 2 valves. **Seeds** *c.* 1cm long, pointed at one end, brown and shining. **Flowering period** February–March. **Distribution** A native of the Caucasus and N. Persia, frequently planted in parks and gardens as an ornamental.

Pittosporum Family
Pittosporaceae

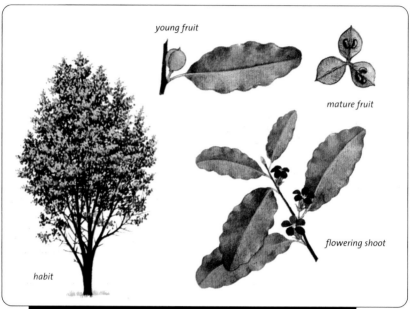

young fruit

mature fruit

flowering shoot

habit

Pittosporum tenuifolium Solander ex Gaertner
Pittosporum

A tree up to *c.* 8m high, sometimes with a very stout bole. **Bark** Dark grey. **Branches** Twigs more or less pubescent. **Leaves** 1–7 x 0·5–2cm (usually 3 x 2cm), entire, oblong to oblong-ovate, obtuse to acute, acuminate, thinly leathery, wavy and crinkled, pale green above, light green below; the petioles are short. Young leaves pubescent. **Flowers** Fragrant, axiliary, solitary on short pedicels; or in small cymes; the bracts fall early; the sepals are narrowly ovate-oblong, subacute to obtuse, silky-hairy when young; the petals are very dark red to purplish or almost black, *c.* 12cm long, the limb spreading to become deflexed; the ovary is hairy; the style is long. **Fruit** A subglobose, 2-valved capsule *c.* 1·2cm in diameter; the valves are glabrous, slightly rough, nearly black and thinly woody when mature. **Flowering period** May. **Distribution and taxonomic notes** A native of New Zealand, cultivated in W. Europe for its attractive leaves. Interesting cultivars include cv. 'Variegatum' with pale cream variegated leaves and cv. 'Silver Queen' with silvery-green leaves. *P. colensoi* Hooker fil., with a taller trunk and stouter limbs than *P. tenuifolium,* is cultivated on a lesser scale, as is the fragrant-flowered species *P. eugenioides* A. Cunn. and the red-flowered *P. ralphii* J. Kirk.

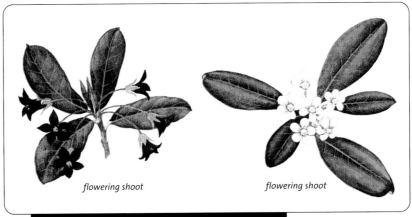

flowering shoot   *flowering shoot*

Pittosporum crassifolium Putterlick

An erect evergreen shrub or small tree up to 10m high with a clustered crown. **Bark** Black. **Leaves** 5–8 x 2–3cm, obovate-oblong, obtuse, dark green above, white-tomentose below, very leathery. **Flowers** Occur in few-flowered cymes; the petals are deep red to purplish-black, oblong. The capsule is 2–2·8cm long, subgobose, white-tomentose, with 3–4 woody valves. **Distribution and taxonomic notes** A native of New Zealand cultivated for ornament and shelter in parts of W. Europe and naturalized in the Scilly Isles. *P. tobira* (Thunb.) Aiton fil. is a species from S. Japan and E. China with leaves of a similar shape but glabrous, and with white or yellowish fragrant flowers, cultivated for ornament in S. and W. Europe.

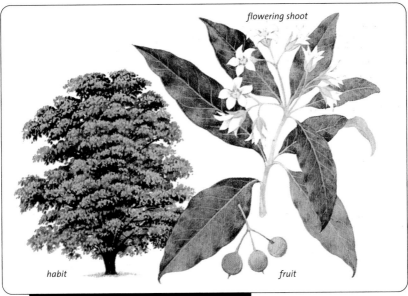

flowering shoot

habit   *fruit*

Pittosporum undulatum Vent.
White Holly or Mock Orange

A glabrous tree up to 20m high with a pyramidal crown. **Bark** Grey. **Leaves** 7–13cm (rarely up to 20cm) long by 2–6cm wide, ovate-lanceolate, acute, wedge-shaped at the base, shining green, somewhat wavy, evergreen. **Flowers** Fragrant and occurring in few-flowered flat-topped cymes; petals white, lanceolate. **Fruit** The capsule is 1–1·2cm long, obovoid, glabrous, with 2 valves, orange when ripe. **Flowering period** May–June. **Distribution** A native of SE. Australia widely cultivated for ornament in S. and W. Europe, becoming extensively naturalized in the Atlantic islands and locally elsewhere.

Plane Tree Family
Platanaceae

Platanus L. Plane Trees

Large, very long-lived deciduous trees with scaling bark. The leaves are alternate with thick petioles. The flowers are unisexual catkins arranged on the same tree in dense globose heads.

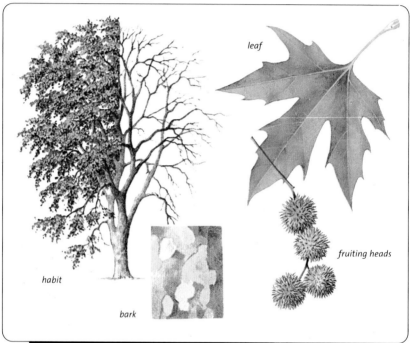

leaf

fruiting heads

habit

bark

Platanus orientalis L. Oriental Plane

A broad, irregularly domed tree up to 30m. The lower branches are often drooping, the lower limbs sometimes resting on the ground. The trunk is often covered with large burrs. **Bark** Fairly smooth and generally pale brown but flaking and scaling to reveal round yellow patches. **Branches** The young shoots are yellow-brown, hairy, but becoming darker with age; the older twigs are grey or reddish-brown. **Leaves** Up to 18 x 18cm, with 5–7 lobes, palmate, yellow-green, with deep, acute sinuses; the lobes are rather narrow and coarsely toothed, the central lobe longer than the rest; the petiole is up to 5cm long, the red base swollen and enclosing the young buds. **Flowers** The male inflorescences are 5–6cm long with 2–7 globose yellowish heads of flowers; the female inflorescences are 6–8cm long with 2–6 flattened globose, dark red heads of flowers. The fruiting catkins grow to 15cm long with heads up to 3cm in diameter, comprised of many 1-seeded carpels surrounded at the base with long spiny hairs. **Flowering period** April–June. **Distribution** W. Asia to the Balkan Peninsula. It is widely planted in parks and gardens elsewhere. Al Bu Cr Gr Yu.

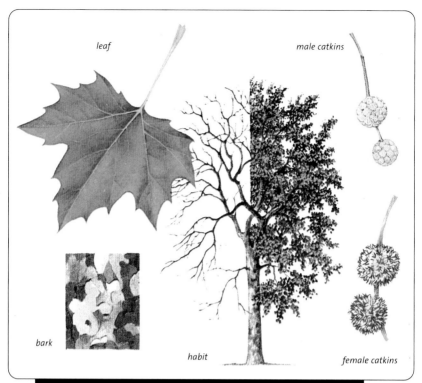

leaf

male catkins

bark

habit

female catkins

Platanus x hispanica Muenchh. London Plane

A dense tree up to 35m. The trunks are very tall; the crown is many-domed, becoming spreading with twisted branches when old. **Bark** Dark grey or brown, regularly flaking to reveal large yellowish or pale patches beneath. **Branches** Young shoots are green with whitish hairs, becoming darker with age; the older twigs are orange-tinged, finally dark grey or brown. **Leaves** Up to 20 x 24cm, usually 5-lobed, usually rounded, palmate, but immensely variable, shiny and smooth except for the woolly veins above, paler below; the sinuses are generally shallow but very variable, cutting one-third to half the length of the blade; the lobes are somewhat triangular with up to 5 forward-pointing teeth on each side. **Flowers** The catkins are 2–8cm long; male flowers are borne on 2–6 yellowish globose heads; female flowers are borne on 2–5 crimson globose heads. The fruiting heads are brown; the seeds, shed in great abundance in the spring, are cylindrical and surrounded with whitish hairs. **Distribution and taxonomic notes** One of the most vigorous-growing trees in almost any environment, due to the shedding bark and shiny short-lived leaves, this makes the London Plane one of the commonest street trees, planted throughout Britain and Europe since the 17th century. Its origins are obscure. It is considered by many writers to be either a hybrid between the Western Plane, *P. occidentalis* L., from N. America and the Oriental Plane, *P. orientalis*, or simply a cultivar of *P. orientalis*.

Rose Family
Rosaceae

One of the largest families of flowering plants, with some 2000 species of herbs, shrubs and trees.

flowering twig

habit

mature fruit

Cydonia oblonga Miller Quince

A small tree 1·5–7·5m high. **Branches** The shoots are woolly when young but become glabrous at maturity. **Leaves** 5–10cm long with entire margins, green-glabrous above, grey-woolly below. **Flowers** Borne singly in the axils of the leaves, 3·8–5cm in diameter and distinctly bowl-shaped; the sepals are toothed; the petals are usually pink but sometimes white, longer than the sepals; the anthers number 15–25; the female part consists of 5 free styles, and 5-carpellate ovaries with thick, cartilaginous walls at maturity and numerous seeds in each carpel. **Fruit** 2·5–3·5cm long, pear-shaped or globose, greenish when young, yellow, woody and sweet-smelling when mature. **Flowering period** May. **Distribution** Plants cultivated for eating in much of C. and S. Europe have much larger fruits (5–12cm long) than NW. European plants. A species which originates in SW. and C. Asia, the Quince has become naturalized in hedges and copses in much of Europe but mainly in the Mediterranean countries. Al Au Bu Co Cz Fu Ge Gr Ho Hu It Ru Sa Si Sp Tu Yu.

Pyrus L. Pears

Small to medium-sized deciduous trees and shrubs, usually with spiny lower and young branches. **Leaves** Alternate, simple or occasionally lobed, the margin toothed or entire, the stipules falling early. **Flowers** Borne in flat-topped clusters; the petals are distinct, larger than the sepals, tapered at the base, and white or pinkish in colour; there are 15–30 anthers which are conspicuously red or reddish-purple, the outer ones maturing before the inner; the female part consists of 2–5 free styles, with the carpels joined together in groups of 2–5, their walls becoming leathery at maturity and each carpel containing 2 seeds.
Fruit A characteristic pome, may be pear-shaped, top-shaped or globose, the flesh invariably containing stone-cells, giving a gritty texture. **Flowering period** For most species April–May.

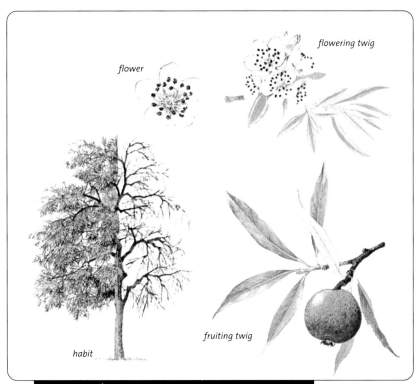

flower

flowering twig

fruiting twig

habit

Pyrus salicifolia Pallas Willow-leaved Pear

A small-domed slender tree about 10m high. **Branches** Main ones more or less horizontal, twigs pendulous and densely white-woolly, especially when young. **Leaves** 3·5–9cm long, narrowly lanceolate, distinctly pointed, the margins entire, somewhat grey in colour with silvery down on both sides at first, but later becoming glossy green above; the petiole is about 1cm long or less. **Flowers** About 2cm in diameter, often opening simultaneously with the leaves; the calyx is persistent, the sepals woolly; the petals are entire or sometimes notched, white; the styles are villous at the base. **Fruit** 2·5–3cm long, pear-shaped, top-shaped or cylindrical, brown when mature; the pedicel is white-woolly. **Distribution** A native of the Caucasus, Persia and Siberia, Willow-leaved Pear is cultivated in Europe. A weeping form, cv. 'Pendula', is the most commonly planted ornamental pear, frequent in parks and gardens.

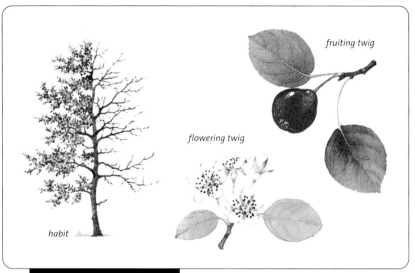

fruiting twig

flowering twig

habit

Pyrus cordata Desf.

A small slender tree or shrub up to 8m high. **Branches** Usually spreading or at right-angles and usually spiny; the twigs are purplish and more or less glabrous. **Leaves** 2·5–5·5cm (rarely as little as 1cm) long, more or less ovate or sometimes heart-shaped, with a toothed margin, and densely hairy when young; the petiole is 2·5cm long. **Flowers** Opening with the leaves. The calyx is deciduous, the sepals 2–3 x 1–1·5mm; the petals are 6–8 x 5–7mm, white. **Fruit** 0·8–1·8cm long, more or less pear-shaped, red and shiny when mature, covered with brown lenticels; the pedicel is slender. **Distribution** An uncommon, sometimes rare species of woods and hedgerows. Br Fr Pl Sp.

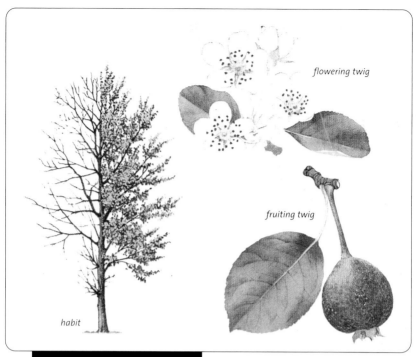

flowering twig

fruiting twig

habit

Pyrus pyraster Burgsd.

A medium-sized round tree 8–20m high. **Branches** May be ascending or spreading and are usually spiny; the twigs are grey or brown, glabrous. **Leaves** 2·5–7cm long, elliptic to orbicular in outline but sometimes heart-shaped; the margin is toothed, sometimes with the teeth confined to the apex, or absent; glabrous when mature; the petiole is 2–7cm long. **Flowers** Appearing with the leaves; the calyx is persistent, the sepals 3–8 x 1–3·5mm; the petals are 1–1·7 x 0·7–1·3cm, pure white. **Fruit** 1·3–3·5 x 1·8–3·5cm, top-shaped or globose, yellowish-brown or black, covered with lenticels; the pedicel is slender. **Distribution** This species is sometimes difficult to identify because it consists of a number of variants of wild and naturalized European pears. The trees are usually solitary and grow in thickets and open woods. Al Au Be Br Bu Cz De Fr Fu Ge Gr Hu It Pl Ru Sd Si Sp.

fruiting twig

Pyrus bourgaeana Decne

A small tree up to 10m high. **Branches** Lower ones spiny; the twigs are grey, glabrous and slightly shiny. **Leaves** 2–4cm long, usually ovate, sometimes almost heart-shaped, the margins toothed, hairy when young, glabrous or papillose on the lower surface when mature. **Flowers** Appearing with the leaves. The calyx is persistent, the sepals 5–7 x 2–2·5mm, the apex with a small point; the petals are 0·8–1 x 0·5–0·7cm, white. **Fruit** 1·7–2·5cm in diameter, top-shaped to globose, dull yellow to almost brown when ripe; the pedicel is thick. **Distribution** An uncommon species, usually found near running water. Pl Sp.

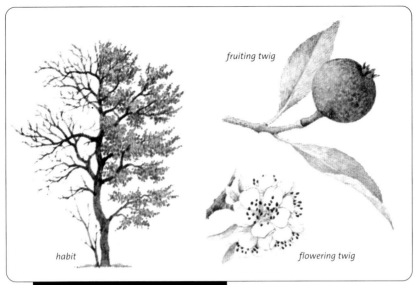

fruiting twig

habit

flowering twig

Pyrus elaeagrifolia Pallas

A small slender tree or sometimes a shrub. **Branches** Spreading and often spiny; the twigs are covered with grey hairs. **Leaves** 3·5–8cm long, more or less lanceolate, toothed at the apex or entire, with dense grey-white wool; the petiole is 1–1·5cm long. **Flowers** Almost sessile clusters, appearing with the leaves. The calyx is persistent, the sepals 5 x 1·5mm; the petals are 1 x 0·7cm, white; the styles are densely hairy below the middle. **Fruit** c. 1·3cm long, pear-shaped to globose, green; the pedicel is thick. **Distribution** An isolated tree of dry places. Al Bu Fu Gr Ru Tu.

fruiting twig

Pyrus salvifolia DC. Sage-leaved Pear or Aurelian Pear

A small tree up to 10m high. **Branches** Thick, somewhat spreading and usually spiny; the twigs are grey, hairy when young, becoming dark brown to black and slightly hairy when mature. **Leaves** 4–7cm long, lanceolate to elliptic, with entire margins, becoming glabrous above, grey-woolly beneath; the petiole is 2–5cm long. **Flowers** In clusters, appearing with the leaves. The calyx is persistent; the petals are glabrous, white; the styles are more or less glabrous. **Fruit** 6–8cm long, pear-shaped or top-shaped, usually woolly when young, yellowish, bitter-tasting; the pedicel is long and woolly. **Distribution and taxonomic notes** *P. salvifolia* is a very variable species and is thought by some authors to be a hybrid between *P. nivalis* and *P. communis*. It is often cultivated, the fruit being used in the brewing industry to make perry. It occurs as an isolated tree on sunny, grassy slopes and in dry woods and may be naturalized in parts of Europe. Au Be Fr Fu Gr Hu Po Ru Yu.

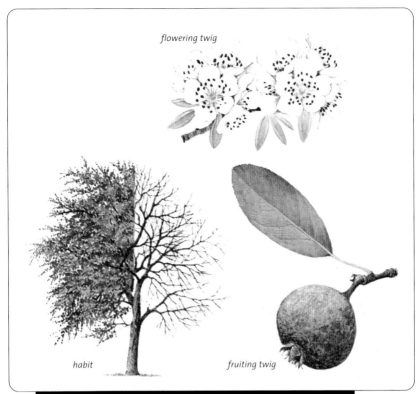

flowering twig

habit

fruiting twig

Pyrus amygdaliformis Vill. Almond-leaved Pear

A small slender tree or dense shrub up to 6m high. **Branches** Spreading, sometimes spiny; the twigs are dull grey and slightly woolly when young. **Leaves** 2·5–8cm long, of variable shape but usually lanceolate to obovate, sometimes 3-lobed, with a shallowly toothed or entire margin, downy when young, becoming glabrous and shiny above and papillose beneath when mature; the petiole is 2–5cm long. **Flowers** In clusters, appearing with, or slightly before, the leaves. The calyx is persistent, the sepals 5–6 x 1·5mm, white and hairy; the petals are 7–8 x 5–6mm, usually notched, white. **Fruit** 1·5–3cm in diameter, globose, yellowish-brown or tawny when mature; the pedicel is thick, about the same length as the fruit. **Distribution** A plant of dry and rough places, appearing as isolated trees. Al Bu Co Cr Fr Gr It Sa Si Sp Yu.

flowering twig

habit

fruiting twig

Pyrus nivalis Jacq.

A medium-sized stout tree 8–20m high. **Branches** Ascending and usually without spines; the twigs are stout, densely woolly when young, becoming glabrous and darker later. **Leaves** 5–9cm long, obovate, the edges of the blade decurrent, running down the petiole, entire or with slightly toothed margins at the apex, sparsely hairy above, but densely greyish and woolly below; the petiole is 1–2cm long, woolly. **Flowers** Opening when the leaves are young. The calyx is persistent, the sepals 6–8 x 3–4mm; the petals are 1·4–1·6 x 1·2–1·4cm, white; the styles are hairy at the base. **Fruit** 3–5cm long, subglobose to globose, greenish-yellow, spotted with purple dots, the flesh sweet when over-ripe; the pedicel is long. **Distribution and taxonomic notes** Narrow-leaved varieties with smaller fruits may be found which tend to cause some confusion with the commonly cultivated pear *P. communis*. Grows in sunny places and dry open woods. Au Bu Cz Fr Hu It Ru Sd Yu.

fruiting twig

Pyrus austriaca Kerner

A medium-sized to largish tree up to 20m. **Branches** Stout, somewhat erect, black and without spines; the twigs are thick and black but covered with grey wool when young. **Leaves** 6–9cm long, more or less lanceolate, the margin toothed towards the apex, becoming glabrous above but with yellowish-grey wool beneath. **Flowers** Appearing with the leaves. The calyx is persistent; the sepals are 5–7 x 3–4mm; the petals are 1·2–1·5 x 1·1–1·3cm, white; the styles are more or less glabrous. **Fruit** 2·5–5·5cm long, pear-shaped or top-shaped, greenish-brown when mature; the pedicel is slender. **Distribution** A species of open places, frequently cultivated and may be naturalized in some countries. Au Cz Fu Hu Sd.

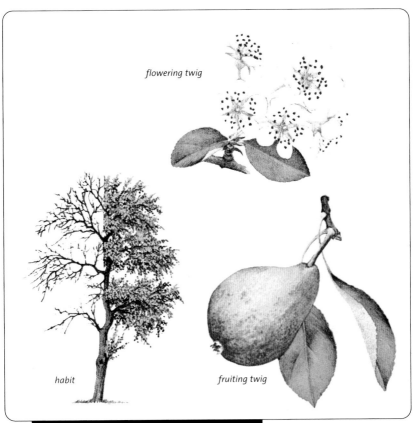

flowering twig

habit

fruiting twig

Pyrus communis L. Common Pear

A medium to tall tree up to 20m high. **Branches** Ascending when young, later spreading, and may be spiny; the twigs are reddish-brown, sometimes slightly hairy but soon becoming smooth and shiny. **Leaves** 5–8cm long, variable in shape but usually ovate to elliptic, the margins finely toothed, sometimes hairy when young but glabrous and glossy green when mature; the petiole is 2–5cm long. **Flowers** Opening before the leaves have fully emerged. The calyx is persistent, the sepals 6–8 x 3–4mm; the petals are 1·2–1·4 x 1–1·2cm, white. **Fruit** 4–12cm long, pear-shaped, top-shaped or globose, usually brown, with sweet-tasting flesh; the pedicel is slender. **Distribution and taxonomic notes** The garden pear, *P. communis* var. *culta* DC., of which more than 1,000 cultivars are known, is probably a hybrid. Many species are thought to be possible parents, including *P. pyraster*, *P. salvifolia*, *P. nivalis* and *P. austriaca*. *P. communis* is a tree of W. Asian origin, now cultivated in orchards throughout most of Europe except the extremely cold northern and dry southern regions. Its cultivated habit is extremely variable and it may be grown in orchards as a standard or half-standard tree or as a cordon. Isolated trees may occur as escapes in hedgerows and woods.

Malus L. Apples

A genus of some 25–30 species of north temperate trees and shrubs, with many cultivars and hybrids raised for both fruit and ornament. The genus is separated from *Pyrus*, its nearest relative, by the styles being united at the base rather than free as in *Pyrus*.

Malus florentina (Zuccagni) C.K. Schneider

A small unarmed tree up to 4m high. **Leaves** 3–6cm long, broadly oval or ovate, truncate or heart-shaped at the base, irregularly sharply lobed with several lobes on each side, dark green above, white-tomentose beneath; the petiole is 0·5–2cm long. **Flowers** 1·5–2cm in diameter, white; the sepals are 3–4mm long, deciduous. **Fruit** *c*. 1cm in diameter, ellipsoid or obovoid, red, with stone cells. **Distribution** A localized native of the S. Balkan Peninsula. Al Gr It Yu.

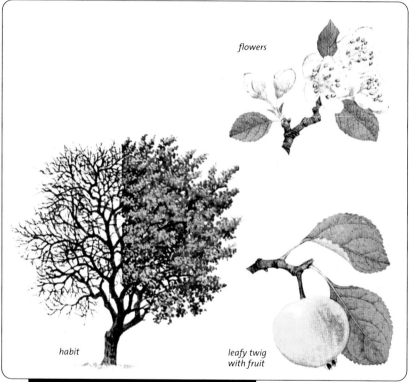

flowers

habit

leafy twig
with fruit

Malus sylvestris Miller Crab Apple

A small tree or shrub up to 10m high. **Branches** Unarmed or, more rarely, thorny. **Bark** Brown and fissured, breaking up into small plates. **Leaves** 3–11 x 2·5–5·5cm, ovate to elliptic or suborbicular, broadly wedge-shaped to rounded at the base, acuminate at the apex, crenate or serrate, glabrous when mature; the petiole is 1·5–3cm long. **Flowers** White, flushed with pink, 3–4cm in diameter; the calyx-tube and peduncles are glabrous or nearly so; the styles are glabrous or sparsely villous at the base. **Fruit** 2·5–3cm in diameter, yellowish-green flushed with red, hard, sour-tasting, subglabrous. **Flowering period** Late May. **Distribution** A native of much of Europe, but rather localized on the mountains in the south. It is of little horticultural importance except as one of the parents in the hybrid orchard apple. All except Au Bl Cr Fi Ic Sa.

flowers

habit

*leafy twig
with fruit*

Malus dasyphylla Borkh.

A small or medium-sized, sparsely spiny tree. **Branches** The twigs are initially tomentose, later becoming glabrous. **Leaves** 3·5–11 x 2·5–5cm, elliptical, crenate, acuminate at the apex, tomentose below; the petiole is 1·5cm long. **Flowers** White, *c.* 4cm in diameter; the styles are glabrous. **Fruit** *c.* 4cm in diameter, yellowish and occasionally red along one side, sour-tasting; the pedicel is 1–5cm but usually 2·5cm long. **Flowering period** May. **Distribution** A native of damp lowland woods along the Danube basin and the northern part of the Balkan Peninsula. Al Au Bu Gr Hu Ru Yu.

habit

leafy twig

flower

Bramley's Seedling

James Grieve

Cox's Orange Pippin

Malus domestica Borkh. Cultivated Apple

A small or medium-sized unarmed tree up to 15m tall. **Branches** The young stems are covered with woolly down. **Leaves** 4–13 x 3–7cm, elliptic-ovate, usually rounded at the base, the margins serrate, slightly tomentose above, densely woolly below. **Flowers** Usually white or pink-tinged, tomentose on the pedicel, calyx tube and on the outside of the calyx. **Fruit** Large, invariably more than 5cm in diameter, indented at base, varying in colour, sweet or sour, usually longer than the pedicel. **Flowering period** May–June. **Distribution and taxonomic notes** The apple is of undoubted hybrid origin, probably derived from *M. sylvestris*, *M. dasyphylla*, *M. praecox* (Pallas) Borkh, and an Asiatic species. More than 1,000 cultivars have been described and are currently grown for their fruit throughout Europe, often escaping and occasionally becoming naturalized.

In addition to edible fruit cultivars there are several species and many hybrids cultivated for their ornamental flowers. The following are some of the most important in Europe:

Malus x magdeburgensis Schoch Magdeburg Apple
A hybrid of *Malus spectabilis* x *pumila* Miller. A free-flowering cultivar with pale green leaves and large pink, semi-double flowers. **Flowering period** May.

Malus spectabilis (Aiton) Borkh. Chinese Crab Apple

A hybrid of *Malus spectabilis* x *pumila* Miller. A large Chinese tree species up to 12m tall, with twisting, pendent branches and large globose flower buds opening into pink or pale pink semi-double flowers up to 5·5cm in diameter. **Flowering period** May.

Malus baccata (L.) Borkh. Siberian Crab Apple

A Chinese species with slender leaves; inflorescence crowded with small white flowers; abundant fruit initially green but becoming bright red and persisting on the tree until late spring. **Flowering period** April–May.

Malus hupehensis (Pamp.) Rehder Hupeh Crab Apple

Another Chinese species, similar to *M. baccata* but with spreading flowers, pink buds, cupped flowers and overlapping petals.

Malus x purpurea (Barbier) Rehder Purple Crab Apple

A garden hybrid, widely planted as a street tree, in parks and small gardens. The buds are deep red; flowers dark pink or purplish, up to 4cm, opening in April–May; a prolific crop of small red or purplish apples is produced in late summer.

Malus halliana Koehne Hall's Crab Apple

Another Chinese species. The leaves are dark green; margins and petioles red. The buds are dark pink, opening into petals with paler inner surfaces. The fruits are globose, *c.* 5mm in diameter, crimson.

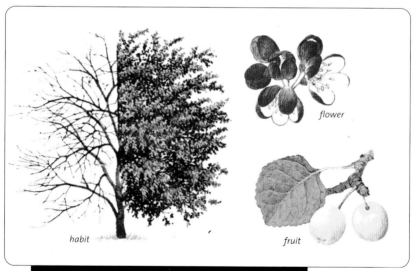

flower

fruit

habit

Malus x floribunda Siebold ex Van Houtte

A Japanese hybrid with an amazing spring profusion of large flowers up to 3cm in diameter, with deep pink buds and flowers paler pink, eventually forming yellow fruits up to 2·5cm in diameter.

Sorbus L. Whitebeams, Rowans and Service Trees

Deciduous trees. **Leaves** Simple, lobed or pinnately divided. **Flowers** In clusters; the petals are white, occasionally pink; there are 15–25 stamens; there are 2–5 carpels, thin-walled in fruit each containing 2 ovules. **Taxonomic notes** Although the widespread species are regular outbreeding trees (eg. *S. domestica, S. torminalis, S. aria*) several local species are apomicts, capable of setting seed without fertilization. Also some species, eg. *S. torminalis* and *S. aria*, frequently hybridize, creating variable hybrid populations. Problems of hybridity and variation between local populations make *Sorbus* species difficult to identify in the field. Some of the more widespread and easily recognizable species are described below.

fruit

flowers

habit

leaf

Sorbus domestica L. True Service Tree

A medium-sized tree up to 20m high with a domed crown. **Bark** Has many small fissures, ultimately shredding, variously shaded orange and brown. **Branches** Spreading or horizontal; the young twigs are green with silky hairs, becoming glabrous later. **Buds** *c*. 1cm long, ovoid, bright, glossy green. **Leaves** Pinnate, the leaflets in 6–10 pairs; each 3–6cm long, oblong, the margins sharply and doubly toothed towards the apex, hairy beneath when young, becoming glabrous. **Flowers** 1·5–1·8cm in diameter, white or creamy. **Fruit** 2–3cm long, more or less ovoid or pear-shaped, greenish or brownish-red, the flesh containing many stone cells. **Flowering period** May. **Distribution** A native of S. Europe, N. Africa and W. Asia, often planted throughout Europe as an ornamental and for its fruit. It has become locally naturalized in C. Europe. Al Au Bu Co Cz Fr Fu Ge Gr Hu It Ru Sd Sp Tu Yu.

fruiting twig

Sorbus vilmorinii C.K. Schneider Vilmorin's Rowan

A native of China, with dark green leaves consisting of 9–12 pairs of leaflets; bears dark pink fruits which become whitish when ripe.

fruit

leaf

Sorbus commixta Hedl. Japanese Rowan

A native of Japan, with leaves consisting of 6–7 pairs of leaflets, glossy green above, pale bluish-green below, turning dark purple in autumn and bearing reddish-orange fruits when ripe. **Flowering period** May; fruits ripening August–September. **Distribution** Both this species and *S. vilmorinii* are planted in parks and gardens or occasionally as street trees.

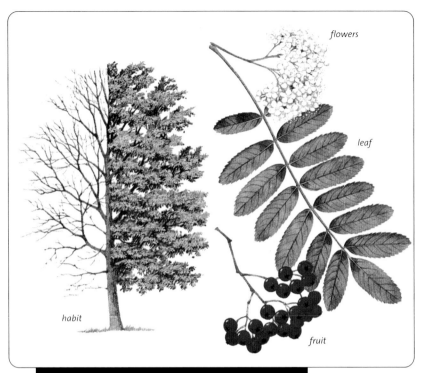

flowers

leaf

fruit

habit

Sorbus aucuparia L. Rowan, Mountain Ash

A small to medium-sized tree up to 20m high with a roughly ovoid, open crown. **Bark** Smooth or faintly ridged, grey or silvery. **Branches** Few and ascending; the twigs are greyish or purplish, hairy at first, becoming glabrous later. **Buds** *c.* 1·7cm long, narrowly ovoid, curved at the tip, dark purple, covered with dense greyish hairs, those on the outer scales appressed. **Leaves** Pinnate, the leaflets in 5–8 pairs; the leaflets are 3–6cm long, oblong, sharply toothed, hairy when young, becoming glabrous; the rachis is round in cross-section, becoming grooved between the leaflets. **Flowers** 0·8–1cm in diameter, creamy-white; the pedicels are woolly; erect or nodding. **Fruit** 6–9mm in diameter, subglobose or ovoid, bright red when ripe, the flesh with a few stone cells. **Flowering period** May. **Fruiting** September. **Distribution** It occurs in much of Europe and is commonly planted as a street tree or garden ornamental. All except BI Cr Fi Sa Tu.

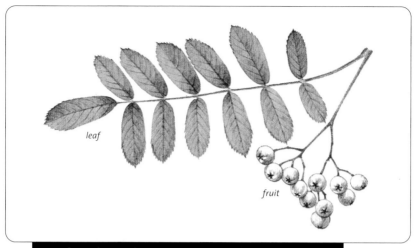

leaf

fruit

Sorbus hupehensis C.K. Schneider Hupeh Rowan

A small tree up to 14m high. **Branches** The twigs are hairy, becoming glabrous. **Buds** Up to 1cm long, pointed, dark red. **Leaves** Somewhat pendent, pinnate, the leaflets in 5–6 pairs; the leaflets are 3·5–7·5cm long, oblong, the margins sharply toothed on the outer half; the rachis is grooved, reddish. **Flowers** *c.* 0·8cm in diameter; white. **Fruit** 6mm in diameter, globose, white or pink when ripe. **Flowering period** May. **Fruiting** September. **Distribution** A native of W. China, the Hupeh Rowan is often planted in parks and gardens.

leaf

Sorbus sargentiana Koehne Sargent's Rowan

A bushy tree up to about 10m high. **Branches** Stout, twigs dark brown. **Buds** Up to 1·5cm long, ovoid, dark red, glossy, resiniferous. **Leaves** Pinnate with leaflets in 4–5 pairs; the leaflets are up to 5cm long, oblong-lanceolate, sharply toothed, softly hairy beneath. **Flowers** *c.* 6mm in diameter, white. **Fruit** 6mm in diameter, numerous, bright red. **Flowering period** June. **Distribution** A W. Chinese species often planted for its colourful autumn foliage. For vigorous growth it is often grafted on to stocks of Mountain Ash.

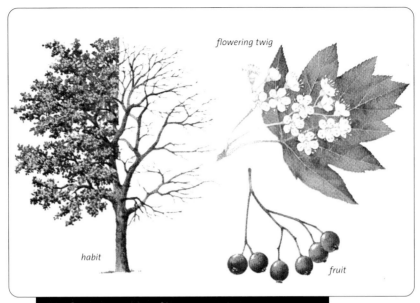

flowering twig

habit

fruit

Sorbus torminalis (L.) Crantz Wild Service Tree

A medium-sized spreading or domed tree up to 25m high. **Bark** Finely fissured, brown or greyish. The twigs are shiny dark brown. **Buds** *c.* 5mm long, globose, shiny green. **Leaves** Simple, 5–10cm long, with 3–5 pairs of triangular-ovate to lanceolate lobes, the margins sharply toothed, dark green on both surfaces, hairy below when young, becoming glabrous later; the petiole is yellowish-green, becoming reddish in autumn. **Flowers** 1–1.5cm in diameter, white; the pedicels are woolly. **Fruit** 1.2–1.8cm in diameter, usually widest above the middle, brown, covered with numerous lenticels. **Flowering period** May–June. **Fruiting** September. **Distribution** A native of much of Europe, occasionally planted in gardens. Al Au Be Br Bu Cz De Fr Fu Ge Gr Ho Hu It Po Pl Sa Sd Si Sp Tu Yu.

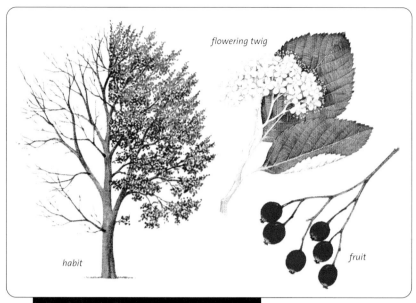

flowering twig

habit

fruit

Sorbus aria (L.) Crantz **Whitebeam**

A medium-sized tree up to 25m high, or occasionally a shrub, with a domed or spreading crown. **Bark** Smooth, sometimes ridged, grey. **Branches** Divergent; the twigs are brown above, green below, hairy at first, becoming glabrous. **Buds** 2cm long, ovoid, green, the tip with white hairs. **Leaves** Simple, 5–12cm long, ovate or elliptical, rounded at the base, the margins shallowly lobed or shallowly and irregularly toothed, the outer edge of each tooth curved towards the apex, with 10–14 pairs of veins, densely hairy, becoming glabrous above, remaining white or greenish-woolly beneath. **Flowers** 1–1·5cm in diameter, white. **Fruit** 0·8–1·5cm long, more or less ovoid, bright red when ripe, with numerous small lenticels. **Flowering period** May–June. **Fruiting** September. **Distribution and taxonomic notes** It is found throughout much of Europe but the southern limits of its distribution are unclear because of confusion with other species. It is often found in gardens and two cultivars are commonly used as street trees: cv. 'Decaisneana' has larger leaves than normal *S. aria* and yellow pedicels with white-flecked fruits; cv. 'Lutescens' has purple twigs and silvery leaves which are smaller than those of *S. aria*. Al Au Be Bl Br Bu Co Cz Fr Fu Hu Ir It Po Ru Sa Sd Si Sp Yu.

leaf

fruit

Sorbus graeca (Spach) Hedl.

A small tree or sometimes a shrub. **Leaves** Simple, 5–9cm long, suborbicular or widest above the middle, not lobed, sharply double-toothed, the teeth even and spreading, with 9–11 pairs of veins, rather leathery with thick greenish-white wool beneath. **Fruit** Up to 1·2cm in diameter, more or less globose, red with large lenticels. **Distribution and taxonomic notes** It is frequently confused with a number of closely related and very similar species throughout Europe. Al Au Bu Cr Cz Fu Ge Gr Hu It Ru Si Yu.

Sorbus rupicola (Syme) Hedl.

A small tree or a shrub. **Leaves** Simple, 8–14·5cm long, more or less ovate or widest above the middle, not lobed, with sharp, coarse and unequal teeth which are curved on the outer margin and pointed towards the apex, with 7–9 pairs of veins, densely white-woolly beneath. **Fruit** 1·2–1·5cm in diameter, more or less globose, bright red with numerous lenticels. **Flowering period** May–June. **Fruiting** September. **Distribution and taxonomic notes** Similar and closely related to *Sorbus graeca*. Br Fu Ir No Sw.

leaf

fruit

Sorbus umbellata (Desf.) Fritsch in A. Kerner

A small tree or sometimes a shrub. **Leaves** 4–7cm long, simple, triangular, broadest above the middle or more or less round, with shallow lobes and coarse teeth towards the apex, the lobes extending up to halfway to the midrib, with 4–7 pairs of veins, densely white-woolly beneath. **Flowers** *c.* 1·5cm in diameter, white. **Fruit** 1·5cm in diameter, globose, yellowish. **Distribution** Al Bu Fu Gr Ru Si Yu.

leaf

fruit

Sorbus mougeotii Soyer-Willemet & Godron

A tree up to 20m high or sometimes a shrub. **Leaves** 7–10cm long, simple, ovate or widest about the middle, shallowly lobed, the large lobes cutting one-quarter of the way to the midrib, more or less smooth above, white or grey, woolly beneath. **Flowers** *c.* 1cm in diameter, white. **Fruit** *c.* 1cm in diameter, more or less globose or slightly longer than wide, red with a few small lenticels. **Flowering period** May. **Fruiting** September. **Distribution and taxonomic notes** A species of the Alps and Pyrenees, thought to have originated as a hybrid between *S. aucuparia* and *S. graeca*. Au Ge It Sp Sw.

leaf

fruit

Sorbus austriaca (G. Beck) Hedl.

A small tree. **Leaves** 8–13cm long, simple, broadly ovate or somewhat elliptical with shallow lobes, the larger lobes extending about one-third of the way to the midrib, the lobes sometimes overlapping, with 8–11 pairs of veins, greyish to white, hairy beneath. **Fruit** Up to 1·3cm in diameter, more or less globose, red and covered with many large lenticels. **Distribution** A tree of hilly and mountainous regions; there are 4 subspecies but only subsp. *austriaca* is widespread in the mountains of Europe. Au Bu Cz Fu Hu Ru Yu.

flowering twig

habit

fruit

Sorbus intermedia (Ehrh.) Pers. Swedish Whitebeam

A medium-sized tree up to 15m high. The bole is short, the crown broadly domed. **Bark** Smooth with shallow and often wide fissures, greyish. **Branches** The twigs are densely hairy when young, becoming glabrous. **Buds** 8mm long, ovoid, green or reddish-brown, covered with grey hairs. **Leaves** 0·8–1·2cm long, simple, elliptic, lobed below the middle, the lobes cut up to one-third of the way to the midrib, the lobes of vigorous shoots often more pronounced, toothed above the middle, green above, with yellowish-grey wool beneath. **Flowers** 1·2–2cm in diameter, white. **Fruit** 1·2–1·5cm long, oblong-ovoid, bright scarlet when ripe with few lenticels; the pedicels are glabrous, greenish-brown. **Flowering period** May. **Fruiting** September. **Distribution** A N. European species, Swedish Whitebeam is commonly planted as a street tree and as an ornamental in parks and occasionally in gardens. Cz De Fi Fu Ge No Po Sw.

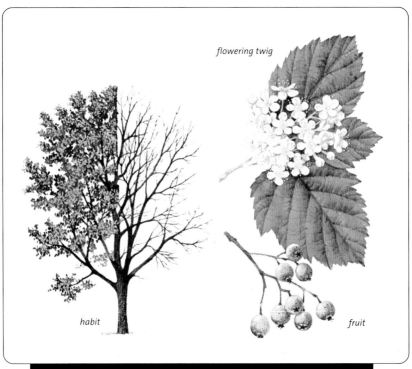

flowering twig

habit

fruit

Sorbus latifolia (Lam.) Pers. Service Tree of Fontainebleau

A medium-sized tree up to 18m high. **Branches** The twigs are reddish-brown, hairy when young, becoming glabrous and shiny. **Buds** 8mm long, ovoid, pale brown. **Leaves** 5–10cm long, simple, broadly elliptical, with 7–9 pairs of veins, more or less triangular lobes, the lobes rounded at the lower edge, unevenly or doubly toothed, hairy, becoming glabrous above, remaining greyish-hairy below. **Flowers** *c.* 2cm in diameter, white; the pedicels are woolly. **Fruit** 1·2–1·5cm in diameter, more or less globose, yellowish-brown with many large lenticels. **Flowering period** May. **Fruiting** September. **Distribution and taxonomic notes** *S. latifolia* and a number of allied species are now known to be apomictic (capable of setting seed without fertilization) and are thought to have originated as hybrids between *S. torminalis* and *S. aria*. A tree first discovered in the forests of Fontainebleau, now frequently found in C. and W. Europe. Fr Ge Pl Sp Sw.

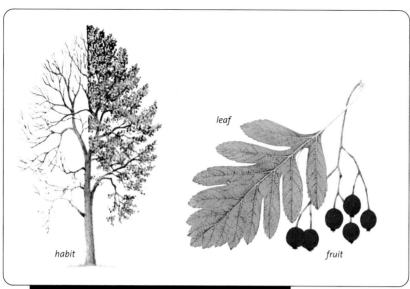

leaf

habit

fruit

Sorbus hybrida L. Bastard Service Tree

A medium-sized tree up to 14m high with a dense ovoid crown. **Bark** Slightly cracked, grey. **Branches** The twigs are pinkish, darker towards the tips. **Buds** 8mm long with few scales, reddish-brown. **Leaves** 7·5–10·5cm long, pinnate with 1–4 (usually 2) pairs of free sessile leaflets towards the base; the remaining portion of the leaf is lobed, the lowest lobes usually cut to the midrib; the margins of the leaflets are toothed towards the tip; somewhat leathery, grey-green above, densely white-woolly beneath. **Flowers** *c.* 1cm in diameter, white. **Fruit** 1–1·2cm in diameter, globose, bright red with small lenticels. **Flowering period** May. **Fruiting** September. **Distribution** Cv. 'Fastigiata' has erect close branches and is often planted in restricted spaces. Woodlands of S. and W. Scandinavia. De Fi No Sw.

leaf

fruit

Sorbus meinchii (Lindeb.) Hedl.

A small tree similar to *S. hybrida*. **Leaves** 4–5 pairs of free sessile leaflets towards the base, the remaining portion of the leaf being a large lobed terminal leaflet, more or less glabrous above, greyish-hairy beneath. **Fruit** Up to 1·2cm in diameter, more or less globose, sometimes slightly longer than wide, red. **Distribution** A species confined to Norway. N.

flowering twig

fruit

habit

Eriobotrya japonica (Thunb.) Lindley **Loquat**

Small evergreen tree or sometimes a shrub, up to 10m high. **Branches** The twigs are hairy. **Leaves** 10–25cm long, broadest above the middle or more or less elliptic, the margins toothed, conspicuously veined, dark green, leathery, glossy above with dense reddish-brown or greyish hair beneath. **Flowers** The inflorescence is a terminal raceme, tightly branched, covered with dense reddish-brown hair. The flowers are about 1cm in diameter, fragrant; the calyx is persistent in fruit; the petals are ovate to almost orbicular, tapering to a point at the base, usually white but often obscured by dense brown hairs; the stamens number 20; the carpels number 2–5, are thin-walled in fruit, each containing 2 ovules; the styles are joined only at the base. **Fruit** 3–6cm long, rounded or elliptical, yellow, fleshy and sweet-tasting. The seeds number one to several. **Distribution** A native of China, the Loquat is cultivated in S. Europe as an orchard tree and sometimes for ornament. It has become naturalized in Cr It Pl Sp.

Amelanchier Medicus **Snowy Mespils**

Small trees or shrubs. **Branches** Lacking spines. **Leaves** Alternate. Stipules falling early. **Flowers** In terminal racemes, sometimes solitary. The calyx is persistent in fruit; the petals are white or pinkish; stamens number 10–20; carpels number 5, fused or partly free with cartilaginous walls in fruit, each containing 2 ovules. **Fruit** Globose, usually juicy and sweet, edible.

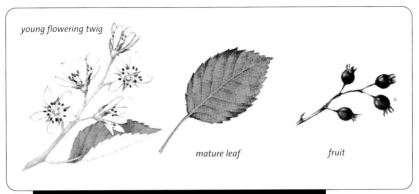

young flowering twig

mature leaf

fruit

Amelanchier ovalis Medicus Snowy Mespil

Usually a shrub, occasionally a tree, reaching 5m. **Branches** Young twigs are woolly. **Leaves** 2·5–5cm long, ovate, coarsely toothed with 3–5 teeth per cm, woolly beneath when young. **Flowers** The inflorescence is a raceme, erect and woolly, with 3–8 flowers; the styles are free. **Fruit** Blue-black. **Distribution** A plant of open woodland, mountains and rocky areas, usually growing on limestone. Al Au Be Bl Bu Co Cr Cz Fr Fu Ge Gr Hu It Pl Po Ru Sa Sd Si Sp Tu Yu.

Amelanchier spicata (Lam.) C. Koch
Similar to *A. ovalis*, being distinguished by the finely toothed leaves, fused styles and hairy apex of the ovary. **Distribution** A N. American species, it is frequently grown as an ornamental in N. Europe where it sometimes becomes naturalized. Fi Fr Fu Ge No Sw.

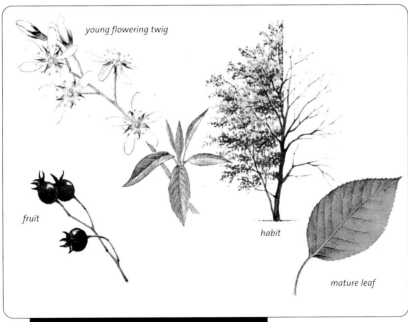

young flowering twig

fruit

habit

mature leaf

Amelanchier grandiflora Rehder

A small tree or shrub up to 9m high. **Branches** The young twigs are hairy. **Leaves** 3–7cm long, elliptical, finely toothed with 6–12 teeth per centimetre, purplish and woolly when young, becoming green and glabrous at maturity. **Flowers** The racemes are many-flowered, usually drooping and somewhat hairy. The petals are 1·5–1·8cm long, narrow; the pedicels are 2–2·2cm long. **Fruit** Dark purple. **Distribution** A species of garden origin, frequently cultivated as an ornamental and occasionally naturalized in W. Europe. Be Br Fr Ge Ho

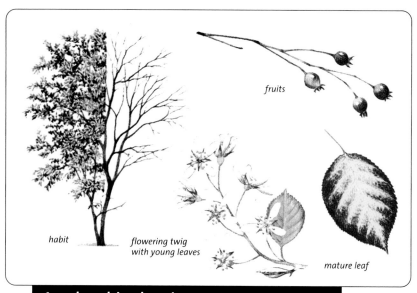

fruits

habit

*flowering twig
with young leaves*

mature leaf

Amelanchier laevis Weig. Allegheny Serviceberry

A small tree sometimes reaching 20m high, many-stemmed or with a single bole. **Branches** The young twigs are nearly glabrous. **Leaves** Up to 8cm long, ovate, pointed at the apex, finely toothed, pinkish-purple and glabrous when young, becoming green. **Flowers** The racemes are many-flowered, drooping, glabrous. The petals are 1–1·8cm long, narrowly oblong; the pedicels are 3–8cm long. **Fruit** 6mm long, more or less glabrous, purple-black when ripe. **Distribution and taxonomic notes** Thought to be a native of E. N. America, it is commonly grown in gardens for its rich red and gold autumn foliage. *A. laevis* has frequently been confused with *A. canadensis*.

Amelanchier canadensis (L.) Medicus
Very similar to *A. spicata* but with leaves more or less oblong and the apex of the ovary glabrous. **Distribution** A native of E. United States, sometimes grown in gardens.

flowering twig

fruit

habit

Cotoneaster frigidus Wall. Himalayan Tree Cotoneaster

A short to medium-sized tree up to 20m. The trunk is usually short or sometimes there are many stems spreading outwards. **Branches** Arching, forming a broadly domed crown. **Bark** Smooth when young, pale greyish-brown. **Leaves** 6–12 x 4–6cm, semi-evergreen, elliptical to obovate, with a wedge-shaped base, the upper surface dark green, the lower surface densely white-hairy. **Flowers** Inflorescence is a dense cluster of white flowers up to 5cm in diameter; the stamens number 20; the styles 2–5. **Fruit** *c.* 5mm long, rounded with bright red flesh. **Distribution and taxonomic notes** A species of Himalayan origin widely planted in large gardens of NW. Europe. *Cotoneaster frigidus* is perhaps less common than its many shrubby relatives. It readily forms hybrids in cultivation with species such as the crinkly leaved *C. salicifolius* Franchet.

flowering twig

habit

mature fruit

Mespilus germanica L. Medlar

A small tree up to 6m, or a spreading, rather tangled shrub. **Bark** Greyish-brown, becoming fissured between oblong plates. **Branches** The young shoots are covered with dense white hairs. **Leaves** 5–15cm long, broadly lanceolate to obovate, entire or minutely toothed, crinkled with distinct sunken veins, dull, yellowish-green and more or less glabrous on the upper surface, paler with dense white hairs underneath. **Flowers** Solitary, 3–6cm in diameter; the sepals are 1–1·6cm long, longer than the petals and triangular-pointed; the petals are white; the stamens number 30–40 with red anthers. **Fruit** 2–3cm long, having 5 carpels with strong walls, brown, somewhat globose with a depressed apex. **Distribution** A woodland species of SE. Europe which has become widely naturalized in C. and W. Europe to SE. England. It is frequently cultivated for the fruit which when soft and over-mature becomes edible. Au Be Br Bu Cz Fr Fu Ge Gr Ho It Ru Sa Sd Si Sp Yu.

Crataegus L. Hawthorns

A widespread group of some 400 northern hemisphere species. Nearly all species can assume the shrubby habit, but several European natives are either true trees or can grow into a tree form. True tree species are widely used in horticulture.

habit

flowering shoot

fruit

Crataegus crus-galli L. Cockspur Thorn

A small spreading tree up to 10m high with a low-domed, rather flattened crown and a short bole. **Bark** Grey or brown, that of young trees smooth, in mature trees finely fissured. **Branches** The twigs are glabrous, purple-brown and carry numerous spines, 7–10cm long. **Leaves** 5–8 x 2–3cm, 3 times as long as broad, widest above the middle, rounded at the tip, the margins sharply toothed, somewhat shiny dark green, turning orange in autumn, glabrous on both surfaces. **Flowers** The inflorescence is a loose cluster of few white flowers, each up to 1·5cm in diameter. **Flowering period** May. **Fruiting** Late October, the fruits persisting on the twigs for some time. **Distribution and taxonomic notes** A species native to NE. America, frequently planted as a street tree or ornamental, particularly for its unique orange autumn foliage. Two hybrids with other American species, *C.* x *lavallei* Hérincq, the Hybrid Cockspur Thorn, with downy shoots and inflorescences and narrower leaves; and *C.* x *prunifolia* (Poir.) Pers., the Broad-leaved Cockspur Thorn, with glabrous, dark purple-brown twigs, shorter spines (1·5–2cm), villous inflorescences and broad leaves, are similarly cultivated for ornament.

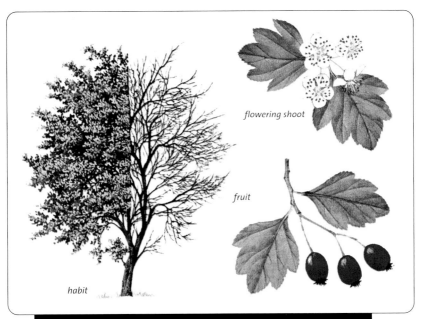

flowering shoot

fruit

habit

Crataegus laevigata (Poiret) DC. Midland Hawthorn

A large shrub and more rarely a tree up to 10m high. **Bark** Divided into rectangular plates, with a grey surface layer cracking to reveal brown below. The occasional axillary spines are up to 1·1cm long. **Leaves** 1·5–6cm long, about three-quarters as broad as long, with 3–5 shallow lobes or more or less entire, the sinuses reaching halfway to the midrib, the lobes somewhat rounded with distinct teeth down to the base, dark shining green, somewhat paler below; petiole is 0·6–2cm long. **Flowers** The inflorescences are few, lax corymbs with up to 9 flowers but often less; the flowers are 1·5–2·4cm in diameter, usually white; there are 2–3 styles. **Fruit** 0·6–1·3cm long, more or less globose, deep red. **Flowering period** May–June. **Fruiting** August–October. **Distribution and taxonomic notes** A species most often found in shady places on moist clay soils, usually in woodlands and particularly oakwoods, although it can also occur on dry limestone slopes. It is much less common and grows in shadier places than *C. monogyna* with which it often forms hybrids. It also produces hybrids with *C. calycina* and its identity is therefore frequently confused. A widespread native of C. Europe but not found in extreme conditions. Au Be Br Cz De Fr Fu Ho Hu Po Ru Sd Sw.

flowering shoot

fruit

habit

Crataegus monogyna Jacq.
Common Hawthorn or Quickthorn

A small tree or shrub up to 18m tall. The bole can be simple or much branched from the base, spreading out into a rather variable crown. **Bark** Usually cracked or fissured into a regular pattern, revealing an orange or pinkish layer beneath the silvery-grey surface layer. Axillary spines are common, up to 1·5cm long, some developing into short lateral branches terminating in spines. **Leaves** 1·5–4·5cm long and up to one and a half times as long as broad, ovate, with 3–5 (rarely 9) lobes, the sinuses usually reaching more than halfway to the midrib, the lobes somewhat pointed with more or less entire margins or a few apical teeth, somewhat leathery, dark shining green above, dull and paler below, with tufts of white hairs in the axils of the veins; the petiole is 1–2cm long, dark pink. **Flowers** The inflorescence is a dense to lax corymb of 9–18 flowers, white to pink, 0·8–1·5cm in diameter, usually in groups of 3; there is 1 style. **Fruit** Globose to ovate, bright red to maroon, 0·7–1·4cm long. **Flowering period** March–June. **Fruiting** May–September. **Distribution and taxonomic notes** A very common native growing in hedgerows, scrub, thickets or woodlands in a variety of habitats but particularly on calcareous soils. It is found throughout Europe and invariably forms hybrids when growing with other species, particularly *C. nigra* and *C. pentagyna*. It is particularly difficult to identify when it forms hybrids with shrubby forms of the Balkan endemics *C. heldreichii* Boiss. and *C. orientalis*. It is commonly planted as a park and street tree. All except Ic.

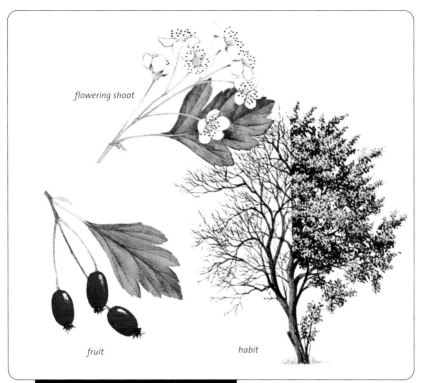

flowering shoot

fruit

habit

Crataegus calycina Peterm.

A shrub or small tree up to 11m with occasional axillary spines 4–11cm long, and rarely with short lateral branches terminating in spines. **Bark** Grey with a brown-red or purple under layer. **Leaves** 2·5–6·5cm long, about as long as broad, oval, with 3–7 lobes; the lobes are acute, the sinuses extending about one-third of the way to the midrib, the basal lobe often cut and finely toothed more or less to the base, bicoloured, usually somewhat villous on the veins below, in the axils and on the petiole; the petiole is about half the length of the blade. **Flowers** The inflorescence is a lax, raceme-like, villous umbel of 4–9 flowers, white, 1·2–2cm in diameter; there are 5 sepals and petals, about 20 red anthers and 1 style. The fruit is large, dark red, 0·9–1·5cm long, ellipsoid. **Flowering period** May–June. **Fruiting** June–September. **Distribution** A shade-tolerant species usually growing in deciduous woods but sometimes also in pine forests. It is more tolerant of extreme continental climates than *C. monogyna* which it replaces in N. and E. Europe. Al Au Be Bu Cz De Fr Fu Ge Gr Hu No Po Ru Sd Sw Tu Yu.

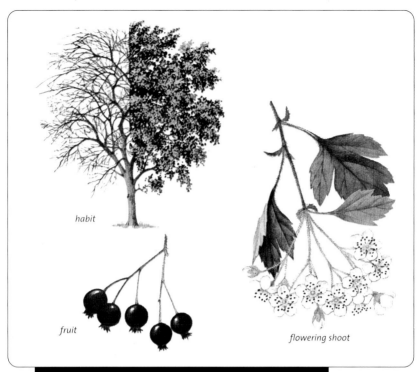

habit

fruit

flowering shoot

Crataegus pentagyna Waldst. & Kit. ex Willd.

A small tree or shrub up to 8m high with graceful, arching upper branches. **Bark** Pale brown on the outside and yellow-brown below. There are occasional stout axillary spines *c.* 9mm long. **Leaves** 2–5cm long and the same wide, broadly or narrowly ovate, laciniate, with 3–7 lobes, the lowest lobes sometimes widely spaced with acute open sinuses, leathery, olive-green above, paler below; the petiole is half to three-quarters the length of the blade. **Flowers** The inflorescence is a lax many-flowered cluster; the flowers are white; there are 5 sepals and petals, about 20 anthers and 3–5 styles. **Fruit** Globose or occasionally ovate, dull black or dark red-black, 0·7–1 x 0·6–1·1cm. **Flowering period** Late May–June. **Distribution** A species of open places, in scrub or forest mainly in E. Europe and the Balkan Peninsula. Bu Fu Hu Ru Tu Yu.

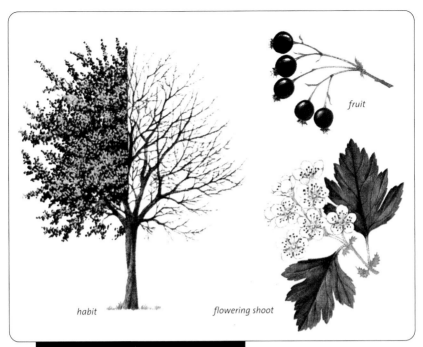

habit

flowering shoot

fruit

Crataegus nigra Waldst. & Kit.

A small tree up to 6m high with occasional axillary spines 0·7–1cm long. **Bark** Ridged and purple-red. **Leaves** 2·5–10cm long x 2–8cm wide, usually slightly longer than broad, ovate to lanceolate, with 5–11 lobes; the lobes are generally shallow, although the lowermost is frequently cut to the midrib, toothed, bicoloured, tomentose; the petiole is one-quarter to one-third as long as the blade. **Flowers** The inflorescence is a somewhat lax cluster of 10–20 flowers, 1·2–1·7cm in diameter, white but often turning pink before falling; there are 5 sepals and petals, *c*. 20 anthers and 4–5 styles. **Fruit** Globose or occasionally ovoid, 0·8–1·3 x 0·9–1·1cm, black with green flesh. **Flowering period** Late April–early May. **Fruiting** May–June. **Distribution** One of the rarer hawthorns, *C. nigra* is a species from the islands and banks of the river Danube and its tributaries, occurring in marshy open woodlands. Hu Ru Yu.

flowering shoot

habit

fruit

Crataegus orientalis Pallas ex Bieb. Oriental Thorn

A shrub or small tree up to 5m with strong lateral branches terminating in spines up to 1cm long. **Bark** Grey-brown, cracking to reveal a reddish-brown under layer. **Branches** The young twigs are hairy. **Leaves** 1·5–4cm long, ovate to triangular, usually slightly longer than broad, with 3–7 lobes, deeply divided with acute sinuses, sometimes slightly fan-shaped, the lobes narrow, dull green, tomentose on both surfaces; the petiole is short, up to 5mm long. **Flowers** The inflorescence is a compact corymb with up to 16 flowers, 1·5–2cm in diameter, white; the sepals have a characteristic hooked tip; there are sometimes 3, usually 4–5 diverging styles. **Fruit** Flattened-globose, brick-red to yellow-orange, 1·5–2 x 0·6–1·2cm, usually broader than long. **Flowering period** June. **Fruiting** August–September. **Distribution and taxonomic notes** A pioneer species from a variety of soils in scrub or degraded forest margins, especially towards mountain tops between 580 and 2000m. A Balkan species, frequently forming hybrids with less well-known Crimean shrubby endemics and other European species, particularly *C. monogyna* and *C. pentagyna*. Al Bu Fu Gr Yu.

flowering shoot

fruit

habit

Crataegus azarolus L. Azarole

A shrub or small tree up to 8m high with stout axillary spines up to 1cm long. **Branches** Tomentose when young, later becoming glabrous. **Leaves** Up to 5cm long, ovate to triangular, usually narrower than long, laciniate, with 3–5 lobes; the lobes are forward-projecting, entire with rounded apices or dentate with a few large teeth; the leaf-base is cuneate and often decurrent on the short petiole which is *c.* 3–8mm long. **Flowers** The inflorescence is a compact corymb with 3–18 flowers, 1·2–1·8cm in diameter; there are 2–3 styles. **Fruit** Globose, slightly flattened at the base and conspicuously angled longitudinally. **Flowering period** March–April. **Fruiting** June–September. **Distribution** A species of humid maquis and sometimes found in oak scrub on limestone. It is native to the E. Mediterranean region and SW. Asia, but as it has been cultivated in France and Italy since Roman times the natural European distribution is somewhat confused. Br Cr Fr It Si Sp Yu.

Prunus L. Cherries and Plums

Deciduous or evergreen trees or shrubs. **Leaves** Alternate, simple with rounded or sharp teeth, petiolate; stipules free, narrow, more or less papery, usually falling early. **Flowers** Solitary or in clusters, corymbs or racemes of up to 100 flowers, pink or white; the 5 petals are joined with the lower part of the sepals to form a tube. **Fruit** Usually has an outer fleshy layer and a single seed contained in the inner stony layer. **Distribution** A temperate genus of *c.* 200 species, of which many are cultivated for fruit and ornament. Natural hybrids are sometimes formed where the parent species grow together. Many artificial hybrids and cultivated varieties have been produced. Some species have been cultivated for so long that their wild origins are not definitely known.

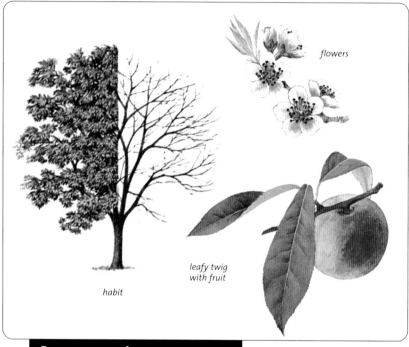

flowers

*leafy twig
with fruit*

habit

Prunus persica (L.) Batsch **Peach**

A rounded, deciduous, bushy tree up to 6m high, but often trained against a wall or as an espalier in orchards. **Bark** Grey-brown, finely fissured. **Branches** Straight; the twigs are smooth, reddish, angular in cross-section. **Leaves** 5–15 x 2–4cm, narrow, oblong-lanceolate to elliptical, long-pointed with small teeth along the margin, almost smooth; the petiole is *c.* 1·5cm long, glandular. **Flowers** Short-stalked, solitary or sometimes in pairs, appearing before the leaves fully develop; the flower tube is about as long as wide; the petals are 1–2cm long, usually deep pink, sometimes pale pink or white. **Fruit** 4–8cm long, globose, covered with a velvety down or rarely smooth, yellow or pale green flushed with red; the fleshy layer is succulent and sweet; the stone deeply grooved. **Flowering period** March–May. **Distribution** The peach or nectarine of commerce, it has been cultivated for so long for its fruit that its natural origins are obscure. It is probably a native of China. It is grown as a field crop or in gardens and is occasionally naturalized in the south. Al Au Bu Co Cr Cz Fr Fu Ge Gr Hu It Pl Sa Sd Si Tu Yu.

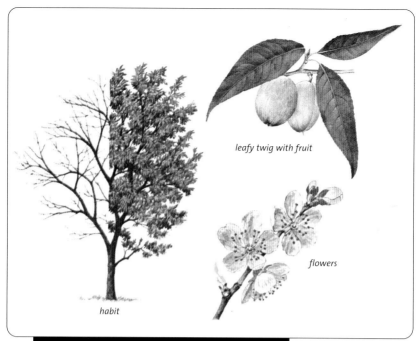

leafy twig with fruit

flowers

habit

Prunus dulcis (Miller) D.A. Webb **Almond**

A small deciduous tree up to 8m, upright-branching when young but becoming broad and bushy. **Bark** Blackish and deeply cracked into small rectangles. **Branches** Spiny in wild trees, straight and without spines in cultivated trees; the twigs are usually smooth. **Leaves** 4–13 x 1·2–4cm, oblong-lanceolate, long-pointed, the margins with small rounded teeth, smooth; the petiole is *c.* 2cm long, glandular. **Flowers** Very short-stalked, mostly produced in pairs before the leaves appear; the flower tube is broadly bell-shaped; the petals are 1·5–2·5cm long, bright pink or rarely white, fading to almost white. **Fruit** 3·5–6cm long, oblong-ovoid, slightly flattened and covered with a velvety down, grey-green; the fleshy layer is rather leathery; the stone has a ridge around the margin, and fine pits. **Flowering period** February–April. **Distribution** The Almond is a tree cultivated for its seeds and ornamental flowers. It is probably native to C. and SW. Asia and perhaps N. Africa. Al Au Bu Co Cr Cz Fr Fu Ge Gr Hd It Pl Ru Sa Sd Si Tu Yu.

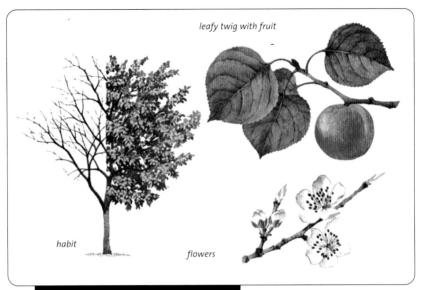

leafy twig with fruit

habit

flowers

Prunus armeniaca L. Apricot

A deciduous shrub or a small, round-headed tree 3–10m high. **Bark** Greyish-brown and finely fissured. **Branches** Tortuous; the twigs are smooth and reddish. **Leaves** 5–10 x 5–9cm, broad, ovate to almost circular, abruptly pointed, the margin with small sharp teeth, squarish or almost heart-shaped at the base; the petiole is 2–4cm long. **Flowers** Very short-stalked, solitary or in pairs, appearing before the leaves; the flower tube is broadly bell-shaped, hairy; the petals are 1–1·5cm long, white or pale pink. **Fruit** 4–8cm long, almost globose, downy, reddish-orange or yellow, the fleshy layer acid becoming sweet, the stone lens-shaped and smooth with 3 narrow ridges along one edge. **Flowering period** March–April. **Distribution** Widely cultivated as a field crop in S. Europe for its fruit, becoming naturalized in a few localities. It is native to C. Asia and China. Al Au Bu Co Cr Cz Fr Fu Ge Gr Hu It Pl Ru Sa Sd Si Sp Tu Yu.

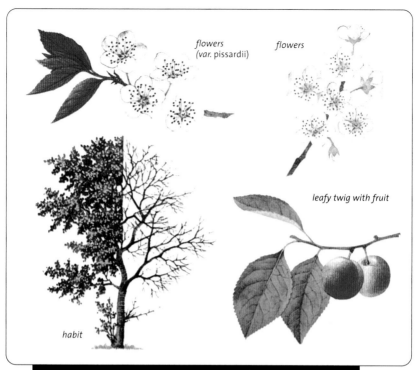

*flowers
(var. pissardii)*

flowers

leafy twig with fruit

habit

Prunus cerasifera Ehrh. Cherry Plum or Myrobalan

A deciduous shrub or round-headed tree up to 8m high. **Bark** Dark brown with rows of lenticels, becoming finely fissured. **Branches** Numerous, fine, sometimes spiny. The twigs are green, smooth and glossy. **Leaves** 4–7 x 2–3·5cm, oblong-obovate, tapering at the base, the margins with regular rounded teeth, smooth and glossy above, the veins downy beneath; the petiole is *c.* 1cm long, grooved, pinkish. **Flowers** Mostly solitary, appearing with or slightly before the leaves; the pedicel is 0·5–1·5cm long, smooth; the flower tube is broadly bell-shaped; the petals are 0·8–1cm long, usually white. **Fruit** 2–3·5cm long, globose, smooth, red or yellow, the fleshy layer becoming sweet; the stone is almost globose, with a thickened margin, smooth. **Flowering period** March. **Distribution and taxonomic notes** The Cherry Plum is commonly cultivated for its fruit, which is used for cooking. *P. cerasifera* var. *pissardii* (Carrière) L.H. Bailey is very commonly planted in gardens and streets of suburban areas for its dark reddish leaves and pale or rosy-pink flowers. A native of the Balkan Peninsula and the Crimea but much planted elsewhere. Al Au Br Bu De Fr Fu Ge Gr Hu It Ru Tu Yu.

Prunus brigantina Vill. in L.

Rather smaller than *P. cerasifera*, with spreading branches and larger, sharper teeth on the leaf margins. **Flowers** In clusters of 2–5, appearing before the leaves; the petals are white. **Fruit** *c.* 2·5cm long, almost globose, smooth, yellow. **Distribution** Native to the SW. Alps on dry slopes up to 1800m. Fr It.

flowers

leafy twig with fruit

habit

Prunus spinosa L. Sloe or Blackthorn

A thickly branched, deciduous shrub or small tree up to 6m, spreading by suckers. **Bark** Blackish-brown. **Branches** Numerous, spreading widely; the twigs are much branched, spiny, usually downy. **Leaves** 2–4·5cm long, obovate to ovate, pointed at the tip, the margins with rounded or pointed teeth, tapering at the base, dull green and smooth above, usually downy underneath on the veins; the petiole is *c*. 1cm long. **Flowers** Mostly solitary, appearing before the leaves; the pedicel is *c*. 5mm long, smooth; the flower tube is broadly bell-shaped; the petals are 5–8mm long, white. **Fruit** 1–1·5cm long, globose or slightly elongated, bluish-black with a blue-grey bloom on the surface; the fleshy layer is very acid and astringent; the stone smooth or slightly rough. **Flowering period** March–April. **Distribution and taxonomic notes** A native of much of Europe except the extreme N. and NE. It is commonly found in hedges and thickets. The fruit is sometimes used for making jams and wines. It occasionally hybridizes with *P. domestica* subsp. *institia*. All except Cr Ic.

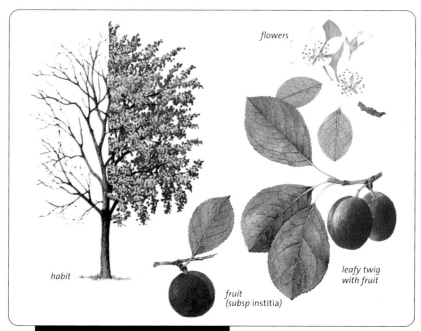

flowers

*leafy twig
with fruit*

habit

*fruit
(subsp* institia*)*

Prunus domestica L. Plum

A deciduous, suckering shrub or tree up to 10m high. **Bark** Dull brown. **Branches** Straight; the twigs are spiny in wild plants but usually without spines in cultivated plants, dull, usually downy. **Leaves** 3–8 x 1·5–5cm, elliptical to obovate, the apex rather blunt to pointed, the margins with regular rounded teeth, smooth and dull green above, downy to almost smooth beneath; the petiole is *c.* 1·5cm long, glandular and downy. **Flowers** Usually occurring in clusters of 2–3, appearing with the leaves; the pedicel is 0·5–2cm long, the flower tube broadly bell-shaped; the petals are 0·7–1·2cm long, white. **Fruit** 2–7·5cm long, globose to oblong, usually pendent, purple, red, yellow or green; the fleshy layer is sweet or acid but not astringent; the stone is rough, rather flattened, slightly pitted. **Flowering period** March–May. **Distribution and taxonomic notes** Widely cultivated for its fruit as a field crop in all except the extreme N. and NE. of Europe. It is often naturalized in hedgerows. The Bullace, *P. domestica* subsp. *institia* (L.) C.K. Schneider, usually has spiny branches and dense down on the young twigs and pedicels, and globose fruits up to 5cm long. The Mirabelle group of plums, damsons and greengages all probably belong with this subspecies. All except Ic.

Prunus cocomilia Ten.
A tree or shrub rather smaller than *P. domestica*. **Leaves** 2·5–4 x 1·2–2·5cm long. **Flowers** Borne on pedicels 2–4mm long with white petals *c.* 6mm long. **Fruit** 1·2–4cm long, oblong, yellow suffused with purplish-red. **Distribution** A native of the mountainous parts of S. Italy, Sicily and the S. Balkan Peninsula. Al Gr It Si Yu.

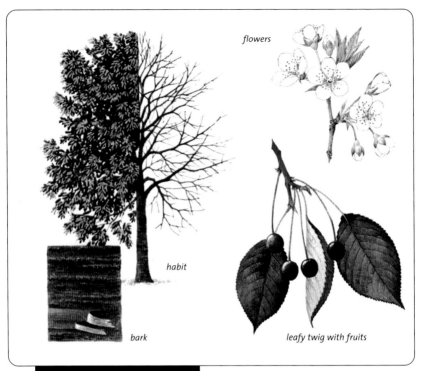

flowers

habit

bark

leafy twig with fruits

Prunus avium L. Gean

A deciduous broad-crowned tree up to 30m high with a well-developed bole. **Bark** Reddish-brown, shiny with horizontal rows of lenticels, peeling in papery strips or later becoming fissured. **Branches** Widely spreading; the young twigs are smooth, reddish above. **Leaves** 8–15 x 4–7cm, ovate to oblong-obovate with a long tapering point, the margin with deep irregular forward-projecting teeth, smooth and dull above, persistently downy on the veins beneath; the petiole is 2–5cm long with 2 conspicuous reddish glands near the blade. **Flowers** Usually occurring in clusters of 2–6, appearing just before the leaves; the pedicel is 2–5cm long; the flower tube is urn-shaped, constricted at the mouth; the petals are 0·9–1·5cm long, white. **Fruit** 0·9–2cm long, globose with a depression at the apex, dark purple-red, rarely yellow or black; the fleshy layer is sweet or bitter; the stone is globose, smooth. **Flowering period** April–May. **Distribution and taxonomic notes** Much of Europe except the extreme N. and E. and rather rare in the Mediterranean region. The Gean is the parental species of the sweet cherries which are widely cultivated for their fruit and often naturalized in Europe. All except Cr Fi Ic.

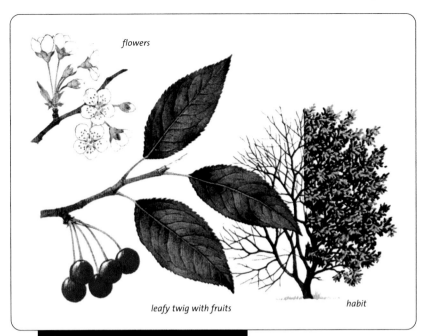

flowers

leafy twig with fruits

habit

Prunus cerasus L. Sour Cherry

Usually a deciduous shrub, but sometimes a small rounded tree up to 8m tall with an ill-defined trunk, often suckering. **Bark** Reddish-brown. **Branches** Spreading, rather untidy; twigs smooth. **Leaves** 3–8 x 1·7–5cm long, ovate to elliptical, abruptly pointed at the tip, the base broad and tapering, the margins with rounded, rather small teeth, smooth and glossy above, sometimes slightly downy beneath when young; the petiole is 1–3cm long with or without glands near the blade. **Flowers** Occurring in clusters of 2–6, appearing just before the leaves; the pedicel is 2–3·5cm long; the flower tube is broadly bell-shap ed; the petals are 0·8–1·5cm long, white. **Fruit** *c.* 1·8cm long, almost globose but slightly depressed above, bright red to blackish; the fleshy layer is soft and acid; the stone almost globose, smooth. **Flowering period** April-May. **Distribution** A species cultivated for its fruit, the sour or Morello cherry, used mainly for preserving rather than as a dessert fruit. Double-flowered cultivars are planted for ornament. Native to SW. Asia but widely naturalized in Europe. Al Au Br Bu Cz De Fi Fr Fu Ge Gr Ho Hu Ir It No Pl Po Ru Sd Sp Sw Yu.

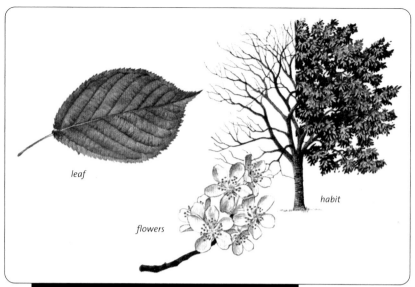

leaf

flowers

habit

Prunus sargentii Rehder Sargent's Cherry

A deciduous tree up to 25m high in the wild but usually smaller in cultivation. **Bark** Purplish-brown, rather glossy, with horizontal rows of lenticels. **Branches** Ascending, spreading at a wide angle; the twigs are slender, dark red, smooth. **Leaves** 9–15 x 4–8cm long, oblong-elliptic to oblong-obovate with a long tapering point, the margins with sharply pointed teeth, smooth; the petiole is 2–4cm long, grooved, deep red, usually with 2 reddish glands near the blade. **Flowers** Usually occurring in clusters of 2–4, appearing slightly before the leaves; the pedicel is 1–2cm long, the flower tube is rather narrowly bell-shaped; the petals are 1·5–2cm long, rosy-pink. **Fruit** 0·7–1·1cm long, ovoid, blackish-crimson, rarely appearing in cultivation. **Flowering period** April. **Distribution and taxonomic notes** Sargent's Cherry is a native of N. Japan, where it never descends below 750m, and the Sakhalin Islands, where it grows at much lower altitudes. The species is widely cultivated for ornament in gardens, parks or as a street tree in various European countries, and is often grafted on to a stock of *P. avium* to improve its performance. Hybrids with *P. subhirtella* and other cherries are occasionally grown.

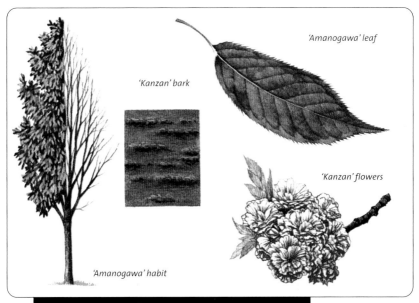

'Amanogawa' leaf

'Kanzan' bark

'Kanzan' flowers

'Amanogawa' habit

Prunus serrulata Lindley Japanese Cherry

A deciduous tree up to 15m though usually much smaller. **Bark** Purplish-brown with horizontal rows of lenticels. **Branches** Usually ascending, spreading widely; the twigs are smooth. **Leaves** 8–20 x 4–9cm, broadly ovate to oblong-obovate with a tapering tip; the margins with sharp, long-pointed spreading teeth; the petiole is 2–4cm long, smooth except for 1–4 reddish glands near the blade. **Flowers** Usually occurring in clusters of 2–4, appearing just before the leaves; the pedicel is 1·5–8cm long; the flower tube is narrowly bell-shaped; the petals are 1·5–4cm long, notched, white or pink. **Fruit** *c.* 7mm long, almost globose, purplish-crimson, rarely appearing in cultivation. **Flowering period** April–May. **Distribution** The Japanese Cherries have long been cultivated in the parks, streets and gardens of Europe for their showy flowers. Their origins are somewhat obscure but they probably originated in C. China and became early introductions to Japan, giving rise to the 'Sato Zakura' or domestic cherries.

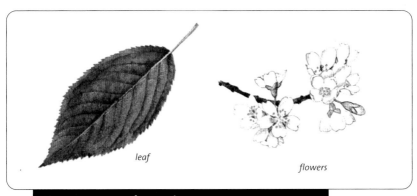

leaf

flowers

Prunus x *yedoensis* Matsum Yoshino Cherry

Rather similar to *P. serrulata*. **Branches** Twigs downy at first, becoming smooth. **Leaves** Glossy above. **Flowers** Usually occurring in clusters of 5–6 with pedicels *c.* 2cm long; petals 1·2–1·8cm long, deeply notched, pale pink. **Fruit** *c.* 1cm long, red and yellow, smooth. **Flowering period** March–April. **Distribution and taxonomic notes** A Japanese hybrid probably between *P. subhirtella* and *P. speciosa* (Koidz.) Ingram (the Oshima Cherry, which is also sometimes cultivated in European parks and gardens), it is commonly planted as an ornamental street tree in suburban areas.

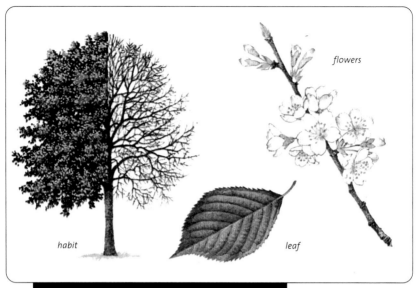

flowers

habit

leaf

Prunus subhirtella Miq. Spring Cherry

A deciduous tree up to 20m high in the wild but usually much smaller in cultivation, with a rather dense crown. **Bark** Greyish-brown. **Branches** Slender; the twigs are crimson, downy and dense. **Leaves** *c*. 6 x 2·5cm, ovate to oblong-lanceolate, long-pointed, the margins with sharp and irregular teeth, the veins downy beneath; the petiole is 0·7–1·2cm long, slightly downy, crimson. **Flowers** Occurring in clusters of 2–5, sometimes on a short stalk, appearing before the leaves; the pedicel is 0·7–1·3cm long; the flower tube is urn-shaped with a rather constricted mouth; the petals are 0·8–1·2cm long, notched, pinkish-white to rose-pink. **Fruit** 7–9mm, globose to ellipsoid, purplish-black. **Flowering period** March–April. **Distribution and taxonomic notes** A Japanese species widely cultivated for ornament in gardens and sometimes as a street tree. Weeping and double-flowered cultivars are often grafted on to *P. avium*. *P. subhirtella* cv. 'Autumnalis', the Autumn Cherry, is the most widespread cultivar, differing principally in producing flowers almost continuously from October to April.

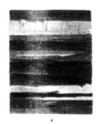

bark (after peeling)

Prunus serrula Franchet Tibetan Cherry

Like *P. subhirtella*. **Bark** Blackish-purple, peeling into strips to reveal a glossy mahogany colour. **Branches** Large, wide-spreading. **Leaves** 4–12 x 1-3cm, lanceolate with a long tapering point; petioles 6–7mm long. **Flowers** Occurring at the same time as the leaves; pedicels *c*. 4cm long; white petals 0·8–1cm long. **Fruit** Bright red, 0·4–1·2cm long. **Flowering period** April–May. **Distribution** A species fairly widely cultivated in parks and gardens for its ornamental bark.

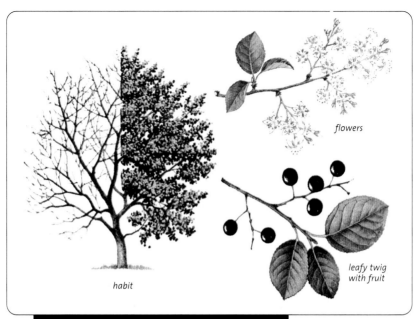

flowers

leafy twig with fruit

habit

Prunus mahaleb L. Saint Lucie Cherry

A deciduous shrub or occasionally a small tree up to 12m high. **Bark** Greyish-brown with rows of lenticels. **Branches** Loosely spreading. The young twigs are covered with short greyish glandular hairs. **Leaves** 3–7 x 2–5cm, broadly ovate to almost round, with a short point, the base rounded or almost heart-shaped, the margins with rounded teeth, smooth and glossy above, slightly downy beneath, especially on the midrib; the petiole is 1·2–1·5cm long with 2 glands near the base. **Flowers** Fragrant, occurring in rounded corymbose racemes of 3–10 flowers at the end of short leafy shoots; the pedicel is 0·8–1·5cm long; the flower tube is bell-shaped; the petals are 5–8mm long, white. **Fruit** 0·6–1cm long, egg-shaped to rather rounded, blackish; the fleshy layer is thin and bitter, the stony layer almost globose, smooth. **Flowering period** April–May. **Distribution** A species native to C. and S. Europe, occurring in open woods and thickets or on dry hillsides. Several varieties are cultivated for ornament and are naturalized in N. Europe. Al Au Be Bu Co Cz Fr Fu Ge Gr Hu It No Pl Ru Sd Si Sp Sw Yu.

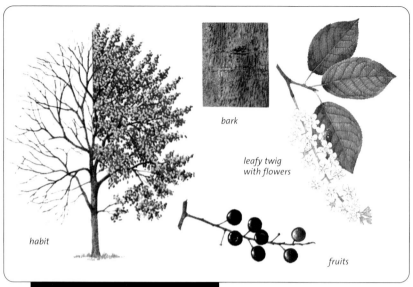

bark

leafy twig
with flowers

habit

fruits

Prunus padus L. Bird Cherry

A deciduous tree, more rarely a shrub, up to 17m high. **Bark** Smooth and dark greyish-brown with a strong rather fetid smell. **Branches** Ascending, slender. The young twigs are finely downy or almost smooth. **Leaves** 6–10 x 3·5–7cm, elliptic to obovate with a tapering apex, the base rounded to almost heart-shaped, the margins with fine sharp teeth, dull green and smooth above, paler beneath, smooth or sometimes downy; the petiole is 1·2–2cm long with 2 or more glands. **Flowers** Occurring in elongated crowded heads, each 7–15cm long with 15–35 flowers carried at the end of short leafy shoots; the pedicel is 0·8–1·6cm long; the flower tube is broadly bell-shaped; the petals are 6–9mm long, white, often irregularly toothed at the margin. **Fruit** 6–8mm long, almost globose, black and shiny; the fleshy layer is bitter, astringent; the stone is almost globose, grooved. **Flowering period** May. **Distribution** A native of much of Europe and N. Asia on most soils, but especially in limestone areas. It is planted as a garden ornamental or occasionally as a street tree. Au Be Br Bu Cz De Fi Fr Fu Ge Ho Ir It No Po Ru Sd Sp Sw Yu.

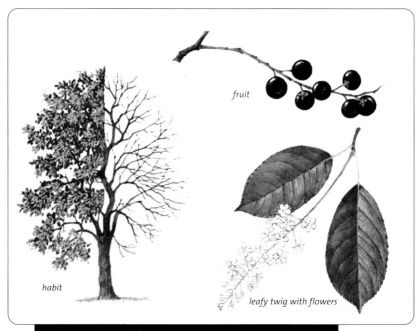

fruit

habit

leafy twig with flowers

Prunus serotina Ehrh. Rum Cherry or Black Cherry

A deciduous tree up to 30m high with a stout trunk. **Bark** Smooth, peeling in strips but later becoming fissured, greyish, bitter and aromatic. **Branches** Spreading; the twigs are slender, purplish-brown above. **Leaves** 5–14 x 2·5–4·5cm, obovate to elliptic-oblong with a tapering point, the margins with tiny forward-projecting teeth, dark green and shining above, paler and slightly downy beneath; the petiole is 0·7–2·5cm long with glands near the leaf-blade. **Flowers** The inflorescence is an elongated head of *c.* 30 flowers, up to 15cm long; the pedicel is 0·3–1·2cm long; the flower tube is broadly cup-shaped; the petals are 3–5mm long, creamy-white. with small teeth at the margins. **Fruit** 0·7–1cm long, calyx persisting at base, globose but slightly flattened, purplish-black, the fleshy layer bitter; the stone is almost globose, smooth. **Flowering period** May–June. **Distribution** A native of N. America, planted for timber in C. Europe and ornament elsewhere, occasionally becoming naturalized. Au Br Cz De Fr Fu Ge Ho Hu Po Ru Sw Yu.

Prunus virginiana L. Choke Cherry

Like *P. serotina* but only up to 5m tall, more commonly occurring as a shrub than a tree; the bark is not aromatic; the leaves are dull green, the margins with sharply pointed spreading teeth; the calyx falling from the ripening dark red fruit. **Flowering period** May. **Distribution** A native of E. to C. N. America, sometimes planted and naturalized in C. and W. Europe. Cz Fr Fu.

ripening fruit

habit

flowering shoot

Prunus lusitanica L. Portugal Laurel

An evergreen shrub or a tree 3–8m (or rarely up to 20m) high. **Bark** Black and smooth or somewhat scaly. **Branches** Spread widely. The twigs are often flushed dark red, smooth. **Leaves** 8–13 x 2·5–7cm, ovate to oblong-lanceolate with a tapering point, the base rounded, the margin with regular, shallow, pointed or rounded teeth, smooth and rather leathery, the upper surface very dark green and glossy, the underside yellowish-green; the petiole is c. 2cm long, flushed dark red, without glands. **Flowers** The inflorescence is an elongated head, 15–28cm long, with up to 100 fragrant flowers, exceeding the leaf in the axil of which it grows; the pedicel is 0·5–1cm long; the flower tube is bell-shaped; the petals are 4–7mm long, creamy-white. **Fruit** 0·8–1·3cm long, ovoid or cone-shaped to almost globose, slightly pointed, purplish-black, smooth; the stone is almost globose with a faintly keeled margin, smooth. **Flowering period** June. **Distribution** A native of Spain, Portugal and SW. France, and much planted for ornament or as a hedge plant elsewhere in W. Europe, occasionally becoming naturalized. Fr Pl Sp.

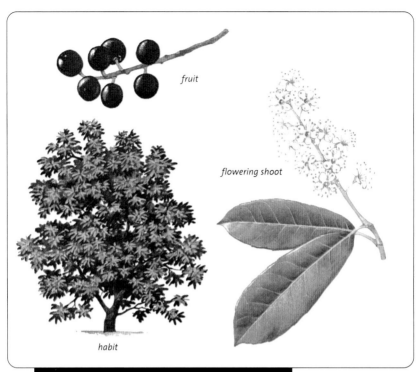

fruit

flowering shoot

habit

Prunus laurocerasus L. Cherry Laurel

An evergreen shrub or a small tree up to 8m high. **Bark** Dark grey-brown with many lenticels. **Branches** Widely spreading; the twigs are pale green, smooth. **Leaves** 10–20 x 3–6cm, oblong to lanceolate with a short tapering tip, the base rounded or tapering, the margins more or less entire or with a few minute teeth, smooth and leathery, the upper surface dark glossy green, the underside yellowish-green; the petiole is *c.* 1·2cm long with 1 or more stalkless glands beneath. **Flowers** The inflorescence is an elongated upright head 8–13cm long with *c.* 30 fragrant flowers, equalling or very slightly exceeding the leaf from the axil of which it grows; the pedicel is *c.* 6mm long; the flower tube is funnel-shaped to bell-shaped; the petals are *c.* 4mm long, creamy-white. **Fruit** 1·1–2cm long, somewhat conical to almost globose, smooth, initially turning from green to red, then becoming blackish-purple; the stone is more or less globose with a faintly keeled margin, smooth. **Flowering period** April. **Distribution** A native of the E. Balkan Peninsula, widely planted for ornament since the 16th and 17th centuries in the S. and W. parts of Europe and frequently becoming naturalized. Many different cultivated varieties have been raised, differing in habit, leaf shape and colour. Br Bu Co Fr Ir Pl Tu Yu.

Pea Family
Leguminosae

Albizia Durazz. Siris

Unarmed deciduous trees or shrubs with twice-pinnate leaves and panicles of rather narrow flower heads. The bisexual or polygamous flowers are in 5 parts, with a tubular 5-toothed calyx and funnel-shaped corolla. The numerous stamens greatly exceed the corolla in length and have the filaments fused at the base to form a tube. The fruit (legume) is long, broadly linear and flat.

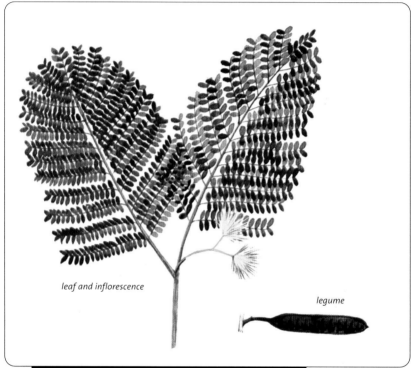

leaf and inflorescence

legume

Albizia lophantha Bentham Plume Albizia

A small tree or shrub up to 7m high. **Branches** Dense, evenly hairy. **Leaves** 16–20 pinnae, each pinna bearing 40–60 leaflets; the petiole is velvety-hairy; each leaflet is *c.* 6mm long, curved, glabrous above, silky and hairy below. **Flowers** The inflorescence is a loose cylindrical axillary spike, 3·5–7cm long, the peduncle densely hairy; the bright yellow flower is *c.* 5mm long, the calyx shortly lobed and less than half as long as the corolla. The stamens are *c.* 1·2cm long, the filaments united at the base to form a tube about as long as or slightly shorter than the corolla. **Fruit** The legume is 7·5cm long, *c.* 1cm broad or sometimes larger, flattened and containing ovate or orbicular seeds. **Distribution** A native of SW. Australia, planted for ornament in the Mediterranean area.

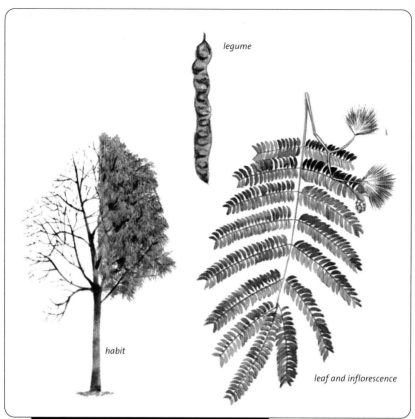

legume

habit

leaf and inflorescence

Albizia julibrissin Durazz. Pink Siris

A small tree rarely exceeding 13.5m high with a rounded or rather flattened crown. **Bark** Smooth. **Branches** Spreading, glabrous. **Leaves** 20–30cm (sometimes up to 46cm) long with 10–25 (occasionally 30) pinnae, each pinna bearing 35–50 (occasionally 80) leaflets; the rachis and rachilla are slightly hairy above, the leaflets 1–1·5cm long, narrowly ovate, curved, green above, whitish beneath, the margins and lower surface with short hairs; the petiole has a cup-shaped gland on the upper surface. **Flowers** The young panicles are hairy with about 10 spreading branches, each terminating in a 20-flowered head; the flowers are 7–9mm long, sessile, pinkish; the stamens are 3·5–4cm long and also pink. **Fruit** The legume is 8–15cm long, brown when ripe, somewhat constricted between each of the 10–15 seeds. **Flowering period** July–August. **Distribution** A woodland and riverside species in lowland Asia, frequently planted as an ornamental and shade tree in S. Europe. In N. Europe it is sometimes used as an annual garden plant.

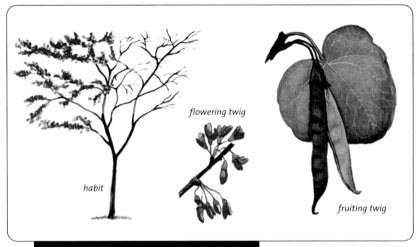

flowering twig

habit

fruiting twig

Cercis siliquastrum L. Judas Tree

A small deciduous tree or shrub up to 10m high, with a rounded or irregular crown and often more than one bole. **Branches** Ascending and spreading, the twigs and buds red-brown or crimson. **Leaves** 7–12cm long, simple, alternate, suborbicular, obtuse or notched at the tip, heart-shaped at the base, glabrous and rather glaucous when young, becoming dark or yellowish-green above, paler and glaucous beneath, digitately veined. **Flowers** Borne in clusters usually appearing before the leaves; the calyx is regularly 5-toothed, brown; the corolla is 1·5–2cm long, pink, the 3 upper petals much smaller than the lower 2. **Fruit** The legume is 6–10cm long, compressed and narrowly winged on the ventral suture, glabrous, becoming red-purple, eventually brown when mature, dehiscent. **Flowering period** May. **Distribution** Typically in dry rocky places in the Mediterranean region, frequently planted as an ornamental and may become naturalized. Al Bu Gr Fr Gr It Pl Si Sp Ru Tu Yu.

flowering twig

male flower

habit

immature fruit

Ceratonia siliqua L. Carob, Locust Tree

A small, monoecious or dioecious, evergreen tree or shrub up to 10m high with a low, dense, domed crown. **Leaves** Pinnate with no terminal leaflet, 2–5 pairs of leaflets, the rachis brown or greenish. Each leaflet is 3–5cm long. **Flowers** The inflorescence is a short axillary raceme; the calyx has 5 short teeth which fall early; corolla is absent. **Fruit** The legume is 10–20cm long, compressed, pendent, green at first, brownish-violet when ripe, indehiscent. **Distribution** A native of dry areas in the Mediterranean region, widely cultivated as a fodder crop and naturalized in many places. Al Bl Co Cr Fr It Pl Sa Si Sp Yu.

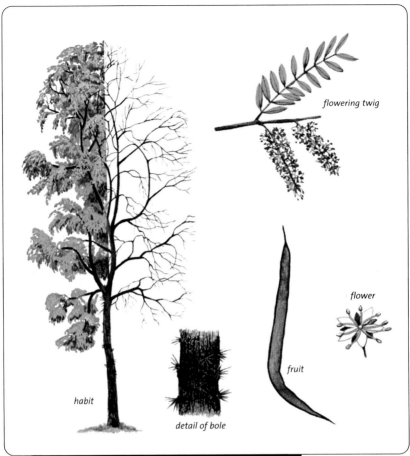

flowering twig

flower

fruit

habit

detail of bole

Gleditsia triacanthos L. Honey Locust

A tall, deciduous, armed tree up to 45m high with a spreading crown. The bole and branches have stout, simple or branched spines, those on the bole often very large and forming clusters. **Leaves** 10–20cm long, pinnate or twice-pinnate; pinnate leaves with 7–18 pairs of leaflets and twice-pinnate leaves with 8–14 pinnae. **Flowers** The inflorescence is a long axillary raceme; the flowers are fragrant, polygamous, 2·5–3mm long; the calyx has 3·5 lobes, the corolla only slightly zygomorphic with 3–5 greenish-white petals. **Fruit** The legume is 3–4·5cm long, compressed, thick-edged, sickle-shaped or spirally twisted, pale green when young, dark brown when ripe, virtually indehiscent. **Flowering period** June. **Distribution** A native of the Mississippi basin in N. America, used as an ornamental and for hedging, especially in S. and C. Europe where it occasionally becomes naturalized. Spineless cultivars are used as park and street trees. Au Bu Fr Ge It Ru Sp Yu.

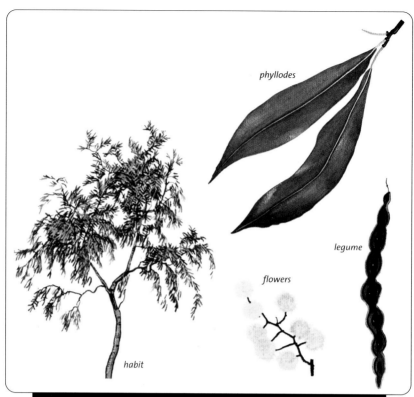

phyllodes

legume

flowers

habit

Acacia cyanophylla Lindley Golden Wreath, Willow Wattle

A dense shrub or small tree up to 10m tall with a solitary or dividing trunk frequently suckering at the base. **Bark** Smooth, initially grey, later becoming greyish-brown and fissured. **Branches** The twigs are often pendulous, somewhat flexible, finely ribbed and glabrous. The phyllodes are variable, 10–20cm (rarely 35cm) long by 0·6–3cm wide (and up to 8cm wide on suckers), linear to lanceolate, straight or sickle-shaped, often pendulous, glabrous, green to glaucous, dull to shiny, with a conspicuous midrib; a gland is usually present on the upper margin near the base. **Flowers** The inflorescences are large heads, 1–1·5cm in diameter, with 25–70 flowers per head occurring on pendulous racemes of 2–8; the flowers are bright yellow. **Fruit** The legume is 6–12 x 0·4–0·8cm, linear compressed, distinctly constricted between the seeds, glaucous when young, later brownish. **Flowering period** March–May. **Distribution** A native of W. Australia, planted widely in S. Europe for stabilizing sand dunes and for ornament. Co Fr Gr It Pl Sa Sp.

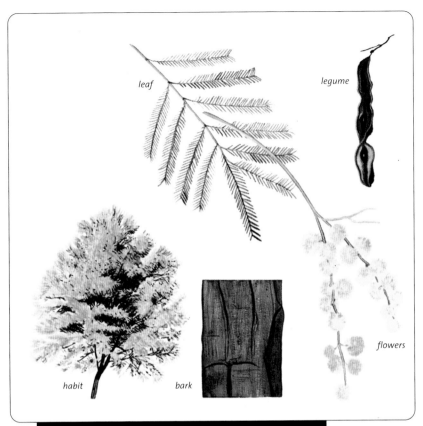

leaf

legume

flowers

habit

bark

Acacia dealbata Link Silver Wattle, Mimosa

A handsome medium-sized tree up to 30m high. **Bark** Smooth, greenish-grey. **Branches** The twigs, young shoots and foliage are all silvery-white to creamy-yellow due to a dense covering of fine, very short hairs. **Leaves** Tripinnate; the leaflets occur in 25–50 pairs, each about 5mm long; the glands are numerous and occur irregularly at the point of insertion on to the rachis. **Flowers** The large terminal and smaller axillary inflorescences are long, spreading racemes or panicles of 20–30 flower heads; the peduncles are rather short and covered with short white or yellowish hairs; the flower heads are bright yellow, 5–6mm in diameter with 30–40 flowers per head. **Fruit** The legume is 4–10 x 1–1·2cm, compressed, and not constricted between the seeds. **Distribution** A native of SE. Australia and Tasmania, planted in many warmer parts of Europe for ornament, for timber and for soil stabilization. It has become widely naturalized in the Mediterranean region. Br Fr It Pl Ru Sa Sp Yu.

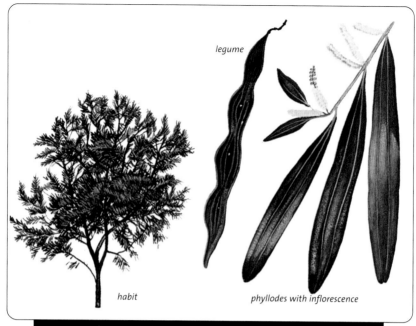

legume

habit

phyllodes with inflorescence

Acacia longifolia (Andrews) Willd. Sydney Golden Wattle

A shrub or small slender tree up to 10m tall, spreading to about 10m in open conditions, with a dense bushy crown and bright green shiny foliage. **Bark** Smooth, dull grey. **Branches** The twigs are stiff, glabrous. **Leaves** The phyllodes are 7–15 x 0.8–3cm, oblong to oblong-lanceolate, straight, striped with prominent longitudinal veins. **Flowers** The inflorescence is a large fluffy cylindrical spike up to 5cm long; the flowers are bright yellow and strong-smelling. **Fruit** The legume is 7–15 x 0.4–0.5cm, linear, terete, almost straight to curled and twisted, distinctly constricted between the seeds, brown when mature. **Seeds** The stalk of the seed is white. **Flowering period** April–May. **Distribution** A native of coastal areas of New South Wales, Australia, widely planted in SW. Europe for ornament and sand dune stabilization. Fr It Pl Sp.

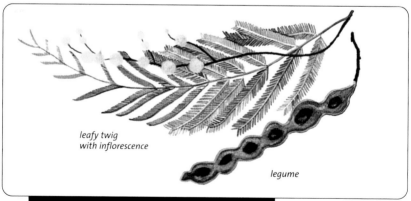

leafy twig with inflorescence

legume

Acacia mearnsii De Wild. Green Wattle

A similar species to *A. dealbata* but rarely attaining more than 15m in height. It is softly yellow, villous. **Leaves** Dark green with 8–14 pairs of pinnae; there are 25–40 pairs of leaflets; the rachis has glands between the pinnae. **Fruit** The legume is 5–7mm wide, distinctly constricted between the seeds and blackish-brown at maturity. **Distribution** Another SE. Australian and Tasmanian native planted for ornament and tan bark in the Iberian Peninsula; naturalized in some areas. Co It Pl Sp.

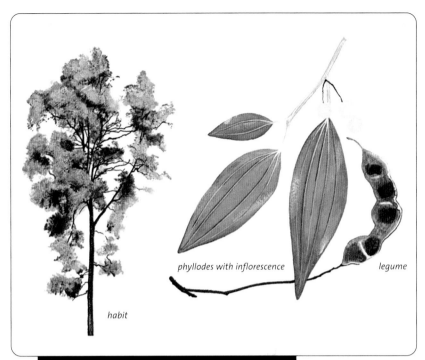

phyllodes with inflorescence

legume

habit

Acacia melanoxylon R. Br. Blackwood

A stout tree with straight erect trunk, up to 40m high although not usually attaining more than 15m. **Bark** Dark grey-brown, rough and furrowed and very persistent even on smaller branches. **Branches** Beginning well down the main trunk, usually horizontal or even pendulous; the crown is dense and rounded; the young twigs are hairy. **Leaves** The phyllodes are 6–13 x 0·7–2cm, lanceolate to obanceolate, slightly curved, bluntly pointed at the apex and tapering at the base, dull, dark green, with 3–5 veins; twice-pinnate leaves sometimes occur on young trees, the pinnae with 14–20 oblong leaflets 5–7mm long. **Flowers** The inflorescence is a short axillary raceme bearing yellow or creamy-white heads, *c.* 1cm in diameter. **Fruit** The legume is 7–12 x 0·8–1cm, compressed, contorted, reddish-brown. **Seeds** The stalk around the seed is scarlet. **Distribution** Another SE. Australian and Tasmanian native, planted for its valuable 'blackwood' veneer timber in SW. Europe, where it has become locally naturalized. Br Fr It Pl Sp.

young legume

phyllodes with inflorescence

Acacia pycnantha Bentham Golden Wattle

A small tree or shrub up to 12m tall; the bole is usually short and thin, suckering freely from the base, the crown shade-giving with the branches curving upwards. **Bark** Dark brown and smooth. **Branches** The twigs are glaucous. **Leaves** The phyllodes are 8–20 x 1–3·5cm (up to 10cm wide on suckers), initially very broad and large, later becoming sickle-shaped, bright, shining green, leathery, 1-veined. **Flowers** The inflorescence is a large raceme of 20–30 deep yellow, fluffy, highly perfumed flowering heads on thick peduncles; the heads are 0·8–1cm in diameter. **Fruit** The legume is 8–13 x 0·5–0·6cm, almost straight, compressed, dark brown and slightly constricted between the seeds. **Seeds** The stalk of the seed is short and white. **Distribution** The Golden Wattle is the floral emblem of Australia and native to temperate regions of Victoria and S. Australia. It is widely planted in S. Europe for tanning and sometimes ornament and has become locally naturalized in S. Portugal and C. and S. Italy. It Pl Sa Sp.

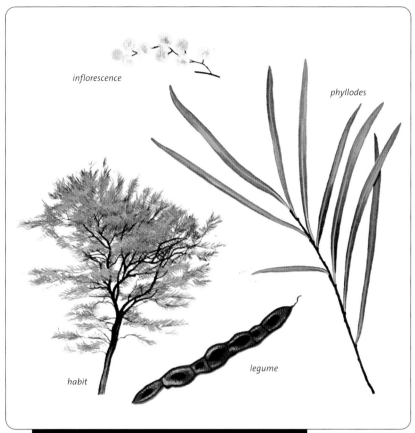

inflorescence

phyllodes

habit

legume

Acacia retinodes Schlecht. Swamp Wattle

A small glabrous tree or shrub up to 10m tall; the bole is short and the branches tend to curve upwards. **Bark** Smooth and grey, later greyish-brown. **Branches** The twigs are usually brown and not pendent. **Leaves** The phyllodes are 6–15 x 0·4–1·8cm, acute to obtuse, with a straight or curved apex, light green. **Flowers** The inflorescence consists of 5–10 heads in short, branched racemes; the heads are 4–6mm in diameter; the flowers are pale yellow. **Fruit** The legume is usually straight and with an almost straight edge, and slightly constricted between the seeds. **Seeds** The scarlet stalk encircles the seed and is bent back upon itself in a double fold. Flowering period June–July. **Distribution and taxonomic notes** A native of S. Australia, widely planted for ornament in S. Europe and locally naturalized. Br Fr It Pl Ru Sp Yu. Shrubby members of the genus are also frequently planted in Europe, i.e. *Acacia farnesiana* (L.). from the Dominican Republic, *A. karoo* Hayne from S. Africa and *A. cyclops* A. Cunn ex DC., which can sometimes be confused with the tree species (see key on p.13 for distinctions).

Laburnum Fabr. Laburnums

Deciduous, unarmed trees or shrubs, the leaves having 3 leaflets. **Flowers** The inflorescences are axillary or apparently terminal in pendulous leafless racemes. The calyx is bell-shaped, 2-lipped, the lips sometimes slightly toothed; the corolla is yellow and the stamens are monodelphous. **Fruit** A legume, slightly constricted between each of the numerous, compressed seeds.

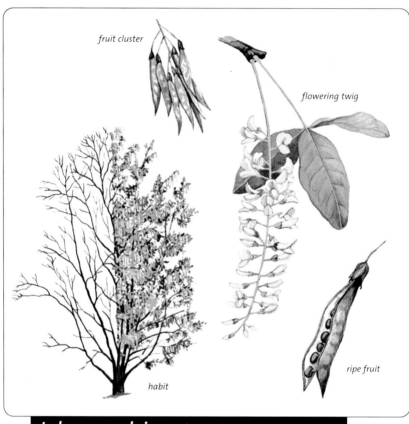

fruit cluster

flowering twig

ripe fruit

habit

Laburnum alpinum (Miller) Berchtold & J. Presl
Alpine Laburnum or Scotch Laburnum

A very small tree or shrub up to 5m high with a short bole. It is similar to *L. anagyroides* but differs in a number of features. **Branches** The green twigs are hairy only when young. **Leaves** The leaflets are green, slightly glossy on both surfaces and more or less glabrous. **Flowers** The racemes are 15–40cm long, slender and rather dense. The corolla is 1·5–2cm long. **Fruit** The legume is 4–5cm long, glabrous, with a narrow wing 1–2mm wide on the upper suture. **Seeds** Brown. **Flowering period** June. **Distribution** A montane species from C. S. and SE. Europe, sometimes planted as a roadside tree. Cultivated specimens may reach 10m in height. Al Au Br Cz Fr It Sd Yu.

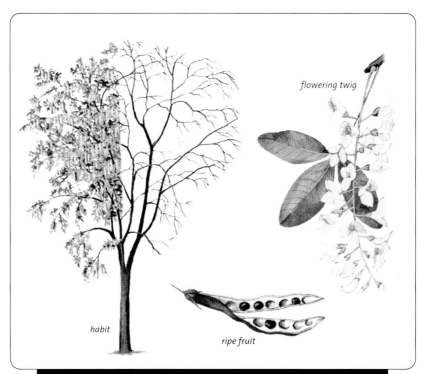

flowering twig

habit

ripe fruit

Laburnum anagyroides Medicus Common Laburnum

A small tree or shrub up to 7m high with a narrow, open, rather irregular crown and slender bole. **Bark** Greenish or brown, smooth, with small warts or flakes. **Branches** Ascending, the smaller ones arching; the twigs are greyish-green with long silky appressed hairs. **Leaves** The leaflets are 3–8cm long, elliptical or wider above the middle, rather blunt with a shortly pointed tip, greyish-green on both surfaces with appressed hairs beneath when young; the petiole is 2–6cm long. **Flowers** The racemes are 10–30cm long and rather loose. The corolla is about 2cm long, golden-yellow and often with brown markings. **Fruit** The legume is 4–6cm long, appressed hairy when young, becoming glabrous and dark brown when mature, the upper suture unwinged. **Seeds** Black. **Flowering period** May–early June. **Distribution** A self-seeding, rapidly growing but short-lived species, the Common Laburnum is one of the most poisonous native European trees. A montane species of S. and C. Europe, of woods and scrub up to 2000m. It is one of the most commonly planted ornamental trees, sometimes becoming naturalized. Au Br Co Cz Fr Ge Hu Ir It Ru Sd Yu.

Laburnum x *watereri* Dippel Voss's Laburnum
A hybrid between *L. anagyroides* and *L. alpinum*, with large flowers, combining the early flowering period of *L. anagyroides* and the long dense racemes of *L. alpinum*. The hybrid and its various cultivated forms have replaced *L. anagyroides* as the most commonly planted Laburnum in some areas.

pods

habit

flowering twig

Sophora japonica L. Pagoda Tree

An unarmed, deciduous tree up to 25m high with an irregular, rather open crown. **Bark** Wrinkled and furrowed, dark or grey-brown. **Branches** Contorted, the twigs glaucous and hairy at first, becoming green and glabrous. **Leaves** 15–25cm long, alternate, pinnate with a terminal leaflet, and 3–8 pairs of leaflets. **Flowers** The inflorescence is a large, finely hairy, terminal panicle, 15–25cm long. The white or pale pink flowers appear only on old trees; the calyx is tubular and slightly 2-lipped; the corolla is strongly zygomorphic, 1–1.5cm long. **Fruit** The legume is 5–8cm long, conspicuously constricted between the seeds, glabrous, greenish, indehiscent or dehiscing very late. **Seeds** There may be many seeds or as few as one. **Flowering period** August–September. **Distribution** A montane plant of thickets and thin woods in E. Asia, it is often planted as an ornamental and may become naturalized in places. Au Fr Ru.

Robinia L. Locust Trees

Deciduous trees with alternate pinnate leaves having a terminal leaflet and usually with spinose stipules. **Flowers** The inflorescence is a pendulous axillary raceme of white, pink or purple flowers. The bell-shaped calyx is somewhat 2-lipped and the stamens are diadelphous. **Fruit** The legume is linear-oblong, flat and dehiscent with 3–10 seeds.

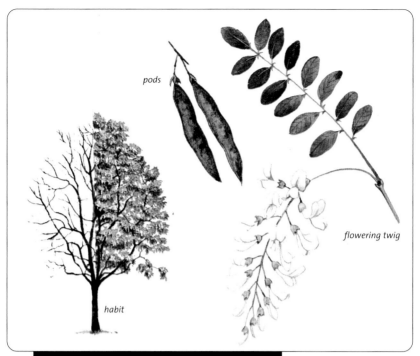

pods

flowering twig

habit

Robinia pseudacacia L. Locust Tree

A medium-sized tree up to 25m high with a broad, rather open crown and short, frequently multiple boles, spreading by root suckers and sometimes forming thickets of young stems. **Bark** Smooth and dark brown in young trees, becoming grey and deeply furrowed into broad twisting ridges in mature trees. **Branches** Twisted and brittle, the young twigs dark and reddish, with short woody stipular spines on strong shoots. **Leaves** 15–20cm long with 3–10 pairs of opposite or subopposite leaflets, each leaflet 2·5–4·5cm long, elliptical or ovate, entire, yellowish-green and glabrous above, slightly hairy but becoming glabrous below, usually with a secondary stipule at the base of the short petiolule. **Flowers** The dense racemes are many-flowered, 10–20cm long; the sweet-scented flowers are 1·5–2cm long, white, rarely pink, with a yellow base to the upper petal. **Fruit** The legume is 5–10cm long, glabrous, often remaining on the tree for some time after reaching maturity. **Flowering period** June. **Distribution** An introduced species, native to thin woods and open places in E. and C. N. America, widely planted in Europe as an ornamental and soil-stabilizer. It has become naturalized in many areas, particularly in S. and W. Europe. Al Au Be Br Bu Cz Fr Ge Gr Ho Hu It Ru Sa Sd Si Sp Tu Yu.

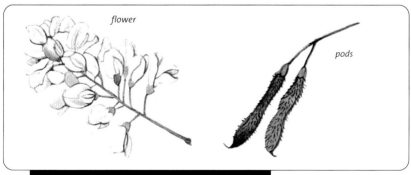

flower

pods

Robinia viscosa Vent. Clammy Locust

A sticky, hairy relative from the SE. of N. America, frequently planted in C. and S. Europe as an ornamental.

Citrus Fruit Family
Rutaceae

Citrus L.

Small trees. **Leaves** Usually simple, alternate, leathery and thin; the petiole is often more or less winged or with narrow margins, with an articulated joint at the meeting of the blade. **Flowers** Solitary or in small spikes emerging from the leaf-axils; the sepals number 4–5; the petals number 4–8; there are 4–10 times as many stamens as petals. **Fruit** A large berry with a thick leathery skin and a soft flesh of large juice-filled hair-cells growing from the inside of the skin. **Distribution** There are more than 60 described species originating from China, SE. Asia and Indomalaysia. Those below are widely cultivated in the Mediterranean region for their edible fruits and for essential oils for the perfume industry extracted from the flowers and fruits.

fruit

Citrus aurantium L. Seville Orange

A small to medium tree up to 10m high with a rounded crown. **Leaves** are 7·5–10cm long, broadly elliptical. **Flowers** Large, and fragrant with the oil of Neroli. **Fruit** c. 7·5cm in diameter with a thick skin, orange when ripe.

flowering twig

fruit (C. sinensis)

fruit (C. bergamia)

habit

Citrus sinensis (L.) Osbeck Sweet Orange

A moderate-sized tree up to c. 10m with a rounded crown. **Leaves** More or less elliptical. **Flowers** Small and very fragrant. **Fruit** The edible orange. **Taxonomic notes** The closely related *C. bergamia* Risso & Poiteau is cultivated in Calabria for the Bergamot oil from the fruit rind. It is a small tree with winged petioles, oblong-ovate leaves and a thick-skinned yellow fruit 7·5–10cm in diameter.

fruit

Citrus deliciosa Ten. Tangerine

A small spiny, spreading tree up to 8m. **Leaves** Narrowly elliptical. **Flowers** Medium-sized. **Fruit** 5–7.5cm in diameter, almost globose, with a thin, easily detachable bright orange rind when ripe.

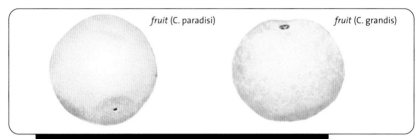

fruit (C. paradisi)   fruit (C. grandis)

Citrus paradisi Macfadyen in Hooker **Grapefruit**

A relatively large, densely leafy tree up to 12m with a rounded crown. **Leaves** 10–15cm long and broadly elliptical; the petiole has very broad wings. **Flowers** Large. **Fruit** 10–15cm in diameter, almost globose, with a thick rind, pale yellow when ripe. **Taxonomic notes** The closely related *C. grandis* (L.) Osbeck, the Shaddock or Pomelo, has a broader petiole and a fruit up to 25cm in diameter.

fruit (C. limetta)

fruit (C. medica)

flowering twig

habit   fruit (C. limon)

Citrus limon (L.) Burm. **Lemon**

A small thorny, rounded tree. **Leaves** *c.* 10cm long, broadly elliptical and minutely toothed; the petiole is narrowly winged and distinctly articulated with the leaf. **Flowers** Small. **Fruit** 6.5–12.5cm in diameter, oblong or ovoid, with a broad protruding apex, a thick, rough to almost smooth, bright yellow rind when ripe. **Taxonomic notes** The origin of the lemon is rather obscure but probably derived from *C. medica* L., the Citron, a small tree with a thick-skinned yellow fruit, 15–25cm in diameter. *C. limetta* Risso, the Sweet Lime, is probably a mutant of the lemon with a shorter, greenish-yellow, sweeter fruit.

Quassia Family
Simaroubaceae

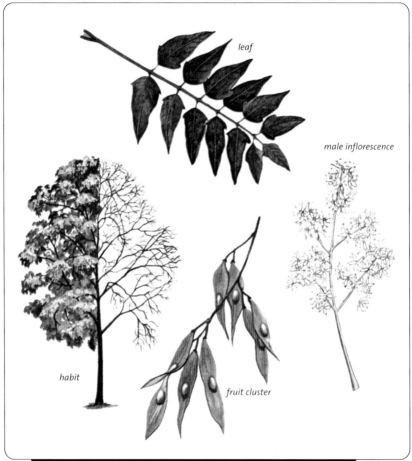

leaf

male inflorescence

habit

fruit cluster

Ailanthus altissima (Miller) Swingle **Tree of Heaven**

A fast-growing deciduous tree up to 20m (rarely 30m) high with an irregular crown and straight cylindrical bole, suckering freely. **Bark** Smooth and grey in young trees, becoming paler and slightly scaly in old trees. **Branches** Stout and ascending; the twigs are smooth, stout and brown, with prominent leaf-scars. **Buds** Small, ovoid, scarlet. **Leaves** Alternate, pinnate, 45–60cm long, more or less glabrous, with 13–25 leaflets; each leaflet is 7–12cm long, lanceolate-ovate, pointed at the tip, unequally cordate at the base, the margin with 2–4 teeth towards the base, each with a large raised gland beneath, fringed, deep red when unfolding, shiny green above when mature and at leaf-fall, pale green beneath, smelling unpleasant when crushed; the petiolule is 0·5–1·5cm long, red. **Flowers** The inflorescence is a large terminal panicle. The flowers are greenish, strong-smelling, 7–8mm in diameter, in 5 parts, polygamous though usually with males and females on separate trees; stamens 10 in male flowers, 2–3 in hermaphrodite flowers; female flowers with 2–5 joined styles. **Fruit** A group of samaras, each samara 3–4cm long with a twisted wing, reddish when young. **Flowering period** July. **Distribution** A native of China, widely planted in Europe for ornament, especially in parks and as a street tree but also for shade and soil conservation, and it has become widely naturalized. Al Au Be Br Bu Co Cz Fr Fu Ge Gr Hu It Pl Ru Sa Sd Si Sp Yu.

Mahogany Family
Meliaceae

leaf

fruit cluster

inflorescence

habit

Melia azedarach L. Indian Bead Tree or Persian Lilac

A short-lived deciduous tree or shrub up to 15m high with a rather open, spreading, often short bole. **Bark** Shallowly furrowed and dark grey. **Branches** The young twigs are sparsely covered in deciduous stellate hairs. **Leaves** Alternate, up to 90cm long, twice-pinnate, with numerous leaflets; each leaflet is 2·5–5cm long, ovate-lanceolate to elliptical, the margin toothed or lobed, dark, somewhat glossy green. **Flowers** The inflorescence is a large loose axillary panicle 10–20cm long, sparsely stellate-hairy when young. The flowers are fragrant, lilac, usually in 5 parts, the petals *c.* 1.8cm long, free-spreading or slightly reflexed; there are twice as many stamens as petals, united to form an almost complete tube with only the anthers free. **Fruit** A drupe, 0·6–1·8cm in diameter, more or less globose or somewhat ovoid, yellow or creamy, containing a hard seed. **Flowering period** June. **Distribution** A native of dry montane regions of E. Asia, widely planted in S. Europe as an ornamental and shade tree and naturalized in the Balkan Peninsula. Cr Gr Yu.

Cashew Family
Anacardiaceae

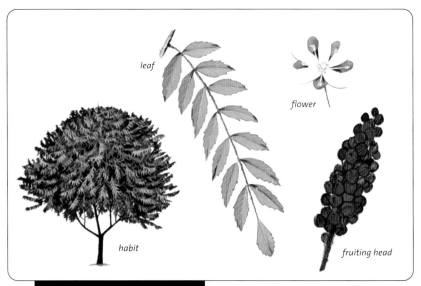

leaf

flower

habit

fruiting head

Rhus coriaria L. Sumach

A small semi-evergreen tree or shrub up to 3m high. **Branches** Ascending, more or less smooth, lenticelled. The young twigs are rather stout, densely hispid. **Buds** Without scales. **Leaves** Alternate, pinnate with 7–21 leaflets; each leaflet is 1–5cm long, ovate to oblong, blunt or pointed at the tip, the margin with large, rather rounded, forward-pointing teeth and occasionally with 1 or 2 lobes at the base, pubescent, especially beneath; the rachis is usually narrowly winged towards the tip, hispid. **Flowers** Dense terminal panicles up to 10cm long; each flower 3–4mm in diameter. **Fruit** A drupe, 4–6mm in diameter, globose with a terminal style, shortly hispid, brownish-purple, one-seeded. **Flowering period** May–July. **Distribution** A native of S. Europe, growing amongst scrub and in rocky places at low altitudes. Al Bu Cr Fr Fu Gr It Pl Si Sp Tu Yu.

leaf and fruiting head

Rhus typhina L. Stag's Horn Sumach

Like *R. coriaria* but deciduous, up to 10m high, often suckering. **Leaves** Leaflets are 5–12cm long, oblong-lanceolate, toothed; the rachis unwinged. **Flowers** The flower head is 10–20cm in diameter, dense; the female flower heads downy. **Fruit** Covered with crimson hairs. **Distribution and taxonomic notes** A native to E. N. America, commonly planted for ornament in parks and gardens, becoming naturalized in favourable localities of C. and N. Europe. Br Bu Cz Fr It Ru Sd Yu. *R. verniciflua* Stokes, the Varnish Tree of Japan, is occasionally cultivated for ornament.

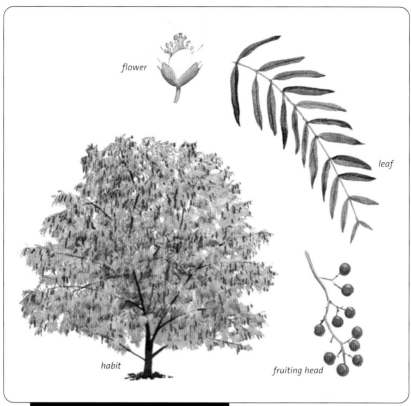

flower

leaf

habit

fruiting head

Schinus molle L. Pepper Tree

An evergreen tree or shrub up to 12m high. **Branches** Slender, pendent. The young twigs are glaucous. **Leaves** Alternate, pinnate with 7–13 pairs of leaflets, each leaflet 2–6 x 0·3–0·8cm long, linear-lanceolate with a slender spine-like tip, often toothed towards the apex, pubescent when young, becoming glabrous, aromatic when crushed; the rachis is often flattened but not conspicuously winged, sometimes terminating the leaf with a spine-like tip, glabrous. **Flowers** In lateral or terminal, lax panicles up to 25cm long, each flower *c.* 4mm in diameter with 5 yellowish-white petals. **Fruit** A drupe, 6–7mm in diameter, globose, shiny, rose-pink, with a solitary seed and a pedicel 2–3mm long. **Flowering period** June–December. **Distribution and taxonomic notes** A native of the mountains of C. and S. America, planted for ornament in S. Europe and more or less naturalized in some localities. Fr Gr It Pl Sa Si Sp. The Brazilian Pepper, *S. terebinthifolia* Raddi, differing in its erect branches, oblong-ovate leaflets, winged rachis and bright red fruit 4–5mm in diameter, is also planted for ornament.

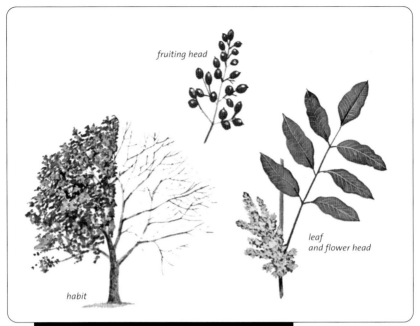

fruiting head

*leaf
and flower head*

habit

Pistacia terebinthus L. Turpentine Tree

A deciduous shrub or small tree up to 10m high. **Bark** Greyish-brown, coarsely fissured. **Branches** The twigs are grey, resiniferous. **Leaves** 3–9 leaflets; each leaflet is 2–8.5 x 1–3.5cm long, broadly ovate to oblong with a small spine-like tip, smooth, rather leathery, shiny dark green; the rachis is rounded in cross-section, unwinged; the petiole is smooth. **Flowers** The flower heads are 5–15cm, lax, with long branches, appearing with the young leaves; the flowers are greenish to brownish. **Fruit** 5–7 x 4–6mm, obovoid with a slender pointed tip, coral-red when young, becoming purplish-brown. **Flowering period** March–April. **Distribution and taxonomic notes** A native of the Mediterranean region, Portugal and SW. Asia, in thickets and open woodland, usually on dry calcareous rocky slopes. Al Bu Co Cr Fr Gr It Pl Sa Si Sp Tu Yu. The similar *P. atlantica* Desf. has lanceolate leaflets with rounded tips, a narrowly winged rachis and a shortly pubescent petiole. A native of SE. Europe and N. Africa. Fu Gr Tu.

fruiting head

leaf
and flower head

habit

Pistacia lentiscus L. Mastic Tree

Usually a spreading evergreen shrub or occasionally a tree up to 8m. **Branches** The twigs are warted, glabrous. **Leaves** Rarely 4, usually 6–12 leaflets without a terminal leaflet; each leaflet is 1–5 x 0·5–1·5cm, lanceolate to oblong with a short spine-like tip, leathery, dark green; the rachis is broadly winged, continued as a spine-like tip to the leaf, the petiole is smooth. **Flowers** The flower heads are in the axils of leaves, 2–5cm long, dense and spike-like; the flowers are yellowish or purplish. **Fruit** *c.* 4mm long, globose with a slender pointed tip, very aromatic, red when young, becoming black. **Flowering period** April. **Distribution and taxonomic notes** A native of the Mediterranean region and Portugal, growing in scrub or woodland margins on dry stony slopes. Hybrids between *P. lentiscus* and *P. terebinthus* occur in parts of France, Italy, Portugal and Sardinia and are known as *P.* x *raportae* Burnat.

habit

fruiting head

Pistacia vera L. Pistachio

A small deciduous tree up to 6m high. **Bark** Greyish-brown, rough, with many short ridges. **Branches** The twigs are grey. **Leaves** Simple or pinnate, usually with 3 (rarely 5) leaflets; each leaflet is 3·5–9cm long, broadly ovate to oblong-ovate, thin-textured, somewhat downy on both surfaces while young, becoming smooth grey-green; the rachis is very slightly winged; the petiole is downy. **Flowers** The flower heads are 7–10cm long, lax, with long branches; the flowers are greenish. **Fruit** 2–2·5cm long, ovoid with a pointed tip, pale reddish-brown with a hard outer layer and an edible seed. **Flowering period** April. **Distribution** Native to W. Asia, widely cultivated around the Mediterranean countries for its edible nuts and naturalized in a few localities. Fr Gr Si Sp.

Maple Family
Aceraceae

Acer L. Maples and Sycamores

Deciduous trees or sometimes shrubs, with long-petioled leaves. The flowers are green or yellowish. The fruit is a samara, winged on the outer side.

fruits

habit

flowering twig

Acer campestre L. Field Maple

Usually a small tree, occasionally up to 26m high, or a shrub, with a domed crown and a sinuous bole. **Bark** Grey or brown with orange fissures. **Branches** Somewhat pendulous but upturned towards the tips; the twigs are brown and covered with fine hairs, darker above than below, often corky, the older ones winged. **Buds** 3mm long, grey or reddish-brown, hairy towards the apex. **Leaves** 4–12cm long, 5-lobed (occasionally 3-lobed), the 2 basal lobes smaller than the upper 3, the upper lobes more or less oblong or wedge-shaped with 2 rounded teeth towards the apex, fringed, hair tufted in the axils of the veins beneath, thick and sometimes leathery, pinkish when young, becoming dark green at maturity; petiole about 5cm, slender. **Flowers** Few, appearing with the leaves in erect hairy heads containing both male and female flowers. **Fruit** In clusters of 4, 5–6cm in diameter, hairy or glabrous, the wings horizontal, green, sometimes tinged with red. **Flowering period** Late April–early May. A very varied species, perhaps due to hybridization. **Distribution** Common in N. Europe, it is cultivated for its autumn foliage; occasionally naturalized. Al Au Be Br Bu Co Cz De Fr Fu Ge Gr Ho Hu Ir It Po Ru Sa Sd Si Sp Sw Tu Yu.

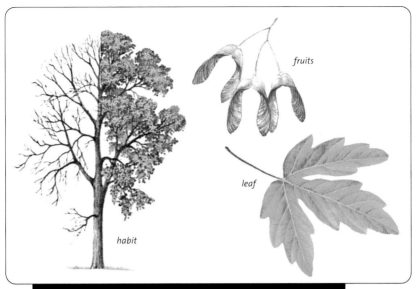

fruits

leaf

habit

Acer heldreichii Orph. ex Boiss. Heldreich's Maple

A medium-sized tree up to 25m high with a high-domed crown. **Bark** Smooth, finely cracked in older trees, grey. **Branches** Ascending, with a few reddish-brown twigs. **Buds** Ovoid, pointed and dark brown. **Leaves** 5–17cm long, with 3–5 deep lobes, the middle lobe free almost to the base, all lobes with 2–3 large teeth on each side, green above, bluish-green below with white or brownish hairs on the veins beneath. **Flowers** Few, appearing with the leaves, in more or less erect, hairless, yellow panicles. **Fruit** 2·5–5cm long, the curved wings usually forming an obtuse angle, reddish, glabrous. **Flowering period** Late May. **Distribution** A montane species of the Balkan Peninsula. Al Bu Gr Yu.

leaf (A. griseum)

leaf (A. davidii)

Among the commonest non-European species planted in parks and gardens are two Chinese species: *Acer griseum* (Franchet) Pax, the Paper-bark Maple, grown for its unusual reddish-brown bark which peels in broad papery strips; and *A. davidii* Franchet, Père David's Maple, one of the Snake-bark Maples with olive-green young bark marked with a bright network of whitish lines. The Paper-bark Maple has hairy twigs and petioles and dark green leaves composed of 3 leaflets, the two lateral ones almost sessile. Père David's Maple has glabrous twigs and either unlobed or up to 5-lobed leaves which are heart-shaped at the base with finely toothed margins. Other commonly planted species include *A. hersii* (Rehder) Rehder, *A. cappadocicum* Gled., *A. macrophyllum* Pursh, *A. saccharum* L. and *A. rufinerve* Siebold & Zucc., all from Asia or N. America.

231

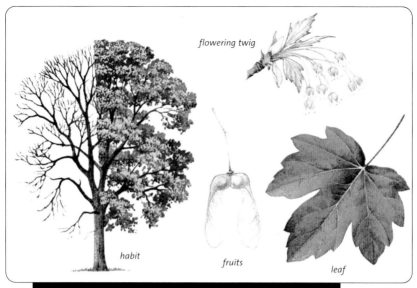

flowering twig

habit

fruits

leaf

Acer hyrcanum Fischer & C.A. Meyer **Balkan Maple**

A small tree up to 16m high with a domed crown. **Bark** Grey-brown, fissured into square plates. **Branches** Ascending or spreading. **Buds** Grey and brown with few scales. **Leaves** Up to 10cm long, with 3 or usually 5 lobes cut halfway to the base, the 3 main lobes parallel-sided with obtuse apices, shallowly toothed on the margins, green above, the lower surface more or less glabrous except for the veins; the petiole is very slender, pinkish or yellowish. **Flowers** Few, opening before the leaves, in subsessile heads with slender pedicels, yellowish. **Fruit** 1·5cm long, the wings diverging at an acute angle or nearly parallel, green, on slender pedicels, in clusters of 6–8. **Flowering period** April. **Distribution** A woodland species from the Balkan Peninsula and the Caucasus. Al Bu Gr Yu.

leafy twig

Acer granatense Boiss.

A species very similar to the Balkan Maple, but differs in having leaves up to 7cm long. The lower surfaces of the leaves, the young petioles and young twigs are all rather densely hairy. **Distribution** It is confined to S. Spain, Mallorca and N. Africa. Bl Sp.

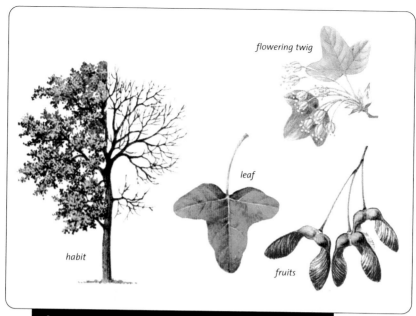

flowering twig

leaf

habit

fruits

Acer monspessulanum L. Montpellier Maple

A small tree up to 12m high or sometimes a shrub, with a broadly domed crown. **Bark** Fissured and cracked, grey or black. **Branches** The twigs are slender, brown, smooth. **Buds** 3mm long, ovoid, orange-brown. **Leaves** 3–8cm long, leathery, 3-lobed, the lobes wide-spreading, ovate, the margins entire, dark green and shiny above, slightly bluish beneath with tufts of hairs in the axils of the lower veins; the petiole is slightly orange. **Flowers** Appearing after the leaves, erect at first, becoming pendent, in yellowish-green heads with long slender pedicels. **Fruit** 1·2cm long, the wings parallel or overlapping, green becoming crimson-tinged, glabrous. **Flowering period** June. **Distribution** A S. European species, growing as far north as S. Germany in rather local populations. It is occasionally planted in large parks. Al Au Bu Co Fr Ge Gr It Pl Ru Sa Si Sp Tu Yu.

leaf

fruits

Acer sempervirens L. Cretan Maple

A small evergreen up to 12m high, but often a shrub, with a low crown. **Bark** Few fissures, dark grey with a few orange patches. **Branches** Twisted; the twigs are brown and shiny. **Leaves** 2–5cm long, 3-lobed, irregularly lobed or undivided with entire wavy margins; the petioles are short, yellowish. **Flowers** Few, erect, in glabrous greenish heads. **Fruit** Has green or occasionally red wings which are almost parallel or spreading at an acute angle. **Flowering period** April. **Distribution** Similar to the Montpellier Maple, but confined to Crete and Greece. Cr Gr.

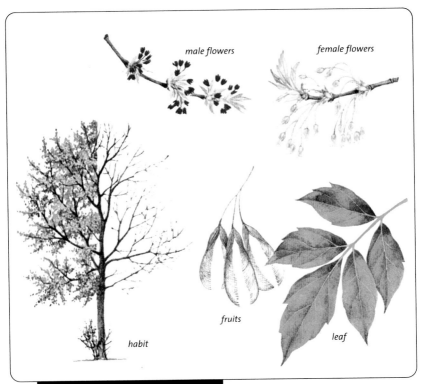

male flowers

female flowers

fruits

leaf

habit

Acer negundo L. Box-elder

A rather small, fast-growing tree up to 20m high. The crown is domed but often irregular due to numerous shoots sprouting from the bole and branches. **Bark** Greyish, smooth at first but becoming shallowly fissured and a darker colour as the tree matures. **Buds** Small, with only 2 scales, white or somewhat silvery. **Leaves** 5–15cm long, pinnate, with 3–5 (sometimes 7) ovate leaflets, the lower with short stalks, the upper sessile and occasionally incompletely divided, but all with shallow, irregularly toothed margins. **Flowers** Dioecious, without petals, appearing before the leaves; male flowers occur in pendent corymbs of 12–16, green or pinkish with red anthers; females occur in loose pendent racemes of 6–12, 5cm long, greenish. **Fruit** 2cm long, glabrous, the wings diverging at an acute angle, brown, maturing early and persisting after leaf-fall. **Flowering period** March. **Distribution and taxonomic notes** A native of E. N. America, widely planted as an ornamental or occasionally to provide shelter and sometimes becoming naturalized. The cv 'Variegatum' is most commonly used as a street tree and is a female form with yellow and green variegated leaves, although it often reverts to the normal green colour. Au Bu Fr Fu Ge Hu Sd Sp.

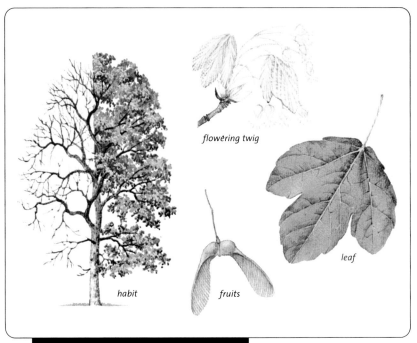

flowering twig

leaf

habit

fruits

Acer opalus Miller Italian Maple

A small tree up to 15–20m high, but often a shrub, with a broad crown. **Bark** Pink-tinged, broken into square plates in young trees, the plates peeling away and leaving orange patches below; in more mature trees the plates curl but do not fall away. **Branches** Twisted and often low and spreading; the twigs are brown with pale lenticels. **Buds** 5mm long, brown, conical and pointed. **Leaves** Up to 10cm long, though usually less, with 3–5 short, broad, acute lobes, if 5 then the 2 basal lobes smaller and less deeply cut than the others; the leaves are at first dark green, glabrous above and generally hairy below, the hairs later becoming confined to the veins; the petiole is red above, green below. **Flowers** Pendulous, large and relatively few in number, pale yellow with slender yellow petioles, forming subsessile clusters with glabrous peduncles, opening just before the leaves emerge. **Fruit** *c.* 2·5cm long, the wings almost parallel, 8–15 in each pendulous cluster, the wings green and pink, the seeds green at first, ripening to red or brown. **Flowering period** April. **Distribution** A montane species of the W. Mediterranean and S. Alps, sometimes planted in parks. Co Fr Ge It Sd Sp.

leaf

Acer obtusatum Waldst. & Kit.

Closely related and very similar to *A. opalus*. It is distinguished by the leaves which are up to 12cm long with sometimes 3, but usually 5, broad blunt lobes. The lower leaf surfaces and the petiole are densely and persistently hairy, as are the peduncles. **Distribution** More easterly than *A. opalus*. Al Co Gr It Si Yu.

flowering twig

fruits

fruits ('Atropurpureum')

leaf ('Atropurpureum')

habit

Acer palmatum Thunb. Smooth Japanese Maple

A small tree up to 16m high, the crown domed, the bole usually very short and often rather twisted. **Bark** Smooth and deep brown on young trees, often with paler markings, but becoming more uniform in old specimens. **Branches** Spreading, ending in slender horizontal twigs which are usually reddish above and green below. **Buds** 2–3mm long, ovoid, often with a reddish tinge. **Leaves** 7–9cm long with 5–7, rarely up to 11 lobes divided halfway or more to the base, all with sharply toothed margins. **Flowers** Clustered, 12–15 together in upright heads, each flower 6–8mm in diameter, dark purplish; the slender pedicels are about 4cm long, green or red. **Fruit** Usually in pendulous clusters, each pair 2cm across, the angle between the wings obtuse, in erect or pendulous clusters, becoming reddish when mature. **Flowering period** April–May. **Distribution and taxonomic notes** A species of lowland and mountain woods in its native Japan. Cultivars are extremely common in gardens and parks, particularly those forms with purple leaves such as cv. 'Atropurpureum' or with scarlet autumn leaves and fruits such as cv. 'Osakazuki'. Also, it is grown as a small, dense, strongly domed shrub.

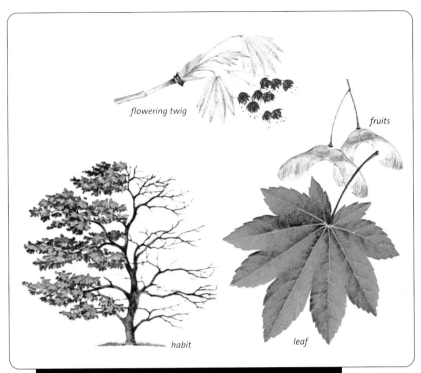

flowering twig

fruits

habit

leaf

Acer japonicum Thunb. Downy Japanese Maple

A small tree up to 14m high with a high-domed crown and a very short bole usually little more than 1m high. **Bark** Greyish-brown, smooth. **Branches** Horizontal or slightly curved upwards; the twigs are often reddish or brownish above. **Buds** Ovoid, pointed, the scales red with a greyish margin. **Leaves** 7–13cm, somewhat broader than long, with 7–11 sharply pointed lobes divided less than halfway to the base, hairy when young but becoming glabrous except on the veins beneath; the margins of the lobes have sharp forward-pointing teeth; the petiole is 3–5cm long, hairy when young, becoming glabrous. **Flowers** Purple, about 1·5cm in diameter, appearing before the leaves in pendulous clusters on long stalks. **Fruit** Each pair is 4–5cm across, the angle between the wings obtuse or horizontal, the seed and the margins of the wings green, hairy at first becoming glabrous; the reddish pedicel is about 2cm long. **Flowering period** April–May. **Distribution and taxonomic notes** This Japanese species is similar to *A. palmatum* and is also grown in gardens. The cv 'Vitifolium' is planted for its bright red autumn foliage.

young fruits

flowering twig

leaf

habit

Acer platanoides L. Norway Maple

A tall tree up to 30m high with a domed spreading crown and rather short bole. **Bark** Grey and smooth or with low ridges. **Branches** Rather sparse, the twigs dull green or tinged with red. **Buds** Ovoid, those at the tips of shoots often with a red tinge. **Leaves** 10–15cm long, with 5–7 pointed, toothed lobes, the basal pair smaller and more narrowly triangular than the rest; bright green and glabrous above, paler beneath with white hairs in the axils of the veins; the petiole is up to 20cm long. **Flowers** Upright clusters of 30–40, each flower up to 8mm in diameter, a strong greenish-yellow, opening before the leaves, and persisting until the leaves are fully open. **Fruit** The pairs of yellowish fruits are 6–10cm across, the angle between the wings wide or horizontal. **Flowering period** March–April. **Distribution and taxonomic notes** A forest tree native to much of Europe but only as a montane species in the south. It is planted as an ornamental in parks and gardens and frequently as a street tree. Numerous cultivars are known, many with red, purple or variegated foliage. Al Au Be Br Bu Cz Fi Fr Fu Ge Gr Ho Hu It No Po Ru Sd Sp Sw Tu Yu. The very similar *A. lobelii* Ten., Lobel's Maple, from the mountains of C. and S. Italy, can be distinguished by its columnar habit and leaves with entire lobes.

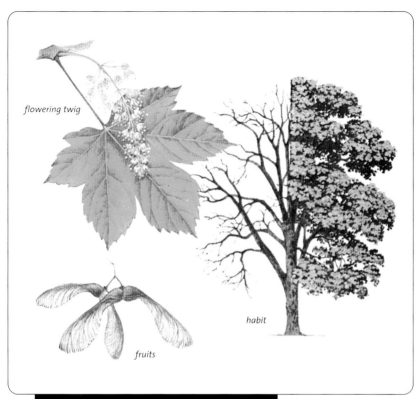

flowering twig

habit

fruits

Acer pseudoplatanus L. Sycamore

A large tree up to 35m, the crown domed and so widely spreading as often to be broader than tall. **Bark** Grey, fissured into irregular rectangles which sometimes flake away leaving slightly orange patches. **Branches** Often stout, the twigs short and rather sinuous, greyish-green with pale lenticels. **Buds** 0·8–1cm long, ovoid, surrounded by reddish scales which gradually curve back and open. **Leaves** 10–15cm long, 5-lobed, the lobes cut about halfway to the base, acute and coarsely toothed, dark green above, paler beneath with hairs around the main veins. The size and lobing of the leaves varies with age: immature trees have larger, more deeply cut leaves and longer scarlet petioles; mature slow-growing trees have smaller leaves and shallow lobes, the lower 2 often smaller than the others, and with shorter pink or green petioles. **Flowers** Numerous, yellowish, in narrow pendulous heads, 6–12cm long, appearing with the leaves. **Fruit** The pairs of fruits are 6cm across, the wings spreading at right-angles, green tinged with red, or brownish when ripe, glabrous. **Flowering period** April. **Distribution** A native montane species of woods and hedges in C. and S. Europe. It is widely planted for shelter and as an ornamental, seeding freely and often becoming naturalized. Al Au Be Br Bu Co Cz De Fr Fu Ge Gr Ho Hu Ir It Pl Po Ru Sd Si Sp Sw Tu Yu.

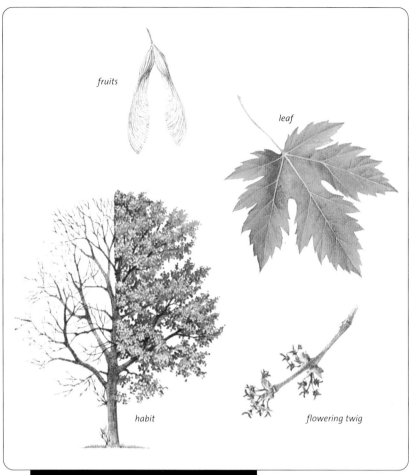

fruits

leaf

habit

flowering twig

Acer saccharinum L. Silver Maple

A tall monoecious tree up to 30m high with a spreading crown. **Bark** Grey, smooth, becoming shaggy as the plant matures, often covered with shoots and suckers. **Branches** Numerous, slender and arching with pendulous brownish or purple twigs. **Leaves** 9–16cm long, 5-lobed, the lobes cutting more than halfway to the base and deeply and unevenly toothed, orange or red above, becoming green, silvery with thick white hair beneath; the petiole is slender, pink. **Flowers** Appearing before the leaves in clusters of 4–5 at the nodes, similar to those of *A. rubrum* but without petals and borne on dark red pedicels. **Fruit** 5–6cm long, the wings diverging at a narrow angle, green, with prominent veins. **Flowering period** March. **Distribution** A N. American species planted in gardens and as a street tree. Cv. 'Laciniatum' is often used in town centres.

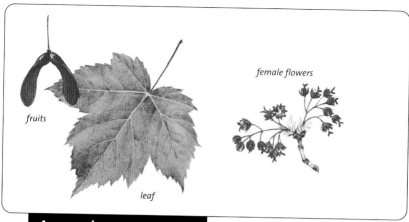

fruits

female flowers

leaf

Acer rubrum L. Red Maple

A fast-growing monoecious or dioecious tree, up to 23m high with an irregular crown. **Branches** Ascending, somewhat arching. The twigs are slender and reddish or copper-coloured. **Leaves** 8–10cm, about as broad as long, with 3–5 lobes cut less than halfway to the base, the basal lobes small, the larger lobes projecting forwards, coarsely toothed, reddish-green above at first, becoming dark green, silvery below; the petiole is red. The flower buds circle the stem, the pedicels lengthening as the flowers mature, the females becoming longer than the males. **Flowers** Red, appearing before the leaves. **Fruit** 1cm long, bright red, the wings diverging at a narrow angle. **Flowering period** March. **Distribution** A N. American species commonly planted as an ornamental in parks, gardens and churchyards.

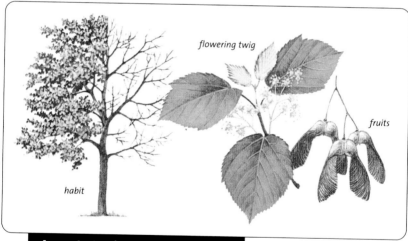

flowering twig

fruits

habit

Acer tataricum L. Tartar Maple

A small, usually monoecious tree up to 10m high, often a shrub. **Bark** Smooth, brown with pale stripes. **Leaves** 6–10cm long, with 3–5 lobes or more usually undivided, oblong, heart-shaped at the base, the margin finely and sharply toothed; the petiole is up to 3·5cm long, whitish or red. **Flowers** Greenish-white, 20–30 in suberect panicles appearing after the leaves. **Fruit** 2·5cm long, the wings more or less parallel, deep red with a thick green outer edge to the wing, hairy at first but later becoming glabrous. **Flowering period** May. **Distribution** A S. and C. European species, on rare occasions found in gardens. Al Au Bu Cz Fu Gr Hu Ru Yu.

Soapberry Family
Sapindaceae

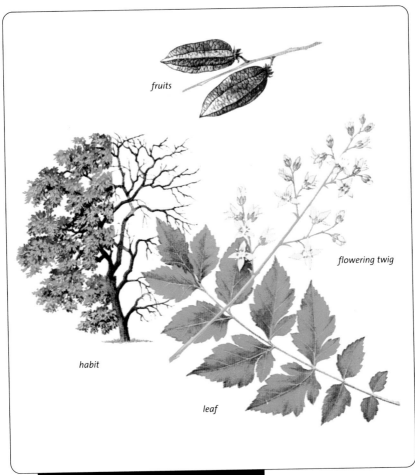

fruits

flowering twig

habit

leaf

Koelreuteria paniculata Laxm.
Pride of India or Golden Rain Tree

A graceful deciduous tree up to 15m high with a gaunt habit when young, becoming more compact at maturity, with soft pithy wood. **Bark** Brown with short fissures down to the orange-coloured underbark. **Branches** The young shoots are minutely downy. **Leaves** Alternate, 15–40cm long, pinnate, sometimes twice-pinnate at the base, with 9–15 ovate-oblong leaflets each 3–8cm long, coarsely and irregulariy toothed or pinnately-lobed, dark green and hairless above, paler beneath. **Flowers** Large terminal pyramidal panicles up to 40cm long and 1cm in diameter, yellow, with 4 petals, 8 or fewer stamens and a 3-celled ovary. **Fruit** Conical, inflated, 3-valved capsule up to 5·5cm long with acute or acuminate valves containing black seeds. **Distribution** A native of E. Asia, widely planted in S. Europe in parks and on roadsides and perhaps naturalized in E. Europe.

Horse Chestnut Family
Hippocastanaceae

fruit and seed

leaf

flower

habit

flower (A. x carnea)

fruit (A. x carnea)

Aesculus hippocastanum L. Common Horse Chestnut

A stout tree up to 25m high with a huge domed crown. **Bark** Greyish-brown, sometimes with a red tinge, scaling or cracking to form large plates or scales. **Branches** The twigs are reddish-brown with pale lenticels. **Buds** Winter buds are strikingly large, up to 3·5cm long, very resiniferous and sticky. **Leaves** 5–7 leaflets; each leaflet is 10–25cm long, obovate, but with a prolonged wedge-shaped base, doubly toothed, glabrous above, tomentose or glabrescent below. **Flowers** Cylindrical or pyramidal panicles, 15–30cm long; the petals are *c.* 1cm long, white and blotched with pink or yellow at the base. **Fruit** Spiny, globose, up to 6cm in diameter, containing a single rounded seed (conker) or 2–3 flattened seeds, each one brown with a large pale scar. **Flowering period** May. **Fruiting** September. **Distribution and taxonomic notes** A native of mountain woods, particularly in the Balkan Peninsula, but is extensively planted for ornament, for timber and as a shade tree in much of Europe except the extreme north. It is frequently locally naturalized in thickets and hedges in W. and C. Europe. A related species, *Aesculus x carnea* Hayne, the Red Horse Chestnut, is also often planted in Europe. It is like the Common Horse Chestnut but is usually smaller in all of its parts, with pink or red petals and a fruit without spines. It is a hybrid between *A. hippocastanum* and *A. pavia* L., a N. American native.

Holly Family
Aquifoliaceae

Ilex L. Hollies

A large genus of evergreen and deciduous shrubs and trees occurring throughout the world, except in Australasia and W. N. America.

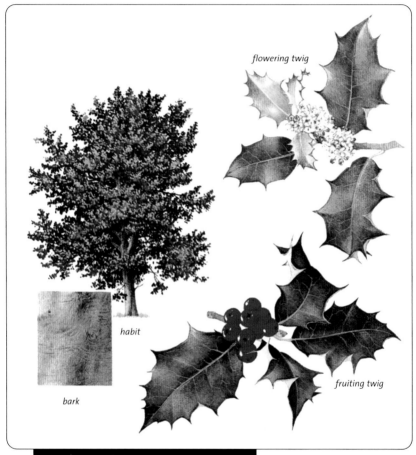

flowering twig

habit

bark

fruiting twig

Ilex aquifolium L. Common Holly

An evergreen shrub or tree up to 10m (exceptionally up to 25m) high with a narrow, rather conical crown. **Bark** Smooth, silvery-grey, becoming warted with age. **Branches** The young twigs are usually bright green, slightly downy, becoming smooth and shiny. **Leaves** 5–12cm long, up to 3 times as long as wide, ovate to oblong-elliptic, usually spiny-tipped, the margin undulate with widely spreading, spine-tipped teeth, becoming flat and entire in the upper parts of large trees, smooth, glossy dark green above, matt dull green beneath: the petiole is c. 1cm long, stout, grooved above. **Flowers** Fragrant, 6–8mm long. The male flowers have large anthers and an abortive ovary; the female flowers have a large ovary and small anthers. **Fruit** 0·7–1cm long, globose, scarlet; the pedicel is 4–8mm long. **Flowering period** May–June. **Distribution** A native of W. Asia and W. and S. Europe, commonly forming an under-storey tree in beech or oak woodland. The Holly is widely cultivated for ornament or shelter and many varieties exist, differing in habit, leaf colour and leaf shape. Al Au Be Br Bu Co De Fr Ge Gr Ho Ir It No Pl Ru Sa Sd Si Sp Sw Yu.

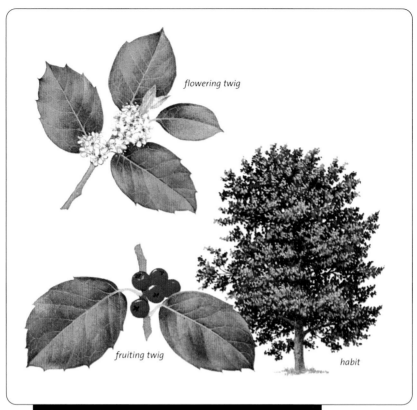

flowering twig

fruiting twig

habit

Ilex x altaclarensis Dallim. Highclere Holly

An evergreen tree up to 20m high with a dense, often domed crown. **Bark** Purplish-grey. **Branches** Rather spreading. The twigs are lined with purple or sometimes green. **Leaves** 5–14 x 3–10cm, ovate to oblong, flat, entire or with up to 10 (rarely 20) small spines directed towards the tip, usually glossy, dark green above, paler beneath. **Flowers** *c.* 1·2cm long; the base of the petals are often tinged purple. **Fruit** *c.* 1·2 x 1cm, oblong-elliptic to globose, scarlet; the pedicel is up to 1·2cm long. **Flowering period** May. **Distribution and taxonomic notes** The Highclere Holly is one of a group of vigorous hybrids derived from the Common Holly and the Canary Holly. They are commonly planted for ornament near the coast, and, being pollution-tolerant, in industrial towns. *Ilex perado* Aiton, the Canary Holly, is similar but with leaves 2·5–6cm long, elliptic-oblong to almost orbicular, the margin entire or with up to 3 short spines directed towards the rounded tip; petiole slightly winged; flowers pinkish; fruit 7–9mm long; pedicel *c.* 1cm long. A native of the Azores, Madeira and the Canary Islands, occasionally planted for ornament in parks and gardens.

Spindle Tree Family
Celastraceae

Euonymus L. Spindle Trees

Unarmed trees or shrubs with opposite leaves and flowers in 4–5 parts. The fruit is a dehiscent capsule, the seeds almost completely enveloped by a fleshy orange aril.

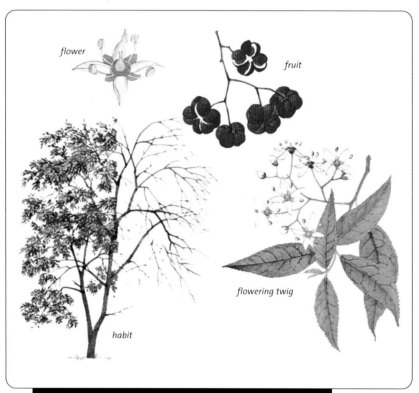

flower

fruit

flowering twig

habit

Euonymus europaeus L. Common Spindle Tree

A small, much-branched, monoecious or dioecious deciduous tree or shrub up to 6m high. **Bark** Smooth and grey at first, becoming shallowly fissured and pink-tinged in older specimens. **Branches** The twigs are green and 4-angled, becoming terete as they mature. **Buds** 2–4mm long, ovoid and pointed. **Leaves** Up to 10cm long, ovate-lanceolate or elliptical with a pointed apex and shallow, sharply-toothed margins, turning purple-orange in autumn. **Flowers** The inflorescence is an axillary cyme with 3–8 yellowish-green flowers in 4 parts. **Fruit** The capsule is pink, 10–15cm wide, with 4 paired rounded segments. **Flowering period** May–June. **Distribution** A common species in much of Europe except for the extreme north and south, growing in hedges and thickets on lime-rich soils. A number of cultivars are known and planted mainly for their large colourful fruits. All except Bl Cr Fi Fr Ic Ru Sd.

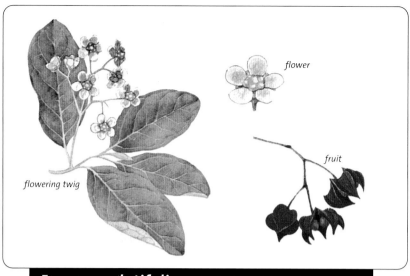

flower

fruit

flowering twig

Euonymus latifolius (L.) Miller Broad-leaved Spindle Tree

Similar to *E. europaeus*, but the twigs are less obviously 4-angled and the buds are 7–12cm long, slender and more pointed, and the leaves are up to 16cm long, sometimes with finely toothed margins. **Flowers** The cymes have 4–12 flowers, the flowers in 5 parts with broad, rounded, pinkish petals. **Fruit** The capsule is 15–20cm wide, 5-celled and more angular. **Flowering period** May–June. **Distribution** A common species in woods and thickets of S. C. and SE. Europe. Al Au Bu Fr Fu Ge Gr It Ru Sd Tu Yu.

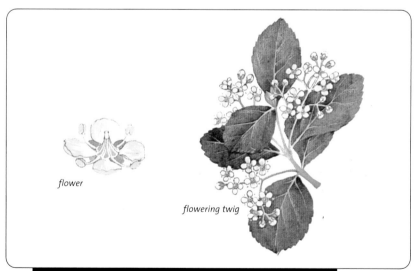

flower

flowering twig

Euonymus japonicus L. fil. Japanese Spindle Tree

An erect evergreen tree or large shrub up to 6m high. **Branches** The twigs are grey, weakly 4-angled. **Leaves** Thick and somewhat leathery, up to 7cm long, elliptical or widest above the middle, pointed or blunt at the tip, with very finely toothed margins. **Flowers** Greenish-yellow, small and in 4 parts, in rather long axillary clusters. **Fruit** The capsule is *c.* 8mm wide, pinkish, with rounded angles. **Flowering period** June–July. **Distribution** A common and variable species of coastal woodland, native to E. Asia. There are numerous cultivars with a wide range of foliage colours; widely planted for ornament, becoming naturalized in some parts of Europe. Bu Fr It Sp Yu.

Box Family
Buxaceae

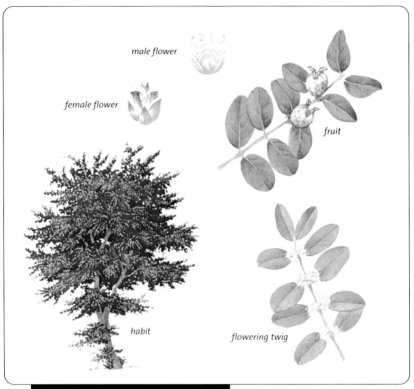

male flower

female flower

fruit

habit

flowering twig

Buxus sempervirens L. Box

A small tree or shrub up to 5m (occasionally 8m) high, rather narrow, often leaning and with more than one bole. **Bark** Smooth and brown at first, becoming corky and finely fissured into small squares, turning grey in old trees. **Branches** The twigs are 4-angled and green, at least when young, with persistent whitish hair. **Buds** Very small, 1–2mm long, terete, pale orange-brown and densely hairy. **Leaves** 1·5–3cm long, ovate, oblong or elliptical, usually notched at the tip, the margins revolute, dark glossy green above, paler beneath, the proximal part of the leaf with persistent white hair; the petiole is very short, *c.* 1 mm long, pale orange and hairy. **Flowers** The inflorescence is a terminal cluster of 5–6 sessile male flowers, *c.* 5mm in diameter, yellow, the bracteoles ovate and acute. **Fruit** The capsule is *c.* 7mm long, subglobose to broad-oblong, brown or grey, the styles 2·5mm long, spreading at right-angles, straight. **Seeds** 5–6mm long, hard, black and shiny. **Flowering period** April. **Distribution** A species of dry hills, usually on base-rich soils in SW. and W. C. Europe, although it is rather local. There are many different cultivars, mainly used for hedging and topiary and sometimes for timber. Al Au Be Br Co Fr Ge Gr It Pl Ru Sa Sd Sp Tu Yu.

Buxus balearica Lam. Balearic Box
Similar to *B. sempervirens* but more upright and with pinkish bark. **Branches** The twigs are stouter, rather stiffly erect and flattened at the nodes, glabrous or quickly becoming so. **Leaves** 2·5–4cm long, the pairs more distant from each other, paler and less glossy. **Flowers** The inflorescence is *c.* 1cm in diameter. **Flowering period** May. **Distribution** A species of damp rocky places in Sardinia, the Balearic Islands and parts of E. and S. Spain, although cultivated in gardens in S. Europe. Bl Sa Sp.

Mallow Family
Malvaceae

flowering twig

habit

Corynabutilon vitifolium (Cav.) Kearney
Flowering Maple

A small tree or shrub 4–9m high, the young shoots covered with white hairs. **Leaves** Alternate, simple, grey-tomentose, usually 10–15cm long, heart-shaped at the base, the margins with 3–5 rather shallow lobes, each lobe pointed and coarsely toothed. **Flowers** The inflorescence is a long-pedunculate, few-flowered axillary cyme, rarely with one, usually 3–5 flowers; each flower is *c.* 7cm in diameter, in 5 parts, the petals rounded and overlapping, usually pale blue or whitish in colour. **Fruit** Splits into several single-seeded segments. **Flowering period** May–July. **Distribution** A native of coastal Chile, cultivated for ornament in Europe in sheltered areas with mild winters.

Buckthorn Family
Rhamnaceae

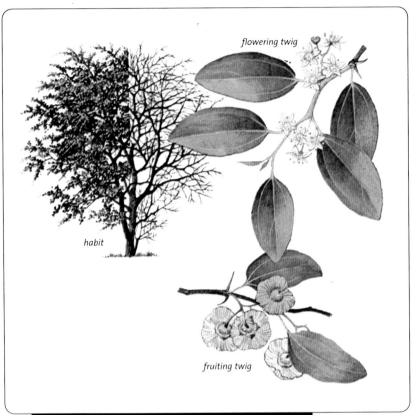

flowering twig

habit

fruiting twig

Paliurus spina-christi Miller Christ's Thorn

A small, profusely branched tree or shrub up to 3m high. **Branches** The twigs are flexible, zigzagging, glabrous or finely hairy. **Leaves** Alternate, in 2 rows along the stems, 2–4cm long, ovate, the margins entire or with small sharp teeth; the stipules are spinose, the spines alternately hooked and straight. **Flowers** Hermaphrodite, 2mm in diameter, yellow, in loose axillary pedunculate cymes. **Fruit** Woody, 1·8–3cm in diameter with a broad, spreading and undulate wing. **Flowering period** July. **Distribution** A species native to the dry slopes in the Mediterranean region, particularly the Balkan Peninsula, and sometimes grown as a hedge plant due to its resistance to grazing. Al Bu Co Fr Fu Gr Hu It Ru Sp Tu Yu.

flowering twig

twig
with young fruits

habit

Zizyphus jujuba (L.) Miller Common Jujube

A small, profusely branched tree or shrub up to 8m high, similar in appearance to *Paliurus*. **Branches** The green twigs are flexible, zigzagging, glabrous, the sterile ones armed with spinose stipules, the flowering ones usually unarmed. **Leaves** Alternate, 2–7cm long, oblong with a blunt apex and shallow bluntly-toothed margins, bright shiny green and glabrous above, slightly hairy below, especially on the veins; the petioles are very short. The 2 spiny stipules are unequal in length, one long and straight, the other short and curved. **Flowers** The inflorescence is a small, few-flowered, axillary cyme with a peduncle shorter than the cyme; the greenish-yellow flowers are inconspicuous, about 3mm in diameter. **Fruit** An ovoid-oblong drupe, 1·5–3cm long, reddish-brown or black when ripe, the flesh sweet. **Flowering period** June–July. **Distribution** An Asian species which is cultivated in S. Europe for the edible fruits. It is sometimes naturalized in hedgerows and orchards. Al Bu Fr Gr It Ru Si Sp Tu Yu.

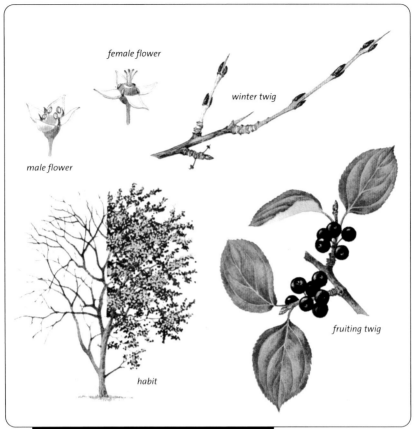

female flower

winter twig

male flower

fruiting twig

habit

Rhamnus catharticus L. Buckthorn

A deciduous dioecious tree or shrub up to 10m high. **Bark** Nearly black on old trees, fissured and scaling to reveal orange patches. **Branches** Opposite, spreading at right-angles to the bole, some of the lateral branches ending in spines, the others forming short spurs bearing the leaves and flowers. The twigs may be glabrous or densely hairy, grey or brown, and have prominent leaf scars. **Buds** Dark with scales. **Leaves** 3–7cm long, opposite or nearly so, ovate to elliptical, the apex blunt or slightly notched, the margins finely toothed, with 2–4 pairs of conspicuous lateral veins, green, turning yellow in autumn; the petiole is much shorter than the blade; the stipules are soft and fall early. **Flowers** The sweet-scented flowers are in 4 or occasionally 5 parts, unisexual, on slender pedicels, solitary or in clusters on the short shoots of the previous year's wood. **Fruit** A globose drupe, 6–8mm in diameter, with 2–4 yellow stones, black when ripe. **Flowering period** May–June. **Distribution** A species of chalky soils, in hedges, thickets and on the edges of woods in much of Europe except the Mediterranean area. Al Au Be Br Bu Cz De Fi Fr Fu Ge Gr Ho Hu Ir It No Pl Po Ru Sd Si Sp Sw Yu.

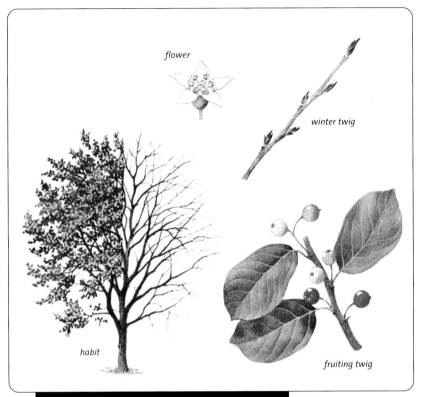

flower

winter twig

habit

fruiting twig

Frangula alnus Miller Alder Buckthorn

A small unarmed deciduous tree or shrub up to 5m high. **Bark** Thin, smooth in older trees, brown with a network of purplish markings. **Branches** Ascending, subopposite, forming an acute angle with the bole but not distinctly differentiated into long and short shoots. The young twigs are green at first, becoming brown with age, slightly hairy and with paler lenticels. **Buds** Without scales but are covered with dense brownish hairs. **Leaves** Widest above the middle, bluntly pointed, entire, hairy beneath when young, but becoming glabrous, with 7–9 pairs of inconspicuous lateral veins, green in summer, turning yellow and red in autumn. **Flowers** Solitary or in clusters on the new wood, in 5 parts, hermaphrodite. **Fruit** A globose drupe 0·6–1cm in diameter, yellow at first, ripening red, eventually black. **Flowering period** May–June (September). **Distribution** Common in marshy woodlands throughout Europe except the extreme north and parts of the Mediterranean region. Al Au Be Br Bu Cz De Fi Fr Fu Ge Gr Ho Hu Ir It No Pl Po Ru Sd Sp Sw Tu Yu.

Lime Tree Family
Tiliaceae

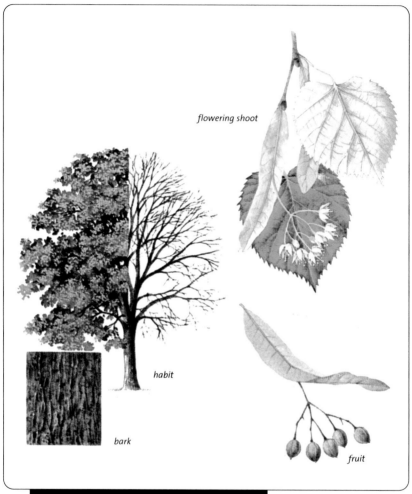

flowering shoot

habit

bark

fruit

Tilia tomentosa Moench Silver Lime

A broad pyramidal or domed tree up to 30m tall. **Bark** Dark greenish-grey, with a network of shallow flattish ridges. **Branches** Variable, usually rather straight, ascending; the young twigs are whitish-tomentose, becoming dark, greyish-green above, bright green beneath. **Buds** 6–8mm long, ovoid, brown and green, pubescent. **Leaves** 8–12cm long, suborbicular, abruptly narrowing to a tapering tip, the base heart-shaped on one side, the margin sharply toothed or slightly lobed, dark green, rather wrinkled and almost smooth above, white-tomentose with stellate hairs below; the petiole is 1·8–5cm long, usually less than half as long as the leaf blade, densely whitish-pubescent. The bracts are lanceolate to oblong-obovate, yellowish-green, pubescent. **Flowers** Dull white, 5–10 carried together in a pendent cyme; staminodes are present; the peduncles are *c.* 3cm long. **Fruit** 0·6–1·2cm long, usually ovoid, slightly 5-angled, the surface minutely warted, downy. **Flowering period** July–August. **Distribution** A species of SW. Asia and the Balkan Peninsula, extending northwards to the W. Ukraine and N. Hungary. It is frequently planted for ornament in city and town parks. Al Bu Fu Gr Hu Ru Tu Yu.

fruit

habit

flowering shoot

Tilia petiolaris DC. Weeping Silver Lime

A rather narrowly domed tree up to 30m tall. **Bark** Dark and pale grey with narrow, shallow ridges and furrows. **Branches** Initially ascending and rather sinuous, becoming conspicuously pendent towards the ends; the young twigs are pale greyish-green, densely pubescent. **Buds** *c.* 5mm long, ovoid, dull green, pubescent. **Leaves** 5–12cm long, rounded-ovate with a short tapering point, deeply cordate or sometimes truncate at the base, sharply toothed, dark green and slightly downy, densely white-tomentose below; the petiole is 6–12cm long, usually about as long as the leaf blade, densely white-pubescent. The bracts are spathulate to narrowly obovate with minute tufts of down. **Flowers** Dull white, 3–10 occurring in a pendent cyme; staminodes are present; the peduncle is *c.* 3cm. **Fruit** *c.* 1·2cm long, depressed-globose, slightly 5-angled, the surface minutely warted, nearly always sterile. **Flowering period** July. **Distribution and taxonomic notes** Some authors consider this species to be an extreme variant of *T. tomentosa*, perhaps most appropriately treated as a cultivar. The origin is not known, but the Weeping Silver Lime may have come from the Caucasus. It is frequently planted in large gardens, churchyards, parks and urban streets.

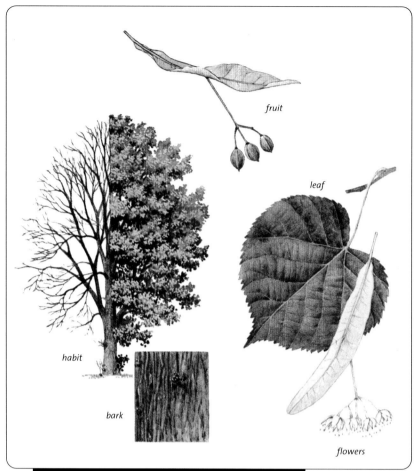

fruit

leaf

habit

bark

flowers

Tilia platyphyllos Scop. Large-leaved Lime

A tall, narrowly domed tree up to 40m high. **Bark** Dark grey, with fine fissures and sometimes flattish ridges. **Branches** Spread at narrow angles; the young twigs are reddish-green, glabrous or pubescent, the hairs often confined to the tip of the twig. **Buds** *c.* 6mm long, ovoid, dark red, pubescent or glabrous. **Leaves** 6–9cm (rarely 15cm) long, broadly ovate, abruptly narrowed into a short tapering tip, symmetrically or obliquely deeply heart-shaped at the base, the margins with regular sharp teeth, soft, dark green above, paler and usually hairy or sometimes almost smooth beneath; the petiole is 1·2–5cm long, often pubescent. The bracts are oblong-obovate, whitish-green, minutely pubescent or glabrous. **Flowers** Yellowish-white, occurring in clusters of 2–6 in a pendent cyme; staminodes are absent; the style is smooth; the peduncles 1·5–3·5cm long. **Fruit** 0·8–1·2cm long, almost globose to pear-shaped with 3–5 strong ridges, tomentose; the shell is woody. **Flowering period** June. **Distribution** A variable species occurring on lime-rich soils in C. and S. Europe, extending eastwards to the W. Ukraine and Asia Minor. It may have been introduced to some parts of NW. Europe. It is frequently planted in parks and as a street tree. Al Au Be Br Bu Co Cz De Fr Fu Gr Ho Hu It Po Ru Sd Si Sp Sw Tu Yu.

Tilia rubra DC.

A species very similar to and often confused with *T. platyphyllos* but with firmer, smoother leaves with a more oblique base, and teeth ending in a hair-like point. **Distribution** S. and CE. Europe. Al Bu Fu Gr Hu Ru Yu.

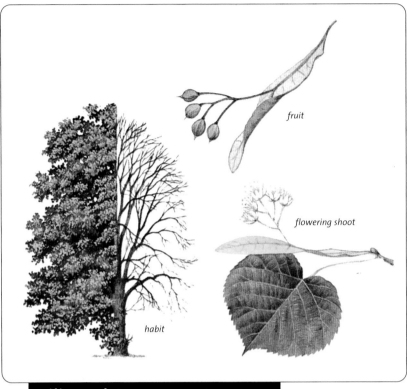

fruit

flowering shoot

habit

Tilia cordata Miller Small-leaved Lime

A tall, irregularly domed tree up to 32m high with a dense crown. **Bark** Grey, very smooth on young trees, becoming dark grey or brown with large cracks and flakes on old trees. **Branches** Ascending, becoming downwardly arched on old trees; the twigs are smooth or almost smooth, brownish-red above, olive below. **Buds** *c.* 5mm long, ovoid, smooth, dark red. **Leaves** 3–9cm long, more or less round, abruptly narrowed into a tapering point, heart-shaped at the base, the margin with fine, sharp teeth, dark shiny green and smooth above, pale beneath, often glaucous with reddish-brown tufts of hairs in the axils of the veins; the petiole is 2·5–4cm long, smooth. The bracts are oblong-lanceolate to obovate, bright, pale green, petiolate. **Flowers** Translucent white, 4–15 carried together in an obliquely erect cyme; staminodes are absent; the style is smooth; the peduncle is 1–2·5cm long. **Fruit** *c.* 6mm long, globose, sometimes slightly ribbed, downy at first, but often becoming smooth; the shell is thin and rather membranous. **Flowering period** July. **Distribution** A native commonly occurring on base-rich soils in much of Europe except the extreme N. and S. It is frequently planted in parks or as a street tree. Al Au Be Br Bu Co Cz De Fi Fr Fu Ge Gr Ho Hu It No Po Ru Sd Sp Sw Tu Yu.

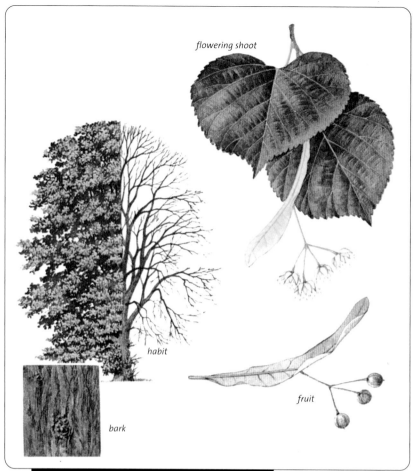

flowering shoot

habit

fruit

bark

Tilia x vulgaris Hayne Common Lime

A tall, irregularly domed tree up to 46m high. **Bark** Dull grey, smooth on young trees, becoming finely fissured or with flattish ridges at maturity; the bole often with dense sprouts and burrs. **Branches** Ascending, becoming arched on old trees; the young twigs are green, smooth or (rarely) slightly downy. **Buds** *c.* 7mm long, ovoid, reddish-brown, usually smooth. **Leaves** 6–10cm long, broadly ovate with a short tapering tip, the base obliquely heart-shaped or nearly truncate, the teeth rounded with a sharp point, dull green above, paler beneath, smooth except for tufts of whitish hairs in the axils of the veins beneath; the petiole is 2–5cm long, green, smooth. The bracts are oblong, yellowish-green, slightly downy on the midrib. **Flowers** Yellowish-white, occurring in clusters of 5–10 in a pendent cyme; staminodes are absent; the style is smooth; the peduncle is 1·5–3·5cm long. **Fruit** *c.* 8mm long, broadly ovoid to almost globose, rounded at the ends, slightly ribbed, downy, the shell thick and woody, often sterile. **Flowering period** July. **Distribution and taxonomic notes** The Common Lime is a hybrid between *T. cordata* and *T. platyphyllos*. These two species commonly hybridize where they grow together in Europe, and the cultivated plant probably originated from a wild hybrid. It is very widely planted for ornament or as a shade tree and in many regions is more abundant than either parent. Au Br Cz Fr Fu Ge Gr Hu It Po Ru Sd Si Sp Sw.

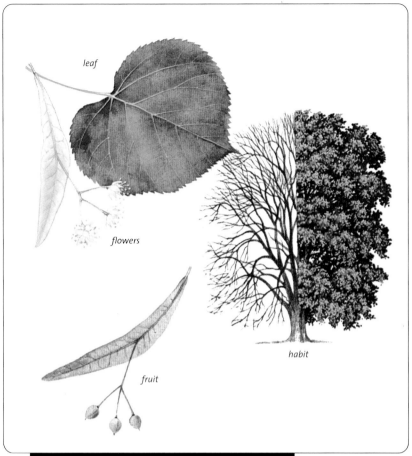

leaf

flowers

fruit

habit

Tilia x euchlora C. Koch Caucasian Lime

A medium-sized, irregularly domed tree up to 20m high. **Bark** Smooth, dull grey, becoming brown and cracked on old trees. **Branches** Ascending at first, rather sinuous, curving downwards and becoming pendulous at the tips of old trees; the twigs are bright green, occasionally reddish-brown above, usually smooth. **Buds** 3–6mm in diameter, yellow and reddish, smooth. **Leaves** 5–10cm long, broadly ovate, abruptly narrowed into a short tapering tip, obliquely heart-shaped at the base, the teeth fine and ending in a slender hair-like tip, dark shining green above, paler beneath with conspicuous tufts of reddish-brown hairs in the axils of the veins; the petiole is *c.* 3·5cm long, smooth. The bracts are rather narrowly obovate to elliptic-oblong, greenish-white. **Flowers** Rich yellow, occurring in pendent cymose clusters of 3–7; staminodes are absent; the peduncle is 2·5–5·5cm long. **Fruit** *c.* 1·2cm long, ovoid to elliptic, tapered at both ends, slightly 5-ribbed, downy; the shell is thick and woody. **Flowering period** July. **Distribution and taxonomic notes** The Caucasian Lime is a rare hybrid between *T. cordata* and *T. dasystyla*, from Crimean oak woodlands. *T. dasystyla* Steven has downy young twigs, tufts of yellowish hairs in the leaf vein axils and a pubescent style. It is rarely cultivated, whereas the hybrid is frequently planted in various parts of Europe for ornament in parks or as a street tree.

Tupelo or Sour-gum Tree Family
Nyssaceae

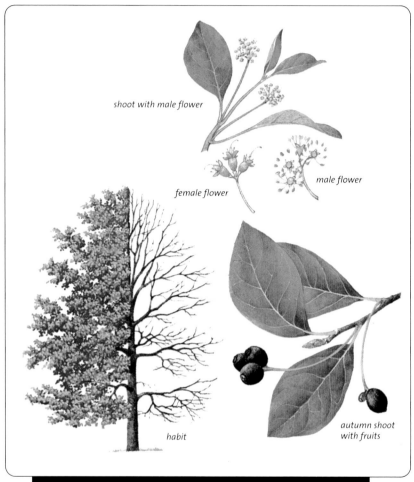

shoot with male flower

female flower

male flower

habit

autumn shoot
with fruits

Nyssa sylvatica Marsh Black Gum, Tupelo or Pepperidge

A deciduous dioecious tree up to 30m high in the wild, with a bole up to 1·5m in diameter and a broadly conical crown. **Bark** Brownish-grey, with cracks separating broad ridges. **Leaves** 5–15cm long x 4–8cm wide, usually ovate or obovate with a tapering base, entire or rarely somewhat toothed, usually glabrous except on the petiole and midrib; the petiole is 1·5–2·5cm long, frequently reddish-tinged. **Flowers** Unisexual, on separate trees, up to 1·5cm in diameter, greenish, produced on slender downy peduncles up to 3cm long; male flowers are numerous, in rounded heads; females are in few-flowered clusters, with 2–4 in each head. **Fruit** A drupe, 1–2cm long, in a cluster, egg-shaped, bluish-black with a 1-seeded stone. **Distribution** A swamp species in E. N. America, introduced as an ornamental into European gardens for its brilliant red and yellow autumn foliage.

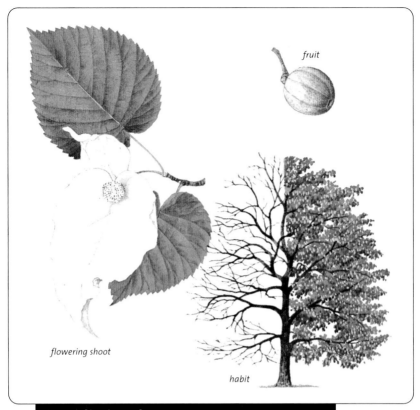

fruit

flowering shoot

habit

Davidia involucrata Baillon
Pocket-handkerchief Tree, Ghost Tree or Dove Tree

A slender deciduous tree 12–20m high, with stout branches and a conical crown becoming narrowly domed at maturity. **Bark** Greyish-brown or purplish-brown with small vertical cracks, and occasionally flaking. The shoots are smooth and dull brown. **Buds** Ovoid, smooth and dark red. **Leaves** 8–18cm long, broadly ovate, heart-shaped at the base, tapering to a slender tip, with 5–9 pairs of veins, the margin with triangular teeth tapering to sharp tips, deep shiny green above, pale and softly pubescent beneath; the petiole is up to 15cm long, pink, yellow-green or sometimes dark red. **Flowers** Small, lacking petals, in dense heads, each with numerous male flowers and 1 bisexual flower; they are conspicuous by the stamens and a large pair of white bracts up to 16cm long x 10cm wide, hanging from the base. **Fruit** 3·5cm in diameter when ripe, rounded, green with a purple bloom. **Flowering period** May. **Distribution** A species native to China, commonly planted in parks and gardens in NW. Europe.

Eucryphia Family
Eucryphiaceae

Several species of *Eucryphia*, a genus of southern hemisphere shrubs, are grown in Europe for their showy flowers. The following 2 cultivars are perhaps the most important: *Eucryphia* x *nymansensis* Bausch, a hybrid between *E. glutinosa* (Poeppig & Endl.) Baillon and *E. cordifolia* Cav. with evergreen leaves and large white flowers 6–8cm in diameter; and *Eucryphia* x *intermedia* Bausch, a hybrid between *E. glutinosa* (Poeppig & Endl.) Baillon and *E. lucida* (Labill.) Baillon with glossy evergreen leaves and white flowers 6cm in diameter.

Buckthorn and Oleaster Family
Elaeagnaceae

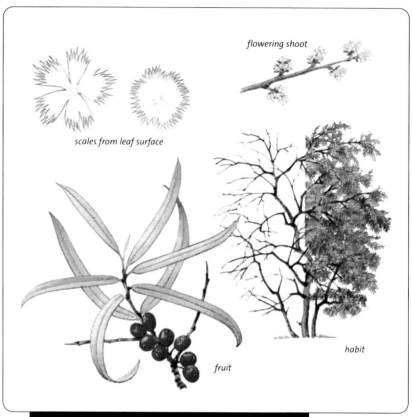

flowering shoot

scales from leaf surface

fruit

habit

Hippophäe rhamnoides L. Sea Buckthorn

A much-branched deciduous dioecious shrub or small tree up to 11m tall, suckering freely from the bole. **Bark** Fissured and scaling on old stems. The twigs are covered with silvery scales. **Leaves** 1–6 x 0·3–1 cm, more or less sessile, simple, entire, covered on both sides with silvery or reddish-brown scales. **Flowers** Greenish, *c.* 3mm in diameter, rather inconspicuous, appearing before the leaves on previous year's growth; male flowers have 4 stamens, the lower flowers sessile, and the flower tube is shorter than the 2 lobes; all female flowers are pedicellate with a flower tube longer than the lobes. **Fruit** 6–8mm in diameter, berry-like, bright orange, containing a single seed. **Flowering period** March–April. **Fruiting** September onwards. **Distribution** A coastal species of stable sand dunes and sea-cliffs, and on river gravel and alluvium in montane regions. It is a native of much of Europe, particularly the NW. It is often planted for ornament, or as a sand dune stabilizer, and has become naturalized in many places. Au Be Br Bu Cz De Fi Fr Fu Ge Ho Hu It No Po Ru Sp Sw Yu.

flowering shoot

fruit

habit

Elaeagnus angustifolia L. Oleaster

A dioecious deciduous shrub or small tree up to 13m high. **Branches** Occasionally spiny. The young shoots are covered with glistening silvery scales, becoming glabrous and dark in the 2nd year. **Leaves** 4–8 x 1–2.5cm, oblong or linear-lanceolate, dull green above and covered with silvery scales beneath. **Flowers** 0.8–1cm long, fragrant, appearing either solitary or in twos or threes in each leaf axil, before the leaves; each flower is a bell-shaped tube, silvery outside and yellow inside; the peduncle is 2–3mm long. **Fruit** Oval, 1–2cm long, succulent, yellowish and covered with silvery scales. **Flowering period** June. **Distribution and taxonomic notes** A native of W. Asia, planted for ornament and widely naturalized in S. Europe, northwards to Czechoslovakia and C. Russia. Al Au Bu Cr Cz Fr Fu Gr Hu It Ru Sp. A related species, *Elaeagnus commutata* Rehder, the Silver Berry from N. America, is often confused with the Oleaster. It differs in having brown twigs and dry mealy fruits. It is cultivated and has become naturalized in many parts of Europe for its silvery foliage and delightfully fragrant flowers.

Tamarisk Family
Tamaricaceae

Tamarix L.

Shrubs or small trees with small, scale-like, clasping or sheathing alternate leaves with sunken, salt-secreting glands. **Flowers** Small, white or pink, in spike-like racemes which may be borne on the current year's growth, the previous year's growth, or both; there are 4–5 sepals and petals; there are 4–15 stamens, 4–5 opposite the sepals and 0–10 opposite the petals; there are 4–5 short styles. In species without stamens opposite the petals there is a more or less fleshy, nectar-secreting disc with 4–5 lobes between the stamens and the ovary. **Seeds** Have a tuft of hairs.

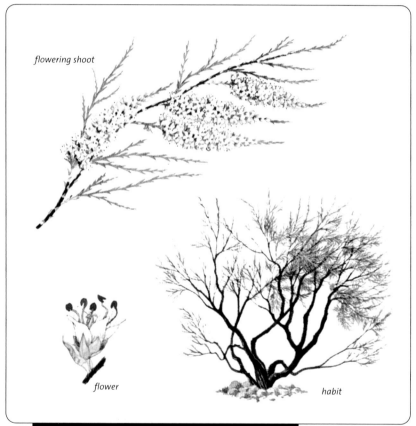

flowering shoot

flower

habit

Tamarix africana Poiret African Tamarisk

A slender tree up to 8m high. **Bark** Black or dark purple-black, and glabrous. **Leaves** 1·5–4mm long, with narrow papery margins, acute. **Flowers** The racemes are 3–6 x 0·5–0·8cm, solitary, usually appearing in spring, but frequently summer in Spain and Portugal; the bracts are triangular, obtuse to acuminate, sometimes exceeding the calyx; the flowers are subsessile, white or pale pink, the flower parts in fives, without stamens opposite the petals; the sepals are 1·5mm long, angular-ovate, acute; the petals are 2–3mm long, angular-ovate, some of them persistent; the stamen filaments are expanded at the base and joined with the lobes of the disc. **Distribution** A species of coastal salt marshes and river banks in SW. Europe but introduced and occasionally naturalized elsewhere. Bl Br Co Fr It Po Sa Si Sp.

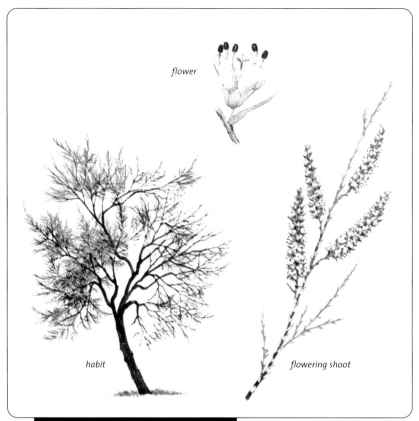

flower

habit

flowering shoot

Tamarix canariensis Willd.

A more or less bushy shrub or tree up to 10m high. **Bark** Reddish-brown. **Leaves** 1–3mm long. **Flowers** The racemes are 1·5–4·5 x 0·3–0·5cm, solitary or clustered, dense, with a papillose axis, usually appearing in summer, but sometimes spring in Spain; the bracts are linear to triangular-acuminate, entire, equalling or somewhat exceeding the calyx; the flowers are pink, with 5 parts, and with 5 stamens opposite the petals; the sepals are 0·5–0·75mm long, finely and deeply divided; the petals are 1·25–1·5mm long, obovate and falling early; the stamen filaments are expanded at the base and joined with the lobes of the disc. **Distribution** A maritime species in dry places of the W. Mediterranean region and Portugal. Bl Fr Po Sa Si Sp.

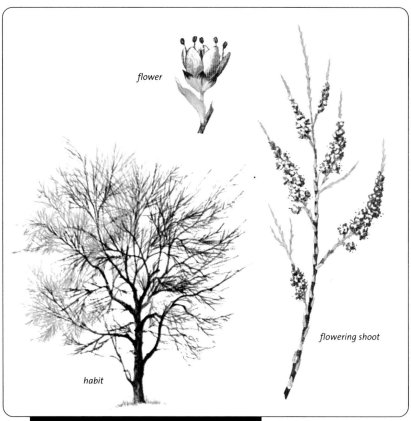

flower

flowering shoot

habit

Tamarix gallica L. French Tamarisk

A small tree or often a shrub up to 8m. **Bark** Purplish-brown to blackish-brown, without papillae. **Leaves** 1·5–2mm long. **Flowers** 2·5 x *c.* 0·5cm, loosely clustered, appearing in spring; the bracts are ragged-edged, shorter than the calyx, the lowermost oblong and blunt, the upper narrowly triangular with a slender, tapering point; the flowers are pink and in 5 parts without stamens opposite the petals; the sepals are 0·7–1·3mm, angular-ovate, acute; the petals are 1·5–2mm long, elliptic to somewhat ovate, falling early; the stamen filaments are not conspicuously swollen at the base but are joined with the lobes of the disc. **Distribution** A common species in SW. Europe, extending to NW. France but frequently cultivated and occasionally becoming naturalized elsewhere. Bl Br Co Fr It Si Sp.

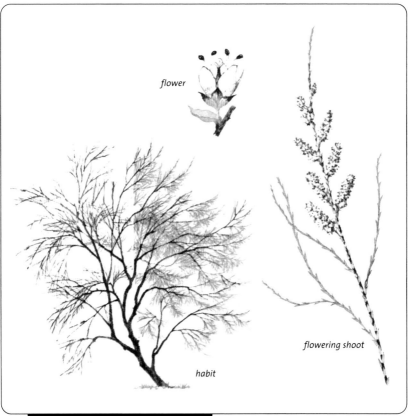

flower

flowering shoot

habit

Tamarix parviflora DC.

A feathery, slender shrub or small tree up to 6m high. **Bark** Smooth, dark brown or purple. **Leaves** 3–5mm long, acute, with a papery margin. **Flowers** The racemes are 3–5 x 0·3–0·5cm, solitary, dense, mostly produced in the spring; the bracts are oblong, obtuse and almost entirely scarious; the flowers are white or pale pink, with 4 (occasionally 5) parts with 0–4 stamens opposite the petals; the sepals are 2–2·5mm long, ovate or somewhat angular, denticulate, the outer keeled and acute, the inner obtuse and shorter; the petals are *c.* 2mm long; the filaments of the stamens opposite the sepals are inserted in shallow sinuses between the lobes of the conspicuous fleshy disc. **Distribution** A native of river banks, hedges and roadsides of the Balkan Peninsula and the Aegean region, but now widely cultivated for ornament in C. and S. Europe. Al Co Cr Gr It Sp Tu Yu.

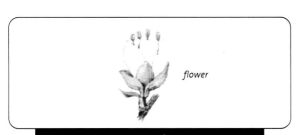

flower

Tamarix tetrandra Pallas ex Bieb.

A remarkably similar species to *T. parviflora* but with black bark, longer and broader racemes, herbaceous bracts and larger flowers (with petals 2·5–3mm long). **Distribution** A montane species, particularly of damp places in SE. Europe and the Balkan Peninsula. Bu Fu Gr Tu Yu.

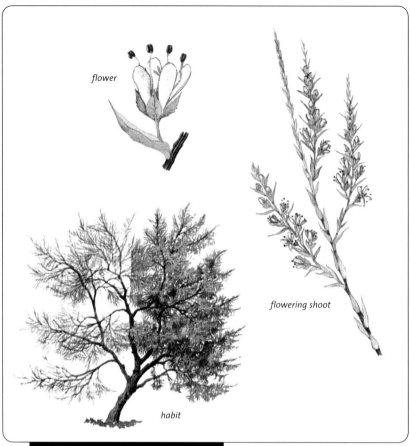

flower

flowering shoot

habit

Tamarix dalmatica Baum

A small glabrous tree. **Bark** Dark brown or blackish. **Leaves** 2·5–4mm long, acute. **Flowers** The racemes are 2–6 x 0·8–1cm, solitary, usually appearing in spring. The bracts are broadly triangular, obtuse to acuminate, often thin and papery, usually exceeding the pedicels and calyx; the flowers are subsessile, white, in 4 (sometimes 5) parts with up to 3 stamens opposite the petals; the sepals are 3·5mm long, keeled, the outer ones angular-ovate, acute, the inner ones obtuse; the petals are 2·5–5mm long, narrowly obovate; the bases of the stamen filaments suddenly expand to surround the disc. **Distribution** A common species of coastal marshes and river banks in the E. Mediterranean. Al Cr Gr It Si Yu.

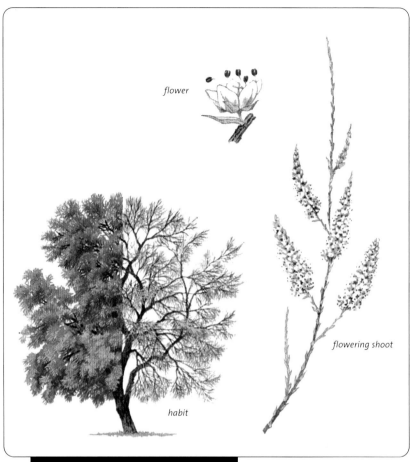

flower

flowering shoot

habit

Tamarix smyrnensis Bunge

A small tree or shrub. **Bark** Reddish-brown. **Leaves** 1·5–3·5mm long, acute. **Flowers** The racemes are 1·5–7 x 0·3–0·4cm long, loosely clustered, the uppermost without flowers at the base, usually appearing in summer; the bracts are narrowly triangular, acute, denticulate, exceeding the pedicels; the pedicel is shorter than the calyx; the flowers are pink, in 5 parts, without stamens opposite the petals; the sepals are *c.* 1mm long, angular-ovate, obtuse or sometimes ragged at the tip; the petals are *c.* 2mm long, ovate-orbicular, strongly keeled, especially towards the base; the stamen filaments are slender and attached between the slightly notched lobes of the fleshy disc. **Distribution and taxonomic notes** A species of coastal salt-marshes and mountain streams in SE. Europe, extending from the Aegean region to the S. Ukraine. Al Bu Cr Fu Gr Ru Tu. The similar Chinese species, *T. chinensis* Louv., the Chinese Tamarisk, is widely planted in Europe for ornament. It has smaller flowers than *T. smyrnensis*.

Myrtle Family
Myrtaceae

Eucalyptus L'Her. Eucalyptus or Gum Trees

Large to medium-sized trees. **Bark** 3 kinds: (i) soft and brittle, shedding in short irregular flakes, lacking in fibre; (ii) hard and long-fibred, shedding in long, broad, thick flakes or strips; (iii) very thin and finely fibred, shedding in ribbons. **Leaves** 3 kinds, passing through juvenile, intermediate and mature stages. **Flowers** The inflorescences are either solitary or in umbels. The buds are surrounded by an operculum of fused calyx segments. **Fruit** A capsule consisting of an enlarged calyx tube with a flat disc surrounded by a rim and opening by valves.

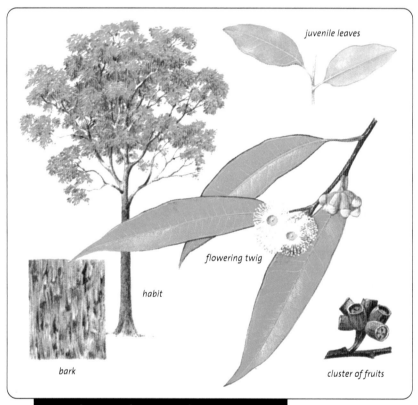

juvenile leaves

flowering twig

habit

bark

cluster of fruits

Eucalyptus botryoides Sm. Bangalay

A dense, shade-giving tree, 12–24m high. **Bark** Slightly fibrous and persistent on the trunk and main branches. **Leaves** Juvenile ones are 5–8 x 3–4cm, opposite for 3–4 pairs, broadly lanceolate to ovate, thin and somewhat wavy, with very fine veins; mature leaves are 10–14 x 3–6cm, alternate, lanceolate to oval, dark green, leathery, pointed, with long petioles; the veins are faint to conspicuous and the intramarginal vein is close to the margin. **Flowers** The inflorescence is axillary, in 6- to 10-flowered umbels on peduncles 7–10cm long. The buds are 1–1·2 x 0·5–0·6cm, slightly angled or 2-ribbed, sessile; the operculum is hemispherical or bluntly conical; the anthers are oblong, with an ovate dorsal gland about half the length of the cells. **Fruit** 7–9 x 7–9mm, sessile, cylindrical or barrel-shaped, with a small disc and 3–4 triangular valves, which are enclosed or only slightly projecting above the rim. **Distribution** A timber, shade or ornamental tree which will grow on a variety of soils but is particular well suited to gravelly, sandy or even marshy soils. A native of SE. Australia (New South Wales and Victoria), now cultivated in It Pl Si Sp.

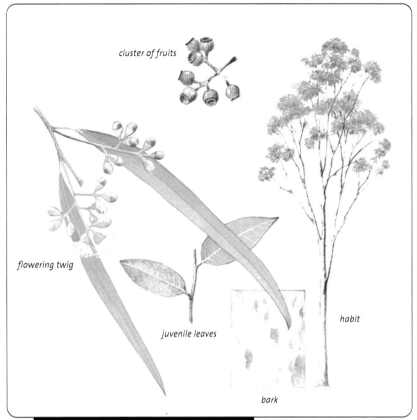

cluster of fruits

flowering twig

juvenile leaves

bark

habit

Eucalyptus citriodora Hooker
Lemon-scented Spotted Gum

A tall graceful slender tree 25–40m high. **Bark** Smooth and deciduous throughout, white or pinkish. **Leaves** Juvenile leaves are 7–15 x 3–6cm, opposite for 4–5 pairs, oblong or lanceolate, rough and bristly; adult leaves are 10–25 x 1–4cm, alternate, narrowly or broadly lanceolate, strongly lemon-scented; the veins are moderately conspicuous but the intramarginal vein is not distinct from the margin. **Flowers** The inflorescence is an axillary branched flattened spike, with 3–5 flowers on peduncles 5–7mm long. The buds are 1–1·2 x 0·7–0·8cm, pedicellate; the operculum is hemispherical; the anthers are somewhat club-shaped, with a gland about half as long as the long cells. **Fruit** *c.* 1 x 1cm, globose or subcylindrical, shortly pedicellate, but strongly contracted at the mouth with a wide disc and 3–4 enclosed valves. **Distribution** An adaptable tree found on a variety of soils but particularly suitable for poor soils. A native of Queensland, this species is cultivated as an ornamental in It Pl Sp.

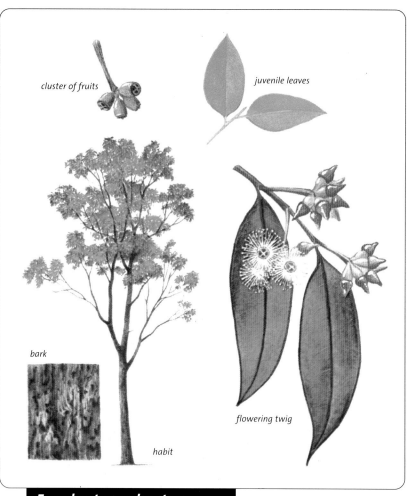

cluster of fruits

juvenile leaves

bark

flowering twig

habit

Eucalyptus robusta Sm.
Swamp Mahogany, Swamp Messmate

A medium-sized shady tree up to 30m high. **Bark** Rough, rather fibrous and persistent throughout, dark in colour. **Leaves** Juvenile leaves are up to 11 x 7cm long, opposite for 4–5 pairs, stalked, thick, broadly lanceolate to elliptic-lanceolate; adult leaves are 10–18 x 4–5cm, alternate, lanceolate to oval, with long apical points, lustrous dark green above, dull green below; the veins are moderately conspicuous. **Flowers** The inflorescence is an axillary umbel of 5–10 flowers, supported by a flat peduncle 2–3cm long; the buds are 1–2 x 0·7–1cm, on short pedicels; the operculum is beak-like; the anthers are somewhat club-shaped with a large oval dorsal gland. **Fruit** 1·2–1·5 x 1–1·2cm, pedicellate, cylindrical to urn-shaped, with an oblique disc and deeply enclosed valves. **Distribution** A lowland plant from marshes, shores of estuaries and brackish water. A native of E. Australia, it is now planted as a plantation tree for its foliage, as a shade tree and a windbreak in Fr It Pl Sa Sp.

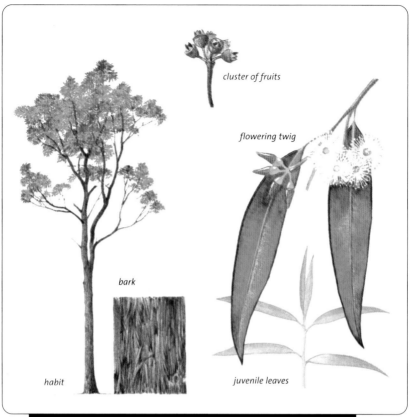

cluster of fruits

flowering twig

bark

habit

juvenile leaves

Eucalyptus resinifera Sm. in White **Red Mahogany**

A large tree with trunk up to 1·2m in diameter at maturity. **Bark** Rough, very fibrous with distinct longitudinal fissures, shedding below but persistent on the branches, reddish in colour. **Leaves** Juvenile leaves are 4–6 x 1·5–2cm, opposite for 3–4 pairs, lanceolate to ovate with short petioles; adult leaves are 10–16 x 2–3cm, alternate, lanceolate, dark green above, paler below, the veins moderately conspicuous. **Flowers** The inflorescence is an axillary umbel with 5–10 flowers on flattened peduncles 1·5–2cm long. The buds are 1·2–1·7 x 0·5–0·6cm, pedicellate; the operculum is very long and pointed, 2–3 times as long as the calyx tube; the anthers are club-shaped to oblong, opening in parallel slits. **Fruit** 5–8 x 5–8mm, ovoid to hemispherical with a small, slightly domed disc and 4 strongly projecting valves. **Distribution and taxonomic notes** A species which is grown on a variety of soils but mostly suitable for sandy coastal areas with subsoil moisture: A native of E. Australia (Queensland and New South Wales) the Red Mahogany is grown widely in sheltered places of the Mediterranean region as a timber tree, for its hard, heavy, fine-grained timber. Fr It Pl Sa Sp. The N. African hybrid *Eucalyptus x trabutii* Vilmorin ex Trabut is similar in general appearance to *E. resinifer* and grown in similar places, but has more oval mature leaves, a shorter operculum and a fruit more tapered at the base.

Valve arrangements

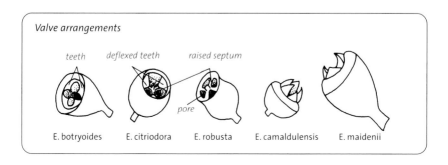

teeth   *deflexed teeth*   *raised septum*

pore

E. botryoides   E. citriodora   E. robusta   E. camaldulensis   E. maidenii

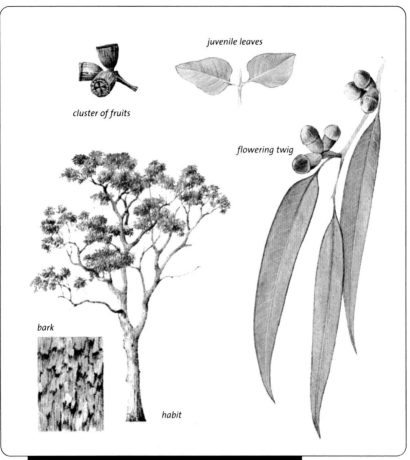

juvenile leaves

cluster of fruits

flowering twig

bark

habit

Eucalyptus gomphocephala DC. Tuart

A medium-sized to large tree up to 43m high. **Bark** Fibrous and persistent throughout, light grey. **Leaves** Juvenile leaves are 5–7 x 4–5cm, opposite for 3–4 pairs, broadly lanceolate; mature leaves are up to 17 x 2cm, alternate, distinctly stalked, thick, narrowly lanceolate, pointed. **Flowers** The inflorescence is an axillary umbel with 3–7 flowers suspended on strap-shaped peduncles, 2·5–3·5 x 1–1·5cm long. The buds are 2–2·5 x 1·2–1·5cm, sessile. The operculum is hemispherical or bluntly conical, mushroom-like and broader than the calyx tube; the anthers are oblong, opening in longitudinal slits and with a large oblong dorsal gland. **Fruit** 1·3–2 x 1·1–1·5cm, sessile, bell-shaped, with a disc forming a conspicuous rim around the strong, shortly projecting valves. **Distribution** Occurring on low-lying coastal plains on sandy loam and calcareous soils. A coastal species of Australia, planted experimentally for reafforestation of sand dunes, since it is resistant to drought, and, owing to its short bole, resistant to wind. It Si Sp.

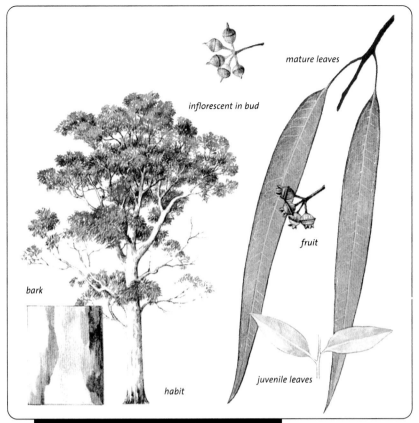

inflorescent in bud

mature leaves

fruit

bark

habit

juvenile leaves

Eucalyptus camaldulensis Dehnh.
Red Gum or Murray Red Gum

A tall tree growing up to (rarely) 40m with a short trunk and a spreading crown. **Bark** Smooth, shedding in plates or strips, mottled buff and grey. **Leaves** Juvenile leaves are 6–9 x 2·5–4cm, opposite for 3–4 pairs, broadly lanceolate to ovate, waxy and bluish; adult leaves are 12–22 x 0·8–1·5cm, alternate, lanceolate, long-pointed, thin, dull and pale green; the veins are conspicuous. **Flowers** The inflorescence is an axillary 5 to 10-flowered umbel on a slender round peduncle 0·6–1·5cm long. The buds are 0·6–1 x 0·4–0·5cm, on slender 3–8mm pedicels. The operculum is beaked, or a long cone; the anthers are obovate, opening in parallel slits, with a small globose dorsal gland. **Fruit** 6–8 x 6–8mm, hemispherical to broadly top-shaped, with a sharp domed disc and 4 sharp triangular curved valves. **Distribution** One of the most variable and widespread species of Australia, it is one of the most widely planted trees in the world's eucalypt plantations. It is usually planted on heavy soils and in Spain is particularly valuable as a timber tree for making mine props and for use as firewood. It was introduced to the Mediterranean region in the early 19th century. Al Co Gr It Pl Sa Si Sp.

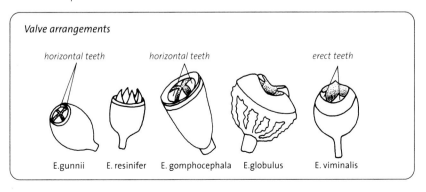

Valve arrangements

horizontal teeth　　　*horizontal teeth*　　　*erect teeth*

E.gunnii　　E. resinifer　　E. gomphocephala　　E.globulus　　E. viminalis

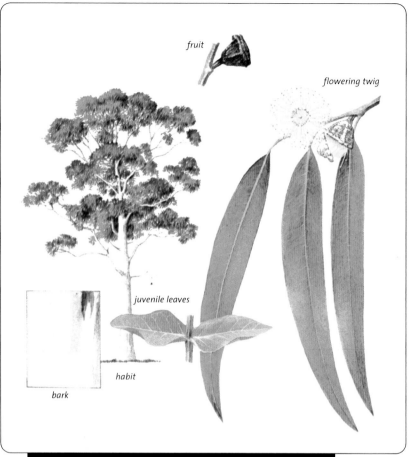

fruit

flowering twig

juvenile leaves

habit

bark

Eucalyptus globulus Labill. Tasmanian Blue Gum

A medium-sized to large tree, reputed to attain 65m. **Bark** Smooth, mostly deciduous but persistent at the base, blue-grey. **Leaves** Juvenile leaves are 7–16 x 4–9cm, opposite for many pairs, broadly lanceolate to ovate, heart-shaped at the base, sessile and even clasping the stem; adult leaves are 10–30 x 3–4cm, or longer, alternate, narrowly lanceolate to lanceolate, sickle-shaped, lustrous dark green all over, leathery, distinctly petiolate; the veins are only moderately conspicuous. **Flowers** The inflorescence consists usually of a single axillary flower but can have an umbel with up to 3 flowers on very short peduncles. The buds are up to 3 x 2cm, glaucous, sessile; the operculum is a flattened hemisphere, peaked, thick and warty; the anthers are obovate, opening in broad parallel slits with a globose gland. **Fruit** 1–1.5 x 1.5–3cm, a flat globe-shape to broadly top-shaped, roughly 4-angled, warty, with one or more short irregular ribs, and with a large, thick smooth disc completely extending over 3–8 valves arranged more or less at disc level. **Distribution and taxonomic notes** An Australian endemic from SE. Tasmania and Victoria. Planted on a tremendous scale in the Mediterranean region. It is grown for its yellow timber, used as a pulp in the paper industry, and as a source of oil from the leaves. It occurs particularly in Sp and Pl, but also in Co Gr It and as an ornamental in Br. In addition to *E. globulus* and the species described on pages 270–279 which have been largely planted in S.C. and SW. Mediterranean Europe, some 30 other species of *Eucalyptus* have been occasionally planted for ornamental purposes in parks and gardens and in small coastal plantations in many parts of NW. Europe. Important examples include *E. rudis* Endl., *E. cladocalyx* F. Mueller, *E. diversicolor* F. Mueller, *E. maculata* Hooker, *E. sideroxylon* A. Cunn. ex Woolls, *E. amygdalina* Labill., *E. pauciflora* Siebold ex Sprengel, *E. punctata* DC., *E. tereticornis* Sm., *E. urnigera* Hooker fil. and *E. coccifera* Hooker fil.

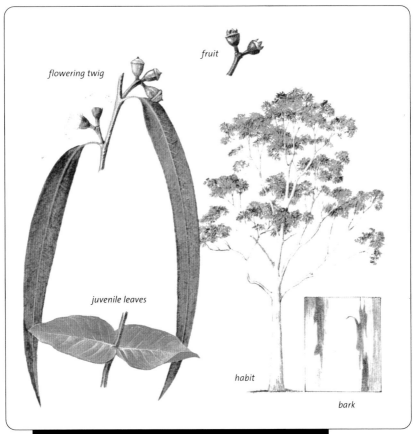

flowering twig

fruit

juvenile leaves

habit

bark

Eucalyptus maidenii Mueller Maiden's Gum

A medium-sized to tall tree 15–46m high. **Bark** Smooth, shedding annually, bluish-white. **Leaves** Juvenile leaves are 4–16 x 4–12cm, opposite for a large number of pairs, ovate to almost orbicular, often heart-shaped at the base, distinctly greyish in appearance; mature leaves are up to 20 x 2·5cm, alternate, narrowly lanceolate to lanceolate, sickle-shaped, dark lustrous green, leathery, petiolate: the veins are conspicuous. **Flowers** The inflorescence is an axillary 3–7 (or more) flowered umbel on a flattened peduncle, 10–15cm long. The buds are *c.* 1·5 x 0·8cm, sessile or pedicellate; the operculum is a peaked hemisphere or beak-shaped. The anthers are obovate, opening in narrow parallel slits with an ovate gland, half the length of the cells. **Fruit** 0·8–1 x 1–1·2cm, subsessile to shortly pedicellate, bell-shaped or conical, waxy on the surface, with a thick, smooth, flat or convex disc partly fused to the strongly projecting valves. **Distribution** A species of good, somewhat heavy soils. A SE. Australian tree cultivated for timber. It Pl Sa Si Sp.

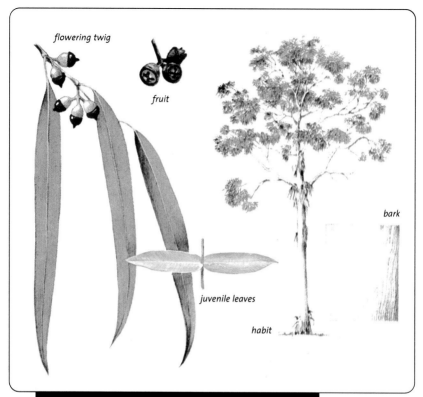

flowering twig

fruit

bark

juvenile leaves

habit

Eucalyptus viminalis Labill. Ribbon Gum

A large tree up to 50m high. **Bark** Rough and persistent at the base or quite smooth throughout, deciduous, often hanging from the branches in long ribbons. **Leaves** Juvenile leaves are 5–10 x 1·5–3cm, slender, lanceolate, opposite for an indefinite number of pairs, sessile to semi-clasping, pale green; intermediate leaves are 8–27 x 4–5cm, broadly lanceolate, pointed, pale green; mature leaves are 11–18 x 1·5–2cm, narrowly lanceolate, alternate, petiolate, flat or undulate, pale green; the veins are faint to moderately conspicuous. **Flowers** The inflorescence is an axillary, usually 3-flowered umbel on an angular 3–6mm peduncle. The buds are *c.* 7 x 5mm, oval to cylindrical, sessile or on short pedicels; the operculum is hemispherical to conical, usually longer than the tube; the anthers are obovate with an ovate gland. **Fruit** 5–6 x 7–8mm, spherical or top-shaped, sessile or with a very short pedicel with a prominent convex or upwardly contracted disc and 3–4 projecting and spreading valves. **Flowering period** August–September. **Distribution** A fairly useful shade and shelter tree with a light, serviceable timber. It grows in Riviera towns and Mediterranean sandy areas. A S. and E. Australian and Tasmanian tree cultivated in It Pl Sp.

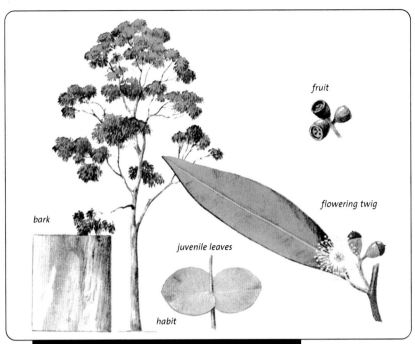

fruit

flowering twig

bark

juvenile leaves

habit

Eucalyptus gunnii Hooker fil. Cider Gum

A medium-sized to large tree up to 30m high. **Bark** Quite smooth, deciduous, green and white or pink-tinged. **Leaves** Juvenile leaves are 3–4 x 2–4cm or larger, elliptical to obovate in outline and somewhat heart-shaped at the base, sessile, glaucous or green; mature leaves are 4–7 x 1·5–3cm, narrow to broadly lanceolate, petiolate, distinctly green; the veins are faint to moderately conspicuous. **Flowers** The inflorescence is an axillary 3-flowered umbel on a slightly flattened or rounded peduncle 3–8mm long. The buds are 6–8 x *c.* 5mm, club-shaped or subcylindrical, sessile or on short pedicels; the operculum is peaked-hemispherical and much shorter than the flask-shaped calyx-tube; the anthers are oblong to orbicular with a large globose dorsal gland. **Fruit** 0·7–1 x 0·8–0·9cm, hemispherical or bell-shaped, with a small depressed blunt disc and 3–5 narrow, slightly projecting valves. **Distribution** A subalpine species planted in cooler parts of Europe, since it is tolerant to cold weather and wet soils. A native species from the highlands of Tasmania, it has been vigorously cultivated from seed in Britain and France.

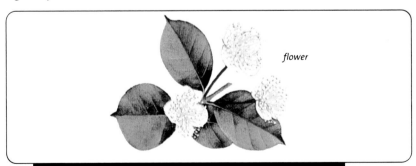

flower

Myrtus apiculata Niedenzu Orange-bark Myrtle

A moderate-sized evergreen tree with a loosely conical crown. **Bark** Orange, flaking readily to leave tapering white streaks below. **Leaves** 2·5 x 1·5cm, alternate, subsessile, oval with a distinct mucronate tip, with a sweet spicy smell when crushed. **Flowers** Solitary in the axils of the leaves; they are globose in bud, red and green in colour, producing masses of white flowers up to 2cm in diameter. **Fruit** A berry, initially red, becoming black. **Flowering period** August–September. **Distribution** A S. American species, planted in gardens.

Pomegranate Family
Punicaceae

flowers

habit

fruit

Punica granatum L. Pomegranate

A deciduous shrub or sometimes a small tree up to 8m high. **Branches** Numerous, slender, mostly ascending or erect. The twigs are spiny or unarmed, somewhat 4-angled, glabrous. **Leaves** Opposite, 2–8 x 0·8–2·5cm, oblong lanceolate to obovate, entire, smooth and shiny, without glands; the petiole is very short; stipules are absent. **Flowers** Hermaphrodite, terminal, often on short side-shoots, solitary or in pairs, each 2·5–4cm in diameter; the sepal tube is funnel-shaped at the base, leathery, persistent, reddish with 5 or more thick, pointed lobes; the 5–7 petals are scarlet or sometimes white, crumpled in bud; the stamens are numerous. **Fruit** 5–8cm in diameter, globose to somewhat oblong, reddish-brown or yellowish, the outer layer leathery, containing several cells each with many seeds; the fleshy layer surrounding each seed is translucent, purplish-yellowish or white, acid, usually becoming sweet; the pedicel is very short. **Flowering period** June–September. **Distribution** A native of SW. Asia but cultivated from antiquity in S. Europe for its edible fruit and often naturalized in the Mediterranean region. Al Bl Bu Co Cr Fr Gr It Pl Ru Sa Sd Si Sp Tu Yu.

Dogwood Family
Cornaceae

flowers

fruit

habit

Cornus mas L. Cornelian Cherry

A small deciduous tree or shrub up to 8m (occasionally 15m) with an open crown. **Branches** Spreading, greyish. The young twigs are greenish-yellow, covered with minute grey hairs. **Leaves** Opposite, 4–10 x 2–4cm, ovate to elliptic, acuminate at the apex, the base rounded or acute, entire, dull green, pubescent; the petiole is *c.* 6mm long. **Flowers** Small umbellate flower-heads, *c.* 2cm in diameter, each containing 10–25 flowers, appearing before the leaves on the previous year's growth; the bracts are 0·6–1 x 0·3–0·6cm, yellowish, pubescent, 4 at the base of each flower cluster, falling readily; each flower is *c.* 4mm in diameter, yellow. **Fruit** Berry, 1·2–2cm long, oblong-ovoid with a sunken apex, pendulous, fleshy, bright red when ripe, acid-tasting; the pedicel is *c.* 6mm long. **Flowering period** February–March. **Distribution and taxonomic notes** A native to C. and SE. Europe but naturalized in some localities, occurring in thickets and other scrub, or among woodland. It is cultivated for its edible fruit and showy winter flowers. Al Au Be Br Bu Cz Fr Fu Ge Gr Hu It Ru Sd Tu Yu. A related species, *C. sanguinea* L., the Dogwood, is usually a deciduous shrub, found throughout Europe except in some parts of the extreme north and south.

Heather Family
Ericaceae

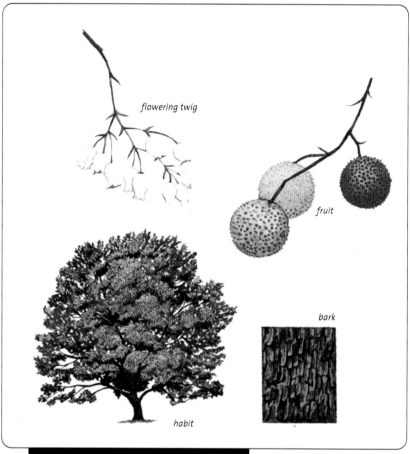

flowering twig

fruit

bark

habit

Arbutus unedo L. Strawberry Tree

A small tree or shrub up to 9m high with a dense rounded crown and usually a short bole. **Bark** At first red, later shredding and obscured by brown, hanging strips. **Branches** Numerous, ascending and sinuous, the young twigs glandular-hairy and pink or red. **Leaves** 4–11cm long, 1·5–4cm wide, oblong-lanceolate, 2–3 times as long as broad, the margins with sharp forward-projecting teeth or almost entire, hairy only at the base, dark glossy green above, paler beneath and with a prominent midrib; the petiole is up to 1cm long, hairy and often red. **Flowers** The drooping panicle is 4–5cm long, the flowers appearing in autumn together with the ripening fruits from the previous year. The calyx is green, 1·5mm long with suborbicular lobes; the corolla 9mm long, white or tinged with pink or green. **Fruit** 2cm in diameter, globose and covered with conical papillae, yellow, becoming scarlet or deep red when ripe, the flesh rather acid. **Flowering period** October–November. **Distribution** A species of evergreen thickets, wood margins and dry slopes in the Mediterranean region but occurring locally as far north as NW. Ireland. It is sometimes planted in gardens. Al Bl Co Cr Fr Gr Ir It Sa Si Sp Tu Yu.

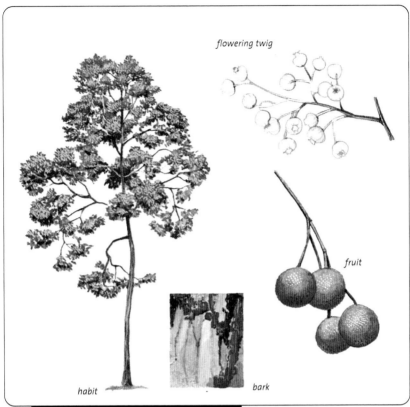

flowering twig

fruit

habit   *bark*

Arbutus andrachne L.
Cyprus or Eastern Strawberry Tree

Similar to *A. unedo* but sometimes reaching 12m in height. **Bark** Smooth and orange-red, peeling in sheets to reveal the yellowish or cinnamon-coloured underbark. **Branches** The young twigs are glabrous, initially yellowish-green, later becoming brown. **Leaves** 5–10cm long, 3–6cm wide, less than twice as long as broad, the young ones sometimes toothed, old ones entire, the midrib pale and prominent above; the petiole is 1·5–2·5cm long. **Flowers** The panicles are erect, the flowers appearing in spring. The calyx is 2·5mm long with ovate, acute lobes. **Fruit** 0·8–1·2cm in diameter, almost smooth or with a slight raised network, orange when ripe. **Flowering period** March–April. **Distribution** An endemic of the Aegean region and S. Crimea. Al Cr Gr Ru Tu.

Arbutus x andrachnoides Link Hybrid Strawberry Tree

A vigorous fertile hybrid between *A. unedo* and *A. andrachne* with the brightly coloured bark of *A. andrachne*, peeling to reveal paler areas. There are at least some glandular hairs on the young twigs and the leaves have toothed margins and red petioles as in *A. unedo*. The flowers may appear in autumn or early spring and the fruits are smaller and smoother than those of *A. unedo*. **Distribution** Common when the parents grow together and sometimes raised in cultivation. The N. American *A. menziesii* Pursh, the Madrona, is sometimes grown in gardens in W. and S. Europe.

Persimmon Family
Ebenaceae

fruit

leaf with female flower

habit

Diospyros lotus L. Date Plum

A small tree up to 14m high with a rounded crown. **Bark** Furrowed and fissured into small plates, dark grey or sometimes pink-tinged. **Leaves** 6–12cm (sometimes up to 18cm) long, elliptic to oblong, rounded at the base, pointed at the tip, the margins entire but wavy, dark glossy green above, somewhat glaucous below, pubescent when young, becoming glabrous above and hairy only on the veins beneath; the petiole is *c.* 1cm long, hairy. **Flowers** Urn-shaped, males about 5mm long, 2–3 in a cluster, females 0·8–1cm long, solitary; the calyx is hairy within and has 4 short fringed lobes; the corolla is reddish or greenish-white, the lobes fringed and recurved, about half as long as the tube. **Fruit** *c.* 1·5cm in diameter, globose, yellow or bluish-black with a dew-like bloom, the flesh sweet but somewhat insipid. **Flowering period** July. **Distribution** Native throughout Asia, it is cultivated in N. Europe for ornament and often becomes naturalized. In S. Europe it is cultivated for its edible fruits. Al Bl Bu Fr Gr It Ru Sd Sp.

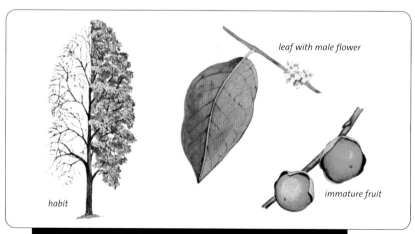

leaf with male flower

habit

immature fruit

Diospyros kaki L. fil. Chinese Persimmon or Kakee

Similar to *D. lotus* but with a scaly bark. **Fruit** 3·5–7·5cm in diameter, ovoid to more or less globose, yellowish or orange, the flesh sweet only when overripe. **Flowering period** June. **Distribution** A native of Japan and E. Asia, cultivated in S. Europe for its edible fruits. Al Bu Fr It Pl Ru.

Storax Family
Styracaceae

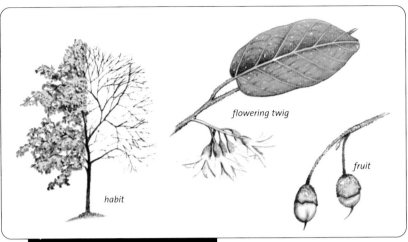

flowering twig

fruit

habit

Styrax officinale L. Storax

A small deciduous tree or shrub 2–7m high with all parts stellate-hairy. The crown is rounded or somewhat flattened. **Bark** Smooth and grey. **Leaves** Alternate, simple, 3–7cm long, ovate to almost oblong, rounded at the base, obtuse at the apex, the margins entire, green above, paler or whitish beneath, both surfaces hairy but the lower one more densely so. **Flowers** 3–6 in terminal or axillary, loose, drooping racemes; the calyx is bell-shaped, nearly entire, greenish and attached to the ovary; the corolla is *c.* 2cm in diameter, bell-shaped and deeply 5-lobed, white; there are 10 or occasionally 12 yellow stamens; the pedicels are 1–2cm long, densely hairy. **Fruit** A dry drupe up to 1cm long, ovoid, greyish and densely hairy, crowned with the remains of the persistent style. **Flowering period** April–May. **Distribution** A species of woods and thickets, often by streams in parts of the Mediterranean from Italy eastwards, and naturalized in France. The aromatic gum storax is obtained by making incisions in the bole and branches. Cr Fr Gr It Tu Yu.

Styrax japonica Siebold & Zucc. **Snowbell Tree**
A similar species to *S. officinale* but up to 11m high. **Flowering period** June–July. **Distribution** A native of China and Japan which produces numerous flowers and is often grown as an ornamental in N. Europe.

Olive Family
Oleaceae

Fraxinus L. Ashes

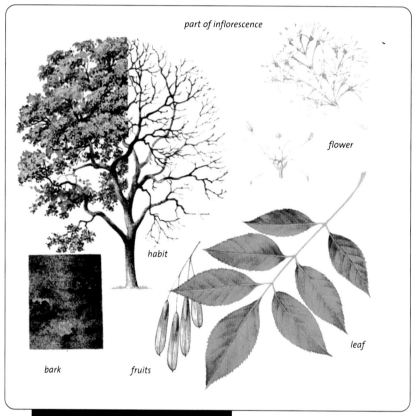

part of inflorescence

flower

habit

leaf

bark

fruits

.*Fraxinus ornus* L. Manna Ash

A medium-sized tree up to 24m high with a domed or somewhat flattened crown. **Bark** Smooth and grey, sometimes dark grey or even black. **Branches** The twigs are grey or yellowish, usually glabrous. **Buds** Greyish or brownish and covered with a whitish bloom. **Leaves** Pinnate with a terminal leaflet, up to 30cm long, each with a grooved rachis and bearing 5–9 leaflets; each leaflet is 3–10cm (rarely as little as 1·5cm) long, ovate or lanceolate with a pointed apex and irregularly sharp-toothed margin, pale beneath with downy brown or white hair on the veins, subsessile to distinctly stalked. **Flowers** The panicles are 15–20cm long, terminal or axillary, appearing after the leaves. The flowers are creamy-white and fragrant, the calyx small, deeply lobed and persistent, the corolla consisting of 4 linear petals, each 5–6cm long. **Fruit** The samara is 1·5–2·5cm long, oblong, widest above the middle or sometimes notched at the apex, with a slender wing, green at first, becoming brown when mature. **Flowering period** May. **Distribution** A common species of woods, thickets and rocky parts of C. Europe and the Mediterranean area. It is frequently found in parks and gardens and sometimes as a street tree. Al Au Bu Co Cz Fr Gr Hu It Ru Sa Sd Si Sp Tu Yu.

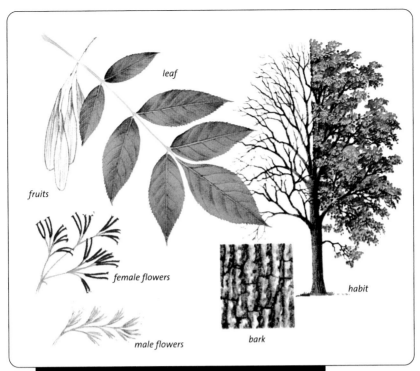

leaf

fruits

female flowers

male flowers

bark

habit

Fraxinus pennsylvanica Marshall Red Ash

A dioecious tree up to 25m high with a domed crown. **Bark** Slightly furrowed and reddish-brown. **Leaves** 22cm (sometimes up to 30cm) long with a white hairy rachis bearing 5–9 (usually 7) leaflets, the largest 8–15cm long, lanceolate to ovate-lanceolate or elliptic, pointed or blunt at the apex and often unequal at the base, irregularly toothed or entire, green and densely hairy beneath, rather thin in texture, subsessile or with the base of the blade decurrent on a short stalk. **Flowers** Axillary, densely hairy panicles appearing before the leaves; they have a persistent calyx but lack a corolla. **Fruit** The samara is 3–6cm long, the wing linear-oblong or widest above the middle, pointed, rounded or notched at the tip, decurrent to about the middle of the cylindrical body. **Distribution and taxonomic notes** A species of wet woods in E. N. America, planted for timber or to provide shelter in C. and SE. Europe, becoming naturalized in places. The Green Ash, var. *subintegerrima* is also cultivated in Europe and differs in its thicker leaves and glabrous young branches, rachis, panicles and lower leaf-surfaces. Au Bu Cz Fu Ge Ru.

Fraxinus americana L. White Ash
A species similar to *F. pennsylvanica* but taller, up to 40m high, with longer petiolules and the bases of the leaflets not decurrent. **Distribution** A wet woodland species of E. N. America planted in E. Europe on a small scale.

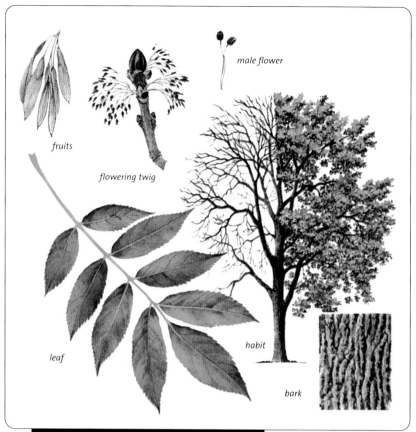

fruits

male flower

flowering twig

leaf

habit

bark

Fraxinus excelsior L. Common Ash

A tall tree up to 40m high with an open, domed crown. **Bark** Pale grey, smooth on young trees, becoming ridged and fissured when old. **Branches** The twigs are strongly flattened at the nodes. **Buds** Conical and black. **Leaves** 20–35cm long with a glabrous or densely hairy rachis bearing 7–13 leaflets or occasionally a large single terminal leaflet; each leaflet is 5–12cm long, oblong-ovate to oblong-lanceolate, with a pointed apex and sharp-toothed margins, the number of teeth exceeding the number of lateral veins, dark green above, pale beneath with dense white hair on the midrib and towards the base. **Flowers** The axillary panicles are globose, on 2nd year twigs, appearing before the leaves. The flowers are purple. Individual trees may be completely male, completely female, completely hermaphrodite, or have a mixture of male and female branches. **Fruit** The numerous samaras form large pendent clusters, each samara 2·5–5cm long, oblong to lanceolate, notched and with a spine at the tip, bright green at first, becoming brown. **Flowering period** April–May. **Distribution** A common species throughout Europe, and frequently cultivated, especially on damp base-rich soils. The grafted cv. 'Pendula', the Weeping Ash, is planted in towns and parks. Au Be Br Bu Cz De Fr Fu Ge Ho Hu Ir It No Po Ru Sd Sp Sw Tu Yu.

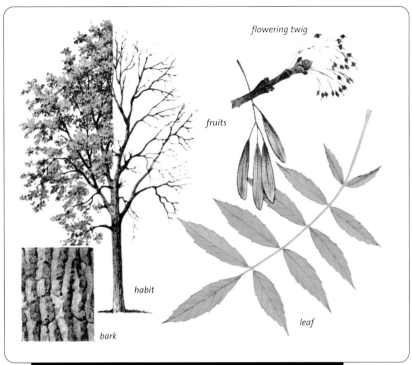

flowering twig

fruits

habit

bark

leaf

Fraxinus angustifolia Vahl Narrow-leaved Ash

A medium-sized tree up to 25m high with a tall irregular crown. **Bark** Has a network of narrow but deep fissures, dark grey and becoming warty in older trees. **Branches** Rather few and ascending, the twigs short, pendulous and glabrous. **Buds** Dark brown and hairy. **Leaves** 15–25cm long, with a glabrous rachis bearing 5–13 leaflets; the petiole is glabrous; each leaflet is 3–9cm long, oblong-lanceolate to linear-lanceolate, long-pointed at the apex and with toothed margins, the number of teeth usually equalling the number of lateral veins, shiny green above, glabrous or hairy at the base of the midrib below. **Flowers** The axillary panicles appear before the leaves; the flowers are hermaphrodite. **Fruit** The samaras form small clusters; each samara 2-4·5cm long, oblong to lanceolate, glabrous, becoming brown when mature. **Flowering period** May. **Distribution** A species of deciduous woods, banks and flood-plains of rivers in S. and EC. Europe. Al Au Bl Bu Co Cz Fr Fu Gr Hu It Pl Ru Sa Si Sp Tu Yu.

Fraxinus pallisiae Wilmott
Similar to *F. angustifolia* but reaching 30m in height with twigs, petioles, rachis and young leaflets densely hairy. **Distribution** SE. Europe. Bu Fu Ru Tu.

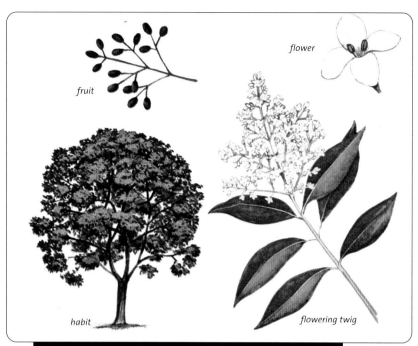

fruit

flower

habit

flowering twig

Ligustrum lucidum Aiton fil. in Aiton **Glossy Privet**

Usually a small evergreen tree up to 15m high, though sometimes a large shrub with a broad, domed crown. **Bark** Smooth or very finely fissured, grey with pale brownish streaks. **Branches** Spreading, the twigs straight, glabrous and marked with white lenticels. **Leaves** Opposite, simple, 8–12cm long, ovate, long-pointed, entire, thick, dark and very glossy green above, much paler and matt beneath; the young leaves are rather reddish. **Flowers** The inflorescence is a loosely-branched conical panicle, 12–20cm long with numerous small fragrant white flowers. The flower has a bell-shaped 4-toothed calyx and a corolla with a long tube expanding into 4 flat lobes. **Fruit** An oval berry *c.* 1cm long, black but with a whitish bloom. **Flowering period** August–January. **Distribution and taxonomic notes** It is a Chinese species grown in S. Europe for ornament and shade, particularly as a street tree, but also for hedging. Its native relative *L. vulgare* L., the Common Privet, is a widespread shrub of European woods, also frequently used as a hedging plant and as an ornamental in gardens.

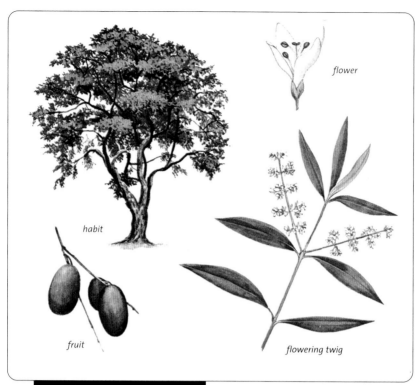

flower

habit

fruit

flowering twig

Olea europaea L. Olive

A long-lived evergreen tree up to 15m high with a broad crown and a thick, gnarled and often very short bole, sometimes dividing into several boles or producing suckers, and often with numerous holes or cavities in the bole and main branches. **Bark** Finely fissured and grey or silvery. **Branches** The twigs are terete or 4-angled and covered with small silvery scales. **Leaves** Opposite, 2–8cm long, lanceolate to widest below the middle, shortly pointed at the tip, entire, leathery, glabrous and dark grey-green above, paler and densely scaly below, more or less sessile or with a very short petiole. **Flowers** Bisexual or polygamous, fragrant, and borne in axillary many-flowered panicles; the calyx has 4 short teeth or shallow lobes; the corolla is white with 4 rather broad lobes. **Fruit** A succulent oily drupe, 1–3.5cm long, ovoid or somewhat globose, green at first, taking a year to become brownish, black or occasionally ivory-white when mature. **Flowering period** July–August. **Fruiting** September–October. **Distribution and taxonomic notes** It grows in open woods and scrub in dry rocky areas. The Cultivated Olive, var. *europaea*, is an important source of oil and is widely grown for its fruit. The Wild Olive, var. *sylvestris* Brot., differs from the common cultivar in having an often bushy habit with spiny 4-angled stems and lower branches, much smaller oval leaves and smaller drupes. Al Bl Co Cr Fr Gr It Pl Ru Sa Sd Si Sp Tu Yu.

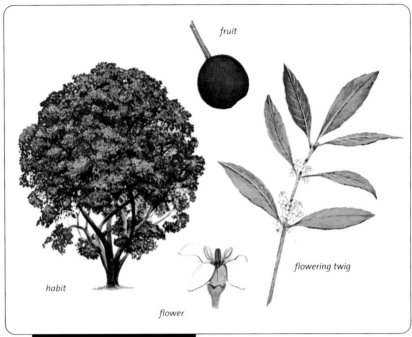

fruit

flowering twig

habit

flower

Phillyrea latifolia L.

A small evergreen tree or shrub up to 15m high with a dense rounded crown. **Bark** Smooth and grey, eventually with a raised network of ridges. **Branches** Rather erect when young but become spreading later; the twigs are slender, grey or brownish and densely hairy. **Leaves** Opposite, simple, making a wide angle with the midrib and forking towards the margin; juvenile leaves are 2–7 x 1–4cm, ovate-cordate to ovate-lanceolate, sometimes lanceolate, with sharply toothed margins; adult leaves are 1–6 x 0.4–2cm, lanceolate to elliptical, the margins entire or very finely toothed, very dark glossy green above, paler and dull beneath, with 7–11 pairs of close lateral veins. **Flowers** Bisexual, borne in short axillary racemes; the thin, yellowish calyx is divided to three-quarters of its length into 4 triangular lobes; the corolla is greenish-white, 4-lobed with a very short but distinct tube. **Fruit** A dry drupe, 0.7–1cm in diameter, globose, bluish-black when ripe. **Flowering period** June. **Distribution** A native of evergreen woods in the Mediterranean region, and occasionally planted in gardens near the coast. Al Bl Bu Co Cr Fr Gr It Pl Sa Si Sp Tu Yu.

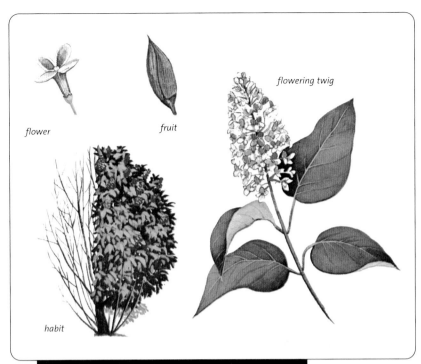

flower

fruit

flowering twig

habit

Syringa vulgaris L. Common Lilac

A small deciduous tree or shrub 3–7m high, with a rounded or oval crown, and suckering easily. **Bark** Spirally fissured, greyish or sometimes russet. **Branches** Terete and shiny brownish-green. **Leaves** Shortly petiolate, opposite, simple, 4–8cm (sometimes up to 12cm) long, ovate or shallowly heart-shaped, the margins entire, glabrous, yellowish-green and slightly leathery. **Flowers** The inflorescences are usually paired, axillary, leafless, conical panicles 10–20cm long, arising from the apical axillary buds. The flowers are fragrant; the calyx is small, shallowly 4-lobed; the corolla is tubular, lilac or occasionally white, 0·8–1·2cm long with 4 valvate, hooded and spreading lobes. **Fruit** An ovoid, pointed capsule, 0.8–1cm long. **Flowering period** May or June. **Distribution and taxonomic notes** A scrubland species native to the rocky hillsides of the Balkan Peninsula, but widely cultivated for centuries throughout the rest of Europe. *S. josikaea* Jacq. fil., Hungarian Lilac, differs from *S. vulgaris* in its elliptical leaves, which are wedge-shaped at the base, and its solitary leafy terminal inflorescences. It is confined to mountains in N. Rumania and the Carpathians but is now naturalized in Germany. Fu Ge Ru.

Bignonia Family
Bignoniaceae

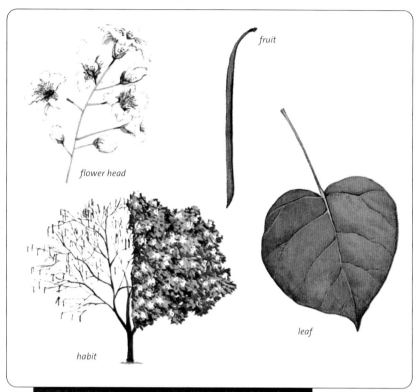

fruit

flower head

leaf

habit

Catalpa bignonioides Walter Indian Bean

A broadly domed deciduous tree up to 20m high. **Bark** Dull grey-brown, usually smooth, finely scaling or sometimes becoming fissured. **Branches** The twigs are stout, smooth, grey-brown. **Buds** Minute, orange-brown, the terminal bud not developing. **Leaves** Opposite, or in whorls of 3, 10–25 x 7–22cm, broadly ovate with short tapering tip, the base rounded or shallowly heart-shaped, the margin sometimes shallowly lobed, light green or occasionally purplish when young, densely pubescent beneath; the petiole is 10–18cm long, flattened, smooth. **Flowers** In broadly conical paniculate heads, 15–25cm long; each flower up to 5cm in diameter, bell-shaped with 5 spreading frilled lobes, white with yellow and purple spots in the throat and on the lower lip. **Fruit** A cylindrical capsule, 15–40 x 0·6–0·8cm, pendulous. **Seeds** *c.* 2·5cm long, flat, papery, with a fringe of long hairs at each end, white. **Flowering period** June–August. **Distribution** A native of SE. United States, frequently planted for ornament in parks and gardens or occasionally as a street tree in W. C. and S. Europe.

leaf

flower

Catalpa x erubescens Carr. Hybrid Catalpa

Like *C. bignonioides* but the bark with coarser ridges and fissures. **Leaves** Up to 38cm (rarely to 60cm) long, often broader than long, broadly ovate to somewhat pentagonal, each corner with a short tapering point, heart-shaped at the base, opening purple, becoming bright green. **Flowers** Heads up to 32cm in diameter, each flower fragrant, 4cm long. **Seeds** Sterile. **Flowering period** July–September. **Distribution and taxonomic notes** A hybrid between *C. ovata* and *C. bignonioides*, frequently planted for ornament in S. and W. Europe.

flower

Catalpa speciosa Engelm. Western Catalpa

Like *C. bignonioides*, but sometimes up to 30m high. **Bark** Scaling ridges and fissures. **Leaves** 12–32 x 7–23m, ovate-lanceolate or occasionally with 3 shallow lobes, the tip long and tapering, the base usually deeply heart-shaped, glossy, dark green above, the underside with pale brown pubescence. **Flowers** Heads up to 20cm long, each flower up to 6cm in diameter. **Fruit** The capsule is up to 50 x 1·5cm. **Flowering period** June–July. **Distribution** A native of the C. United States, occasionally cultivated for ornament.

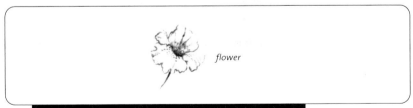

flower

Catalpa ovata G. Don fil. Yellow Catalpa

Like *C. bignonioides* but the leaves up to 25 x 25cm, more or less pentagonal with short tapering points on the corners, heart-shaped at the base, dark green. **Flowers** Heads up to 25cm long; each flower *c.* 2·5cm in diameter, dull white suffused with yellow, spotted red inside. **Fruit** The capsule up to 30 x 0·8cm. **Flowering period** July–August. **Distribution** A native of China, planted for ornament.

Figwort Family
Scrophulariaceae

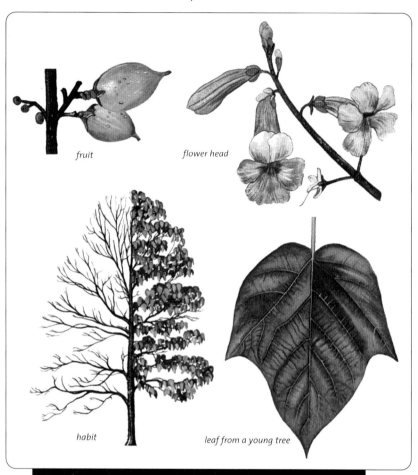

fruit

flower head

habit

leaf from a young tree

Paulownia tomentosa (Thunb.) Steudel **Foxglove Tree**

A deciduous tree up to 12m (rarely to 26m) high with a domed crown. **Bark** Smooth and grey. **Branches** Rather few, widely spreading. The twigs are rather stout, purplish-brown, with numerous lenticels. **Buds** Minute, purplish. **Leaves** Opposite, up to 45 x 25cm, broadly ovate with a long tapering tip, the base deeply heart-shaped, the margin entire or with up to 3 lobes on young trees, the lobes with tapering tips on either side of the base, pale green and softly pubescent above, densely grey-pubescent beneath, especially around the prominent veins; the petiole is 10–15cm, occasionally up to 45cm, densely pubescent. **Flowers** Upright paniculate heads, 20–30cm long; each flower densely brown-pubescent in bud, becoming pale to deep violet, suffused yellowish inside the tube, up to 6cm long, tubular, with 5 widely spreading lobes. **Fruit** A capsule, up to 5 x 2cm long, ovoid with a beak-like tapering tip, glossy and glutinous, splitting to release numerous seeds; the pedicel is *c.* 1·5cm long, stout, pubescent. **Seeds** *c.* 8mm long, winged, whitish. **Flowering period** May. **Distribution** A native of China, commonly planted for ornament in gardens, or occasionally as a street tree, especially in S. Europe.

Myoporum Family
Myoporaceae

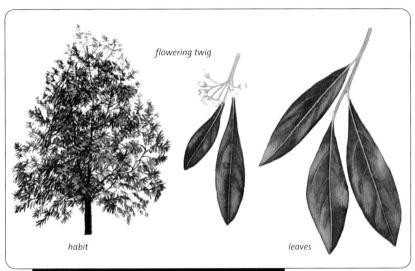

flowering twig

habit

leaves

Myoporum tenuifolium G. Forster

An evergreen glabrous tree or shrub up to 8m high, but very variable in size, with a rounded crown. **Bark** Very finely fissured, greyish-brown. **Leaves** Alternate, 4·5–10cm (rarely 17cm) long; the narrow leaves are 1·5–3cm wide, elliptic-oblong to lanceolate or even linear, sharply contracted at the base and pointed at the apex; the leaves are broad, up to 5cm wide, widest below the middle and rather blunt at the apex, the margins usually entire but sometimes with a few teeth, glossy green above, with numerous translucent glands; the petiole is 0.5–1cm long. **Flowers** Clustered in small dense axillary cymes of 5–9, or occasionally solitary, on slender pedicels up to 1cm long; the calyx is 2–3mm long, divided to halfway into 5 narrow, acute, rather rigid lobes; the corolla is white, spotted with purple and bearded on the inside, nearly bell-shaped, the tube 4–5mm long, the limb 1–1·2cm in diameter, with equal spreading lobes shorter than the tube; the 4 functional stamens protrude shortly from the corolla. **Fruit** A small, slightly fleshy drupe, 7–9mm in diameter, almost globose or ovoid, becoming purple when ripe. **Flowering period** April. **Distribution** A native of Australia and New Caledonia, planted for shelter in W. Europe and becoming naturalized in some places. BI Pl Sp.

Honeysuckle Family
Caprifoliaceae

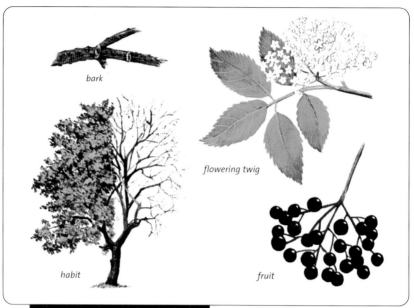

bark

flowering twig

habit

fruit

Sambucus nigra L. Elder

A small deciduous, much-branched tree up to 10m high, though frequently a shrub. **Bark** Extensively grooved and furrowed, brown or greyish, becoming corky in older specimens. Vigorous erect shoots often grow from the base of the bole. **Branches** Arching, with a large white central pith. **Leaves** Opposite, pinnately compound, with 5–7 or sometimes 9 leaflets; the leaflets are 4·5–12cm long, more or less ovate, pointed, sharply toothed on the margins and sparsely hairy beneath. **Flowers** The inflorescence is a flat-topped corymbose cluster, 10–24cm in diameter, with 4–5 primary branches; the heavily scented flowers are in 3–5 parts with white petals and anthers. **Fruit** A globose drupe with 3–5 stone-cells; the young fruits are green, ripening to black or occasionally red, the clusters drooping when mature. **Flowering period** June–July. **Distribution and taxonomic notes** A species of damp woods, hedges and waste places, widely cultivated for its fruit in S. Europe. All except Cr Fi Ic Ru Sw. The Alpine Elder, *S. racemosa* L., is similar in appearance but distinguished by its scarlet fruits.

flowering twig *fruit*

Viburnum opulus L. Guelder Rose

A spreading deciduous tree up to 4m high. **Branches** The twigs are angled, greyish, hairless. **Buds** Have scales. **Leaves** 3–8cm long with 3 or sometimes 5 irregularly toothed lobes, and filiform stipules. **Flowers** The inflorescence is 4·5–10·5 in diameter, the outer flowers sterile and much larger than the inner, fertile ones. **Fruit** Red, almost globose, often persisting after the leaves have fallen. **Flowering period** June–July. **Distribution** It grows in damp woods, hedges and thickets throughout much of Europe. Al Au Be Br Bu Cz De Fi Fr Fu Ge Ho Hu Ir It No Po Ru Sd Sw Yu.

flowering twig *fruit*

Viburnum lantana L. Wayfaring Tree

A deciduous tree up to 6m high. **Branches** The twigs are terete, greyish, stellate, hairy. **Leaves** 4–14cm long, ovate or widest above the middle, rough, toothed on the margins, densely stellate-hairy beneath; stipules are absent. **Flowers** The inflorescence is 6–10cm in diameter, the flowers are fertile and uniform. **Fruit** Ovoid and slightly flattened, red at first but turning black. **Flowering period** May–June. **Distribution** A species of hedges, thickets, edges of woods and rocky places, especially on chalky soils. Al Au Be Br Bu Cr Cz Fr Fu Ge Gr Hu It No Sd Sp Sw Yu.

flowering twig *fruit*

Viburnum tinus L. Laurustinus

A dense evergreen tree up to 7m high. **Branches** The twigs are usually glabrous, weakly-angled. **Leaves** 3–10cm long, ovate-lanceolate or ovate-orbicular, entire, globose and shiny above, sparsely hairy beneath; stipules are absent. **Flowers** The inflorescence is 4–9cm in diameter, the flowers are fertile and uniform. **Fruit** More or less globose and dark blue. **Distribution** A species of woody and stony places in S. Europe, sometimes forming thickets and often grown for ornament or to provide shelter. Al Bl Br Co Fr Gr It Pl Sa Sd Si Yu.

Agave Family
Agavaceae

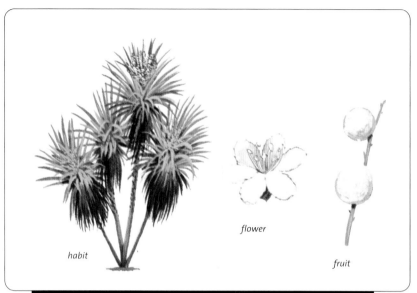

habit

flower

fruit

Cordyline australis (G. Forster) Hooker fil. **Cabbage Palm**

A small evergreen tree up to 13m high with a cylindrical trunk, becoming forked after flowering, and frequently suckering at the base. **Bark** Pale brownish-grey. **Leaves** 30–90 x 2·5–8cm, linear to linear-lanceolate, gradually tapering to a sharp point, dark green or yellowish-tinged, usually in a single rounded cluster on top of each stem, erect, the lowermost drooping to hide the trunk, sessile, with numerous parallel veins. **Flowers** In large terminal panicles, 60–120 x 30–60cm; each flower fragrant, *c.* 1cm in diameter, with 6 narrowly oblong lobes, creamy-white; there are 6 stamens. **Fruit** A berry, *c.* 6mm long, globose, white or bluish-white, containing several black seeds. **Flowering period** June–July. **Distribution** A native of New Zealand, commonly planted for ornament in streets, parks and gardens in coastal areas of W. and S. Europe.

habit

Yucca aloifolia L., Spanish Bayonet

Similar to *Cordyline australis* but up to 10m high, forming a stoutish, smooth trunk, much branched above. **Leaves** 50–100cm long, the margins with small teeth, bluish-green. **Flowers** 4–6cm in diameter, white, tinged with purple at the tips of the lobes. **Fruit** Elongated, blackish-purple when ripe, succulent, pedicellate. **Distribution** A native of SW. United States grown for ornament in S. Europe and occasionally escaping from cultivation.

habit

Dracaena draco L. Dragon Tree

Also similar to *Cordyline australis* but gradually forming a stout, much fluted and convoluted trunk, dichotomously branched above to form a dense, broadly-domed canopy. **Leaves** Bluish-green, tinged reddish at the base. **Flowers** Greenish-white. **Fruit** Up to 1.5cm long, globose, reddish-orange, 1-seeded. **Distribution** A native of the Canary Islands and Madeira, commonly planted in streets, parks and gardens in the Mediterranean countries.

Banana Family
Musaceae

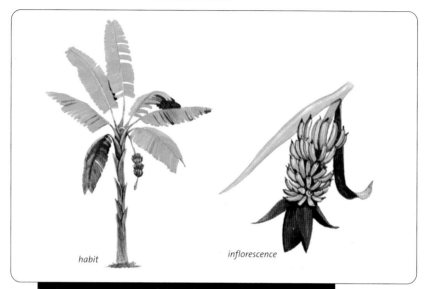

habit

inflorescence

Musa cavendishii Lambert ex Paxton **Banana**

A tree-like herb with shoots up to 3m high which fruit once and then die. The plant grows again every year by means of suckers from a stout tuberous stock. **Leaves** Arising from the base; the sheaths are very long, fibrous, persistent, tubular, with free margins but tightly wrapped round the sheaths of younger leaves to form a rigid false stem; the blade is 120–200 x 40–60cm, oblong, blunt at the tip, the margin entire but readily splitting to the midrib. **Flowers** The inflorescence is a long drooping spike up to 1m long. **Fruit** A berry (the banana), 12–18cm long. **Seeds** Numerous but sterile. **Flowering period** March–September. **Distribution** A native of tropical Asia but cultivated in small orchards and gardens along the Mediterranean coast. Cr Gr Si Sp.

Palm Tree Family
Palmae

habit　　　*inflorescence*　　　*leaf*

Arecastrum romanzoffianum (Cham.) Bell Queen Palm

A monoecious tree with a single slender trunk up to 10m high and 70cm in diameter. The bole is smooth and distinctly ringed. **Leaves** Pinnate and up to 5m long; the leaflets are narrow, less than 3cm wide, long, soft, drooping from the centre, green on both surfaces. **Flowers** The inflorescence is up to 1m long, hanging from the axils of the lower leaves, covered with cream-coloured flowers. **Fruit** Yellow, ovoid, beaked. **Distribution** A native of C. and S. Brazil, cultivated as a street tree in the Mediterranean region.

habit　　　*fruit*　　　*leaf*

Howeia forsterana (C. Moore & F. Mueller) Bell Sentry Palm

A monoecious tree with a single slender trunk up to 15m in height. The bole is grey, smooth and covered with leaf-scars. **Leaves** Pinnate, up to 5m long, with a prominent midrib and widely-spaced flat leaflets; each leaflet is narrowly lanceolate, green on both surfaces although spotty and scaly below; the petiole is long, up to 1·5m, usually ascending and arching only slightly. **Flowers** The inflorescence is about 1m long, hanging, and branched. **Fruit** Ovoid, up to 6cm long, densely packed on the spadix. **Distribution** A native of Lord Howe Island; one of the more popular Mediterranean palms cultivated in parks and gardens.

habit

Jubaea chilensis (Molina) Baillon Chilean Wine Palm

A monoecious tree with a single stout bole up to 30m tall and 2m in diameter. The bole is grey, smooth and covered with rhombic leaf-scars. **Leaves** Pinnatifid, up to 4m long with many leaflets; each leaflet can be up to 70cm long, 3cm in diameter and divided at the apex. **Flowers** The inflorescence emerges from the lower leaf axils and is a dense terminal panicle of yellowish flowers. **Fruit** Globose, ovoid and yellow. **Distribution** The Chilean Wine Palm is perhaps the hardiest of the southern hemisphere palms, growing further south of the equator than any other species. It endures drought and low temperatures and performs particularly well on the French Riviera. It is the largest palm to be widely planted in the Mediterranean region.

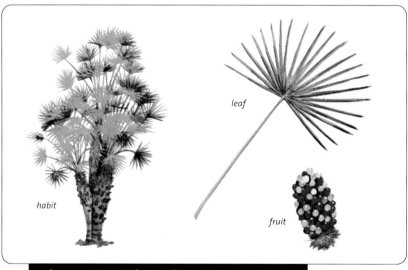

leaf

habit

fruit

Chamaerops humilis L. European Fan Palm

A small stemless or short-stemmed, dioecious or polygamous shrub or tree up to 2m high in the wild, or 3m high in cultivation. The bole is grey and covered with grey or whitish fibres and old leaf-bases. **Leaves** Palmate, up to 1m in diameter, deeply divided and very stiff; the segments are sword-shaped and split at the apex, green, grey-green or powdery-blue, firm and not drooping. **Flowers** The inflorescence is up to 35cm long, inconspicuous and often hidden in the leaves. **Fruit** Up to 4·5cm in diameter, globose, oblong, yellow or brown. **Distribution** The only native palm of Europe, occurring on sandy ground mainly near the coast in the W. Mediterranean region. Bl Fr It Pl Sa Si Sp.

leaf

habit

inflorescence

Livistona australis (R. Br.) C.F.P. Mart.

A monoecious tree with a slender trunk attaining 20m or more in height. The bole is invariably covered with brown leaf-bases and untidy brown fibres until a considerable age. **Leaves** Palmate, up to 1·5m in diameter, circular in outline with a rib extending several centimetres into the centre of the leaf; the segments are glossy green, with a prominent yellow central nerve giving a golden-green appearance, soft, drooping at the tips and frequently with threads hanging from the segments; the petioles are long, slender, spiny and toothed. **Flowers** The inflorescence appears from amongst the leaves and is at first covered by a very woody spathe, later to become much branched, bearing long-branched fruit clusters. **Fruit** Spherical, about 2cm in diameter and reddish-brown. **Distribution** A distinctive native of E. Australia, grown as a street and park tree in S. Europe.

Phoenix L.

Large dioecious trees with long stems. **Leaves** Pinnatifid with many induplicate, slender lanceolate lobes or segments, the ones towards the base shorter than those towards the tip; the petiole is stout, shorter than the blade and unarmed. The spadices are stalked with a few simple branches. **Flowers** Yellowish; the males have slender filaments; the females have ovaries with 3 carpels. **Fruit** A berry, usually developing from 1 carpel only. **Seeds** Deeply grooved along the ventral side.

leaf

cluster of fruits

habit

Phoenix canariensis (hort. ex Chabaud). Canary Island Date Palm

A stout tree up to 20m high, the persistent leaf-bases forming a massive bole up to 1·5m in diameter. **Leaves** Pinnate, 5–6m long, forming a dense crown of up to 200, strongly ascending but the lower ones hanging with age; the leaflets are in 150–200 pairs, usually in several ranks leaving the stem at various angles, short and narrow, long-pointed, light green, induplicate, straight; the spines at the base of each leaf-stalk gradually become longer and are followed by small leaflets which eventually become full-sized; the petiole is short, spiny and strongly ascending. **Flowers** The much-branched inflorescence grows up to 2m and emerges from the axils of the leaves. **Fruit** Occuring in heavy clusters, each one globose-ovoid, up to 3cm in diameter, orange. **Seeds** Wrinkled. **Distribution and taxonomic notes** A native of the Canary Islands frequently planted as an ornamental in subtropical parts of the world, particularly in the Mediterranean region and SW. Europe, as a street and garden tree. It is sometimes naturalized. A smaller, several-stemmed species with non-succulent fruits, *P. theophrasti* W. Greuter, is endemic to Crete.

single fruit

cluster of fruits

leaf

habit

Phoenix dactylifera L. Date Palm

A fairly tall dioecious tree up to 35m tall, suckering freely at the base; the bole is covered for years with old leaf-bases which later form a characteristic scarred pattern. **Leaves** Pinnate, up to 4m long, forming a lax sparse crown of about 20–40 leaves, the upper ones ascending, the lower ones curving downwards; the leaflets are up to 50cm long, induplicate, grey-green, glaucous, rigid, sharp-pointed, occurring in several ranks. **Flowers** The inflorescence is hanging in fruit. **Fruit** is 2·5–8cm in diameter, deep orange when ripe, edible and sweet. **Distribution** The true Date Palm provides the staple food of millions in the Middle-East and the S. Mediterranean region. It is planted on a small scale in S. Europe for ornament, and for dates in SE. Spain. Sp.

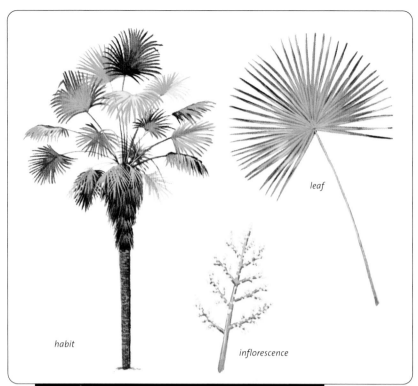

leaf

habit

inflorescence

Trachycarpus fortunei (Hooker) H.A. Wendl.
Chinese Windmill Palm

A monoecious tree with a single slender trunk up to 14m high. The bole is covered for a long time with persistent, dense, long, brown, fibrous leaf-bases, giving a matted appearance. **Leaves** Palmate, up to 1m in diameter, divided almost to the base; the segments are pointed, stiff, glaucous below and dark green above; the petioles are up to 50cm long, toothed, and covered with dense long brown fibres at the base. **Flowers** The inflorescence is a pedunculate densely branched spadix, covered with many fragrant yellow flowers. **Fruit** 3-lobed, kidney-shaped, about 2cm long, purplish-black when ripe. **Seeds** Grooved on the ventral side. **Distribution** A hardy native of C. and E. China, widely planted on roadsides and in parks in the Mediterranean region.

leaf

fruits

habit

Washingtonia filifera (J.J. Linden) H.A. Wendl.
Petticoat Palm

An hermaphrodite tree up to 20m tall and 1m in diameter with a single bole. The upper part and sometimes the whole of the bole is covered with the remains of dead leaves, forming a 'petticoat'; if the leaves are removed the leaf-bases form a compact but irregular covering and the surface of the bole is grey and marked with vertical chinks or ridges, more prominent than the growth rings. **Leaves** Up to 2m in diameter, fan-shaped in outline, divided more than halfway to the base, very persistent and covered with many long threads attached to the segments and sinuses; the petiole is up to 2m long and 15cm in diameter; each leaf consists of up to 50 grey-green segments. **Flowers** The inflorescence emerges from the axils of the lower leaves and is covered with numerous small white flowers, at first erect, the remains later hanging. **Fruit** Ovoid and lightly wrinkled. **Distribution** A native of S. California, W. Arizona and NW. Mexico, conspicuously planted in parks, gardens and roadsides throughout the Mediterranean region.

Bibliography and further reading

Bean, W.J. 1970–1976
Trees and Shrubs Hardy in the British Isles (8th edition) vols I–III.
John Murray, London.

Chittenden, F.J. 1951
The Royal Horticultural Society Dictionary of Gardening.
Clarendon Press, London.

Corner, E.J.H. 1966
The Natural History of Palms.
Weidenfeld & Nicholson, London.

Dallimore, W. & Jackson, A.B. 1966
A Handbook of Coniferae and Ginkgoaceae, ed. 4.
Arnold, London.

Lancaster, R. 1974
Trees for your Garden.
Floraprint, Nottingham.

McCurrach, J.C. 1960
Palms of the World.
Harper & Brothers, New York.

Miller Gault, S. 1976
The Dictionary of Shrubs.
Rainbird/Ebury Press, London.

Penfold, A.R. & Willis, J.L. 1961
The Eucalypts.
Leonard Hill/Interscience, London & New York.

Phillips, R. 1978
Trees in Britain, Europe and North America.
Pan, London.

Polunin, O. & Everard, B. 1976
Trees and Bushes of Europe.
Oxford University Press, London.

Stafleu, F.A. *et al.* (editors) 1978
International Code of Botanical Nomenclature.
Bohn, Scheltema & Holkema, Utrecht.

Tutin, T.G. *et al.* (editors) 1964-1980
Flora Europaea, vols 1-5.
Cambridge University Press, Cambridge.

Wilkinson, G. 1978
Epitaph for the Elm.
Hutchinson, London.

Vicomte de Noailles & Lancaster, R. 1977
Mediterranean Plants and Gardens.
Floraprint, Nottingham.

Glossary

abortive imperfectly developed, not functional

acuminate gradually tapering into a slender point

acute sharply pointed

alternate staggered singly around the stem (usually leaf arrangement)

anther part of the stamen containing the pollen

apomict plant which reproduces by seed not formed as a result of sexual fusion

appressed parts pressed closely together but not joined

aril outer layer surrounding a seed, usually fleshy, derived from the seed stalk

articulated jointed

ascending sloping or curving upwards

auricles rounded lobes at the base of a leaf

axil upper angle between a stem and a leaf or bract

basic soils rich in free basic ions, eg. calcium or magnesium

berry fleshy fruit without a stony layer surrounding the seeds

bifid split deeply into two

blade expanded, flattened part of a leaf

bloom whitish or bluish covering, very easily removed
(as on the outside of some grapes)

bole lower branch-free part of a trunk

bract scale-like or leaf-like structure, from the axil of which an inflorescence
or part of an inflorescence emerges

bracteole scale-like or leaf-like structure, from the axil of which
a single flower emerges

bud developing shoot or flower, often protected by scales and the growth
suspended during unfavourable conditions

burr lumpy outgrowth from a trunk, often covered with sprouting shoots

buttressed base of the trunk surrounded by tapering flanges or ridges

callus swelling, usually surrounding diseased or damaged tissue on a branch or trunk

calyx sepals of a flower considered as a whole

carpel functional unit of the female organ of a flower; may be separate or joined,
resulting in a partitioned ovary

catkin elongated, crowded inflorescence of inconspicuous, wind-pollinated flowers

ciliate margin surrounded by regularly projecting hairs

clone group of individual plants arising from an original plant without
sexual reproduction; many cultivars are clones

columnar narrow, almost parallel-sided crown

compound leaf made up of several distinct leaflets

cone inflorescence of a conifer, often woody and conical, composed of scales
and bract

coniferous cone-bearing

contiguous parts touching at the margins but not fused

coppiced cut down regularly to the base, yielding long poles

cordate heart-shaped; often restricted to the base of a leaf with a rounded lobe
either side of the stalk

coriaceous leathery textured, like the leaves of many evergreens

corolla petals of a flower considered as a whole

corymb short, broad and more or less flat-topped inflorescence,
developing like a raceme

crenate margin with shallow, rounded teeth

cuneate wedge-shaped or tapering leaf-base

cupule cup-like structure at the base of a fruit, composed of bracts
(eg. the acorn cup of oaks)

cyme more or less flat-topped inflorescence, each growing point
terminated by a flower

deciduous dropping off; usually referring to leaves which fall in autumn

decurrent the base continued down the stem as a wing

decussate leaves in pairs on opposite sides of the stem, but each pair
at right-angles to the next

deflexed bent sharply downwards

dehiscence process of opening of a dry fruit to shed its seed

dentate margin with sharp teeth

diadelphous stamen arrangement of some species of the Pea family:
9 fused in a bundle and 1 separate

digitate leaflets spreading like the fingers of a hand; palmate

dioecious with separate male and female flowers borne on different plants

dorsal back or outer surface of an organ

double-toothed margin with large teeth, each of which has smaller teeth

drupe fleshy fruit with the seed(s) surrounded by a stony layer

ellipsoid solid body, widest at the middle, elliptic in longitudinal section

elliptic outline, widest at the middle, rounded and narrowed towards each end

endemic native to a restricted region, usually a single country or smaller area

entire margin unbroken by teeth or lobes

fastigiate branches more or less upright (as in Lombardy Poplar)

filament part of the stamen, the stalk supporting the anther

filiform thread-like; long and very slender

fluted with deep vertical grooves

fruit ripe seeds and surrounding structures, either fleshy or dry

glabrous without hairs

gland a small vesicle containing oil or other liquid, within,
on or protruding from the surface of a plant

glaucous covered with a bluish or whitish layer

globose globe-shaped body, more or less round in cross-section

hermaphrodite flowers possessing both functional male and female parts

hispid covered with rather long, stiff, bristly hairs

hybrid a plant originating from the fertilization of one species by another

incised deeply cut

indehiscent not releasing the seeds

indumentum general term for the hairy covering of any part of a plant

induplicate folded or rolled inwards or upwards

inflorescence flower cluster including the stem bearing flowers and bracts

involucre joined bracts, usually surrounding the base of a short dense inflorescence

juvenile (i) young (ii) first-formed

keeled having a raised ridge or sharp folded edge, resembling the keel of a boat

laciniate divided deeply into narrow segments

lanate woolly; densely covered with long, curly, intertwined hairs

lanceolate lance-shaped in outline; widest below the middle,
about 3 times as long as wide

lateral at the side

legume a dry fruit splitting along its length above and below to release its seeds;
typically, the fruit of a species of the Pea family

lenticel rounded or elliptical pore in bark, usually raised

linear narrow and more or less parallel-sided

locule division of an ovary that has internal walls

maquis thicket of tall shrubs and scattered trees, characteristic of countries
bordering the Mediterranean

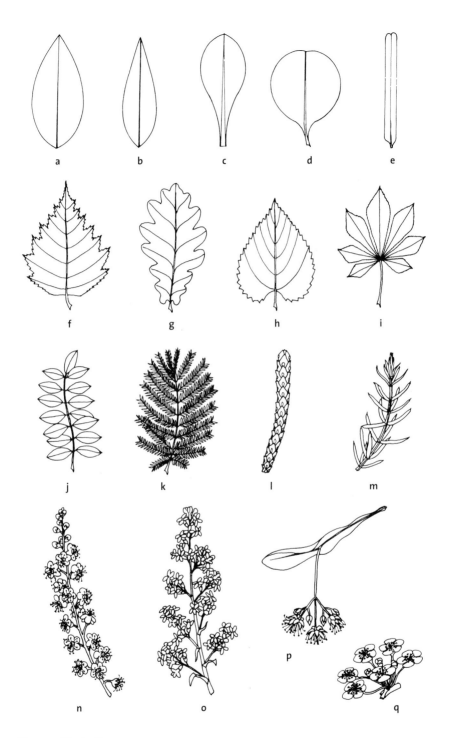

Glossary illustrations

Leaves and inflorescences, somewhat simplified.

a Ovate. **b** lanceolate, tip acute. **c** spathulate, tip obtuse. **d** orbicular. **e** linear, tip emarginate.
f tip acuminate, margin double-toothed or biserrate, base truncate.
g margin lobed, base auriculate. **h** margin dentate, base cordate. **i** palmate.
j pinnate, leaflets elliptic. **k** twice-pinnate. **l** leaves rhombic, arrangement decussate.
m arrangement whorled. **n** raceme. **o** panicle. **p** cyme (pendent). **q** umbel.

membranous thin, dry, somewhat papery

midrib central or main vein of a leaf

monodelphous stamens united into a bundle by the fusion of their filaments

monoecious with separate male and female flowers, both on the same plant

mucronate narrowing abruptly into a small, sharp point

nectary nectar-secreting gland, usually within a flower

node point on a stem where a leaf or leaves arise

ob- prefix meaning 'inverted', eg. obovate = ovate but broadest above the middle

obtuse blunt

operculum rounded cover or lid

opposite in pairs at the same level on the stem (usually leaf arrangement)

orbicular (in outline) rounded

outbreeding species in which the flowers are usually fertilized by pollen
from a different plant

ovary female part of the flower immediately enclosing the ovule

ovate outline, widest below the middle, rounded towards each end

ovoid solid body, widest below the middle, ovate in cross-section

ovule structure which contains the egg and develops into a seed after fertilization

palmate leaf with more than 3 leaflets arising from the same point

panicle branched inflorescence with each branch developing like a raceme

pepillae small slender projections from a surface

pedicel stalk of a flower

peduncle stalk of an inflorescence or group of flowers within an inflorescence

peltate organ with the stalk attached near the centre of a surface,
rather than at the margin

perianth sepals and petals together

pericarp wall of a fruit

patiole stalk of a leaf

patiolule stalk of a leaflet

phyllode flattened, leaf-like petiole with no blade (as in *Acacia*)

pinnate compound leaf with many leaflets arranged either side
of a central stalk (rachis)

pinnatifid leaf cut into lobes either side of a central intact region

pioneer among the first species to colonize open ground

pith (i) spongy tissue in the centre of most stems
(ii) the whitish, inner skin of a citrus fruit

placenta area in the ovary where the ovules are attached

pollard tree cut back repeatedly to 2–3m above the ground

polygamous with male, female and hermaphrodite flowers on the same or
on different plants

pome fruit where the seeds are enclosed first by a tough cartilage-like layer,
then by the fleshy receptacle (eg. apple)

procumbent trailing; lying near to the ground

pubescent covered with short, rather soft hairs

pyramidal crown which is widest at the base, gradually tapering above

raceme an inflorescence, usually elongated, which continually adds new, stalked
flowers to the tip; the oldest flowers are thus at the base

rachilla stem-like axis bearing leaflets or flowers, arising from a main rachis

rachis stem-like axis bearing leaflets or flowers

receptacle enlarged upper part of flower stem from which the parts of a flower arise

recurved curved backwards

reflexed bent sharply backwards

remote widely spaced

reticulate marked with a network of ridges; netted

revolute curved underneath (usually leaf-margins)

rhomboid lozenge-shaped; shaped like the diamond of playing cards

samara indehiscent dry fruit with a wing formed from part of the wall

scabrid covered with short stiff hairs

scarious thin, dry and membranous

seed fertilized, ripened ovule, sometimes including the outer layers of a small dry fruit; the dispersed reproductive unit

sessile stalkless

simple leaf not divided into leaflets

sinuate margin wavy when viewed from above

sinus depression in a margin, between two teeth or lobes

spadix spike-like inflorescence, sometimes branched, surrounded by one or more sheaths, at least while young

spathe bract-like or petal-like sheath enclosing an inflorescence

spathulate spoon-shaped; expanded suddenly towards the tip

spike raceme-like inflorescence with stalkless flowers

spired narrowly conical; shaped like a church spire

sprout young shoot, sometimes clustered around the base of trunks or from burrs

stamen male reproductive organ of a flower, consisting of anther and filament

staminode sterile stamen, often much reduced

sterile (i) (stamens) not producing viable pollen

(ii) (plant) not producing seed capable of germination

stigma surface receptive to pollen; part of the female reproductive organs of a flower

stipule appendage at base of petiole, either scale-like or leaf-like

stomata pores, usually in a leaf or stem surface, through which gas exchange takes place

stomatiferous area bearing stomata

stone seed enclosed by a hard layer formed from the inner layers of fruit wall

stone-cell hard, gritty enclosures in a fleshy fruit (eg. pear)

strobilus cone-like structure bearing male or female reproductive organs

style part of the female reproductive organs of a flower, connecting the stigma to the ovary

sub- prefix meaning 'almost'

subalpine at the limits of the tree-line

sucker shoot arising directly from a root, often away from the main trunk

suture junction, often a line where splitting open occurs

terete circular in cross-section; without grooves or ridges

terminal at the end or tip, usually of a branch

tomentose densely covered with rather short, soft hairs

tripinnate (leaf) pinnate with 3 levels of division; the main stalk bears 2 rows of secondary stalks, each bearing 2 rows of tertiary stalks with 2 rows of leaflets

truncate with a squarish, transverse tip

tubercle a short, blunt, smooth projection

tuberculate with tubercles

twice-pinnate (leaf) pinnate with 2 levels of division; the main stalk bears 2 rows of secondary stalks with 2 rows of leaflets

umbel inflorescence with all the pedicels or peduncles arising from the same point

undulate margin wavy when viewed from the edge

valve segment, usually of a fruit, that separates during dehiscence

ventral front or inner face of an organ

villous covered with long shaggy hairs

viscid sticky, glutinous

whorl arrangement with more than two organs arising at the same level around a stem

wing (i) thin, expanded portion of a seed, fruit or other organ

(ii) side petals of a flower of the Pea family

zygomorphic divisible into equal halves in one plane only

Index

Page numbers in **bold** type refer to illustrations